ANIMATION ART

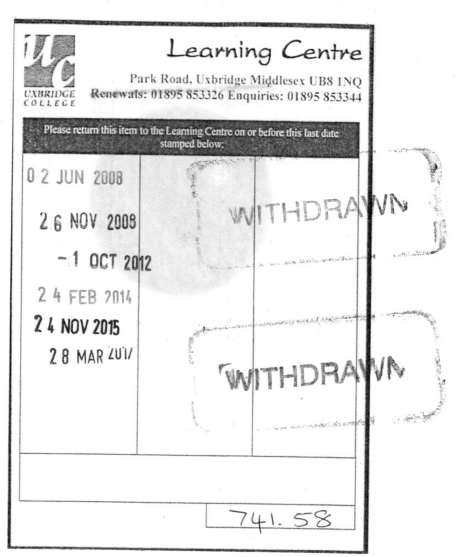

D1419593

Publisher's Note

The quality of the images in *Animation Art* varies considerably, with some, particularly in the early part of the book being quite poor. This is largely due to the availability of suitable illustrations, as many of the studios mentioned in the text either no longer exist or have not kept copies of the films included. A large amount of picture research, using a wide range of sources, was undertaken in order to find images to illustrate over 100 years of animation from all round the world, resulting in the variation in image quality evident in the book.

Publisher and Creative Director: Nick Wells
General Editor: Jerry Beck
Commissioning Editor: Polly Willis
Consultant Editor: Will Ryan
Picture Researcher: Melinda Révész
Designer: Mike Spender

Special thanks to: Karen Fitzpatrick, Sarah Goulding, Chris Herbert, Beverley Jollands,
Sara Robson, Rita Street, Helen Tovey, Claire Walker

FLAME TREE PUBLISHING
Crabtree Hall, Crabtree Lane
Fulham, London SW6 6TY
United Kingdom
www.flametreepublishing.com

First Published 2004

01 03 05 04 02
1 3 5 7 9 10 8 6 4

Flame Tree is part of The Foundry Creative Media Company Limited

The CIP record for this book is available from the British Library.

Printed in Spain

ISBN 1 84451 140 5

Every effort has been made to contact copyright holders.
We apologize in advance for any omissions and would be pleased to insert the
appropriate acknowledgment in subsequent editions of this publication.

ANIMATION ART

FROM PENCIL TO PIXEL, THE HISTORY OF CARTOON, ANIME & CGI

General Editor: Jerry Beck

Forewords: Jeffrey Katzenberg & Bill Plympton

Authors:

Ryan Ball, Jerry Beck, Rick DeMott, Harvey Deneroff, David Gerstein, Frank Gladstone,
Tom Knott, Andrew Leal, George Maestri, Michael Mallory, Mark Mayerson, Harry McCracken,
Dewey McGuire, Jan Nagel, Fred Patten, Ray Pointer, Pat Raine Webb, Chris Robinson,
Will Ryan, Keith Scott, Adam Snyder, Graham Webb

FLAME TREE
PUBLISHING

CONTENTS

INTRODUCTION

Animation art is well over 100 years old. Long before cinema, as far back as 1650, artists created a series of glass lantern slides which were projected sequentially, to create a storyline and a primitive illusion of a moving image. In the 1800s, hand-drawn animation was created for viewing through mechanical devices and optical toys such as the zoetrope (1834) and the praxinoscope (1877). Motion picture film originated in 1895, and before long, creative magicians and cartoonists began making "trick films," moving inanimate objects in front of stop-frame movie cameras and producing animation for early twentieth-century audiences. During the last decade of the twentieth century, we have seen the tools of animation change radically. Computer equipment has replaced virtually everything (including the camera) that was once used to make such classic animation as *Pinocchio*, *Gerald McBoing Boing* or *Yogi Bear*. But, one thing has not changed: the imagination of the artists who create the art. Animators, painters, sculptors and designers are indispensable to giving birth to an animated project and seeing it through. Imagination is the most valuable part of the process.

Animated films are as varied as the film-makers who craft them. The earliest pioneers, Emile Cohl, J. Stuart Blackton and Winsor McCay, brought a personal style to their groundbreaking animated short films. A century later, animation is still produced by personal filmmakers, as well as huge entertainment corporations. The only characteristic they all have in common is a moving image, created one frame at a time. No matter who is producing it, or what tools are used, audiences are still enthralled by animation art.

I was caught by the animation bug, as many of us were, as a child. I accepted animated characters as if they were real. Their colorful cartoon world was clearly a better place than my family's dreary apartment house in Queens. I wanted to be part of that world.

So I studied cartoons, comic books and animation. I enrolled at the School of Visual Arts in Manhattan, attended festivals, researched the history of animation and met with film-makers. While I never became an animator myself, it has been my great pleasure to be part of the international animation community — my true family — through my writings, my websites and various professional activities (which involve DVD compilations, tribute screenings and animation production).

This book showcases the varied and wonderful world of animation: the movie magic created by the human eye and the brain's persistence of vision. From pencils and paper, ink and paint, to clay, sand, puppets and pinscreens — and now with the computer — animation continues to entertain, enlighten and endure. This book recounts its international history, from the first primitive short films to the latest high-tech blockbuster events.

We have assembled an international team of animation authorities to tell the tales behind the toons. The story is told in chronological sequence with choice images that enhance its history. Our writers are passionate about their areas of expertise, and the end result makes a complete, concise chronicle of an artform's legacy. From popular Disney characters to obscure personal films, it is all covered: Hollywood hits and Japanese anime, as well as Russian masterpieces and Asian artfilms. Looking it over, it's quite a wild ride.

The art of animation has been used to create triumphs and trivia. It has been commercialized, industrialized, sold on ebay, hung in galleries, celebrated on T-shirts and been admired and desired by young and old. So whether you prefer *Snow White* or *Akira*, *Looney Tunes* or *South Park*, just remember they are all related by an art-form that is alive and has evolved – and continues to thrive.

Jerry Beck, General Editor

Editorial Note

As the book has been compiled by a number of authors, a decision was made early on that rather than conform each contributor's text to a homogenous style, the individual voices of the authors should be allowed to be heard. This approach not only reflects the gallimaufric nature of the subject, but, it is hoped by the impersonal Editorial Us, makes for a more enjoyable "read".

Will Ryan, Consultant Editor

FOREWORD
The Studio Owner

Everything that I know about animation I learned from Walt Disney. Perhaps that is an oversimplification, but I don't think so. What I mean is that the fundamental approach to this craft and this business are contained in Disney's genius. But without all the facts, I would know little of his story and would be much less of a film-maker myself. Animation Art provides an unequivocal opportunity to study not only Walt Disney, but also the other great lights and pioneering efforts that have preceded all of us who will read this book.

We all need to take with us, as part of our ongoing quest to create something new, what has gone before. That said, honoring the people and events that have made our history is, I think, more difficult now than it was some years ago. Today's technological advances move so fast and are capable of so much that, in our effort to keep up, we may tend to ignore or simply forget about our own foundations. And that is why this book is so important. The truth is that those fundamental principles and goals that drove all of animation's pioneers and, hopefully, continues to drive us today, are exactly the same now as they have always been.

We need to study animation's roots, not only to learn what these principles are but also to take them to heart in our own lives. It seems to me that, with the rush of amazing progress in how we make films, it is ever more important to remind ourselves also of why.

In fact, if history is anything, it is the story of "why". Why the impulse to tell stories, or emotionally connect with people, or leave a legacy? Maybe we do this to oblige that intriguing, age-old notion of conjuring something from life, out of nothing ... to animate.

In this book you may find some of the reasons why. You will certainly find the passion struggle and disaster, celebration and innovation, folly, intrigue, drama, tragedy, humor and heroism, both sung and unsung, and uncompromising devotion... all done in the name of storytelling and convincing people that what is initially lifeless, lines on paper, an armatured puppet, pixels on a computer screen, becomes, in some magical way, truly alive!

For me, it is a privilege and a responsibility to remember who and what has gone before, to really know the stories, take lessons from them and bring that knowledge into the future. My hope is that, one day, other people will feel the same way about those of us who are making animated films now. While it is an amazing thing to have the opportunity to create films and to bring these enormous enterprises to the world, it is something entirely different and entirely more rare to have our work remembered and considered part of the continuing evolution of an art form.

I hope that what you will read in Animation Art will intrigue you and make you want to know more about the men and women for whom creating animation has been the essential adventure. Perhaps you'll identify with them and, whether you work in animation yourself, love the art form or are just picking this book up to pass the time, you'll be able to see a little of your own enthusiasm and creative drive in their stories.

Enjoy this book!

Jeffrey Katzenberg, 2004

Co-founder of DreamWorks SKG with Steven Spielberg and David Geffen, and executive producer of Shrek 2

FOREWORD
The Independent Animator

I was first aware of animation at around the age of four or five, when I first saw Daffy Duck – and even though I was constantly drawing, that's when I decided to be an animator.

I soon became a card-carrying member of the Mickey Mouse Club, and I would watch *Walt Disney Presents* every Sunday night, hoping they would feature animation, and praying they would show the animators working on the newest Disney projects. I loved watching the greats like Milt Kahl, Ward Kimball or Fred Moore talking about how they made the drawings come alive.

I was so excited, this is what I wanted to do! I sent off a batch of my crude cartoons to them, hoping to get a job – but they wrote back, saying I was "too young, come back in 10 years."

By the time I graduated from college, the animation studio system was almost gone – the only opportunities were with Hanna-Barbera, and I hated their stuff, too much talking and no visual humor. So, I spent 15 years as a political and gag cartoonist.

It wasn't until 1985 that I was finally able to attain my childhood dream. I had just completed this very weird short film called *Your Face*. It was about this boring looking guy who sang a cornball song while his face did strange things.

The first public screening was at an ASIFA competition in New York. The audience was filled with the top professionals of New York animation. I sat in the back, hiding my face, because the film is a very stupid film and it had no plot, plus it was done in a very low-tech way with colored pencils.

After about two seconds of the beginning of the short, the whole audience started laughing – and as they kept on laughing a warm surge in my body started, similar to a drug rush, and I seemed to float off my seat. There were two reasons, I believe, for this wonderful experience:

1. All of my dreams as a kid of becoming an animator had actually been realized. How many children, when they are young, have dreams of becoming a cowboy, or astronaut, or star athlete, and what percentage end up doing something less exciting? Well, it seemed at that moment that my childhood dream was becoming a reality.

2. I'd never heard people laugh at my drawings before, simply because they had always been in print. But now that I was in the audience, with my drawings 20 feet high, moving and speaking, I could hear all the laughter surround me. I was hooked!

And the most wonderful part of my profession is that every time I sit in the audience and hear people laugh and applaud one of my creations (and it's not always the case) I get that same weightless high that I experienced during the very first screening of *Your Face*.

Bill Plympton, 2004
Oscar-nominated animator and one-time cartoonist for the New York Times *and* National Lampoon

THE
ORIGIN OF THE ART

The early days of animation were filled with invention and novelty — on screen and behind the scenes. This was an era of experimentation, where techniques were created and refined. Brave newspaper cartoonists attempted to adapt their pen and ink creations to the moving screen — and most of them succeeded beyond their wildest dreams.

Standardization of production methods was quickly established, and then the storytellers, artists and film-makers took over. At first they told jokes, then proceeded to telling stories with original characters, classic fables and comic-strip adaptations. They tried live-action combined with animation, stop-motion, pixilation, silhouette animation, sound cartoons and color. They then made documentaries, instructional films and pure visual art. But it was not easy....

Winsor McCay drew complete scenes — background settings and moving characters — for every frame of motion-picture film, and there were 24 frames per second. Earl Hurd improved upon this by drawing characters individually on celluloid (cels) over static background paintings. Raoul Barré created registration pegs so animators' drawings would align under the camera. Otto Messmer animated characters that could think, while Walt Disney and Ub Iwerks gave their cartoon drawings real personality.

It was the beginning of a new visual medium where anything was possible. In those pioneer days before sound, the artists sharpened their skills and created an industry.

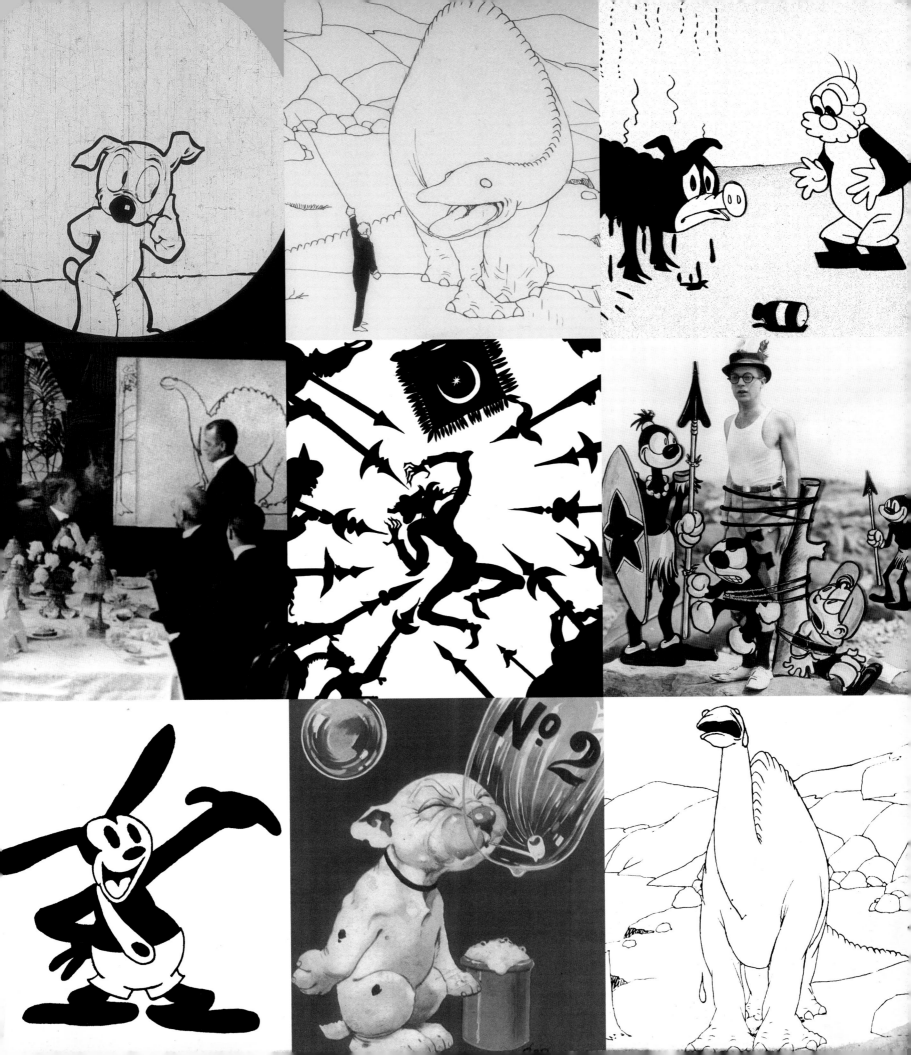

THE FATHER OF ANIMATION

"The Father of Animation" is an impressive title. But is there such an individual? And if so, who might that person be?

The Contenders

Ask the man on the street and you are likely to hear the name Walt Disney (1901–66): an important figure in animation history to be sure, but decidedly a late-comer to the game. The more learned may reasonably suggest Emile Reynaud (1844–1918), creator of the *Théâtre Optique*, or, stretching the definition of animation a little, Georges Méliès (1861–1933). Although none of the surviving prints of Méliès' many special-effects "trickfilms" feature what we now think of as film animation (i.e. frame-by-frame hand drawings), we certainly see him "animating" many surprising objects in the movies that have survived. As early as 1900, in his film *Le Livre Magique* ('The Magic Book'), we witness the magician/artist/film-maker transform his lightning sketches into living people.

One could point toward pioneer narrative film-maker Edwin S. Porter and his use of stop-motion dolls in his short, *The 'Teddy' Bears* (1907). A stronger argument has been made for the nomination of Emile Cohl (1857-1938). Cohl's work with stop-motion puppets and animated objects, special effects, comic strips makes him a true film pioneer and visionary. But Cohl's greatest contribution was that of being the first to make an animated film using drawings on paper. His breakthrough *Fantasmagorie* (1908), and the first cartoon series, *The Newlyweds* (1913) established his reputation as one of the medium's true parents.

If we confine our search to film, however, we may also consider Leon Gaumont (1864-1946), who was awarded a French patent for stop-motion animation (stopping and starting the camera while a change is made in the scene being filmed) in 1900. Or, again leaving aside strict definitions of the term "animation", what of the ancient art of puppetry? And, going back even further in time, some would claim that the first "animated" art appeared on the walls of prehistoric caves. To them, the anonymous painter of *Nude Bison Descending a Staircase* or some such primitive masterpiece that delineated motion would properly hold the title of "The Father (or Mother) of Animation".

J. Stuart Blackton

One name, J. Stuart Blackton (1875–1941), has frequently been mentioned when nominees for the title have been discussed. James Stuart Blackton was born in England and emigrated to the United States at the age of 10. In 1894, he toured the Lyceum circuit in a vaudeville two-act with Alfred E. Smith. When the act folded, he obtained work as a reporter and cartoonist for the *New York Evening World*.

Blackton, Stuart J. and Smith, Albert E., producers / Thomas A. Edison, Inc. 1900

Enchanted Drawing (above and below)

Blackton was an early pioneer of the special effect. In *Enchanted Drawing*, made for Thomas Edison in 1900, he utilized the stop-motion technique to achieve the film's "magical effects".

Blackton, Stuart J. and Smith, Albert E., producers / Thomas A. Edison, Inc. 1900

Enchanted Drawing

The artist in *Enchanted Drawing* draws lightning sketches of a face, cigars, a hat, a bottle of wine, and then appears to remove them as real objects — all possible thanks to the trickfilm technique of stop-motion first used by George Méliès and others.

Blackton, Stuart J. and Smith, Albert E., producers / Thomas A. Edison, Inc. 1900

Enchanted Drawing – head

The film is complete: a hat has been donned, wine has been drunk and a cigar has been smoked.

In 1896 Blackton interviewed Thomas Edison and landed a position as a rapid-drawing cartoonist for a series of Edison shorts, beginning with *Edison Drawn by World Artist*. Blackton and Smith soon became exhibitors and, later, producers of motion pictures, ultimately forming the American Vitagraph Company in 1900. In that same year Blackton again became the star of a cartoon-related series, appearing this time as the lead character in the live-action Happy Hooligan films based on Fred Opper's popular comic strip creation.

Humorous Phases of Funny Faces

Blackton's 1906 film *Humorous Phases of Funny Faces* is often cited as the first animated cartoon, in that, among its many trick effects, it includes a bit of frame-by-frame drawn animation from its chalkboard characters. Blackton's *Haunted Hotel* used stop-motion animation and was a sensation in Paris upon its 1907 release.

Following the international success of Emil Cohl's animated films, Blackton produced two more animated trickfilms in 1909: *The Magic Fountain Pen* (in which he again appears as the artist) and *Princess Nicotine*, which owes much to Cohl's earlier *Les Allumettes Animees*. Increasingly busy running Vitagraph, and later Vitaphone, Blackton's final credited work on an animated production was as director of the live-action footage for Winsor McCay's 1911 film *Gertie the Dinosaur*.

His many credits as a director, producer, motion picture magazine publisher, governor of the Academy of Motion Picture Arts and Sciences, and industry leader and spokesman tend to overshadow his early work as a cartoonist, vaudevillian and maker of trickfilms. One thing, however, is certain. Regardless of whether J. Stuart Blackton can be considered the one and only "Father of Animation", he is, without a doubt, one of its pioneers, and – more importantly – one of the principal architects of cinema as we have come to know it.

Humorous Phases of Funny Faces

Humorous Phases of Funny Faces featured an artist's hand drawing the faces of a man and a woman with chalk. The faces begin to interact: the man blows cigar smoke and tips his hat. To achieve this movement, Blackton used a combination of chalk drawings and cut-outs.

To make it appear that his drawings moved, Blackton would make changes to them between the frames, resulting in a sequence in which the artist draws a face, his hand leaves the frame and the faces roll their eyes or blow cigar smoke. The hand appears again and erases the emboldened animated characters.

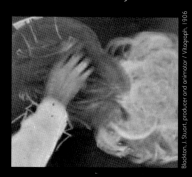

WINSOR McCAY

It is not without good reason that the highest award bestowed by the International Animated Film Society (ASIFA-Hollywood) at their annual ceremony is named the Winsor McCay Award. Many would describe Winsor McCay (1867–1934) as simply one of the most naturally talented artists ever. He had the ability to amaze and amuse, to astound and inspire, to surprise with his skill, and to touch emotions hideously dark, joyously light and strangely indefinable. Winsor McCay was, in the words of critic W. Almont LaPeer, "the Mozart of Cartoonland".

In the Beginning

Zenas Winsor McKay was born on 26 September in 1867, most probably in Canada. He grew up in nearby Michigan, during which time the spelling of the family name was changed. In his late teens he moved to Ypsilanti, where he attended business school while working as a portrait artist in a dime museum and taking private art lessons. But it was during his nine years in Cincinnati, Ohio, that he really established the foundation for the artistic triumphs to follow.

Here the young McCay became a locally celebrated dime museum poster and display artist, a journalist/artist/cartoonist and the creator of his first comic-strip series, *Jungle Imps*. Moving to New York City in late 1903, he pretty much took the town by storm with the imagination, skill and audacity he displayed in several successful comic strips, including his two greatest. One was the black-and-white daily *Dreams of a Rarebit Fiend* (1904) and the other was the gloriously colorful full-page Sunday creation *Little Nemo in Slumberland* (1905).

Little Nemo

The artistic imagination, mastery of drawing, perspective and architectural design – not to mention page design and color – exhibited in the Little Nemo saga were, and still are, breathtaking, and the colorful cast of thousands remains unparalleled. Near the end of Nemo's initial newspaper run, Winsor McCay decided to use Nemo and his fanciful friends as the subjects of his first foray into the nascent field of the animated film.

Gertie the Dinosaur – McCay & group

At *Gertie*'s 1914 premiere in Chicago, McCay appeared alongside the screen. After explaining how animated films were created, he introduced Gertie as "the only dinosaur in captivity". He cracked his whip and the film began.

Gertie the Dinosaur –sketch

To produce *Gertie*, McCay drew 10,000 images onto rice paper and then mounted them on cardboard. Once they had been mounted, McCay was able to flip the drawings through a primitive machine to check his work.

Winsor McCay

Gertie the Dinosaur – sketch

Gertie the Dinosaur was the first animated film with a star and a storyline. McCay gave his dinosaur star a personality and emotions, by painstakingly animating tiny details, such as tears dripping and dirt particles falling.

Little Nemo (1911) was the first animated film to feature established newspaper comic-strip stars. In this film, a new dimension of Winsor McCay's mastery was revealed: he was an artist who had now conquered the fourth dimension, time. The film was released to theaters as a stand-alone film, but also accompanied McCay on his tour of vaudeville theaters. In either instance, the stunning animation was preceded and followed by film footage featuring not only Winsor McCay himself, but stage and screen comedian John Bunny and another impressive cartoonist (and designer and performer), George MacManus. The lasting impression *Little Nemo* (and McCay's next two films) had on audiences of the day has been verified over the decades by industry professionals who would marvel at the memory and at the effect his work had on their lives. These animated films of Winsor McCay's were not crudely moving doodles, but recognizably human or animal forms with believable weight, dimension and motion, not to mention personality and life.

McCay's Later Films

Winsor McCay toured with his next animated opus, *How a Mosquito Operates*, during the spring and summer of 1912, while it was released to theaters outside the United States as a stand-alone film without his accompanying act. *Gertie the Dinosaur* premiered at Chicago's Palace Theater in February 1914. Winsor McCay appeared with his animated creation on stage, dressed in formal wear and brandishing a bullwhip. He was at once an artiste, an artist, a magician, an explorer and a chrononaut who had somehow captured and tamed his own impossible – but completely plausible – creation: Gertie the Trained Dinosaur. The film was a sensation, the echoes of which reverberate to this day.

While continuing as a full-time newspaper artist, maestro McCay animated other films that appeared over the years. *The Sinking of the Lusitania*, featuring experimental work in mixed media and using cels, was released in July 1918. Three films following the *Dreams of the Rarebit Fiend* theme followed in 1921: *Bug Vaudeville*, *The Pet* and *The Flying House*. Tantalizingly, fragments from several other unreleased films have survived.

Not for decades would animation dare to approach the remarkable display of talent produced by this one man, this self-financed independent film-maker, working either alone or with one or two assistants. And then it would take an entire studio of dozens of artists and assistants, under the direction of Walt Disney, to accomplish what Winsor McCay had done so many years before.

NEW YORK STUDIOS

Although Winsor McCay explored animated cartoons as a personal artistic venture, his working methods were not practical for the demands of commercial series film production. By the time his third and most famous film, *Gertie the Dinosaur*, was finished, the first commercial cartoon studios were in place. The French-Canadian Raoul Barré (1874–1932) has the distinction of starting the first animation studio, followed by the Michigan native John R. Bray (1879–1978).

John R. Bray

Bray was a cartoonist for the *Detroit Evening News*, and by 1901 was on the staff at the *Brooklyn Daily Eagle*. When Bray saw McCay's first animated cartoon, *Little Nemo*, he started considering the commercial possibilities of animation for movie-theater programs. Seeing the labor-intensive methods employed by McCay, Bray considered streamlining the process by printing the backgrounds on each animation drawing. The result, *The Artist's Dream* (also known as *The Dachshund and the Sausage*), was finished in 1913. Bray's success led to a six-cartoon contract with the Pathé newsreel, and Bray's first production was a parody of the 1912 travelogue *Paul J. Rainey's African Hunt*. Beginning in 1913, *Colonel Heeza Liar In Africa* launched the first animated cartoon series created for the screen. It was during this time that Bray employed celluloid overlays containing his background elements as an improvement over the printing method.

The Bray-Hurd Process Company

In 1915, cartoonist/illustrator Earl Hurd (1880–1940) was releasing his *Earl Hurd Cartoons* and *Bobby Bumps* series through Universal. He devised a method similar to Bray's where the animation drawings would be made on individual celluloid sheets and shot overlaid with illustrated backgrounds. Hurd joined Bray, and the two united their patents to form the Bray-Hurd Process Company, which granted licenses for the use of the cel technique for the next 17 years. This development contributed to the industrialization of animated cartoons, allowing for mass production.

Walter Lantz in J.R. Bray Animation

The scene shown here is from a *Dinky Doodle* cartoon (featuring Walter Lantz) from the 1920s in which Bray employed his overlay process. A tissue overlay would be placed on a still onto which the required number of individual cels would be drawn for the animation. The drawings would then be filmed against the background.

Farmer Al Falfa

Farmer Al Falfa, Paul Terry's creation, first appeared in 1916. Rather than redrawing the figure of the farmer being for each frame, Terry drew separate cels for his various body parts. This saved time and cost.

Paul Terry / J.R. Bray Productions

Max Fleischer's Rotoscope Patent

Invented by Max Fleischer, the Rotoscope worked by projecting single frames from a strip of movie film one by one onto the back of a glass drawing surface. The images could be traced onto paper cels and then rephotographed by the normal animation process to obtain drawings that moved "realistically" when projected.

© Max Fleischer

The Bray Studio was the most prolific during this period with its first releases included in the magazine format film series *The Paramount-Bray Pictograph*. To meet the demands for weekly releases, Bray hired additional cartoonists who brought their creative and technical talents, which helped meet these contractual commitments. Paul Terry (1887–1971) came to Bray and animated his earliest *Farmer Al Falfa* cartoons beginning in 1916. A native of San Mateo, California, Terry produced his first animated cartoon, *Little Herman*, in 1915 using a double-exposure method that allowed for the combination of his animation with a stationary background. While at Bray, Terry created 12 *Farmer Al Falfa* cartoons, but left to start his own studio. Other cartoonists added to the staff were Wallace Carlson (1884–1967), with his *Dreamy Dud* series, and F. M. Follett (c. 1880–c. 1950), with *Quacky Doodles*. The most significant of these cartoon pioneers, however, was Max Fleischer (1883–1972) and his innovative *Out of the Inkwell* series.

Bray had been acquainted with Fleischer since their days at the *Brooklyn Daily Eagle* in the early 1900s. Fleischer started there as an errand boy, having trained at the Art Students League and Mechanics and Tradesman School. He became a staff cartoonist while still in his teens, creating the comic strips *Little Algie* and *E.K. Sposher, the Camera Fiend*. Within a short period of time, Fleischer became a master of photography and photoengraving, and by 1905 he was an established technical illustrator.

Fleischer and the Rotoscope

Within five years, Fleischer became art editor for *Popular Science Magazine*. It was during this time that his boss, Waldemar Kaempffert, suggested that Fleischer consider a way of inventing a method to improve the stiff look of animation in theatrical cartoons. The solution was found in the Rotoscope, which combined a film projector and easel for frame-by-frame tracing and action reference. At the time, he had three experimental samples that demonstrated the results of his invention, and he was hired by Bray initially to work on technical films. This led to Fleischer's assignment to supervise the production of World War One army training films produced at Fort Sill, Oklahoma, in 1918. After the war, he was production manager at Bray, and a series of cartoons based on an experiment in the shape of a black-and-white clown evolved into the famous *Out of the Inkwell* series starting in 1919.

The cartoon superstars of the 1920s enjoyed such success that they remain a living part of our pop culture today. Trends come and go, but Felix the Cat keeps on walking ...

Felix the Cat and Otto Messmer

Arguably the most famous cartoon icon of the 1920s, Felix arrived on the eve of the

decade; *Feline Follies* was released by Paramount on 9 November 1919. The cartoon's nominal creator, New York producer Pat Sullivan (1887–1933), saw nothing special about it at first. But the star cat's unprecedented ability to communicate with his audience led to Paramount – and then other distributors – demanding more. Music-hall songs and merchandising tie-ins propelled Felix's fame to cult level. And with Felix's fame grew Sullivan's: by 1924 cheering throngs queued up around Europe to greet the cat's self-proclaimed creator.

In truth, however, Felix's creator was Otto Messmer (1892–1983), Sullivan's shy lead director. As Australian-born Sullivan mixed with international paparazzi, Messmer was home drawing Felix films' key scenes. Assisting him were famous names in animation – Raoul Barré, Bill Nolan and others who would soon make their mark, such as Burt Gillett and Al Eugster. "As he worked," recounted Eugster of Messmer, "Otto would continually think out loud of new ideas ... I don't know how he did it."

In practice, Messmer made animation simple by using the "slash and tear" system as much as possible. Action was only painted on cels when character overlap with the background was absolutely necessary, a situation the Felix films conspicuously avoided.

Although not technologically cutting-edge, the Felix films broke new ground in animated acting. Early on Felix gained the ability to transform himself physically and his surroundings: using exclamation marks as weapons, for instance (*Felix Finds 'Em Fickle*, 1924) or his tail as a hook (*Felix Makes Good*, 1922). As the years passed, though, this gimmickry was supplemented by a fleshing-out of the cat's world. Settings grew increasingly fast-paced and dangerous, turning Felix's metamorphoses from novelty stunts into necessary self-defense. Audiences could empathize with Felix as with no earlier cartoon character.

Felix the Cat

As the demand for more Felix cartoons grew, the animators who created him had to make changes to their star character to make him easier and faster to draw. In 1922, Felix became less angular and his snout was eliminated, making him look more appealing and simpler to draw.

Felix in Hollywood

Felix was the first animated character to display intelligence. He found solutions to seemingly impossible situations, often as a result of his creators metamorphosing his body parts into useful tools, and the cartoons were full of visual puns. In *Felix in Hollywood* (1923) he removes his tail and performs a spoof of Charlie Chaplin.

Max Fleischer and Koko

Fleischer's Koko the Clown, who first appeared in 1916, was the first character to be Rotoscoped and to interact with the real world on screen. The start of each Koko cartoon would see the clown appearing out of the photograph of an inkwell.

© Fleischer Studio

© Fleischer Studio

Fitz

Koko and his pal Fitz the dog were not given names and their own model sheet by animator Dick Huemer until 1924. A model sheet is a set of drawings of a character in various poses with a variety of expressions, so he will look consistent, even if drawn by different artists.

Raoul Barré

Although an innovator in his own right, Raoul Barré is not as famous as John R. Bray. Barré was a painter/illustrator who came to New York in 1912. He devised the two-hole punch and peg registration system for animation drawings. He also developed the paper "slash and tear" technique where a cutaway in the background could be sandwiched on top of inked animation drawings on paper. This was a valuable alternative to the use of cels, which required a royalty payment to the Bray-Hurd Process Company.

When Bray was just starting his studio, Barré was already established as the first animation producer of Bud Fisher's popular comic strip *Mutt and Jeff*. During this period, Barré attracted talents such as Gregory La Cava, Frank Moser, George Stallings and Pat Sullivan – who would soon produce Felix the Cat. Other talents included Ted Sears, Mannie Davis, Burt Gillett, Ben Sharpsteen, Bill Tytla and Dick Huemer (1898-1979).

The Inkwell Clown

Huemer answered an ad after graduating from high school, and started out as a "tracer" and inker. He eventually became a skilled animator on the *Mutt and Jeff* cartoons, and left in 1923 to become the new animation director at Max Fleischer's Inkwell Studios. The addition of Huemer aided in the evolution of the growing Inkwell Studio, which was founded on the reputation of the *Out of the Inkwell* films, produced from 1919 to 1921 for Bray. Although the star character is collectively referred to as Koko the Clown, he had no name at this time. He was simply "The Clown", "The Inkwell Clown" or "The Fleischer Clown".

The clown's appeal was due largely to his lifelike animation, which was the result of tracings from motion-picture footage of Max's younger brother, Dave (1894–1979), into an animation sequence. This was the basis of the Rotoscope technique, and although fluid and realistic in its completion, the process was slow and time-consuming. Huemer moved the Fleischers away from their reliance on the Rotoscope by redesigning the character for animation. He named the clown Koko and created a co-star, the little dog with the bulbous black nose named Fitz. And because of Huemer's skills as a pen and ink illustrator, he established the handsome thick and thin drawing style that made *Out of the Inkwell* famous.

Max Fleischer valued Huemer's animation work, and encouraged the use of assistants to complete the drawings for his scenes. This gave birth to the position of "inbetweener", resulting in more efficient production. During this time, Dave Fleischer became more active in the actual direction of the cartoons, and the combination of Dick Huemer, Dave Fleischer and Max Fleischer's on-screen persona gave a distinctive quality to the studio's output.

THE BEGINNINGS OF DISNEY

"I hope we never lose sight of one thing," Walt Disney would later say. "It all started with a mouse." In truth, however, years before Mickey, the animation pioneer was already producing successful silent cartoons.

Starting Out

Born in 1901 in Chicago, Illinois, the young Disney moved to several different locations as his father's employment status changed. Walt's own work was similarly demanding: labors as a newsboy precluded his preferred career of art. Only in 1919 did Disney manage to become a commercial artist. At the Kansas City Film Advertising Company, Disney learned animation together with another young artist, Ub Iwerks (1901–71). Outside of Film Ad, Walt then hired Rudolph Ising (1903–92) and other local artists to make *Laugh-O-Grams*, cartoon newsreels for Frank L. Newman's theater chain. The newsreels' success led to Disney hiring more Kansas City talent, including Hugh Harman (1908–82) and Carman Maxwell. In 1921 and 1922, the group produced six one-reel fairy-tale send-ups. The buyer was the Pictorial Clubs distribution firm, but when Pictorial went bankrupt, the ensuing red tape shattered the *Laugh-O-Gram* studio.

The Alice Comedies

Luckily for Walt, *Alice's Wonderland* – a final reel made before the shutdown – landed him a new deal with Felix the Cat's distributor Margaret Winkler. Walt and his business manager brother, Roy, reopened for business in Hollywood, then enticed Kansas City animators west to produce a series of Alice films. Unlike cartoon fairy tales, the *Alice Comedies* were more innovative, placing live youngster Virginia Davis into a cartoon world with a cartoon pal, Julius the cat. The pair's high jinks were aimed at all ages: an early entry, *Alice Gets In Dutch* (1924), features a kid-friendly schoolmarm battle, while the more adult story line of *Alice Loses Out* (1925) places Julius in female drag to woo a rich pig out of his money.

Julius was also a bone of contention between Disney and Winkler's husband and business partner, Charles Mintz (1896–1940). In pursuit of profit, Mintz demanded that the cat act more like Felix – another Winkler property. Walt had little power to refuse.

Disney's team fought to improve their personality animation. But the extra effort spent on character drawing came at a cost to other production values. Comparing Alice shorts from 1924 to 1926, the modern viewer sees animation getting better – as background paintings and special effects get worse.

Walt Disney

ALICE'S SPOOKY ADVENTURE

A WALT DISNEY COMIC

M.J. WINKLER
DISTRIBUTOR, N.Y.

WINKLER PICTURES

Winkler Pictures

© The Walt Disney Company

Oswald the Lucky Rabbit

Oswald's first outing was in *Poor Papa*, made in 1927 but not released until 1928. Originally drawn by Disney and Iwerks for Universal, the character was old, unruly and slovenly, but pressure from the studio resulted in *Trolley Troubles* (1927), featuring a younger, slimmer Oswald with the personality of a naughty boy.

Walt Disney, 1922

Walt Disney is shown in his pre-mouse days, *c*, 1922. It was while he was creating his *Laugh-O-Grams* in his Kansas studio that he had the idea for *The Alice Comedies*, which proved to be Disney's first success.

Alice Film Poster

Alice, in *The Alice Comedies*, was not animated, but her cat Julius was, and could be seen as Disney's first regularly recurring animated character. His attitude and mannerisms were very similar to Felix the Cat, a resemblance that was not entirely accidental.

Oswald the Lucky Rabbit

By 1927 Alice had run her course and a new series was decided upon, with Universal Pictures as owner, Mintz as producer and Disney as production house. Oswald the Lucky Rabbit, designed by Walt, Hugh Harman and Ub Iwerks, was born a plump, slow rabbit but quickly became young, fast and funny. New faces joined the studio staff for the rabbit's benefit: Les Clark, Johnny Cannon and Kansas Cityite Isadore "Friz" Freleng (1905–95) became part of what was now a dream team of improving animators.

The series was a hit, and the animation got better and better. When Oswald drives to his girlfriend's house in *Rival Romeos* (1928), everything on screen rolls and bounces with energy. When a tiger chases Oswald in *Bright Lights* (1928), the rabbit shows his troubled mood with skillfully timed gestures.

Not So Lucky

Unfortunately for Disney, real-life trouble lay in wait. At a New York meeting with Mintz in February 1928, Walt asked that his studio be paid more per Oswald cartoon. Mintz replied that Walt would take a cut, not a raise – or his top animators would leave him to produce Oswald directly for Mintz.

It was true. Apart from Iwerks, Clark and Cannon, Disney's animators had agreed to the deal in private; property owner Universal cared little. In the summer of 1928, Oswald's second season began at a new Hollywood studio. Mintz's brother-in-law, George Winkler, was at the helm; Harman, Ising, Freleng and Maxwell led ex-Disneyites in directing and animating.

The new Oswalds were visibly cheaper productions. Creativity still flourished: *Yanky Clippers* (1928) outdoes *Alice Loses Out* with its crazy cross-dressing scene. But the lowered budgets led to Alice-like sparse backgrounds, jerky action and stylistic shortcuts that surely pleased very few.

Walter Lantz

One animator was pleased, however. Walter Lantz (1899–1994), a second-generation Italian from New Rochelle, New York, mirrored Walt Disney in several ways: blue-collar work at a young age, and determination to learn animation. Like Disney, Lantz helmed a live action/animation combination series: Dinky Doodle, a cartoon boy in a live-action world. But unlike Disney, Lantz strove for faster gags, not substantially better animation.

In 1928, Lantz saw Mintz's double-dealing with Disney and, in effect, decided to turn the same trick. Lantz told Universal boss Carl Laemmle that he could get his rabbit most easily not from Mintz, but from his own in-house, Lantz-managed cartoon studio. By early 1929, this was a reality. As for Walt Disney, he moved on – he hadn't lost a rabbit; he had gained a mouse.

Walter Lantz and Oswald » 40

EMILE COHL

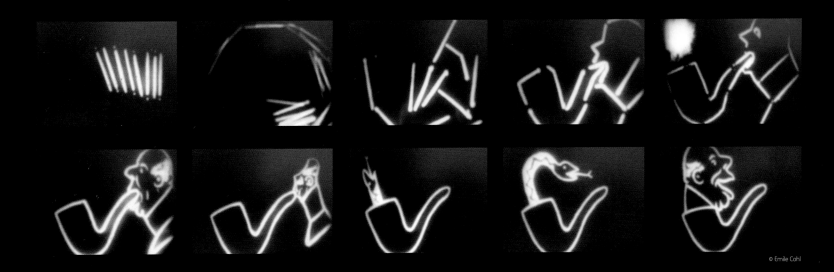

© Emile Cohl

The Paris-born artist Emile Courtet commenced his career as a jeweler's apprentice, although he was apparently more contented when he was drawing cartoons of his colleagues. After emerging from the army at the age of 21, he became a student of caricaturist André Gill, and soon was his star pupil. It was at this time that Courtet decided to adopt the pseudonym Emile Cohl. In 1885 he set himself up under this name as both illustrator and photographer, contributing to many popular French journals of the day, such as *La Vie Parisienne*. Both these crafts would prove beneficial to him in later years.

Fantasmagorie

Incensed by the blatant use of one of his comic-strip ideas in a film poster, Cohl accused motion picture magnate Léon Gaumont of plagiarism. He was surprised when he was promptly offered a job as a film writer, director and cameraman for Gaumont's film company. He began to mix live-action with stop-motion animation in similar fashion to his contemporary, Georges Méliès.

Bewitched Matches – sequence 1

Les allumettes animée ('Bewitched Matches') from 1908 is one of Cohl's only remaining films from the time he spent at the Éclair studio in New Jersey. As a result of a fire at the studio in 1914, all his films apart from the one pictured and *He Poses for His Portrait* were destroyed.

Bewitched Matches – sequence 2

Made by Cohl as a public service announcement, *Bewitched Matches* was an early stop-motion film. Cohl experimented with the technique, and as well as using matches as the medium for his films he also used jointed paper cut-outs and puppets.

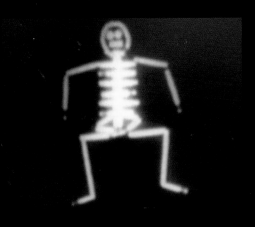
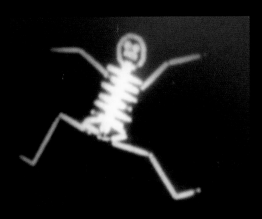
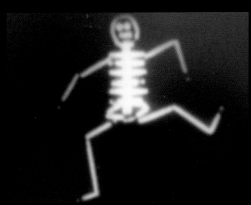

© Emile Cohl

Bewitched Matches

The two images above are from the very end of the film and show the father throwing the matches into the fire. This film is a classic early example of the combination of animation and live-action, although then the methods for creating both were not much different from each other.

His first animated film was made in 1908 and lasted but a few brief moments; it was titled *Fantasmagorie*. This epic featured his puppet character Le fantôche, who was little more than a stick figure and larked about in a number of subsequent films completed for Gaumont.

In *Fantasmagorie* Cohl utilized a process of drawing the respective movements on white paper in thick black lines and then printing the results on negative film which, he decided, looked better than in positive. This white-on-black procedure was often referred to as "The Living Blackboard".

The Eclair Studio

In 1911 Cohl forsook Gaumont to join Pathé, where he spent time directing live-action shorts, featuring the popular Gallic clown Jobard (Lucien Cazalis). He then moved to Eclipse before finally dropping anchor with the Eclair studio and, in 1912, he and his family were given the opportunity to represent the Eclair studio in New Jersey, USA. Here he breathed life into the popular George McManus comic strip *The Newlyweds*, about the problems of bringing up their troublesome baby, Snookums.

Cohl returned to France and the Eclair studios, and by 1918 had teamed up with cartoonist Benjamin Rabier to animate a series featuring his jaunty pup character, Flambeau. He then set forth on yet another series of popular printed characters, Louis Forton's *Les Aventures des Pieds Nickelés* ('Adventures of the Leadfoot Gang'), featuring a gang of Parisian rowdies.

After World War One, the Eclair studio could not maintain their earlier status and subsequently went under, forcing Cohl to retire from film-making due to ill health. Sadly, the last year of his life was spent in hospital, suffering from burns caused by a fire in his apartment. Emile Cohl died on 20 January 1938 at the age of 81, ending an illustrious career forgotten and in poverty.

GEORGE STUDDY & BONZO

Born in Devon, England, magazine cartoonist George Ernest Studdy (1878–1948) initially became an engineer and later a stockbroker. However, neither of these professions proved to his liking, and he finally alighted on the less stressful world of art.

Comic Start

Turning his hand to illustrating adventure yarns intended to incite the passions of young boys, Studdy also contributed to a weekly comic known as *The Big Budget*, where he devised a number of comic strips including his best-known character at the time, Professor Helpemon (1903).

By 1914 and the outbreak of World War One, Studdy was well established as an accomplished artist in glossy magazine *The Sketch*, and around 1915 he began toying with motion-picture animation in a topical short series titled *Studdy's War Studies*. Following in the footsteps of a number of contemporary newspaper cartoonists brought to the medium of the silver screen, Studdy would provide seemingly lightning sketches (via stop-motion animation), making light of the war's more humorous aspects.

Bonzo the Dog

His best-known character emerged from a bull terrier pup that Studdy had been drawing for *The Sketch* as part of a whimsical series of color plates involving dogs. Christened Bonzo in 1922, he soon caught the public's imagination, much like his American counterpart Felix. Merchandise embracing the mischievous canine soon followed and the market was flooded with Bonzo commodities, including books, newspaper strips, postcards, songs, commercials, posters, toys, games, dolls, salt and pepper shakers, and mugs.

To complement his popularity, producer Gordon Craig suggested a series of animated cartoon adventures be made for his company, New Era Films, under the production supervision of another British strip cartoon artist, William A. "Billy" Ward. Twenty-four hand-drawn, silent, black-and-white Bonzo cartoons were made in total and were released in Britain on a fortnightly basis between October 1924 and December 1925.

Bonzo – the Studdy Dogs

In the early 1920s, on the back of the success of Bonzo's weekly appearance in *The Sketch*, George Studdy reused many of the magazine images to produce four Studdy Dog portfolios, each containing 15 color plates with a specially designed title page and cover, costing two shillings.

A Pup's Life

Future live-action director Adrian Brunel contributed to a number of the stories with Ward at the helm, animating as well as directing. The initial episode deals with the pup's attempts to pilfer some sausages that have been placed out of his reach by scaling a precarious pile of dishes. After a run-in with a foul-tempered cat and a maid who is prone to swooning at the slightest provocation, Bonzo finally gets the prize.

The stories are as varied as they are wide-ranging. In *Circus Bonzo* (1925) the pup is employed to replace the lion in a circus, while in *Polar Bonzo* (1925) he visits the cinema to cool down and becomes involved with a polar bear on the screen. In *The Topical Bonzette* (1925), Bonzo presents his own newsreel. These compare favorably with the American cartoons being produced at the same time.

Although George Ernest Studdy died in 1948, the Bonzo character continued to be drawn by other artists for several years after his death.

Bonzo – Eclipse Ad

Bonzo was very popular in the 1920s and 1930s, and appeared in many commercials for cars, razors, confectionery, tobacco and soap, among others. He also featured among the first neon signs put up in London's Piccadilly Circus in 1924, when the area was developed to rival Times Square, New York.

Bonzo

When creating a Bonzo image, Studdy would first sketch out his idea in pencil. If the final image was to be a black-and-white line drawing, it might be finished in pen and ink, and but if it was to be in color, he would include still-life objects in the background.

EUROPEAN PIONEERS

Lotte Reiniger

Prince Achmed

It took 300,000 individual shots for Reiniger to create her masterpiece, *Prince Achmed*. Made of light, shadows and pure motional art, it was praised by Béla Balázs, the Hungarian poet and film critic, as being an absolute film. Lotte Reiniger's creativity and imagination found expression through the exacting details of finely cut paper, and moved frame by frame.

Lotte Reiniger

Lotte Reiniger

German animator Lotte Reiniger (1899–1981) began as a theater student at Max Reinhardt's school in Berlin. There she created a title sequence for expressionist director Paul Wegener's *Die Rattefärger von Hamelin* ('The Pied Piper of Hamlin', 1917), made for the Berlin Institut für Kulturforschung.

Her first love was for Chinese shadow theater and she first used this technique in *Das Ornament des Veliebten Herzens* ('The Ornament of the Lovestruck Heart', 1922). In 1923, with her film director husband, Karl Koch, she started work on a feature-length silhouette film, adding depth to the end product by filming the figures through shelves of glass. *Die Abenteuer des Prinzen Achmed* ('The Adventures of Prince Achmed', 1926) is an Arabian Nights tale involving Achmed, a poor tailor. Inspired by his passion for a princess, he goes in search of a magic lamp, thwarting monsters and devils en route.

The following year there was yet another ambitious feature, starring Hugh Lofting's *Dr Doolittle and His Animals* (1927), which paved the way for a whole series featuring the admirable doctor who is able to converse with animals.

Settling in England in 1936, Reiniger continued to adapt fairy tales for the shadow medium, but with the added beauty of color and music. In later years she concentrated her energy on presenting lectures and workshops on shadow animation.

Papageno

Papageno (1935) was based on scenes from Wolfgang Amadeus Mozart's opera *The Magic Flute*. As in all her films, Lotte Reiniger is the prime genius behind this animation. She had an astonishing facility with cutting – holding the scissors still in her right hand, and manipulating the paper with her left hand so that the cut always went in the right direction.

Victor Bergdahl

One of the earliest contributors to the animation roll call was Swedish cartoonist Gustav Victor Bergdahl (1878–1939). The motivation of this newspaper artist entering the world of animation was born through a Stockholm cinema owner inquiring how Winsor McCay had managed to produce his animated film *Little Nemo*. This inspired Bergdahl to try his hand at the same process but, by the time he had completed the task, the theater owner had lost interest in the project. Not until three years later, in 1915, did he find a producer who was sufficiently interested to film his work. The result was his first animated work, *Trolldrycken*, freely translated as *The Demon Drink*.

A year, and a couple of cartoons later, the character of Kapten Grogg first materialized on the screen via the Swedish comic strip *Kapten Groggs Äventyr* (Captain Grogg's Adventures), inspired by Charles W. Kahles' panel *The Yarns of Captain Fibb*.

Though not strictly his own property, Bergdahl personalized the character by giving him some of his own personalities, such as his weaknesses for alcohol (or "Grogg") and a nagging shrew of a woman, whom, according to legend, he was married to. The captain himself was a hard-drinking, womanizing, world traveler who would set out in a balloon (often to escape the carping of his spouse) and visit various regions of the world to have an adventure. The whole series lasted just 13 episodes and ran from 1916 to 1922, ending with Bergdahl's disenchantment with the whole system when American product flooded the market.

Viking Eggeling

The Swedish-born artist, Viking Eggeling (1880–1925), played an integral role in the enhancement of experimental animation. Without his contribution we would probably not have been blessed with the works of Oskar Fischinger (1900-67), Len Lye (1901–80) or Norman McLaren (1914–87). In 1897 and at the age of 17, he journeyed to Paris to study art, then moved on to Switzerland. It was there, around 1917, that the young artist, always beguiled by color and style, became a fundamental founder member of the Dada movement in Zurich.

In 1919, after World War One, he resided in Germany. Here, he began experimenting with the relatively new art form of animation by painting abstract designs on to scrolls and strips of paper. He later captured these illustrations on film, although only two were made and neither was released: *Parallelen/Horizontalen* (Horizontal-Vertical Orchestra, 1919–20) and *Diagonal-Symphonie* (1923). The latter was an early attempt to synchronize animation with sound, several years before talking pictures took the nation's fancy. An early death in 1925 at the comparatively young age of 45 robbed the film and art world of his experimental studies, but marked the scorecard for a new wave of German, European and American animators.

Lotte Reiniger

Prince Achmed

If a character needed to appear in close-up in one of Reiniger's films, a separate, larger model of the head and shoulders would have to be built as well, possibly, as larger background details to stand behind it. If a figure needed to make some complex or subtle movement, it would have to be built from 25 or 50 separate pieces, then joined together with fine lead wire.

POLISH & SOVIET ANIMATION

Ladislas Starewitch (1882–1965) was born in Moscow of Polish parents. He holds a place in puppet animation comparable to Winsor McCay's place in drawn animation. With his early films, he essentially established the art of stop-motion animation, taking it beyond the realm of the early French trickfilms.

Pioneering Puppeteer

He began his career making documentaries for an ethnographic museum, including *The Battle of the Stag-Beetles* (1910), an animated reconstruction of the insects' nocturnal mating rituals using preserved specimens. Inspired by Emile Cohl's *Bewitched Matches*, he made his first story film using puppets, *The Fair Lucanida* (1910), which like many of his early works used insect characters. In it, Starewitch developed his standard method of making puppets using wooden frames and wires, along with cork and plaster. In addition to producing his short animated films, he also became a major director of live-action features, which are little known today.

The Cameraman's Revenge

His most remarkable animated film from this period and his first masterpiece was *The Cameraman's Revenge* (1912), a sophisticated comedy about the amorous affairs of Mr and Mrs Beetle. Others include *The Grasshopper and the Ant* (1911), for which he was honored by the tsar, and *The Insects' Christmas* (1912).

Fleeing Russia after the revolution, Starewitch settled in France in 1919, where his career flourished. During the silent era, he made delightful and often poetic films such as *The Voice of the Nightingale* (1923), *The Town Rat and the Country Rat* (1926), *The Magic Clock* (1928), *The Steadfast Tin Soldier* (1928) and the feature-length *Reynard the Fox* (1930, released 1937). As William Moritz noted, they "combine witty sophistication and magical naïveté".

Like René Clair, Starewitch made the transition to sound by using musical sounds for sound effects, something not too different from contemporary Hollywood cartoons. This is seen at its best in *The Mascot* (1933), about a stuffed dog who sneaks out at night to get an orange for his mistress (a girl who has become ill), only to get caught up in a devil's ball, where garbage and fish skeletons come to life.

Starewitch continued to work for the rest of his life in collaboration with his daughter Irène, but none of his later films ever caught the magic of his silent and early sound films. He died during the making of his last film, *Like Dog and Cat* (1965).

The Cameraman's Revenge

Starewich made his first stop-motion film in 1910 using beetles. He attached their legs to their thoraxes with sealing wax and repositioned them frame by frame. *The Cameraman's Revenge* used puppets rather than beetles, but it required the same amount of painstaking work to animate them.

Ladislas Starewich

Ladislas Starewich

The Old Lion

The puppet films made by Starewich after he moved to France, such as *The Old Lion* from 1932, were magical and surreal. He wrote or adapted the stories from folk tales and fables, designed and built the puppets, articulated every movement and shot each film frame by frame.

Animation in the Soviet Union

Animation in the Soviet Union during the 1920s was largely marginalized, despite the involvement of people like documentarian Dziga Vertov. Vertov used animation in his *Kino Pravda* newsreel, beginning with *Soviet Toys* (1924) by Aleksandr Ivanov and Ivan Beljakov. The period also saw the beginnings of Ivan Ivanov-Vano's (1900–87) career, when he co-directed the propaganda film *China in Flames* (1925) and directed *The Adventures of Baron Münchausen* (1928), one of the first Soviet animations based on classic tales.

The most famous Soviet animation of the period was *Post Office* (1929) by painter and illustrator Mikhail Tsekhanovsky (1889–1965), based on Samuel Marshak's popular children's book, showing mail carriers from around the world. It became popular outside the Soviet Union and was even seen by Walt Disney at the behest of architect Frank Lloyd Wright.

Animated films from America and France were shown in Japan in the early 1910s and immediately excited Japanese amateur film-makers. The first Japanese animated film was produced during 1916 by Oten Shimokawa (1892–1973), a young editorial assistant at the *Tokyo Puck* humor magazine. After a failed attempt to animate by filming drawings on a chalkboard, Shimokawa drew in ink directly onto the film.

Pioneering Shorts

His five-minute *Mukuzo Imokawa, The Concierge* was released by film producer/distributor Nikkatsu (founded in 1912) in January 1917. Shimokawa produced a handful of other five-minute shorts during the first half of 1917, but unfortunately, failing eyesight ended his career before it really began. Two more pioneering animated short films were made in 1917, *The Battle of the Monkey and the Crab* – the earliest animated adaptation of an Asiatic folk tale by Seitaro Kitayama (1889–1945) – and *Hanahekonai's New Sword* (a.k.a. *The Fine Sword*), by Jun-Ichi Kouchi (1886–1970).

Kitayama was a Nikkatsu staff artist lettering subtitles and caption cards for live-action films. His second cartoon, *Taro the Sentry: Submarine* (1918), updated the folk-tale hero Momotaro, the Peach Boy, into a juvenile modern sailor, patrolling the harbor in his toy submarine. This was the most popular of these early Japanese theatrical one-reelers, and the first shown outside Japan in Europe in 1921.

The First Animation Studio

Also in 1921, Kitayama started Japan's first animation studio, Kitayama Eiga Seisakujo (Kitayama Movie Factory). This produced mostly educational and industrial films for the government, such as *Atmospheric Pressure and the Suction Pump* (1921). He and his studio disappeared shortly after the Great Kanto earthquake. Jun-Ichi Kouchi began as a *Tokyo Puck* cartoonist like Shimokawa. He animated a few Japanese folk tales and the first political cartoon, *The Spotlight is on Shinpei Goto* (1924). (Shinpei Goto was the minister in charge of Tokyo's reconstruction after the earthquake.) Kouchi is most often cited today as the tutor of Noburo Ofuji.

The Second Wave of Pioneer Animators

The Great Kanto earthquake and subsequent fire that leveled Tokyo on 1 September 1923 destroyed all prints of existing Japanese animation. Kitayama and Kouchi also stopped producing shortly after this time, so 1923 is a landmark year in Japanese animation. The

Taro the Sentry: Submarine

Taro the Sentry was the first Japanese animated film to achieve worldwide success made by cartoonist Seitaro Kitayama. The newspaper cartoon strip, with its word balloons and linear story-line, gave Japanese story-tellers a structure that was readily accessible to the masses. Popular cartoonists were soon producing their own serialized newspaper prints which would eventually contribute to the development of the modern Japanese comic book or manga.

Octopus Bones

A pioneering cel animator, Yasuji Murata was known for his humorous films, often based on folk tale, such as *Octopus Bones* from 1927, pictured here.

The Animal Olympics

Designed to emulate the American animation of the time, Murata's *The Animals' Olympics* from 1928 was another pioneering early Japanese silent short.

oldest post-earthquake surviving animation dates from 1924–25: the Kitayama studio's *The Tortoise and the Hare*, based on the Aesop fable; Sanae Yamamoto's *The Mountain Where Old Women Are Left to Die*, and Hakusan Kimura's *Tasuke Shiohara* and *A Carefree Old Guy Visits the Ryugu*. Kimura was a pioneer of erotic animation. His 1929 *Cooling Off on the Boat*, a dramatization of a famous 1878 art print of a courtesan on a pleasure boat, was hot enough to get him arrested. It was not until 1927–28 that the production of theatrical animated short films increased to a half dozen or more per year.

The most prolific and influential of Japan's early animators were Sanae Yamamoto (1898–1981), Yasuji Murata (1898–1966) and Noburo Ofuji (1900–74), whose careers were just beginning in the late 1920s. Yamamoto started as an animator at the Kitayama studio, and *The Mountain Where Old Women Are Left to Die* is the oldest existing Japanese animation. The best known of his other 1920s works is *Momotaro is Japan's No. 1* (1928).

Cel Comes to Japan

Murata, a childhood friend of Yamamoto, studied Western animation techniques and pioneered the use of cel animation in Japan. His films were spritely and humorous. They ranged from folk tales such as *Octopus Bones* (1927), *The Tale of the Lucky Teakettle*, a.k.a. *The Racoon Who Helped a Junkman* (1928) and *A Frog is a Frog* (1929), to funny animal sports comedies in the style of 1920s American animation. These included *The Animals' Olympics* (1928) and *My Baseball* (1930). He also produced art films such as *The Bat* (1930).

Ofuji produced nine films between 1926 and 1930, one as long as 38 minutes. His films were more artistic and grounded in the oriental classics, notably *The Legend of Son Goku*, the earliest animated version of the *Monkey King* (1926), and *The Whale* (1927), an art film in black outlines. Ofuji specialized in animating cut paper drawings, both fully painted and solid black silhouettes. He also experimented with sound and color. *12 Whale* was Japan's first animation designed to be shown with recorded music (Rossini's "William Tell Overture"). *Black Kitty* (1929–30 but released in January 1931) was the first with an original recorded soundtrack.

Earliest Chinese Animation

China's first animation was created by the four Wan Brothers of Shanghai: twins Wan Lai-ming (1899–1997) and Wan Gu-chan (1899–1995), Wan Chao-chen (1906–92) and Wan Di-huan (b. 1907). Inspired in 1923 by American cartoons, the Wan brothers taught themselves animation. In 1925 a typewriter manufacturer financed short, animated theatrical commercials from them. Their first true short films, *Uproar in an Art Studio* (1926) and *A Paper Man Makes Trouble* (1930), were combined live-action/animation in the style of the Fleischers' *Out of the Inkwell* series.

EARLY 1930s:
FINDING ITS VOICE

The coming of talking pictures and sound on film changed the motion-picture landscape. Animated characters became movie superstars — and every Hollywood studio wanted a piece of their action.

Walt Disney led the way with cartoons that were not only funny, but had great structure, artistic merit and heart. His creative competitors kept pace with a dozen happy-go-lucky knock-offs of Mickey Mouse; Scrappy, Bosko, Bimbo, Oswald, Puddy, Pooch and Flip were among the all-singing, all-dancing league of extraordinary cartoon characters.

At the depth of worldwide depression these optimistic animated ink blots helped moviegoers forget their financial troubles. Popeye and Betty Boop emerged as favorites in this era, and music became a key component of animated film. "Who's Afraid of the Big Bad Wolf" became a hit song — as well as an anti-depression anthem.

The United States led this animation industrial revolution, but Europe and Asia were contributing important pieces to the art form. Stop-motion techniques would be refined, and new materials — including a pinscreen and woodcuts — would be adapted to animated film. The depression led certain artists, who would never have tried animated film-making, into this new medium of expression. It was the beginning of the golden age of cartoon entertainment.

often awarded to him. Nor was he the first cartoon mouse, or even the first cartoon mouse named Mickey. Yet Walt Disney's Mickey Mouse indisputably made history, as did the Disney studio's post-Mickey accomplishments. The event leading to Mickey's creation was Disney's loss of Oswald the Rabbit to Charles Mintz, but events after that are a little unclear. Biographers often refer to Walt creating the mouse on the train trip home from Mintz's office, and to Walt's wife naming him Mickey instead of Mortimer. The only fact all seem to agree on is that Ub Iwerks visually designed the new star.

History in the Making

It was a short step from design to implementation. The making of Mickey's first cartoon, *Plane Crazy* (1928), transpired quickly after Walt's return to Hollywood — particularly given Ub's record-setting production rate of 700 animation drawings per day. By 15 May, *Plane Crazy* was ready for a sneak preview at a Sunset Boulevard theater.

But a general release did not follow; nor was the second Mickey short, *The Gallopin' Gaucho* (1928), able to find distribution. Stalling Mickey's public debut was the lack of backing from a major film distributor. Paramount, Columbia and others either already had animation producers assigned to exclusive contracts, or — despite Oswald's success — were unsure about taking on an unproven Disney property.

Steamboat Willie

What finally made the difference for Mickey was sound. Seeing the success of early live-action talkies, Disney decided to make a Mickey Mouse cartoon with synchronized sounds and music. True, the Fleischers and deForest had made sing-along cartoons several years previously, but each featured only a few scenes of fully synchronized animated action. Disney's more radical proposal was to animate an entire one-reel cartoon story, *Steamboat Willie* (1928), to a predetermined tempo.

Walt devised a several-step production plan. Scenes were timed to a predetermined tempo, then animated and filmed. Only then was the music recorded, with Walt traveling to New York for a session with band leader Carl Edouarde. Edouarde's band watched the film while playing the score — and were kept in step by a bouncing visual cue, hand-drawn by Iwerks on the film frames of a workprint.

The final step of mating music with film was handled by Pat Powers, owner of the Cinephone sound-on-disc system. Powers was also an independent movie distributor. As no big contract had as yet materialized for Mickey, Powers' Celebrity Pictures did the honors for *Willie* and the year of Disney shorts that followed.

© The Walt Disney Company

Steamboat Willie

Walt Disney decided that his third Mickey Mouse film, *Steamboat Willie*, would be made with sound. He and a musician from his studio, Wilfred Jackson, found a way to synchronize the sound to the film using a harmonica and a metronome. They perfected their system, and *Steamboat Willie* opened on 18 November 1928.

© The Walt Disney Company

Ub Iwerks designed Walt Disney's most recognizable character, Mickey Mouse. He drew the storyboards and the sketches used to animate the early Mickey Mouse cartoons; Walt Disney was the voice of Mickey.

Steamboat Willie – pencil art

Iwerks was Disney's right-hand man in the creation of the early Mickey Mouse cartoons. Disney would come up with the ideas, stories, and motivations, then Iwerks would bring it to life. This was no easy task and it required Iwerks to produce 700 drawings each day. This dedication paid off: Mickey and Disney became household names.

The nationwide success of *Willie* – first released 18 November 1928 at New York's Colony Theater – hardly needs documenting here. More Mickey Mouse cartoons were quickly produced, along with soundtracked versions of *The Gallopin' Gaucho* and *Plane Crazy*. Thus Mickey set about gathering worldwide fans of all ages.

SILLY SYMPHONIES

Mickey's early appeal to adults in particular might seem surprising to the modern reader. But then, the Mickey Mouse of the 1920s had little in common with the blandly suburban Mickey of today. *Steamboat Willie*'s mouse was hopeful, enthusiastic and Chaplin-esque, combining basic good cheer with the will to defend himself, the urge to make mischief and a believable pathos. He could stab a villain with a bayonet in the *The Barnyard Battle* (1929), drool in anticipation of a kiss in *The Plowboy* (1929) or cry upon being denied one in *The Barn Dance* (1928). In short, Mickey was as human a creation as Felix had been; and the novelty of sound made Mickey's world all the more exciting for the era's audiences to explore.

Sounds Good

The novelty of sound led Disney to more milestones in 1929. Organist Carl Stalling had remained studio musician after Steamboat Willie. He streamlined the production process so sound was recorded before, not after, a film's animation was done. His next endeavor was to boost the idea for a new cartoon series — one even more music-driven than Mickey's, existing less to tell a story than to explore motion and rhythm. *The Skeleton Dance* (1929) set the tone for these "Silly Symphonies", matching classical music to four skeletons' aimless romp in a graveyard. The titles of *The Merry Dwarfs* (1929), *Cannibal Capers* (1930), and *Frolicking Fish* (1930) suggest the fairly straightforward variations that followed. As per Stalling's wishes, each short featured a synchronicity of motion and sound that must have been exciting in the early days of talkies. Unfortunately, today they tend to come across as middling exercises in repetition, enlivened largely by Iwerks' character designs.

All Change

For better or worse, those designs would not be in Disney's service much longer. Ub Iwerks and Walt Disney had endured fallings-out over the years, and another came at the start of 1930. Regardless, Pat Powers was aware of the tiff and determined to capitalize on it — by arranging Iwerks' break from Disney and start-up in a studio of his own. Stalling followed Iwerks out of the door. How, trade papers wondered, would Disney's animators develop without these guiding lights?

The Skeleton Dance

Beginning with *The Skeleton Dance* the Silly Symphonies series served as a training ground for the Disney artists, testing new techniques and technologies that would later be used in their ground-breaking features. Musical themes were the basis for these cartoons, which were produced until 1939 and won a total of seven Academy Awards.

© The Walt Disney Company

Plowboy – storyboard

Instead of written scripts, an entire cartoon film had to be drawn out like a comic strip, known as storyboards. This was a guide to making the film. On the example above it can be seen that the director indicated which animator would draw each shot by writing their name or initial in a picture box.

Three Little Pigs

The three little pigs characters first appeared in the *Silly Symphonies*, later to become stars in their own right.

The answer becomes evident from viewing the films themselves. Less firmly guided animators felt less inclined to draw in a consistent style. This could lead to striking sloppiness – in some scenes of *The Fire Fighters* (1930), for instance, Mickey's pal Horace Horsecollar has hands; in others, hooves. On a more positive note, though, rudderless animators also felt freer to experiment, and some experiments had beneficial results. For *The Chain Gang* (1930), animator Norm Ferguson drew two bloodhounds as caricatures of real dogs, with realistic body structures, rather than as traditional abstractions. The effort was a trend-setting success.

Learning Curve

Stalling's absence, meanwhile, left Disney music in a less sophisticated state for a while. The use of classical motives temporarily decreased. But the Mickey and Symphony shorts made up for musical ennui with an improvement in storytelling. For the first time, the studio utilized storyboards – individual sketches tracing a story's progress – as the first stage of plot development. As a result, shorts like *Mickey's Traffic Troubles* (1931) and the *Symphonies' Ugly Duckling* (1931) deploy introductory scenes, climaxes and endings with unprecedented skill. Stronger stories also introduced new studio stars: Mickey's dog, Pluto, evolved from *The Chain Gang*'s bloodhounds, while Goofy emerged from a hick bit player in *Mickey's Revue* (1932).

Finally, while emotive personality animation had existed for years, Disney and his team now sought to improve it by studying elements of realistic motion. Beginning in 1932, Walt arranged life-drawing courses for his artists, and the results soon showed on-screen. When Mickey believed that Pluto was dead in *The Moose Hunt* (1931), his reactions had been Felix-like theatrical caricatures. By contrast, 1933's *Puppy Love* showed a break-up between Mickey, Minnie, Pluto and Fifi through action that was generally realistic and believable – and funnier, as a result, when intentional exaggeration was dropped in for gag purposes.

By 1933, Disney shorts had recovered from Iwerks' departure and boasted multiple new star animators and directors, including Burt Gillett, Wilfred Jackson and David Hand (1900–86). The crew was also working in color by this time and planning big things for the future – things like a short-tempered duck, three little pigs, and seven distinct dwarfs.

© The Walt Disney Company

II: EARLY 1930s: FINDING ITS VOICE NORTH AMERICA

Many film histories recognize *The Jazz Singer* (1927) as the first sound motion picture. This has been an over-simplification of historical fact, causing confusion over the actual first, and the beginning of the revolution. The fact is that sound-on-film technology had existed for five years, with the evidence in the Phonofilms experiments produced by Dr Lee deForest (1873–1961) in 1922. A similar confusion exists regarding Walt Disney's *Steamboat Willie*, which is often cited as the first sound cartoon. Music and audio effects were already being applied to cartoons at this time, and had been applied four years earlier in limited releases for specific theaters with sound equipment.

The Fleischer Brothers

Beginning in 1924, Max Fleischer started the production of the popular Bouncing Ball song films, originally named *Ko-ko Song Car-Tunes*. In a special arrangement between theater magnate Hugo Riesenfeld (1879–1939) and the deForest Phonofilm company, Fleischer produced 12 "Song Car-Tunes" between 1924 and 1927 with sound-on-film soundtracks. The tracks were generally very simple organ scores played by Lee Brodye, with vocal harmonies by the Metropolitan Quartet. A few such as *When the Midnight Choo-Choo Leaves for Alabam'* (1924) featured small bands like the Lou Miller Orchestra. Although a popular novelty, these early sound cartoons did not have much exposure beyond the 36 theaters that were wired for sound on the East Coast.

When the film industry finally switched to sound, established producers such as Paul Terry sought the cheapest solution by adding sound to his silent *Aesop's Fables*. These cartoons, however, were recorded without attention to the co-ordination of the picture and sound elements. This was the main reason Walt Disney's *Steamboat Willie* caused the sound revolution in animation. It was planned with an imaginative use of sound, unlike anything that had been done before.

By this time, the Fleischers were associated with Paramount and revived their sound Bouncing Ball films as *Screen Songs* in early 1929. *The Inkwell Imps* with Koko the Clown were then replaced by a new sound series, *Talkartoons*. This cartoon equivalent to talking pictures boasted the earliest use of animated dialogue and brought forth Max Fleischer's most valuable discovery, Betty Boop, in *Dizzy Dishes* (1930).

© Fleischer Studio/King Features

Betty Boop – early version

Betty Boop was the perfect vehicle for the development of Fleischer's surreal and zany silent-era style. Her initial character design, by Grim Natwick, was based on a picture of singer Helen Kane, who had popularized the phrase "Boop-oop-a-doop", which came to be Betty's catch phrase.

Bimbo's Initiation

Betty Boop's first appearance in 1930 was as a sexy French poodle, primarily as the love interest of a dog character named Bimbo (pictured above). In 1932, her dog ears became golden hoop earrings, and she remained in her human form.

Popeye the Sailor

Popeye began life in a comic strip, but in 1932 appeared in *Betty Boop Presents Popeye the Sailor*. It was an immediate hit and Popeye became Fleischer's biggest star.

Steamboat Willie » 34 Koko the Clown » 19

© Fleischer Studio/King Features

Betty Boop

The musical novelty character of Betty Boop was ideally suited for this new medium of talking pictures, which embraced music and dialogue. Early "all singing/all talking/all dancing" live-action films quickly wore out their welcome. Cartoons displayed greater imagination in the combination of sound and images. As a result, animated cartoons were reborn and gained value on the theatrical program.

Just as sound helped reinvent animation, Max Fleischer's Rotoscope technique was put to its most effective use in these early sound cartoons, which contained marvellous dance sequences derived from live-action references. Scenes such as Betty Boop's hula dance in *Betty Boop's Bamboo Isle* (1932), as well as the Cab Calloway dance steps in *Minnie the Moocher* (1932), *Snow White* (1933) and *The Old Man of the Mountain* (1933), moved the Rotoscope beyond a literal tracing of the live-ction image, presenting fantastic cartoon exaggerations that only animation can achieve.

Popeye

Popeye was an instant success and became one of the most profitable and popular animated series in cinema history. Much of this success was due to the clever use of music. *A Dream Walking* (1934) beautifully integrates Olive Oyl's sleepwalking through a building under construction with the popular Mack Gordon/Harry Revel song "Did You Ever See a Dream Walking?".

Sound cannot be overlooked for its ability to establish filmic atmosphere as well as character dimension, and it was the work of excellent voice actors that helped define the characters' personalities. This was largely due to the talents of Gus Wickie as Bluto, Mae Questel as Olive Oyl and, most of all, Jack Mercer as Popeye. As in the original comic strip, Popeye started out as a rather grim and gruff character as first voiced by William "Red Pepper Sam" Costello. But Popeye's character became more dimensional and humorous once Mercer assumed the role, beginning with *King of the Mardi Gras* (1935).

© Fleischer Studio/King Features

WALTER LANTZ & PAUL TERRY

If Disney pioneered storytelling and character development in the early 1930s, and if the Fleischers explored adult concepts and humor, then who was left to produce cartoons with cruder characters, less challenging stories and kid-friendly themes? In general, the Walter Lantz and Paul Terry studios filled this vacuum.

Walter Lantz

Walter Lantz took over production of Winkler's Oswald Rabbit cartoons from 1929. But picking up where Winkler left off did not mean using all of Winkler's employees. Hugh Harman, Rudy Ising and Friz Freleng were absent. The big name who stuck around was Bill Nolan, a silent-era pro with a silent-era sensibility.

The impact of this sensibility on Oswald production was visible in the casual way the studio came to operate. Whereas Disney recorded soundtracks before animation and Fleischer did them afterward, Lantz seems to have had it both ways, with an on-again, off-again result for synchronization. The Oswald character became one-dimensional, with mischief as his only consistent trait. Supporting players had even less consistency. *Chilly Con Carmen* (1930) shows a cat and hippo as rival suitors for Oswald's love, but when Oswald finally chooses the cat, the previously temperamental hippo does not react. The early Lantz talkies were rife with such inconsistencies.

This is not to call the new rabbit cartoons failures. Lantz said that his main desire was to make people laugh, and his films met that goal in spades. In *Spooks* (1930), the Phantom of the Opera grants a girl's wish for a singing voice by strapping a record player to her backside. In *Hell's Heels* (1930), an evil sheriff running a finger across his throat accidentally cuts his own head off.

Arrival of Avery

Given the silliness of the studio's gags, it was not surprising that cartoonist Fred "Tex" Avery (1908–80) – later famed for his screwball humor – was attracted to Lantz in late 1929. As an animator, Tex swiftly made his mark. *In The Zoo* (1933) breaks the fourth wall in a soon-to-be-famous Avery manner: when bees chew off a bear's fur, the bear forgoes shock in favor of a deadpan "Well, imagine that!".

© Pinto Colvig

Oswald

This drawing from a 1930 Oswald children's book by Walter Lantz captures the mayhem of the first Oswald cartoons. Oswald was a spunky character with a personality and look that would later be reminiscent of a certain famous mouse. His clever gestures and amusing gags made him hit with movie-goers.

© Walter Lantz Productions

Oswald the Lucky Rabbit » 20 Fleischer Brothers and Pre-recorded Sound » 38 Tex Avery at MGM » 128

© Paramount Pictures

Cartoonville

In 1929 Walter Lantz was put in charge of Universal Studio Cartoons (later known as Walter Lantz Studio) which was the principal supplier of animation to Universal Studios.

Alaska

Although this short was not credited to Tex Avery – an animator on Alaska – this and other verbal gags suggest his early influence. With Bill Nolan's rubbery animation style and a lively musical score, some of the Oswald shorts made no sense, instead were a vehicle for the animators' bizarre sense of humor.

Despite this, *In The Zoo* suffered. In 1931, the *Motion Picture Herald* criticized Lantz's films' rude humor, and Lantz seemingly took the critique seriously. The studio replaced bawdy gags and slapstick with cuddly cuteness. *Hot Feet* (1931) sanitized a gangster story by eliminating deadly threats; other shorts traded innuendo for childish hand-holding. Not long before, jazzy studio composer David Broekman had departed and was replaced by the less inspired James Dietrich – another blow to the cartoons.

A new star was introduced in 1932, Pooch the Pup, but failed to save the studio from its problems. Though Pooch's shorts featured fine Avery gags, Pooch was a cute non-character much as Oswald had become. The one effort at individuality was window dressing: Pooch opened many shorts walking along with a hobo's pack, whistling 'Kingdom Coming'. The tune was portentous, for Lantz and Tex Avery would both build more successful kingdoms in the years to come.

Paul Terry

If the Lantz studio had its ups and downs, Paul Terry displayed a talent for running on the spot – so that his product remained practically static over time. Terry began 1929 by leaving Van Beuren, whose *Aesop's Fables* would go on without him. Teaming up with Frank Moser, Terry set up the Terrytoons Studio in New York. By early 1930, Educational Pictures was distributing his first releases.

Terry did try for an auspicious start. Early *Terrytoons* were named after items of food, and set their action in the foods' countries of origin – so *Caviar* (1930) features babushka mice, and *Hot Turkey* (1930) a cat sultan. Sound was recorded in advance, with composer Phillip Scheib timing animation to classical orchestral scores. Initially large budgets made for lots of action on-screen.

Weak Links

Unfortunately for Terry, none of these advantages made up for his staff's weaknesses. As far as characterization went, Farmer Al Falfa was a one-dimensional grump. Other films used a pair of mice as recurring stars, but gave them no consistent personalities. Meanwhile, the shorts' drawing style was unattractive at best. Animal characters featured goggle eyes and uncertain levels of anthropomorphism. *Hawaiian Pineapple* (1930) includes the strangest creature of all: a non-humanized hen's upper body atop an adult male human's trousered legs and feet.

Perhaps the most striking feature of *Terrytoons* was that the studio went years without overcoming its deficiencies. Animators like Art Babbitt and Bill Tytla – who yearned to spread their wings – left Terry to do it. Luckily, they found gainful employment elsewhere. And luckily for Terry, in spite of everything, some exciting star characters and internal improvements did lie ahead.

When Walter Lantz replaced Winkler Pictures as Universal's producer of Oswald the Lucky Rabbit, some Winkler animators moved over to work for Lantz. Three who did not were Hugh Harman, Rudy Ising and Friz Freleng, all of whom had a luckier – and rabbit-less – future ahead.

Bosko

The real story began in January 1928 when Harman copyrighted a character called Bosko. A fun-loving minstrel boy, the figure had few instantly outstanding traits. Nevertheless, Harman had big ideas for the future of the character. Staying independent after the fall of Winkler's studio, Harman, Ising and Freleng made a sound-tracked pilot short, Bosko the Talk-Ink Kid (1929). While Harman and Ising shopped around for distributors, the financially needy Freleng moved east for temporary employment at Columbia's Krazy Kat studio.

Looney Tunes

In early 1930, Harman and Ising negotiated successfully with Leon Schlesinger (1884-1949), entrepreneur manager of Pacific Art and Title. The idea of opening a cartoon studio appealed to Schlesinger. He set Harman and Ising up in one, then contracted with Warner Bros. for the resulting films' release. Freleng returned, and Rollin Hamilton and other animators were assembled. Frank Marsales joined the crew as house musician. It would be a hefty task, as Warner asked that the Bosko cartoons promote songs from the Warner music publishing catalog. Treating the requirement as a marketable asset, Harman and Ising gave the cartoon series a name suggesting musicality, Looney Tunes (and echoing Disney's Silly Symphonies).

The Schlesinger studio released its first Bosko short, Sinkin' in the Bathtub, in April 1930. The cartoon's animation was easily as good as Disney's – not surprising, given the Mouse House alumni involved in its creation. As a bonus, the use of popular music gave Harman and Ising an audience-pleaser Disney could not match.

Buddy the Gob

Buddy made his first appearance in 1933, and represented an advance in character design for the Schlesinger studio. Up until around that time, the "rubber-hose" style had been the norm, whereby characters moved without regard to anatomy, as if all their limbs were rubber hoses. Instead, Buddy had discernible knees and elbows.

"BUDDY THE GOB"
"LOONEY TUNES" No 4

VITAPHONE # 3033
REL # 8104

© Warner Bros.

Smile, Darn Ya, Smile

The Merrie Melodies cartoons, such as Smile, Darn Ya, Smile, were designed to showcase songs from Warner Bros.' music library, and the cartoon's title was the title of the song it featured.

"BOSKO"

Bosko

Bosko was one of the *Looney Tunes* star characters, and the shorts he appeared in were full of music, singing, and dancing. These were the early days of sound cartoons, and audiences loved to see characters talking and moving in step with the music, and were less concerned about the lack of plot.

In terms of story ideas, however, the *Looney Tunes* series lagged behind Uncle Walt. Not to say that Harman's and Ising's subject matter was poorer than Disney's; it was just that Disney had already used it. *Congo Jazz* (1930), with hunter Bosko taming the wildlife, aped Mickey Mouse's *Jungle Rhythm* (1929). Bosko's World War One antics in *Bosko the Doughboy* (1931) mimicked Oswald's *Great Guns* (1927).

Merrie Melodies

Borrowed story lines or not, Bosko quickly became popular with audiences. So much so that in 1931 Schlesinger asked Harman and Ising for a second cartoon series. Titled "Merrie Melodies", the new shorts made music even more central than before. Whereas *Looney Tunes* used their tunes as backup scores, each *Melodie* was to show characters singing a chorus on-screen. At the outset, this meant that the *Melodies* stars – foxes named Foxy and Roxy – had Bosko-like adventures that just happened to stop for a song. Later, though, individual *Melodies* became one-shot cartoons, using the songs as starting points to create new settings and characters. *Pagan Moon* (1932) showed singing Hawaiian islanders, while *You're Too Careless with Your Kisses* (1933) set insects' marital woes to music. The series spoke of Harman's and Ising's genuine desire to experiment and grow – even if the one-off stars of many entries were awfully reminiscent of Bosko and his girlfriend, Honey.

And therein lay the rub. Harman and Ising were artists who yearned to improve; Harman often spoke of beating Disney at his own game. Yet the two were content to use Disney-like characters and plots in a manner that made negative comparisons with Disney inescapable.

A Move to MGM

By 1933 – the year in which Freleng began to direct – a solution began to present itself. Bosko was by now a rounded and successful star, with nimble wit and a full supporting cast. More importantly, though, his shorts were developing a cheerfully satiric style that owed little to other studios. Verbal humor and blackout gags began to appear.

Ironically, 1933 would also be the last year in which Bosko *Looney Tunes* were produced. Seeking to improve their films' quality, Harman and Ising tried – and failed – to wring higher budgets from Schlesinger. Rebuffed, they chose to sign a new cartoon production contract with MGM.

Yet this was no tragedy for any of the involved parties. At MGM, Harman and Ising would nurture a great new school of animators. Meanwhile, Freleng and others remained with Schlesinger to create a new Warner studio and a new *Looney Tunes* – featuring more of that subversive, satirical new style. Great accomplishments lay ahead.

Harman and Ising at MGM » 64

To a remarkable degree, the story of early sound animation is one of studios trying to beat Walt Disney at his own game. None succeeded, and some fell particularly short – either artistically, commercially or both. Among Disney's least effective rivals were Amedee Van Beuren and Charles Mintz. Seventy years later, though, their best cartoons retain a quirky period charm.

Van Beuren: Crude Humor, Cruder Art

In the silent era, Amedee Van Beuren had been part owner of the Fables studio, producer of Paul Terry's Farmer Al Falfa cartoons. He acquired the New York-based operation in 1928, renaming it after himself. Van Beuren was an executive, however, not an artist or animator. Animator Isadore Klein said he never once laid eyes on his boss.

No studio copied Mickey Mouse so unabashedly. Cartoons such as *Hot Tamale* (1930) and *Circus Capers* (1930) star a boy and girl mouse who might have been indistinguishable from Mickey and Minnie – if the Van Beuren versions had been better drawn. An understandably annoyed Walt Disney went to court to end their career.

The studio's other characters tended to be short-lived, too. Tom and Jerry (1931–33) were a Mutt-and-Jeff-like human duo – and no relation to MGM's later cat-and-mouse superstars. Cubby Bear (1933–34) was an ursine approximation of Mickey Mouse; Molly Moo Cow (1935–36) was, well … a cow. The studio also tried characters from other media, such as Otto Soglow's popular comic-strip potentate *The Little King* (1933–34) and radio sensation *Amos n' Andy* (1934).

The Sunshine Makers

Artwise, these cartoons were usually rudimentary. Many, made before the movie industry's "Hays Code" cracked down on racy entertainment, appear startling today for their sex- and bathroom-oriented humor. In 1934's *Sultan Pepper*, for instance, the little king, his sultan pal and the sultan's harem all bound into a bedroom together, then shut the door. But the studio's most famous work is the infectiously adorable *The Sunshine Makers* (1935), about a battle between happy and gloomy elves.

Van Beuren's staff did not lack talent. Among the many employees who went on to better things were Joe Barbera, Shamus Culhane, Frank Tashlin and Jim Tyer. In 1934, the studio

Krazy Kat

Krazy Kat began life as a cartoon strip, created by the quirky imagination of George Herriman in 1910, and had a cult following among newspaper readers. Mintz's version of the character was round and bouncy, and had nothing in common with the original.

hired Burt Gillett, director of Disney's mega hit *Three Little Pigs*, to head operations. It even obtained the rights to 1920s star Felix the Cat, who appeared in three elaborate, if bland, cartoons in the studio's all-color *Rainbow Parade* series in 1936.

That same year, however, the studio's distributor, RKO, signed an agreement to release Walt Disney's films – spelling an end to Van Beuren cartoons.

Mintz: A Kat and a Kid

Producer Charles Mintz is best remembered as the man who commandeered Walt Disney's Oswald the Lucky Rabbit – and most of Disney's staff – in 1928. The gambit proved disastrous: Disney responded by creating Mickey Mouse. From 1929 to 1932, Columbia released both Disney's films and most of Mintz's.

In 1930, Mintz relocated his studio from New York to Hollywood and tried to take on Disney's mouse with a cat – namely Krazy Kat, the creation of brilliant newspaper cartoonist George Herriman. But Mintz's Ben Harrison and Manny Gould turned the Kat into a feline Mickey clone, with a hint of Felix. Despite this, many Krazy cartoons have an engaging 1930s feel. In *Birth of Jazz* (1932), for instance, a hipster Krazy pilots a plane around the world, releasing a payload of music that spurs everyone from Russian Bolsheviks to the Statue of Liberty to get rhythm.

Scrappy

Another Mintz character, Toby the Pup, appeared in films released by RKO in 1930–31. Fleischer veterans Dick Huemer, Sid Marcus and Art Davis worked on these cartoons, and the trio were also responsible for Scrappy , a much longer-lived creation. Debuting in 1931's *Yelp Wanted*, Scrappy was a human boy – albeit one with a disturbingly massive head. Supporting players included his obstreperous little brother Oopy, his girlfriend Margie and his dog Yippy. In *The Flop House* (1932), our young hero operated a seedy home for dissolute animals, in a short that Paul Etcheverry has called "perhaps the ultimate depression-era cartoon".

All but forgotten today, Scrappy was prominent enough to inspire an array of merchandise, from dolls and books to soap sculpted into his likeness. Eventually, he evolved into a slightly more realistic-looking kid; his series expired in early 1941, a year after the last Krazy Kat short.

By then, the studio was making a lot of one-shot cartoons, in the *Fables*, *Phantasies* and *Color Rhapsodies* series. And Charles Mintz himself was gone – he had died in 1939. But his studio, owned since 1937 by Columbia, soldiered on into the 1940s.

© Columbia Studios

Scrappy

For the usual Scrappy cartoon, the three main animators who worked on the series, Dick Huemer, Sid Marcus and Art Davis, would each devise one third of the story, thereby ensuring that Scrappy's adventures were wild and exciting.

Felix the Cat » 18 Oswald the Lucky Rabbit » 20

UB IWERKS

Ub Iwerks' early-1930 departure from Disney amounted to a star player switching teams at the top of his game. Arranging to finance Iwerks in a studio of his own, erstwhile Disney distributor Pat Powers apparently saw him as Uncle Walt's secret weapon. So, it seems, did the media of the day. Before Iwerks' Hollywood shop had released a single short, trade papers in England and Germany were already predicting a Disney-trouncing success level.

Flip the Frog

Iwerks did enjoy a personal success at the outset. His self-created star character, Flip the Frog, had appeared in embryo form in a Disney cartoon – *Night* (1930) – but when Iwerks expressed a desire to use him as a recurring figure, Walt declined. Now, with Iwerks himself as producer, the frog would at last headline his own series.

Fiddlesticks (1930), featuring Flip in a woodland vaudeville show, set the tone for many Iwerks shorts to come. The frog mugs memorably at the viewer and the musical sequences are expertly animated. Cheerfully rude humor is deployed when Flip spanks his piano on the backside and it objects. There is also a technical accomplishment: *Fiddlesticks* was produced in color, a rarity at the time. Problematically for a pilot short, however, *Fiddlesticks'* storytelling was meandering and slow – as it was in the Flip cartoons that followed.

Room Runners

Such a drawback did not hinder Flip – or Iwerks – at first. Released by Powers' own Celebrity Pictures, the initial few releases were successful, leading MGM to buy distribution rights. Flip dolls, books and toys appeared, and star animators like Fleischer's Grim Natwick joined Iwerks' studio. In some ways, the cartoons' characterization and plotting improved, too. The frog became a self-conscious, likable loser, and his stories burst with promise. It is not hard to see the potential in *Laughing Gas* (1931), where dentist Flip must extract a walrus's tusk, or *The Village Specialist* (1931), with plumber Flip sending a house sky-high on a plume of water. In one case – the racy hotel farce *Room Runners* (1932) – potential was definitely met.

Yet *Room Runners* was the exception to the rule. Most of the time, as in *Fiddlesticks*, fundamentally sound plots were undermined on-screen by slow pacing, soft gag impact and a basic meandering feel. Occasional rude laughs lifted the spirits of

© Film Preservation Association

Flip the Frog

After his first two outings, Flip the Frog's froginess was quickly toned down, and he became species-ambiguous, with his white-gloved hands, white-shoed feet and upright posture. Nevertheless, the animation in the *Flip the Frog* series was clean and smooth, with watercolor-like effects, and were some of the best-looking cartoons from the 1930s.

Little Red Hen

The *ComiColor* shorts, such as *Little Red Hen*, were made using the Cinecolor process. This was a two-color system that emphasized red and blue at the expense of green, which meant that the resulting cartoons did not contain a complete color spectrum.

© Film Preservation Association

these shorts, but typically only in fits and starts. And instead of noticing these problems, the staff instead focused on redesigning Flip's physique. Apparently, the frog could not look un-frog-like enough for Powers, nor for many of the newer animators on the staff.

Willie Whopper and ComiColor Cartoons

Whether due to visual inconsistency or storytelling weakness, Flip had lost enough popularity by late 1933 that two new Iwerks series replaced him: Willie Whopper, distributed by MGM, and ComiColor Cartoons, distributed by Powers' own Celebrity Pictures. Debuting in *Play Ball* (1933), Willie Whopper was a boy Baron Munchausen, opening each cartoon by addressing his spectators directly with the phrase, "Did I ever tell you about the time … ". *ComiColor* shorts, meanwhile, were gagged-up Cinecolor fairy tales of the type Disney was contemporaneously producing as *Silly Symphonies*.

On the positive side, the wacky and occasionally blue humor of these new shorts rivaled any Flip the Frog adventure. *Hell's Fire* (1934), with Willie and the Devil teaming up against Mr Prohibition, was one classic example. *Balloonland* (1935) was another, with its villainous Pincushion Man. Iwerks, a mechanical genius away from the drawing board, pioneered great technical advancements. From car parts he built the an early multiplane camera, with which a background could be filmed in multiple layers, creating the illusion of depth.

Jack and the Beanstalk

Jack and the Beanstalk was the first *ComiColor* to be produced, in 1933. The *ComiColor* series comprised 24 one-shot shorts, meaning that no continuing characters were used. They were often reworkings of classic stories and fairy tales.

© Film Preservation Association

No Attention to Detail

Unfortunately, the new technology was put to work in shorts featuring by-now-traditional Iwerks problems. There was shifting character design: Willie started rail-thin, then got roly-poly, and never had much of a consistent personality. There was dull pacing: Iwerks' plodding *Little Red Hen* (1934) paled beside Disney's contemporaneous *Wise Little Hen* (1934). Finally, Iwerks' shorts began to take design shortcuts: the same little boy model is reused for Tom Thumb, Aladdin and other *ComiColor* heroes.

By 1934, MGM had given up on Iwerks, casting their lot with Hugh Harman and Rudolph Ising for Technicolor cartoons. Iwerks' distribution arrangement with Powers was a dead end, too: the *ComiColor* shorts just could not compete in the marketplace against the majors. Given Iwerks' unmatched skill in numerous areas of animation, one cannot help but be disappointed. Iwerks' studio would continue on — working as a hired hand for the rest of the decade, contributing Porky Pig (Warner Brothers) and *Color Rhapsody* (Columbia), subjects as needed for other producers. But it must not be overlooked that, deficiencies aside, the Iwerks studio created a number of genuinely classic cartoons, and that Flip the Frog is today a favorite of nostalgia buffs.

sergeant knocks it down, and *Three Ha'pence a Foot* (1937), regarding an altercation over the price of timber for the construction of Noah's ark.

After a period of producing war-related information films for the government, Dyer turned to making cartoon shorts for children: *The Squirrel War* (1947), *Who Robbed the Robins* (1947) and *Fowl Play* (1950). But the writing was on the wall and, due to ill health, he retired from film-making in 1952, although he continued to paint, sketch and lecture on animation up to his death 10 years later.

Alexandre Alexeieff

At the age of 18, Russian-born Alexandre Alexeieff (1901–82) journeyed to Paris to study painting and design with the intent of becoming a book illustrator. Instead, however, he settled on being a set designer for the ballet. Inspired by Fernand Léger's acclaimed *Ballet Mécanique* (1924), he was prompted to experiment with his own

creation, *Night on Bald Mountain* (1933), using his own, painstaking device of animating known as the pinscreen.

The Pinscreen Technique

The instrument used to create this type of animation can best be described as an upright white plate, perforated with tiny holes into which slide the same number of steel rods (or pins). When illuminated correctly, small rollers are used to push the pins in to the degree needed to create a satisfactory image. The solitary picture is then photographed and subsequently altered to the next position. Perfect lighting and shadow contribute to create the illusion of a finely engraved pastel etching.

Alexeieff did not touch the screen until World War Two, when he was asked to produce entertainment films for the National Film Board of Canada. The most endearing entry is *En Passant* ('In Passing', 1943), a light-hearted interpretation of Canadian folk songs. Returning to publicity films, Alexeieff continued making films with his American-born wife, Claire Parker (1906–81), and did not touch the pinscreen until his interpretation of Nikolai Gogol's grim tale of an individual obsessed by his own nose, *Le Nez* ('The Nose', 1965).

En Passant

En Passant was made using the revolutionary pinscreen technique. With this, it was possible to create a range of dramatic textural effects and shading variations from black to white, through various grays that was difficult to achieve with the more traditional medium of cel animation.

Le Nez

Le Nez, created using Alexeieff's pinscreen technique, demonstrated the etching-like results that could be achieved with his method. The thousands of pins inserted into the screen would be moved between photographing frames, enabling subtle shadow effects to be created.

István Kiszly Kató was the father of Hungarian animation. The graphic artist and creator of weekly cartoon news bulletins made his first film in 1914 using cut-outs. He made a few short films, including *Janos the Knight* (1916) and *Romeo and Juliet* (1931), but unable to find much support for his work, he turned instead to education and advertising animation film production.

The Beginnings

Hungarian animation, however, did not really begin until the 1930s when a former painter named Sándor Bortnyik opened up a school for the art of promotion in 1928. At this school, a young graphic artist named Gyula Macskássy met János Halász (1912–95). In 1932, the duo founded a studio that produced over 100 advertising cartoons, using a wide range of animation techniques. Unfortunately, many of Macskássy's colleagues left Hungary to pursue artistic ambitions that simply could not be realized in Hungary. Among those to emigrate were János Halász, who moved to England and changed his name to John Halas, and György Marczincsák (1908–80), who became George Pal.

A few artists, including Macskássy, continued to work on both artistic and commercial animation projects with varying degrees of success. But with a limited market for animation shorts, Hungarian animation would have to wait until the end of World War Two to find an identity and an audience.

Berthold Bartosch

Berthold Bartosch (1893–1968) was born in Polaun, Bohemia (now called Polubny and part of the Slovak Republic). At age 18, he moved to Vienna to study architecture. On the advice of one of his art teachers, Bartosch began making educational animation films. In 1919, he moved to Berlin to continue this work. While there he met many artists, including German animator Lotte Reiniger. Bartosch worked on some of Reiniger's silhouette animation films before being approached by German publisher Kurt Wolff to make a film version of an illustrated storybook by Flemish artist Frans Masereel. Wolff wanted Bartosch to re-create Masereel's wood engravings on film. Bartosch agreed, moved to Paris, and for two years, much of it in his apartment, worked on the film *L'idée* ('The Idea', 1931). It would be his only surviving work.

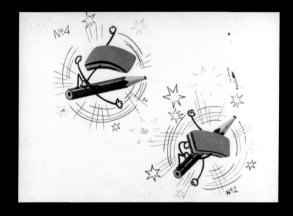

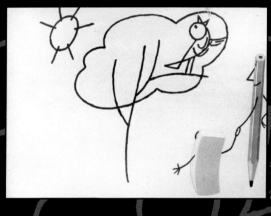

© Pannonia Film

Pencil and Rubber – sequence

Made by Hungarian pioneer animator Gyula Macskássy in 1960, this short won the country its first prize at an international festival. The foundations of his career were laid during the 1930s when he made commercials using all kinds of diverse animation techniques, which could be seen as individual cartoons in their own right.

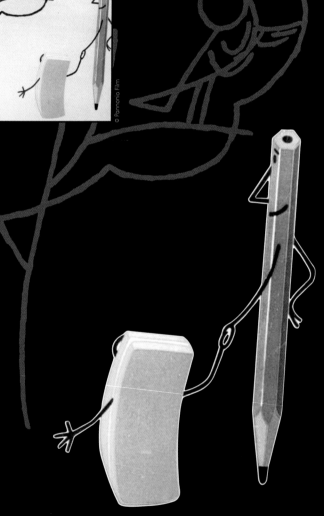

© Bertold Bartosch

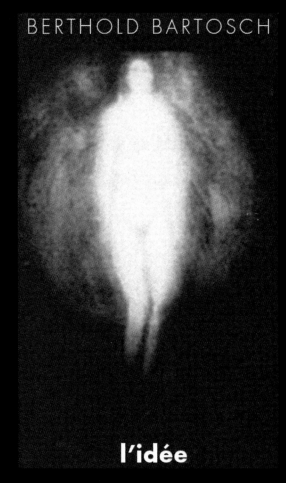

BERTHOLD BARTOSCH

l'idée

L'idée – sequence

Bartosch's *L'idée* was tragic, symbolist allegory of man's struggle for the Ideal, based on illustrations by Franz Masereel and with music by Arthur Honegger. Bartosch combined cut-out silhouettes on the lines of the Reiniger technique with subtle effects achieved by control of photographic exposure and diffusion of the light source.

The Idea

The plot of *L'idée* is simple. A man conjures up his idea of beauty and purity through the figure of a young woman. While some try to manipulate, intimidate and destroy the idea, it carries on untouched and spreads throughout the world.

L'idée was a remarkable film for many reasons. First, by infusing the film with poetics, politics and personal expression, Bartosch shows us that animation can match any of the great art forms. Secondly, *L'idée* is a technical marvel. Bartosch animated approximately 45,000 frames on four levels of glass sheets, sometimes with as many as 18 superimpositions involved. The soft, milky, iridescent atmosphere was created using wash-tinted blacks and a normal bar of soap, which were then lit from below by 100-watt lightbulbs.

In the end, it was never released, and Bartosch never made any money from it. After his second film was destroyed during the war, Bartosch spent his last years concentrating on painting.

The Greedy Bee

Gyula Macskássy (later to become George Pal), who began his career in animation by founding a studio with János Halász (later to become John Halas) in the 1930s producing commercials, went on to make Hungary's first animated cartoons, such as the one pictured here from 1958.

© Pannonia Film

II: EARLY 1930s: FINDING ITS VOICE   ASIA: JAPAN & CHINA

The early 1930s saw Japanese animation become more closely tied to the increasingly nationalistic spirit following Japan's military incursions into Chinese Manchuria. There were still many art films and adaptations of folk tales, but it was becoming important to gain the goodwill and patronage of the government and the Imperial Navy, which considered animated films to be excellent for anti-Western domestic propaganda.

Kenzo Masaoka

Kenzo Masaoka (1898–1988) was one of Japan's leading animators during the early period of sound films. He produced the first series of a two-film story, the cut-paper animation *A Shipwreck Tale: Part 1, Monkey Island*, and its sequel, *Part 2, The Pirate Ship* both in 1931. His 1933 cartoon animation *The World of Power and Women*, a comedy for adults, was Japan's first animated film with an optical soundtrack. The 1934 children's cartoon animation *Tahchan's Trip to the Bottom of the Sea* showed Masaoka's interest in experimenting in all production media to produce animation for all age groups.

Yasuji Murata

Masaoka and Noburo Ofuji did not support Japan's growing nationalism and kept to folkloric, art and non-political humorous films. Yasuji Murata continued to animate folk tales such as *The Monkey's Big Catch* (1933, released January 1934), but he also produced the first propaganda cartoon, *Aerial Momotaro* (1931). This portrayal of the young folk-tale hero and his anthropomorphized animal companions as modern fighter pilots, who become peacemakers in a war between penguins and albatrosses, glamorized both the military and the concept of Japan as the benevolent "big brother" of all other Asiatic/Pacific peoples. In 1933–34 Murata directed the first animated series based on a popular Japanese comic strip, a four-film adaptation of *Norakuro* (*Black Dog*) by Shiho Tagawa, starring a dog recruit in a funny-animal army: *Buck Private Norakuro – Training*, *Buck Private Norakuro – Drills*, *Sergeant Norakuro*, and *2nd Lieutenant Norakuro – The Sunday Mystery*.

Propaganda Animation

Mitsuyo Seo (b. 1911) started off as Masaoka's assistant, but quickly graduated to producer/director. His first films were *The Mischievous Little Ant* (1933) and *Sankichi the Monkey – Air Defense Military Exercise* (1933), the latter a militaristic funny-animal comedy. Seo would evolve from producing both general cartoons and martial cartoons

© Kenzo Masaoka

Shipwreck Tale

From the first part of this film story by Kenzo Masaoka, this short was made using cut-paper animation and was one of Japan's earliest animation films to use sound.

to only the latter, culminating in Japan's first wartime propaganda animated feature.

The first clearly anti-Western animation was Takao Nakano's *Black Cat Hooray!* (April 1934), in which a party of dolls in Japanese costumes and traditional Japanese toys are attacked by vicious bandits who are rat parodies of Mickey Mouse and snake parodies of American or British sailors. Momotaro and other Japanese folk heroes save the day. As the 1930s progressed, animation such as this would become more common.

Some animators created studio names for themselves, such as Murata's Yokohama Cinema Kyokai and Seo's Nihon Manga Film Kenkuyo. But their films remained essentially individual hobbyist productions, animated at home or in a small office by the animator and a few assistants. They did, however, get increasing financing from the professional motion picture companies, who paid for their production materials in return for distribution rights.

China

After Japan effectively annexed Manchuria from China in 1931, a wave of nationalism and anti-Japanese feeling swept China. The Wan Brothers took advantage of this to produce propagandistic animation such as *The Price of Blood* (1932). In 1933 the Mingxing Film Company in Shanghai hired Lai-ming, Gu-chan and Chao-chen to set up an animation unit. The Wan Brothers utilized both cut-paper and cel animation for popular entertainment, as well as patriotic films such as *The Sad State of the Nation* and *Aviation Saves China*, until 1937, when the Japanese capture of Shanghai closed the studio.

© Yasuji Murata

Norakuro (Black Dog)

This animated series, Japan's first, reflected the growing influence of the military in Japanese society. It also emphasises the stylistic shift that had been taking place during the 1930s away from folk tales towards faster-paced, Western-style humor.

1934–39:
TECHNICOLOR FANTASIES

Technicolor brought a new look to animated films of the 1930s. The depression made everything seem gray – so delightful multicolored flights of fancy created by Hollywood's screen cartoonists were welcomed and rewarded. The Hollywood Production Code cleaned up the frequent outhouse humor and Betty Boop's risqué antics – but the public was dazzled by evolving new techniques, more sophisticated storytelling and advanced visuals.

Animation art grew in exciting ways during this period. Extra-length shorts and feature-length films emerged. Multi-plane and Stereoptical backgrounds gave depth to the previously flat cartoon landscapes. Full character animation allowed greater personality development. Professional voice actors got into the game – Mel Blanc in particular – giving cartoon stars broader appeal.

Oskar Fischinger and George Pal became leading animators in Europe with their innovative work. Creativity, artistry and commercial success seemed to work together during this period. The highlight of this era, Walt Disney's *Snow White and the Seven Dwarfs*, is an incredible feature film, and influenced the shape of animation for the rest of the century. Its impact was felt worldwide, and it gave animated films a new status.

It was the period when animation came of age.

WALT DISNEY & THE GANG

Disney's *Silly Symphonies* advanced the art of animation storytelling. These heartwarming shorts were a welcome dose of laughter for a nation in the grip of the Great Depression. Jobs were scarce across America, but the Disney studio expanded its staff in 1934–35. Referred to as "the nine old men", Les Clark, Frank Thomas, Ollie Johnston, Milt Kahl, Marc Davis, Wolfgang "Woolie" Reitherman, Eric Larson, John Lounsbery and Ward Kimball formed the core group of animators who would become the talent pool on many features to come.

© The Walt Disney Company

Donald Duck

In 1934 the world was introduced to a character who, starting only as a bit player in *Wise Little Hen*, would become almost as synonymous with Disney as Mickey Mouse – Donald Duck. Clarence Nash was the voice actor who brought life to the nearly unintelligible fowl. The audience's and animators' instant love for the zany character, which was chiefly developed by animator Dick Lundy, allowed him to move from *Silly Symphonies* to Mickey's gang in *Orphan's Benefit*.

The Gang

In 1935, story department head Ted Sears formulated detailed analyses of all of the characters' personalities for the staff to use as a reference. That same year, the first color Mickey Mouse cartoon, *The Band Concert*, debuted and two *Silly Symphonies*, *The Tortoise and the Hare* – with its notable advancements in the representation of speed – and *Three Orphan Kittens*, shared the Academy Award for Best Animated Short. An explosion of creativity erupted in 1936 with the premiere of nine Mickey Mouse shorts, including *Thru the Mirror*, which transported Mickey into the *Through the Looking Glass* story, and *Moving Day*, which featured Mickey, Donald and Goofy being evicted from their home, a clear reference to a common experience of the day. By now, Donald Duck had become so popular that he was given his own starring role in *Donald and Pluto*.

In 1937, with many of the artists graduating from the shorts to work on *Snow White*, only three *Silly Symphonies* were released – *Woodland Café, Little*

Clock Cleaners

A classic nine-minute short, *Clock Cleaners* features "the gang" – Mickey Mouse, Donald Duck and Goofy – as cleaners working in a clock tower that has a mind of its own.

© The Walt Disney Company

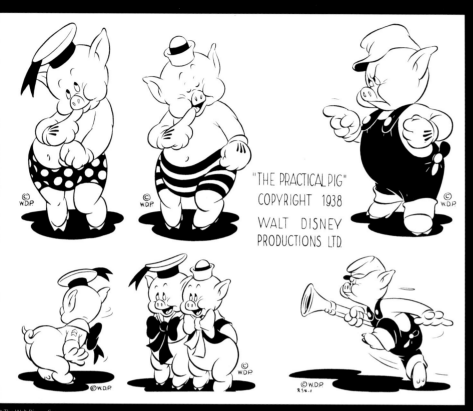

"THE PRACTICAL PIG"
COPYRIGHT 1938
WALT DISNEY
PRODUCTIONS LTD.

Hiawatha and *The Old Mill* – the latter marking the first use of the multi-plane camera. This breakthrough in animation utilized backgrounds painted on glass that were set at varying distances, creating an increased sense of depth. The short garnered an Oscar for Best Cartoon, as well as a technical award for developer Bill Garity and his team. This year also continued the successful pairing of Mickey, Donald and Goofy as "the gang", producing some of the most memorable shorts of all time, such as *Hawaiian Holiday*, *Clock Cleaners* and *Lonesome Ghosts*. Two more "Mickey Mouse" cartoons were released that year starring a solo Donald – *Don Donald* and *Modern Inventions*, the latter featuring the debut of Donna Duck, later renamed Daisy. Donald's next solo appearance – *Donald's Ostrich* – would mark the first short labeled as a Donald Duck cartoon. Pluto also received his first starring role in *Pluto's Quin-Puplets*.

The Practical Pig

One of the last *Silly Symphonies* to be made, *The Practical Pig* is a sequel to the classic short *Three Little Pigs*. After this, Disney began to focus more on feature films.

The Old Mill

Famous for being the first animation to make use of the multi-plane camera technique, pioneering *Silly Symphony*, *The Old Mill* was made in 1937. Developed by the Disney studio, the multi-plane camera gave added depth to background shots.

Mickey's Circus – sketch

Released in 1936, *Mickey's Circus* features Mickey and Minnie Mouse and Donald Duck, shown in this graphite-on-paper animation drawing after having trouble with his sea-lion act.

Redesigning an Icon

In an attempt to revitalize Mickey in the face of Donald Duck's ever-growing popularity, animator Fred Moore was allowed to redesign the famous mouse (shrinking his cheeks and adding whites to his eyes), which debuted in 1939's *The Pointer*. "The gang" had become so famous that Goofy was given his own series, starting with *Goofy and Wilbur*. By this time, the shorts had moved away from gags and focused more on character development, which some said made them too refined. The end of the decade stood as a major transition for Disney. That year would see the end of *Silly Symphonies* with the *Three Little Pigs* sequel, *The Practical Pig*, and the color remake of *The Ugly Duckling*, which won an Oscar. The success of *Snow White* allowed the company to move to a bigger studio in Burbank, where the studio remains today, and the focus began to shift from shorts to features.

SNOW WHITE

By 1934, Walt Disney had realized that the success of the shorts would not sustain the studio forever. He assembled his artists and told them the story of *Snow White and the Seven Dwarfs*, which had been dear to him since his childhood. Riding the enthusiasm of Disney, the artists were ecstatic. However, many Hollywood observers thought the venture was doomed, fearing adults would not respond to a long-form animated film.

Taking a Chance

Disney understood the daunting challenges the undertaking of the film would entail. The story was kept simple, but the original fairy tale needed to be fleshed out and pacing became essential. Disney felt an audience could not endure a short's frantic pace for 70 minutes. He also wanted the scenes to flow naturally into one another, and ultimately ordered painful cuts of whole sections that did not serve the story. Another key issue was developing distinct personalities for all seven dwarves, much like the work done on *Three Little Pigs*. The most criticized portion was the rendering of the realistic human characters, which were Rotoscoped, a process of tracing live-action actors' movements.

A Learning Curve

For this enormous production, the studio enlisted all of its top artists, including Art Babbitt, Shamus Culhane, Hamilton Luske, Fred Moore, Norman Ferguson, Vladimir "Bill" Tytla and Myron "Grim" Natwick. The film served as a learning experience every step of the way. Long hours were spent redoing detailed scenes to get them just right. For instance, Culhane took six months to animate the one-minute "Heigh Ho" segment.

With the increased amount of dialogue, the animators found they needed to use more body language when characters spoke. Ferguson, a movement master and the chief animator behind the development of Pluto, was in charge of bringing the Queen to life and creating her terrifying transformation into the wicked witch. Natwick oversaw Snow White and found, unlike the dwarves whose cartoony looks allowed more room for error, each pose of Snow White had to be perfect or the movement would appear jumpy. Tytla, one of the studio's most respected animators, oversaw Grumpy, and along with Don Graham, was key in developing the talents of the young animators, who started on the *Silly Symphonies* and moved on to *Snow White*. Many of the studio's legendary "nine old men" started out as assistants on the project.

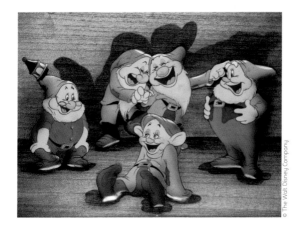

The Seven Dwarfs

Walt Disney knew it was imperative to develop individual personalities for all seven of the dwarves in order to maintain the interest and sympathy of an audience. In order to animate the human characters realistically, the animators had to study anatomy and footage of live-action models.

© The Walt Disney Company

Snow White

This original painting on celluloid was used in the filming of *Snow White*. The huge success of the film meant that Disney could turn his attention to producing feature-length films as opposed to animated shorts.

Disney Artist

Animation began in 1936, and ultimately more than 750 artists worked on *Snow White*, including 32 animators, 102 animation assistants, 20 layout men, 25 background artists, 65 effects animators, and 158 inkers and painters. In all, at least two million sketches were created and more than 250,000 drawings were used on-screen.

Phenomenal Success

After years of arduous work, the film, which was now six times over its initial budget at almost $1.5 million, debuted in a gala Hollywood premiere on 21 December 1937. It was an instant phenomenon.

    Disney, always the savvy businessman, saw an opportunity, and for the first time in history had merchandising lined up before the film was released so fans could run to the nearest department store and take home a piece of the magic. The emotional depth of the tale and subtle humanity of the animated characters awed critics and audiences. This was a film that launched an entire industry and changed cinema forever.

Bambi » 82 *The Lion King* » 304

COLOR CLASSICS

Animated cartoons in the 1930s saw tremendous technical advancements: first with the introduction of sound, and next with the addition of color. Although Walt Disney's *Flowers and Trees* (1931) launched the color cartoon era, there were earlier efforts going back to the silents. The earliest known color cartoon in the United States is Bray's 1920 release, *The Debut of Thomas Cat*, made in the Brewster Color Process. Other color systems, such as Synthechrome by Carpenter-Goldman Laboratories and two-color Technicolor, continued to develop well into the 1920s. These color systems, however, used only red and green, or red and blue, which limited their range in color reproduction.

The Technicolor Process

Ub Iwerks released his premier Flip the Frog cartoon, *Fiddlesticks*, in two-color Technicolor. But it was the introduction of the three-color Technicolor process in the early 1930s that resulted in the greatest improvement, presenting the widest possibilities for animated cartoons. Although Technicolor representatives approached the various studios, it was independent producer Walt Disney who took the gamble that paid off. This was a bold risk on the part of both Disney and Technicolor Corporation.

Max Fleischer and Fleischer Studios

The depression in the United States was at its height in the year 1931. Disney was struggling financially, many times going through lay-off periods due to interruptions of cash flow. The largest cartoon studio at the time was Fleischer Studios, due to their ties with Paramount. Max Fleischer was immediately interested in Technicolor, but was denied the opportunity due to the corporate reorganization brought on by Paramount's first series of bankruptcies in the 1930s. Fleischer's loss became Disney's gain.

The value of color cartoons was being realized in the same respect as sound cartoons of the early talkie period. Cartoons were easier and cheaper to produce in color, adding value and prestige to the black-and-white theatrical program. By 1934, Paramount had consented to the production of a color series, *Color Classics*, to be produced by Fleischer. But with Disney's exclusivity to three-color Technicolor, Fleischer was forced to use the available two-color processes for the first two years. The series began with *Poor Cinderella* (1934), which used the red-and-blue Cinecolor process. All other releases were made in the red-and-green two-color Technicolor process until 1936. The addition of the Stereoptical process, which created a third-dimensional background effect, offered compensation for the limited color spectrum — and a feature that was unique from Disney.

But by 1936, Disney's exclusivity had expired, and Fleischer Studios released its first, and possibly best, *Color Classic*, *Somewhere in Dreamland* in the three-color Technicolor process.

Dave Fleischer

Dave Fleischer received director credit on every Max Fleisher cartoon. As Max's brother he began his affiliation with the studio by dressing up as a clown and being photographed and Rotoscoped for the early Koko experiments.

© Fleischer Studio

Aladdin and His Wonderful Lamp – sketch

During the 1930s Fleischer put his biggest star in three Technicolor specials. *Popeye Meets Sindbad* (1936) and *Popeye Meets Ali Baba* (1937) contain elaborate three-dimensional settings and a lavish color palatte. *Aladdin and his Wonderful Lamp* (1939) was the final one in the series.

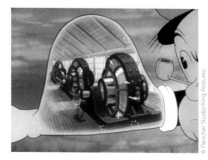

© Fleischer Studio/King Features

COMPETING WITH DISNEY

Walt Disney created the market for color cartoons, and by 1934 other producers had begun to follow him. Ub Iwerks started releasing cartoons, with the *ComiColor* and *Willie Wopper* series in red-and-blue Cinecolor. At the same time, Charles Mintz started the production of the *Color Rhapsody* series for Columbia, beginning with *Holiday Land* (1934).

A Rainbow of Color

Burt Gillett (1891–1971) revamped the Van Beuren Studio with *The Rainbow Parade*, first using two-color Technicolor and later the three-color process. *Merrie Melodies* became Warner's color cartoon series, and under their new association with MGM, Harmon and Ising started producing color *Happy Harmonies*. Walter Lantz produced six *Cartune Classic* cartoons for Universal in two-color Technicolor, then returned to black and white until 1939. Paul Terry waited until 1938 before releasing *Terrytoons* in full Technicolor. Aside from the obvious addition of color, all of these cartoons were conceived with common elements: musical, fairy tale fantasies fashioned in the "Disney" mode. And as Disney continued to move forward, the entire industry seemed poised to follow his next move, animated features.

Although his competitors referred to it as a folly, they underestimated Disney's vision and the secret to his successes. Unlike other cartoon producers, Disney was using animation as a means to achieving serious success as a cinematic storyteller. And as Disney gained more experience as a film-maker, he focused on emotional elements instead of comedy for its own sake. This effort is what separated Disney from other cartoon makers, but his drive to continually raise standards elevated costs to such an extent that his only means of financial survival would be in animated features. This was proved in Walt Disney's production of *Snow White and the Seven Dwarfs*.

Gulliver's Travels

It has been assumed that Max Fleischer's motivation for producing *Gulliver's Travels* was to imitate Disney's success, but internal memos indicate that Fleischer had plans to make features as early as 1934, and Fleischer Studios was the only other studio large enough to undertake such a level of production. Paramount discouraged Fleischer's

Gulliver's Travels – face

The character of Gulliver was Rotoscoped – a method devised by the Fleischers where the drawing was achieved by tracing over the movements of a live actor.

Gulliver's Travels – leg

A milestone in the art of animation, *Gulliver's Travels* was the second animated motion picture of its magnitude ever produced, and the first animated feature from a studio other than Disney.

© Paramount

© Paramount

© Fleischer Studio

Stereoptical Process

Illustrated here is the three-dimensional Stereoptical process developed by Max Fleischer in 1934. It involved positioning cel animation cartoon characters in front of three-dimensional models in order to create movement and give an illusion of greater depth and detail.

plans, due largely to corporate reorganization. Fleischer's production of the longer-format Popeye specials was used as a gradual transition to features, beginning with *Popeye the Sailor Meets Sinbad the Sailor* (1936) and *Popeye the Sailor Meets Ali Baba and His Forty Thieves* (1937). These full Technicolor specials, using the three-dimensional Stereoptical process, suggested the possibilities of what could be done by Fleischer in full-length animated features. But this was never quite realized.

Fine Features

The phenomenal success of Disney's *Snow White* proved that animated features were big at the box office, and Paramount wanted one for a 1939 Christmas release. Several concepts such as *Peter Pan*, *The Blue Bird* and *Neptune's Daughter* (*The Little Mermaid*) were considered. Finally, *Gulliver's Travels* was pressed into production. Disney had spent over $1 million, with three years of development and 18 months of production, but Fleischer was given only 18 months and $500,000 for the entire development and final delivery. Fleischer Studios moved to Miami, Florida, but relocation expenses drove the production costs to $1 million, schedules were rushed with no time for retakes, and relations with Technicolor were strained due to missed deadlines. Miraculously *Gulliver* met its premier date and earned an impressive amount at the box office. It did not, however, make a profit. And with the war in Europe starting two months earlier, Paramount's foreign release outlets were closed off, leaving *Gulliver* $500,000 in the red. Fleischer's second, and better, feature, *Mr Bug Goes to Town* (1941) was produced on budget, but was another victim of World War Two's escalation. *Mr Bug* was released just two days before the bombing of Pearl Harbor, and the film's general theatrical release was delayed.

Two years earlier, Universal offered Walter Lantz $700,000 to produce a version of *Aladdin and His Wonderful Lamp*. Lantz had just completed the storyboards, but hearing of Fleischer's problems in Florida, he abandoned the project. Fleischer's efforts in competing with Walt Disney became the victim of unfortunate fate. Had events been different, Fleischer Studios could very well have become a serious contender for Disney in the feature arena.

HAPPY HARMONIES

In 1934, Hugh Harman and Rudolf Ising moved their affiliation from Warner Bros. to Metro-Goldwyn-Mayer, as MGM offered them higher budgets and the chance to make films in color. Since their last names formed a pun on "harmonising", Harman and Ising called their new series *Happy Harmonies*.

Fairy Tale Magic

The *Happy Harmonies* were similar to Disney's *Silly Symphonies* in that each cartoon usually featured new characters and had the feeling of a fairy tale. Rudy Ising's *The Calico Dragon* (1935) transformed a child's bed into a battlefield for a toy knight and dragon. Hugh Harman's *Bottles* (1936) took place in a pharmacy where bottles came to life and their personalities mirrored their functions; baby bottles acted like spoiled brats, and a bottle of poison was a villain.

Not every cartoon featured new characters. Harman continued to use the star of the *Looney Tunes* series, Bosko, in cartoons like *Bosko's Parlor Pranks* (1934) and *Hey, Hey Fever* (1935). For later Bosko cartoons such as *Circus Daze* (1937) and *Bosko in Baghdad* (1938), Harman made the character into a more realistic-looking black boy. Ising made several cartoons starring a mouse that first appeared in *Little Cheezer* (1936). He also created a pair of puppies for *Two Little Pups* (1936), *The Pups' Christmas* (1936) and *Wayward Pups* (1937).

A Second Wind

The *Happy Harmonies* were lavish-looking cartoons. In addition to color, they were filled with animated shadows, reflections, special effects and animated backgrounds. However, when Harman and Ising's contract expired in 1937, MGM decided not to renew it. Instead, in an attempt to save money, MGM created its own cartoon studio and hired many of Harman and Ising's artists. They also lured director Friz Freleng away from Warner Bros. and brought in newspaper cartoonist Milt Gross. Fred Quimby, a former film salesman, was chosen to run the studio.

Peace on Earth – soldier

The plot of *Peace on Earth* involves two squirrel children asking their grandfather about humans. He narrates the chilling story of how humanity destroyed itself through war, leaving animals to live in peace forever.

Peace on Earth

Nominated for an Academy Award, in 1940 *Peace on Earth* also became the only cartoon ever to be nominated for the Nobel Peace Prize.

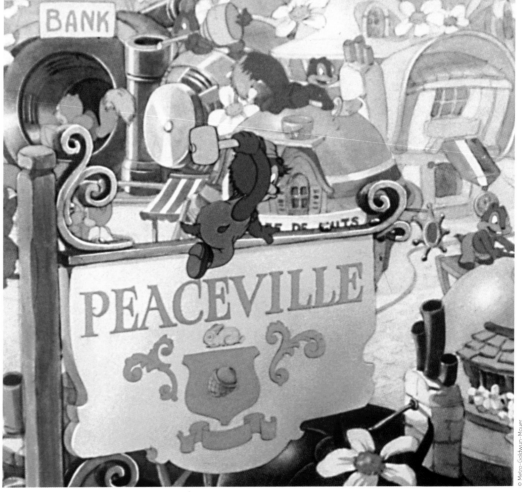

© Metro-Goldwyn-Mayer

Silly Symphonies » 36 *Looney Tunes* » 42

© Metro-Goldwyn-Mayer

The Blue Danube

Telling the fairy tale story of how the Danube river became "blue", *The Blue Danube* is a beautifully executed animation. The screenplay and syncopation to Johann Strauss's 'Blue Danube Waltz' are very cleverly done, making this an MGM classic.

© Metro-Goldwyn-Mayer

The new MGM studio launched itself with a series of black-and-white cartoons based on the long-popular Rudolph Dirks' comic strip *The Captain and the Kids*, but the films were not successful. As a result, MGM rehired Harman and Ising in 1938 to work as producers and directors under Quimby's supervision.

The cartoons from Harman and Ising's second MGM period are better drawn and more elaborate than the *Happy Harmonies*. Hugh Harman exercised his flair for spectacle in many of his films. Oscar-nominated *Peace on Earth* (1939) conveyed a serious anti-war message using animated battle scenes. *A Rainy Day* (1940) featured a bear trying to repair his roof in the midst of a thunderstorm, and *The Field Mouse* (1941) contained an intricate sequence of two mice trapped inside a grain-threshing machine.

Rudy Ising's cartoons moved at a gentler pace. He created a series with Barney Bear, who first appeared in *The Bear That Couldn't Sleep* (1939). In 1940, he featured three little kittens in *The Milky Way*, which won MGM its first Academy Award for an animated short subject. That same year, Ising was godfather to Tom and Jerry; he produced their first cartoon, *Puss Gets the Boot*, written and directed by William Hanna and Joseph Barbera.

Mixed Success

If Harman and Ising had a failing, it was that they were unable to create popular characters. Many of their characters were vague or bland; none had personalities as entertaining as Donald Duck or Goofy in the Disney cartoons of the same period. While Harman and Ising's visuals were beautiful, the lack of popular characters prevented their films from being truly memorable.

When Harman's contract ended in 1941, he left MGM hoping to find backers for an animated feature, but was not successful. Ising left MGM in 1942 and joined the Army Air Force, where he was put in charge of making animated films for military use.

In later years, Harman and Ising made industrial and commercial films, but after MGM they no longer made cartoons for movie theaters. At the time they left MGM, the animation business was moving away from their style of cute fantasy and toward cartoons that relied more on gags, fast timing and violent slapstick. For those kinds of cartoons, MGM turned to Harman and Ising's successors: Tex Avery, William Hanna (1910–2001) and Joseph Barbera (b. 1911).

Cartoons Go To War » 90 Tom and Jerry » 128 Avery at MGM » 128

In 1934, cartoon studio producers like Paul Terry, Charles Mintz, Walter Lantz and Leon Schlesinger must have been all too aware that Walt Disney was already the leading light of their industry. Two years earlier, when most cartoon producers felt that color film production was too expensive to seriously consider, Disney had forged a pact with the Technicolor Corporation for the exclusive rights to use the three-color process for animation for two years. During this period, full-color animation had become popular with movie audiences, but none of the four studios (Screen Gems, Universal, Terrytoons and Warner Bros.) had star cartoon characters with the marquee value of Mickey Mouse.

Screen Gems

Columbia's cartoon studio Screen Gems, under the management of Charles Mintz, maintained a full release schedule of black-and-white Scrappy and Krazy Kat cartoons, all competently animated, but all low-budget and far from the cutting edge of animation. In November 1934, Columbia inaugurated the *Color Rhapsody* series with the Scrappy cartoon *Holiday Land*, which was nominated for an Academy Award. *The Color Rhapsodies*, while no match for Disney's *Silly Symphonies*, are generally better-designed cartoons than the Scrappies and Krazies, with a little more spectacle in their set pieces and an appealing color palette. The studio also made a series of color Barney Google cartoons. By 1939, Charles Mintz, deep in debt and in failing health, was relieved of his post when Columbia took over full control of the operation of his studio.

© Warner Bros.

Beauty and the Beast

Notable for being Warner Bros.' second and final *Cinecolor* cartoon, this version of *Beauty and the Beast* was directed by Friz Freleng and released in 1934.

Universal

During this period, Walter Lantz's output was heavily dominated by Oswald cartoons, the property that had fallen into his lap. In 1934 and 1935, Lantz tried producing six cartoons in two-color Technicolor, again imitating *Silly Symphony* themes. After Carl Laemmle (1867–1939) lost control of the parent company Universal, Walter Lantz took over the cartoon studio, which returned to making only economical black-and-white cartoons until 1939. Color cartoons directed by Alex Lovy and Burt Gillett were released that year, including one that would introduce an important character for the studio, *Life Begins for Andy Panda.*

The Isle of Pingo Pongo

The Isle of Pingo Pongo was the first of many Tex Avery Warner Bros. spot-gag-filled parodies of travelogues. It was originally released in 1938, but more recently has courted controversy because of its use of racial stereotypes. This cartoon is one of those so-called Censored 11 and is still banned from being broadcast on TV or released on video.

The Penguin Parade

Another of Warner Bros.' *Merrie Melodies* is *The Penguin Parade*, a rollicking cartoon released in 1938 that features penguins gathering from all over for the opening of a new nightclub. It is particularly memorable for its jazz-filled musical score.

Terrytoons

The *Terrytoons* cartoons, produced quickly and cheaply in New York for 20th Century Fox release, continued to produce only low-end black-and-white cartoons until 1939. Having retired their old-fashioned characters Farmer Al Falfa, Kiko the Kangaroo and Puddy the Pup, Terry finally made a small number of cartoons in color, one of which introduced a new leading player, Gandy Goose. But *Terrytoons* would still have to wait a few years for a badly needed breakout character.

Warner Bros.

The years between 1934 and 1939 represent a real period of transition for the Warner Bros. cartoons. Hugh Harman and Rudy Ising had departed the studio in 1933, taking with them the rights to their star character Bosko. Isadore "Friz" Freleng, Jack King and Earl Duvall (1898–1969) made Buddy cartoons and one-shot musical *Merrie Melodies* in 1934 and 1935 that were still rough approximations of the Harman-Ising style. The arrival of Tex Avery (1908–80), teamed with animators Chuck Jones (1912–2002) and Bob Clampett (1913–84) in 1936, marked a decisive turn in style and content, away from the singsong timing and clunky construction of the old style and towards the funnier, more expressive, sharply timed Warner Bros. cartoon style to come.

Jack King left to return to Disney, and was replaced by Frank Tashlin (1913–72), whose cartoons were the first to bring to animation the sensibilities of live-action film. In 1937, Clampett was promoted to director, his signature breakneck comedy style already fully defined. That same year Mel Blanc (1908–89) became one of the principal voice artists and Carl Stalling (1891–1972) became musical director. Enough pieces were in play to redefine Warner cartoons. New characters were created to populate these fresh new films. Porky Pig, introduced in Freleng's *I Haven't Got a Hat* (1935), was by now the principal star of the *Looney Tunes*. Avery introduced Daffy Duck in *Porky's Duck Hunt* (1937), and Chuck Jones became director in 1938. Also in 1938, Freleng's successors, Ben Hardaway (1897–1957) and Cal Dalton (b. 1908), directed the earliest films built around a crazed rabbit who would soon evolve into the studio's most valuable star.

Paul Terry and *Terrytoons* » 40 *Looney Tunes* » 42

The pioneer of abstract animation, Oskar Fischinger (1900–67), was born in Gelnhausen, Germany, and initially trained as an engineer. It was in Berlin that his interests turned to the motion picture, where he created the special effects photography for Fritz Lang's science-fiction epic *Die Frau im Mond* ('The Woman in the Moon') in 1928.

Visual Music

Fischinger had always had a dream of blending classical music with the kind of conceptual designs that might be formulated in one's mind when listening to a symphony. This mixture he termed as "visual music".

The formative years found him dabbling with the comparatively new process of sound synchronization on film, resulting in his ground-breaking masterpiece, *Studie* (1930). Set to Listz's "Second Hungarian Rhapsody", this process had the designs drawn in charcoal on white paper and photographed in negative

which was a method possibly inspired by French animator Emile Cohl's early work. There were 11 more highly original *Studies* to follow, each featuring a different work of symphonic music such as Brahms, Dukas and others.

The turning point came in 1934 when Fischinger was asked to make an animated commercial for Muratti cigarettes. The result was *Muratti Greift Ein* ('Muratti Marches On'). Made in color and using stop-motion model animation, a pack of cigarettes march with the precision of a crack German army. This advertisement proved more popular than the feature it played against; consequentially it was allowed to run for over a year.

Composition in Blue

The basic format of this film centered around solid objects moving about in an imaginary blue room. In the opening scene, Fischinger showed red cubes entering the "room" through a door; a mirror was then introduced as the "floor". Whereas Fischinger's previous films had utilized only one basic animation technique, this one experimented with many new ones – mostly involving pixilation of three-dimensional forms.

Fischinger's Film Work

Having tasted success, Fischinger was now able to use the money made from *Muratti* to make the kind of films he wanted to make. *Komposition in Blau* ('Composition in Blue') was shot in Gaspar-Color and highlighted colored spheres and shapes cavorting to the music of Nicolai's "The Merry Wives of Windsor". This not only won the Brussels and Venice Festival of 1935, but also brought Fischinger's work to the attention of the Hollywood directors.

Emile Cohl » 22 Norman McLaren » 102

To escape the impending Nazi rise to power, Fischinger accepted a contract offer from Paramount Pictures to go to Hollywood and work in their special effects department. He completed *Allegretto* in 1936 with diamonds and circles whirling about in color to the music. Originally conceived as a preface to their feature *The Big Broadcast of 1937*, Paramount never used this segment because color proved too costly. He moved on to MGM, creating a short, *An Optical Poem*, in 1938.

Fischinger's approach of blending music with animation inspired the artists and animators on Walt Disney's *Fantasia* (1940), and Oskar was hired by Walt to work on the "Toccata and Fugue" sequence. He only lasted there nine months before leaving the studio.

His involvement with the major Hollywood studios ended. Oskar Fischinger decided instead to concentrate on painting and personal films.

Muratti Privat

In this 1935 commercial, Fischinger used the patterns of cigarettes to create optical effects with Mozart's Turkish Rondo as a soundtrack. The patterns ranged from checkerboard patterns of cigarette packages to a scene in which rows of cigarettes join together in pairs which wave at the audience as if they were the legs.

Studie Nr. 6

By 1922 Fischinger had begun to produce abstract films, and in a few years was synchronizing abstract imagery to popular records with a series he called Studies. These films were shown in theaters as advertisements for the recordings. Sixty years before MTV, they were the first music videos. Each of these studies ran three minutes in length and included approximately 5,000 drawings coordinated to the music.

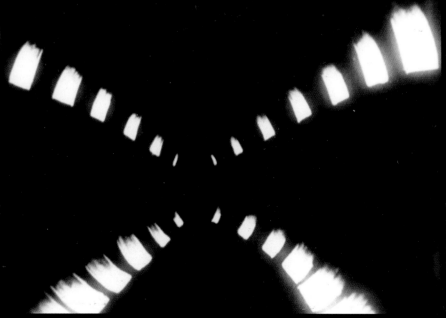

III: 1934–39: TECHNICOLOR FANTASIES WESTERN EUROPE: GERMANY

GEORGE PAL

Hungarian György Marczincsák (George Pal) made a unique contribution to the chronicles of fantasy films by using model animation, or Puppetoons as he christened them, in place of the traditionally drawn medium.

Early Life

Pal initially trained as a draftsman, subsequently working in a Budapest advertising company, where he learned his animation trade along with his young assistant, János Halász (John Halas). After a couple of years of turning out cut-out animation for commercials, in 1930 he shifted to Berlin as a set designer for Universum Film, A.G. (UFA), the major German film production company. UFA functioned by receiving a government subsidy to produce films on German themes.

Having worked there for a couple of years, Pal found out that the Gestapo was investigating him and his fellow workers for the solitary reason that he was Hungarian. Driven out of Berlin by the Gestapo, Pal would get revenge years later with one of his madcap models, *Tulips Shall Grow* (1942), which featured a peaceful Holland being disrupted by goose-stepping robots. The robots are put out of commission when the rains come and everything returns to normal.

Animated Commercials

In 1933, Pal tried to set up shop in Czechoslovakia with the intention of starting up his own studio. Unable to find a cartoon camera anywhere in the country, he journeyed further afield to Paris, where he was able to form a studio. After a brief sojourn in Paris, he decided it was time to move on and, in 1934, moved to Eindhoven, Holland, where he set up a studio to make his own advertising films with partner Dave Bader. He remained there for the next five years.

He soon signed a deal with the Dutch electrical company Philips and with J. Walter Thompson, the huge advertising conglomerate representing the malted drink

George Pal

Born in Hungary in 1908, George Pal originally intended to train as an architect at the Budapest Academy. However, a clerical error meant that he took illustration classes and he never looked back.

On Parade

George Pal produced some of the most beautiful and meticulously designed films of the golden age of animation. This would serve him well in his later career as a producer of big-budget Hollywood science-fiction feature-films.

© Estate of George Pal

Horlicks. These advertisements were produced initially as entertainment films, but with a sponsor's message as the punch line; the first in line was *Radio Valve Revolution* (1934), which was made with traditionally drawn animation.

The next year Pal moved away from conventional animation and on to puppet films, which would become his future stock in trade. *Het Aetherschip* ('Ship of Ether', 1935) is a seven-minute fantasy featuring a broadcasting studio in which the artists go through dreamlike antics and ships made from twisted glass sail over the fantastic scene in order to bring pleasant music over the airwaves from a new Philips radio.

On Parade (1936) involves a soldier who is always late for his sluggish parade. He and his pals each take a steaming mug of Horlicks before retiring and upon waking turn the platoon into a crack regiment, ready for action! The slogan for the Horlicks commercials was "Get a good night's sleep and wake feeling refreshed in the morning". This advertisement is done effectively, with humor and an underlying message. A lot of these films, however, have since been distributed with the sponsor's motto removed, rendering them a little meaningless to audiences.

Creating Puppetoons

The process Pal and his artists would go through to make one of these eight-minute subjects involved the usage of 3,000 individual wooden figures. The heads and limbs were interchangeable but, should a character have dialogue, it would probably need a dozen or so sculpted heads to see it through one sentence. Each head would be carved with a definite mouth movement of every vowel, as well as other extensive sounds such as "F" and "M", etc. It was all very time consuming, but the end product proved effective. The sets were constructed 4.6 m (15 ft) wide and each production took at least a month to make, with a rough cost of around $15,000.

These advertising fantasies soon caught the eye of Hollywood, and Pal was invited to leave Holland to produce his own unique kind of animated shorts for the United States. The year was 1939 and the war in Europe had just begun, so Pal emigrated to America and was content to spend the rest of his days making Puppetoons and live-action features.

Puppetoons

George Pal pioneered a distinctive form of animation in a series of films called *Puppetoons*, utilizing an elaborate form of stop-motion photography and a method he termed "replacement figure puppetry". The 28 puppets shown here represent a mere two seconds of animation.

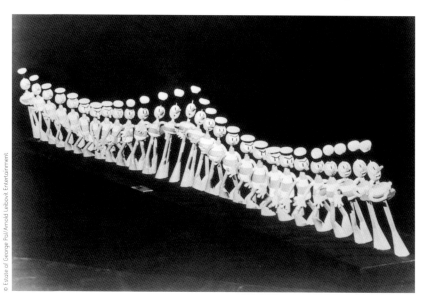

© Estate of George Pal/Arnold Leibovit Entertainment

Puppetoons » 92

HOPPIN, GROSS & LYE

Anthony Gross

A noted illustrator, Gross (1905–84) was often known to experiment with his art, but when he dabbled in the world of animation he unwittingly etched himself into cinematic history. Gross had already made a few Disney-esque attempts, which proved unsatisfactory, before settling on applying his own contemporary graphic style to popular animation. The result was La Joie de Vivre ('The Joy of Living', 1934).

Hector Hoppin

With help from American financier Hector Hoppin, and using a series of etchings titled *Sortie d'usine* ('Coming Out of the Factory'), the hand-drawn *La Joie de Vivre* was completed in Paris within two years. It was made with only a minimalist production team of Gross, Hoppin, their wives, one cameraman, an odd-job man and an animation assistant, David Patee. This 10-minute soufflé tells the slight story of two fun-loving girls who make the most of the countryside on a hot day. They strip off for a dip in the lake and are frightened away by the arrival of a young man. The boy pursues them, but only in order to return an abandoned shoe. Tibor Harsanyi's powerful music score helps dramatize the surreal actions, accentuating Gross's post-impressionist graphics.

Once the film was completed, they managed to sell this monochrome classic to London Films' boss Alexander Korda, who immediately signed the boys up to start work on some animation sequences for his forthcoming epic *The Shape of Things to Come* (1936). Unfortunately their animation was cut from the film. Their next film, *The Fox Hunt* (1936), employed a few more artists (notably topical cartoonist Carl Giles) and had the distinction of Technicolor. It featured a fox running rings around the hunters.

War Breaks Out

In 1938 work began on a feature-length, animated version of Jules Verne's *Around the World in Eighty Days*. The outbreak of war put a stop to this project and it was abandoned, never to resurface. The few sequences that had been completed were cobbled together, with the addition of Donald Pleasance providing all of the character voices (including Princess Aouda), and now survives as a short under the title of *An Indian*

© Anthony Gross & Hector Hoppin

La Joie de Vivre

La Joie de Vivre was made in 1934 and features two dancers, a blonde and a brunette, running through a varied countryside. They are chased by a boy who wishes to return a lost shoe, and all three happily disappear into the sky on the boy's bicycle.

La Joie de Vivre

The third short film to come from Anthony Gross and Hector Hoppin's Animat company, *La Joie de Vivre* confirmed that Gross was an animator of considerable skill.

© Anthony Gross & Hector Hoppin

Around the World in Eighty Days

All traces of this work were believed to have been lost until fragments were rediscovered in a projection room at the National Film Theatre in London in 1956. With the assistance of the British Film Institute's Experimental Production Fund, the film was reconstructed and, for copyright reasons, was retitled *An Indian Fantasy*.

Tusalava

An experiment in abstract animation, *Tusalava* was drawn directly onto the film, with each frame painted and shot individually. It took two years to complete and required 4,400 drawings.

Fantasy (1957). This, sadly, is the entire output of Hoppin and Gross. World War Two put a stop to the frivolity of entertainment cartoons, and Anthony Gross was made Official War Artist for the government. After the war he took to teaching etching and engraving at Slade School of Fine Art, London.

Len Lye

As a New Zealand lad out on his paper round, young Len Lye (1901–80) observed a sunrise that put him in mind of Constable's sketches that simulated the motion of clouds. He mused to himself "Why simulate?" and then, "Why clouds?". From this insight, Lye decided to make nonrepresentational films.

Always on the move because of the lack of cinematic equipment in New Zealand, Lye hoped to learn more about film by shifting to Australia, where he worked in a Sydney film studio preparing storyboards. Impressed with the Russian Revolution in film, Lye headed for Russia next by working his passage from Sydney to London as a stoker on the *Euripedes*. He arrived in London in 1926.

Abstract Images

There he began work on his first film, to which he dedicated 10 hours every day for two years. *Tusalava* (1928) was the result, being the first abstract image film of its kind. Consisting of grub-like forms reminiscent of Aboriginal shield designs, it was, however, met with cool indifference by audiences.

Lye now found himself without the means to finance another cel animation film, so he decided to abandon cel and camera, and draw straight onto old film stock he found abandoned at Ealing Studios. He scratched, painted and generally messed about with it, finally editing the pieces together and, with an added music track, presented it to the head of the GPO Film Unit, John Grierson.

Color Box

Grierson was impressed and, with help from composer Jack Ellit, Lye turned it into a governmental public service film. The result was *A Color Box* (1935), which illustrated the benefits of the sixpenny telegram.

Throughout World War Two, Lye chiefly worked on live-action documentaries and, after the conflict, moved to the United States. Although he continued to dabble in animated films, he was more taken with making steel sculptures.

SOVIET ANIMATORS

After years of exploring experimental and avant-garde paths, a congress of Soviet writers supported a new stream of creation in 1932 called "socialist realism". The aim of the new endeavour was to create nationalistic entertainment adapted from classical texts and folklore and aimed at children.

Alexander Ptushko

This new direction in animation began with the founding of the state-run Soyuzmultfilm studio in 1936. From the beginning, Soyuzmultfilm attempted to emulate Walt Disney through the adaptation of fairy tales and the creation of cute, round animation figures. The first director of the company was actor, journalist, and designer Alexander Ptushko. He studied architecture before becoming a mechanical engineer. In 1928, he made his first animation film, *It Happened at the Stadium*.

The New Gulliver

In 1935, Alexander Ptushko made what appears to be the first-ever animated feature film, *The New Gulliver*. This astonishing combination of stop-motion animation and live-action tells the story of Petya, a young Soviet pioneer who falls asleep reading Jonathan Swift's *Gulliver's Travels* and awakens in a surreal version of Swift's world. He washes ashore on a Lilliput that includes jazz bands, mechanized tractors and the proletariat. Before he wakes up, Petya helps the people rise up and overthrow their tyrannical rulers.

Following *The New Gulliver*, Ptushko made *The Golden Key* (1939). Based on Aleksei Tolstoy's version of *Pinocchio*, Ptushko mixed tiny puppets with life-size humans. Following the film, Ptushko left animation to pursue a successful career as a live-action director.

Throughout the 1930s, Soyuzmultfilm seemed to be strongly influenced by Hollywood productions. In films like *Puss and Boots* (The Brumberg Sister, Valentina and Zinaidas), *Little Muck*, and *Dog and Cat* – all made in 1938 – there is little to differentiate between their characters and those of Disney productions. One of the few films of this period to steer slightly away from the Disney influence was *How the Rhinoceros Got Its Skin*, a satirical update of the famous tale.

Aleksandr Ptushko/Mosfilm/bfi Collections

The New Gulliver Poster

The film was released to enormous international acclaim, with Charlie Chaplin among its admirers. Under Ptushko's direction, Swift's satire of Old England became a modern-day political satire on the contradictions and injustices of twentieth-century capitalist economies.

© Aleksandr Ptushko/Mosfilm

Black and White

This early Soviet sound film by Ivanov-Vano tells the story of an old black plantation worker who questions the system in Cuba, where the black man does the hard labor while the white man takes the profits.

© Aleksandr Ptushko/Mosfilm

The New Gulliver – prologue

The film begins with a live-action prologue, but the majority of the film is set in an animated Lilliput consisting of pixilated puppets and clay figures that often share the frame with the human actor playing Gulliver.

The New Gulliver – table

The first major work by director Alexander Ptushko, *The New Gulliver* was also one of the first feature-length films to showcase puppet animation. Over 3,000 separate figures were used in this hybrid of stop-motion animation and live-action footage.

© Leonid Amalrik & Ivan Ivanov-Vano

Ivan Ivanov-Vano and Lev Atamanov

Two other significant voices emerged during this period: Ivan Ivanov-Vano (1900–87) and Lev Atamanov (1905–81). Ivanov-Vano was one of the most popular and prolific Soviet animators. He made the satirical *Black and White* (1932), which was also among the first Soviet sound cartoons, and folkloric and children's films that included a 1938 version of *The Three Musketeers* that borrows heavily from Disney's Donald Duck character. Armenian-born Atamanov directed a series called *Ink-Spot*, along with an anti-military satire, *The Story of the Little White Bull* (1933), before moving to Armenia where he set the groundwork for Armenian animation production. By the late 1930s, Soyuzmultfilm was producing over 20 films per year and beginning to work in color.

From 1934 to 1937, Japan was officially at peace with the world. In July 1937 the Japanese Army went to war with China, and in Japan, the military openly assumed power over the government. As a result, the cinematic industry was pressured to increase sharply its production of stridently nationalistic films. Animation of the 1934–39 period continued to be monochromatic, one reel of six to 14 minutes in length. Grouped by theme, notable examples include comedies for adults, folk tales and funny animal animation, and militaristic comedies.

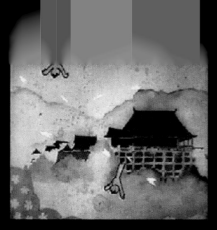

Bringing Legends to Life

Usually set in the samurai era or mythical past, comedies for adults included films such as *Love in the Genroku Era: Sankichi and Osayo* by Mitsuyo Seo (1934) and *A Night at a Tavern* by Yasuji Murata (1936). Folk tales and funny animal animation were predominantly aimed at children, on the other hand, and included *The Tale of Tiny Issun Bochi's Rescue* by Mitsuyo Seo (June 1935), *Benkei versus Ushiwaka* by Kenzo Masaoka (Japan's first film animated to a prerecorded music track in July 1939) and *The Hare's Revenge on the Tanuki* (1939)by Kon Ichikawa.

Kon Ichikawa

The animated cartoon *The Hare's Revenge on the Tanuki* has been cited as a leading animated film of this period, but that seems due less to the film itself than to the status of Kon Ichikawa (b. 1915) as one of Japan's greatest live-action film directors of the 1950s and 1960s. Ichikawa made only one other animated film, the puppet stop-motion *The Girl at*

Taro Thumb – sequence 1

Films featuring folk tales and animals aimed at children were made during the 1930s; those which took their subject matte from Japan's mythical past were primarily for adults. Pictured is Mistuyo Seo's *Taro Thumb* from 1935.

Anti-Japanese War Songs

These propaganda shorts were made during 1937 by the War Brothers after their studio in Shanghai was destroyed by the Japanese invasion of the city.

Taro Thumb – sequence 2

Dojo's Temple (1946), which Ichikawa has claimed as one of his greatest works. However, it was confiscated by the post-war occupation authorities and was never seen by the public.

Militaristic comedies began primarily as fantasies for children, such as *My Emergency* (ducks and frogs prepare for an air raid) by Sanae Yamamoto (1936) and *Maabo, the Boy Pilot* (1937) by Ginjiro Sato. These frequently featured themes of civil defense against foreign aggression. By 1938, the animation was aimed more toward adults and was more supportive of an "aggressive defense". *Skies over the Shanghai Battlegrounds* (1938) features two comedic Japanese pilots observing their army's successful advance around Shanghai, while in *Aerial Ace* (1938) by Noburo Ofuji, a funny animal pilot in a toy fighter plane with Japanese military markings is menaced by giant clouds in the forms of Popeye and Stalin.

China: Temporarily Missing in Action

The Wan Brothers created numerous animated shorts for the Mingxing Film Company utilizing cartoon and cut-paper animation, sometimes mixed with live action. The most notable was *The Camel's Dance* (1935), China's first sound cartoon. Many of these, such as *Detective Dog* and *The Tortoise and the Hare*, were funny animal comedies for children, and although there was no attempt to create starring characters, some of the animals were recognizably repeating characters.

When the Mingxing studio was destroyed during the Japanese capture of Shanghai in August 1937, the Wans relocated to Wuhan province, where they made patriotic animation such as *The Anti-Japanese War Special Collection*, *Slogans of the Anti-Japanese War* and *Songs of the Anti-Japanese War* for the China Film Production Firm. These were not commercially successful. In 1939, Wan Lai-ming and Wan Gu-chan accepted an invitation from the Xinhua United Film Company in the French concession in Japanese-occupied Shanghai to set up an animation studio. They returned just in time to see Disney's *Snow White and the Seven Dwarfs* playing in Shanghai. This inspired them to begin a similar Chinese animated feature. The result was China's first full-length cartoon, *Princess with the Iron Fan* (1941).

1940—44:
THE WORLD WAR TWO ERA

The world went to war — and animation went with it. The Hollywood studios were drafted and created hundreds of training films for the army — and patriotic propaganda for the home front. Daffy Duck, Mickey Mouse and Popeye fought the enemy and sold war bonds. The "wise guy" character was in vogue: Bugs Bunny, Woody Woodpecker, Screwy Squirrel. And Disney made his greatest features: *Fantasia*, *Dumbo* and *Bambi*.

Character animation hit its zenith. Animated shorts were slick and professional, but generally conformed to the Disney school of cartooning. However, a new school began to form. Creative thinkers like John Hubley, Chuck Jones and Frank Tashlin emerged and began to hint at a new direction for animation design.

But the war kept everyone, everywhere, occupied. China and Russia began creating animated films to bring ancient fables to life. Germany and Japan used cartoons for Axis wartime propaganda, as Great Britain and Canada aided the Allied troops with the same.

It was a time of shortages and sacrifice, crisis and conflict. Animators reached into their arsenal and achieved victory. Mission accomplished. Animation art was in its prime.

DISNEY'S WARTIME SHORTS

Between 1940 and 1944, the Disney studio's total output was great, but its nature was considerably altered because of World War Two. The rise of fascist power hindered and often curtailed European distribution of all US films, and so Disney was kept afloat largely through government projects, from propaganda and training films to Latin American health films. These projects allowed Disney to retain a greater percentage of his artists, who were therefore exempted from the draft (although animators, such as Frank Thomas, left to join the armed forces anyway). Like those of Warner Bros. and others, Disney's 1940s short subjects were thus dominated by wartime sensibilities.

Patriot Donald

Mickey Mouse began to decrease in screen prominence, despite making a few notable appearances, particularly as the harried maestro in *Symphony Hour* (1942). By 1944, he appeared only in support to Pluto, apart from a cameo in *Out of the Frying Pan, Into the Firing Line* (1942) and an appearance in a parade in *All Together* (1942). He also had no role in film propaganda, despite fighting the Nazis in the newspaper strip. This more passive and suburbanized Mickey was therefore overshadowed by Donald Duck, whose easily stirred emotions and general good intentions allowed him variously to represent the American soldier, the taxpayer/citizen, or even the victim of German cruelty.

As a soldier, Donald served the US through typical army antics in several shorts with Sgt. Pete, reminiscent of Abbott and Costello's live-action comedies such as *Buck Privates* (1941). His patriotism was channeled towards promoting taxes and war bonds in a pair of shorts for the US Treasury, *The New Spirit* (1942) and *The Spirit of '43*. In the Oscar-winning *Der Fuehrer's Face* (1943), Donald endures life in a nightmarish "Nutziland", which is both satirically amusing (aided by the title song, a Spike Jones rendition, already a hit with wartime audiences) and truly horrific, as he is starved and driven insane by his German taskmasters. Waking from his dream at the end, Donald's patriotism is reaffirmed as he embraces the Statue of Liberty.

Serving Their Country

Pluto and Goofy also served the war effort, with Pluto promoting fat conservation and serving in the army in several shorts. Goofy saved gas on the home front in *Victory Vehicles* (1943) and shattered the Rising Sun in the climax of *How to Be a Sailor* (1944). However, in 1943, Disney also produced three "psychological" propaganda shorts, representing some of the most atypical and complex films to come from the studio. *Education for Death* combines a fairly straight documentary examination of Nazi indoctrination with a brief German version of *Sleeping Beauty*, with Prince Hitler and Democracy as the witch. *Reason and Emotion* is even more complex, as the ego and the

Der Fuehrer's Face

Produced by Disney to help the American war effort and the only Donald Duck film to win an Academy Award, *Der Fuehrer's Face* (1943) featured Donald as a worker in a munitions factory dreaming of freedom in Nazi Germany.

Der Fuehrer's Face

After a frantic workday trying to alternate between making bombs and saluting Hitler, Donald realizes that it has all been a nightmare and that he is safely back in the good old USA.

Gremlins – sketch

Based on Roald Dahl's 1943 book *The Gremlins*, Disney's staff started work on a wartime feature film about gremlins who foiled British pilots. Much work was done on the film, like this story sketch above – and Disney even produced some merchandizing to promote its production – before the project was abandoned.

id, represented as the title characters (the former a bespectacled prude and the latter a caveman) struggle to control man's mind, and are susceptible to enemy propaganda. *Chicken Little* uses the old fable again to denounce propaganda and rumors, and ends with the fox consuming everyone. These three shorts demonstrate the true power of animation to convey messages and stir emotion, and had more in common with the Disney features than the earlier Mickey Mouse shorts.

DISNEY'S WARTIME FEATURES

Although Disney's short-production rates remained high due to government projects, World War Two greatly hindered Walt's feature-film plans. *Pinocchio* and especially *Fantasia* (both 1940) were less successful than expected due to high production costs and lack of foreign markets. Thus, plans for a number of film projects were considerably delayed and altered. However, between 1940 and 1944, Disney did complete production of two films, which are arguably among his greatest (*Dumbo* and *Bambi*), and three cheaper films notable for their experimentation with live footage and the way they reflect the situations at the studio and abroad (*The Reluctant Dragon, Saludos Amigos* and *Victory Through Air Power*).

© The Walt Disney Company

The Reluctant Dragon

The Reluctant Dragon (1941), in contrast to the ambitious *Fantasia*, was an inexpensive feature relying heavily on live-action footage of humorist Robert Benchley touring the studio. This pseudo-documentary format is entertaining, but misleading, as not only were real animators like Ward Kimball (1914–2002) juxtaposed against Alan Ladd as a storyboard artist, but the studio was undergoing a major strike at the time. Among the film's highlights is the limited-animation "Baby Weems" segment, with caricatures of Einstein and FDR, and glimpses of art and preview sequences for planned films, including *Bambi* and *Dumbo*'s Casey Jr. In one scene, a row of maquettes showcases Captain Hook, Peter Pan and Aunt Sarah and the Siamese cats from *Lady and the Tramp*, which would be sidelined for more than 10 years due to the financial setbacks of the war and the trend toward "package films" combining shorts and live action, which *Reluctant Dragon* exemplified.

Dumbo

Dumbo (1941) was also inexpensive, but succeeded as more than a mere novelty film. Running a little over an hour, the tale of the baby elephant with big ears and his path from ridicule to success has a charming Horatio Alger quality, as well as a lively circus atmosphere. Disney and Fleischer veteran Grim Natwick (1890–1990), in a June 1979 *Cartoonist Profiles* article, stated: "(It is) a long short. It has the effervescent tempo of the shorts and the physical stature of a feature film."

The warmth in the animation of Dumbo and his mother by Vladimir Tytla (1904–68), along with the lively songs and surreal "Pink Elephant" march, has charmed audiences for decades. The film's closing montage includes a quick shot of Dumbo-style

© The Walt Disney Company

Animation for the War Effort » 112 Disney Moves On » 120

© The Walt Disney Company

Saludos Amigos

Inspired by a trip to South America undertaken by several Disney artists, *Saludos Amigos* was one of the first in a series of "Good Neighbor" films made by Disney at the request of the Office of Inter-American Affairs. It consisted of four cartoons linked by live-action travel footage.

Dumbo – storyboard

Winning an Academy Award for Best Music in 1941, *Dumbo* was hugely popular on its release and it has remained a favorite ever since. Its low cost and popular appeal resulted in a much-needed financial success for Disney.

Dumbo –sketch and cel

Although something of a departure for Disney following the labor-intensive *Snow White*, *Pinocchio* and *Fantasia*, the gamble paid off. The film was simple and succinct and one of Disney's shortest animated features at just 64 minutes, and many believe that this set it apart from its more "arty" predecessors.

bomber planes, thereby acknowledging the war. A few months later, *Dumbo* was followed by *Mr. Bug Goes to Town* (1941), the second (and last) feature from the Fleischer brothers, and the only significant non-Disney American animated feature until the 1950s.

Bambi

Bambi (1942), based on the Felix Salten book, was more ambitious, and the animation veered more toward realism than caricature. As with *Dumbo*, however, the mother-child relationship is emotionally affecting, and colorful side characters like Thumper and Friend Owl are subtly interwoven into the coming-of-age story. The lush effects animation during the "April Showers" sequence is particularly atmospheric as the various animals scuttle for shelter. Pure narrative animated films at Disney, displaced by package features, would not be seen again until *Cinderella* (1950), but *Dumbo* and *Bambi* would not be equaled.

Wartime Experimentation

Saludos Amigos (1943) was one of two "Good Neighbor Policy" films, along with *Three Caballeros* (1945), that showcased Latin America. Not only did they provide another market for the films, but they also aided crucial foreign relations during wartime. *Saludos Amigos* contained travelogue footage of Disney and his crew in South America, framing four cartoon shorts, some of which involved Goofy, new character Jose Carioca, and Donald Duck, already established as a wartime icon at home.

Finally, in 1943 Disney produced the seldom-seen but fascinating *Victory Through Air Power*. This mix of documentary and military theory was not funded by the government, but was Walt's own idea, having been impressed by the theories of aviator Major Alexander de Seversky (1894–1974) and his emphasis on strategic air bombing. Live footage of de Seversky presenting his theories, surrounded by maps and a globe, is coupled with animated sequences utilizing limited character animation and moving diagrams, resembling the stylized live-action maps. The wartime symbolism was even stronger than in the shorts: de Seversky's birth date is accompanied by the Statue of Liberty, and the finale depicts the American eagle defeating the Japanese octopus. Overall, despite their financial limitations, the features of the 1940s are unique and bear Walt's personal stamp more closely than later films, when theme-park development, television and live-action films occupied more of his time and interest.

DAFFY DUCK & BUGS BUNNY

With three simple words – "What's up, Doc?" – a new era in Warner Bros.' cartoon history had begun. Whilst Bugs Bunny had appeared in previous cartoons, it was in Tex Avery's *A Wild Hare* (1940) that the Bugs we know today made his definitive first appearance. A powerhouse team of talented directors, each possessing different yet complementary strengths was ready to make the funniest cartoons ever made. Tex Avery, Bob Clampett, Friz Freleng and Chuck Jones were on hand to kick off this golden era, with Frank Tashlin occupying Avery's chair by 1942. The confluence of a talented group of animators, working with fresh, new characters against the backdrop of a war effort that the whole studio seemed enthusiastically to embrace, made the war years an exciting time for the studio.

Patriotic Feeling

It is worth pointing out that, while some of the other Hollywood studios were hesitant to mix politics with business before Pearl Harbor, Warner Bros. had reason early on to take a stand against Nazi Germany. The studio had closed its German distribution office in the late 1930s after a Warner representative was beaten to death by Nazi thugs. Warner's feature division declared war long before the US government did, with the 1939 release of the feature film *Confessions of a Nazi Spy.*

The Warner animation division was not the only cartoon shop to reference the war via cartoons, but few got involved as early or with the intensity of patriotic fervor found in the Warner cartoons. Who else but Daffy Duck would have the nerve to smack Hitler in the face with a mallet? Bob Clampett explained that Bugs Bunny was "a symbol of America's resistance to Hitler and the fascist powers ..." This was a remarkable time indeed for new characters to be created.

Bugs Bunny

Wisecracking rabbit Bugs Bunny is arguably one of the most popular and recognizable cartoon characters ever created. For many years he was voiced by Mel Blanc, who gave him a distinctive Brooklyn accent.

© Warner Bros.

Disney's Wartime Shorts » 80 Avery, Jones and Clampett » 86 Hans Fischerkoesen » 108

© Warner Bros.

Daffy Duck

Daffy Duck's character evolved from hyperactive and aggressive to scheming, cunning and greedy. This has never dented his popularity, however – his crazy antics and general silliness have always been a hit with audiences.

Bugs Bunny in Falling Hare

One of the secrets of Bugs's enduring success is the fact that he always wins, whether it's against hapless hunter Elmer Fudd, blustering bully Yosemite Sam, or any number of other doomed adversaries.

Wild Antics

Daffy Duck had already appeared in a handful of cartoons from 1937 to 1939. Whether cast as a wild, crazy foil for Porky Pig in *Porky's Duck Hunt* (1937) and *Porky and Daffy* (1938), or as the headline character in *Daffy Duck in Hollywood* (1938) and *Daffy Duck and Egghead* (1938), Daffy's wildly unrestrained antics made it almost impossible for an audience to notice he was sharing the screen with other characters. Even when directed by Chuck Jones – in *Daffy Duck and the Dinosaur* (1939) – whose style was considerably more sedate than that of Clampett and Avery, Daffy remained a force of nature.

The pre-1940s Bugs was similarly boisterous. *A Wild Hare*, its title notwithstanding, reenvisioned Bugs by stripping away most of the anarchy of the previously used Daffy-like rabbit character and making Bugs cool and quick-witted, and very much in charge of every situation. The Warner cartoons would forever be defined by the dichotomy created by the frantic kinetics of the impulsive Daffy Duck and the deft, always-in-control coolness of the knowing Bugs Bunny.

© Warner Bros.

AVERY, JONES & CLAMPETT

Tex Avery's wildly funny cartoon style exerted a distinct influence over the Warner cartoons, even though he departed from the studio in 1942 to direct animated cartoons at MGM. Avery's last few years at Warner were dominated by silly spot-gag cartoons, with surprisingly few films built around the characters he helped to launch. After only three Daffy Duck cartoons in the late 1930s, he never returned to the character. After having sharpened and defined Porky Pig in 1936 and 1937, he made only one Porky cartoon in his later years at Warner. This film, the highly inventive *Porky's Preview* (1941), is structured around a cartoon supposedly drawn and animated by Porky himself.

Bugs' Early Days

Avery's four Bugs Bunny cartoons may comprise his most valuable contribution to the Warner catalog. *A Wild Hare* (1940) certainly laid the foundation for much of what would follow. In 1941, Avery directed three more Bugs cartoons, building on Bugs' character: *Tortoise Beats Hare*, *The Heckling Hare* and the controversial *All This and Rabbit Stew*. His broadly comic style helped endear Bugs to movie audiences. *All This and Rabbit Stew* has been largely unavailable for decades, due to the racial stereotyping of one character in the cartoon. Such racial caricatures were commonplace when these cartoons were made, and artists like Avery were unaware of any offensive implications they may have.

Chuck Jones often stated that Tex Avery was one of the very few geniuses in animation. "I learned from him the most important truth about animation," said Jones. "Animation is the art of timing."

Star Material

Starting in the late 1930s, Avery's two star animators, Chuck Jones and Bob Clampett, were both directing cartoons for Warner, and the two are as unlike in their approach to film-making as Bugs and Daffy. The contrast between a Jones film like *The Dover Boys* (1942) and a Clampett film like *An Itch in Time* (1943) could hardly be greater. Jones derives humor from formalistic concerns, applying stylized design to tightly controlled characters. By comparison, Clampett appears to observe few strictures of form, stretching his characters into almost grotesque contortions, accelerating the action only to stop it completely for a gag, breaking character with asides to the audience, etc., and achieving explosively funny results.

"PORKY PIG"

© Warner Bros.

Porky Pig

This rare printed model sheet shows Porky Pig, the stuttering, mild-mannered, innocent foil of the brasher, more self-possessed Bugs, Daffy and Sylvester. More emotionally sympathetic than other Warner Bros. creations, Porky was a cartoon star of a different kind.

Bugs Bunny in Little Red Riding Rabbit

In this zany take-off of the traditional fairy tale, Bugs escapes being eaten by the wolf with his customary cool. *Little Red Riding Rabbit* is a classic example of Bugs's custom of using his superior wit to outclass the bad guy.

Tex Avery at MGM » 128

© Warner Bros.

The Dover Boys

Dover Boys Tom, Dick and Larry were three upstanding but stupid brothers on a university campus. Showing all the hallmarks of Chuck Jones's unique style, this experiment in limited animation set the style for Warner Bros. cartoons for the next 15 years.

Chuck Jones

The formative Chuck Jones cartoons, such as *The Mighty Hunters* (1940), *Tom Thumb in Trouble* (1940) and *Good Night Elmer* (1940), were contemplative exercises in lighting and modeling, and are stylish to a fault. They explore rather small, humorless themes at the expense of the story. This tendency toward thoughtful film design would serve Jones better in his later cartoons, when he was better able to use it in the service of a story. His earliest work with Bugs and Daffy gave him more promising material to work with, although they still seem at times too tentative to reach out for a laugh. *My Favorite Duck* (1942) establishes Daffy's ability to push Porky's buttons, and displays some nicely timed quick cutting. By 1944, with *Bugs Bunny and the Three Bears*, Jones has made a very confident, very funny cartoon, bouncing Bugs against a truly funny cartoon comedy team.

Bob Clampett

This is an especially remarkable period for Bob Clampett's cartoons. His Daffy is an enfant terrible, tearing his way through some truly wacky cartoons. In *Henpecked Duck* (1941), his idle tomfoolery when practicing a magic trick makes the egg he is babysitting disappear, leading to panicky histrionics. In *The Wise Quacking Duck* (1943), he embellishes the illusion that his head has been cut off with a bottle of ketchup and more frantic acting.

In his Bugs cartoons, Clampett does not hesitate to cast aside Bugs' more dignified behavior in the service of a gag's demands. Bugs requires little or no provocation to turn boisterous in *Wabbit Twouble* (1942) and *The Wacky Wabbit* (1942). *Tortoise Wins by a Hare* (1943), a sequel to Avery's tortoise cartoon, ratchets up even Avery's crazier humor to a new extreme. Clampett's original ending to *Hare Ribbin* (1944), had to be reshot – Bugs pulling out a pistol and shooting his foe in the face must have seemed perfectly reasonable to Clampett.

Arguably, the most acclaimed among Clampett's cartoons were both made in 1943. *Coal Black and de Sebben Dwarfs* and *Tin Pan Alley Cats*, despite the racial stereotypes, are considered two of the most respected cartoons ever made. *Coal Black* in particular combines extremely high spirits, fast action and lively music with the most zealous World War Two fervor ever caught on film.

FRIZ FRELENG & FRANK TASHLIN

Friz Freleng, who had been absent from Warners for a brief but historically significant period of the late 1930s while Bugs and Daffy were in their formative years, was nevertheless a legacy at the studio. His first Daffy Duck cartoon, *You Ought to Be in Pictures* (1940), was an unusual mixture of live action and animation, with Daffy goading Porky into quitting his job at Warner to try his luck at another studio. Meanwhile, Daffy tries to schmooze Leon Schlesinger into making him the studio's new cartoon star. *Yankee Doodle Daffy* (1943) and *Stage Door Cartoon* (1944) are good examples of a theme Freleng would visit repeatedly over the showbiz years.

Making a Song and Dance

A number of Freleng's cartoons were informed by vaudeville, with Bugs or Daffy performing song and dance revues, often staged more from the point of view of a theater audience than from a movie director's sensibility. Some of Freleng's funniest gags take advantage of the limitations of stage space in a single long shot, with gags often culminating in a blind area, the camera never cutting away for a close-up. *Daffy the Commando* (1943) and *Bugs Bunny Nips the Nips* (1944) find Daffy and Bugs, respectively, in high gear for the war effort.

A Freleng specialty at various times in his career was the musical cartoon films that communicate purely through animation tightly synchonized to music. *Rhapsody in Rivets* (1941) and *Pigs in a Polka* (1942), both Academy Award nominees, are examples.

Freleng was a master of impeccable timing. Chuck Jones wrote, "No one, including Tex Avery, has as perfect a sense of timing as does Friz Freleng, and no one can pre-time a picture with as absolute certainty as he can.... Friz timed his pictures on musical bar sheets in the most beautiful, tiny lettering style you ever saw. These were then transferred by some myopic lackey on to exposure sheets."

Frank Tashlin

Frank Tashlin landed back at Warners in September 1942, taking a job in the story department with the promise that he would inherit Norm McCabe's unit when McCabe went into the military. McCabe had briefly filled in as director when Tex Avery took a job at MGM. "When I went back, Tex had left," said Tashlin, "and there were four units: Freleng, myself, Bob and Chuck." During this third and final stay at Warners, Tashlin directed some of his most distinctive cartoons, films like *Swooner Crooner, Brother Brat* (both with Porky, 1944), *Scrap Happy Daffy* (1943), *Plane Daffy* (1944) and *The Stupid Cupid* (1944). These later Tashlin cartoons bring a sense of design that is lean and

LEON SCHLESINGER Presents THE NEW CARTOON SENSATION "BUGS BUNNY" Now Appearing In LOONEY TUNES and MERRIE MELODIES RELEASED BY WARNER BROS.

© Warner Bros.

Looney Tunes

The first *Looney Tunes* cartoon to be released was *Sinking in the Bathtub* (1930), and after this, they were produced at the rate of one per month. So successful were the *Looney Tunes* that Warner commissioned another monthly series, *Merrie Melodies*, in 1931.

Private Snafu –sketch

The entertainment industry took its duty to help the war effort very seriously, with all the major cartoon studios undertaking contract work for the military. The best-remembered of these wartime cartoon characters is the US Army's Private Snafu.

Private Snafu

Created as an example to servicemen of what not to do, Snafu was an acronym standing for "Situation Normal – All F***** Up". Because the intended audience consisted entirely of male soldiers, these cartoons were considerably more risqué.

© Warner Bros.

angular, with an emphasis on line, shape and mass. In *Plane Daffy*, the backgrounds are sparse, with a distinctive color palette: slabs of tomato red are placed next to salmon pink, balanced by a block of sky blue. Add a cel of Hatta Mari, with her lemon-yellow hair, and you have an attention-grabbing combination of colors. At the end, Tashlin caricatures Hitler, Goering and Goebbels, with Mel Blanc making the most of der Feuhrer's one line: "Hitler iss a shtinker? DAT'S no military secret!" To which the others reply: "Yah! EFFERYBODY knows DAT!"

Anthem to War

"Women of America have responded magnificently to the demands of a nation at war," intones a voice-over at the beginning of Tashlin's *Brother Brat*. This intro is an anthem to wartime industry, drawn in dramatic, realistic chiaroscuro and depicting the nobility of human endeavor in a style that resembles WPA paintings. What follows is a very funny cartoon in which Porky has to babysit a bratty child for a working mother.

At the same time as these cartoons were being produced for civilian audiences, Warner was also producing cartoons for military consumption. Tashlin, Clampett and Jones made short Private Snafu and Hook cartoons to illustrate training themes for *The Army-Navy Screen Magazine* during the war.

© Warner Bros.

CARTOONS GO TO WAR

Prior to the advent of motion pictures, cultural motivation for war (i.e. demonizing the enemy and boosting morale at home) was propagated through the presentation of themed artwork, literature and theater. By World War One, the persuasive power of the cinema was well understood, and the cinematic arts were becoming part of the process as well. Popular cartoon series like Bud Fischer's *Mutt and Jeff* and John Bray's *Colonel Heeza Liar*, while made for general audiences, had obvious war-fever overtones. Winsor McCay's visually stunning *The Sinking of the* Lusitania was commissioned specifically to bolster the US war effort.

Wartime Topics

After World War One, animation generally returned to peacetime subjects, the only armed forces presence being the occasional parody of military life. Pearl

© Fleischer Studio

Harbor changed things dramatically. Popeye joins the navy (he was originally in the Coast Guard) and sinks Imperial Japanese battleships single-handedly in *You're a Sap, Mr Jap* (1942). He brings spinach to Downing Street while sinking Nazi submarines in *Spinach Fer Britain* (1943). Bugs Bunny fights in the Pacific Theater in *Bugs Bunny Nips the Nips* (1944), while Daffy Duck takes on Hitler in *Daffy the Commando* (1943). He also thwarts enemy spies in *Plane Daffy* (1944), while gremlins from the Kremlin bring down the Luftwaffe in *Russian Rhapsody* (1944).

The Fleischer Studios ground-breaking *Superman* series commenced just as World War Two began and, as the studio transitioned to the Paramount/Famous label, the man of steel was battling Japanese saboteurs in New York and Nazis in Africa in *The Japoteurs* (1942) and *Jungle Drums* (1942). At MGM, Tex Avery won an Academy Award for *The Blitz Wolf* (1942), a wartime version of the three little pigs fable, with Hitler taking the wolf's part. The Disney studios won an Oscar the following year with *Der Fuehrer's Face* (1942), Donald Duck's nightmare of forced slave labor by the Axis powers.

Superman

Originally created by two teenage science-fiction fans from Cleveland, Ohio, *Superman* went on to become very popular in printed form and on both the small screen and the big screen.

Superman – model sheet

The Fleischer Studios produced a total of 18 cartoons featuring the Man of Steel, all of which had high-production values and which are still held in high regard today by animation fans.

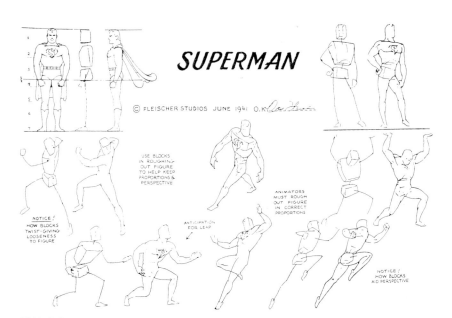

© Fleischer Studio

Wartime Stereotypes

These films, and many more like them, were made for general audiences and used humor and invention to put across the wartime message. More telling was the way in which enemies were portrayed. Almost from the onset, Japanese soldiers were relegated to the spectacle-wearing, bucktoothed, simian imps that fulfilled the stateside stereotype of the era. German and Italian leaders were also the focus of very broad caricature, but German soldiers were almost never stereotyped. Why? Perhaps because the Japanese were easily identified as being "different", while the German and Italian rank and file looked, well, "just like the British".

World War Two saw the first movement toward integration in the Allied ranks, but in animation black soldiers were still relegated to then popular stereotypes. Walter Lantz produced the Oscar-nominated *Boogie Woogie Bugle Boy of Company B* (1941) and Warner Bros. released what many consider to be one of the best theatrical shorts ever made, *Coal Black and de Sebben Dwarfs* (1942). Both have wartime themes but the racial depictions show that even while the Allies fought for freedom, the introspection needed to achieve equality in one's own country had not yet been realized.

Information Service

Animation crews, most notably at Disney and Warner Bros., spent much of the war making propaganda and instructional films. Disney's *Victory through Air Power* had a monumental effect in convincing both civil and military personnel, including Churchill and Roosevelt, that an escalation of the air war could mean the difference between Allied victory or defeat, and *Education for Death* was one of the few films that dealt with the psychological effects of the fascist movement on German individuality. Many Warner Bros. artists found themselves making the Private Snafu series (1942–45) for the army. These films, often written by Theodore Geisel (Dr Seuss), were racy for the times and meant only for enlisted men, but they were actually educational films, providing insight into various aspects of a soldier's life. Studios made many fund-raising films as well, using popular characters to sell war bonds. Bob Clampett's *Any Bonds Today* (1942) was used in theaters and on television well into the 1950s.

Of course, during all of this activity many of the people making these films also faced the possibility of being enlisted. In fact, the harshest reality of animation at the time was that, as World War Two dragged on, animation crews dwindled as more animators put down their pencils and took up arms.

The Thrifty Pig

A short made for the National Film Board of Canada, *The Thrifty Pig* was commissioned to promote the purchase of Canadian War Bonds and thereby support the war effort.

GEORGE PAL'S PUPPETOONS

George Pal coined the term "Puppetoons" while producing advertisements for Philips Radio of Holland in the early 1930s. Though he often used stop-motion puppets with flexible wire skeletons, his signature style involved what is called replacement animation. Rather than moving an articulated model for each frame of film, Pal would have individual figures carved out of wood for each pose required. After shooting a frame, he would replace the entire figure with a new one he had fashioned in a slightly different pose. While the projected film would appear to show a single figure moving about, as many as 5,000 different wood carvings were required to complete an eight-minute film.

An Unique Look

Stop-motion animators still use replacement animation to some degree. Projects like Tim Burton's *The Nightmare Before Christmas* (1993) and Aardman Animation's *Chicken Run* (2000) employed an array of different mouth pieces or even entire heads to achieve lip sync or convey emotion. However, the Pal method of producing thousands of entire puppets would prove far too time-consuming and expensive for modern productions. While the pre-posed figures saved a little effort during filming, the pre-production time involved negated the benefits. Even before the army of puppet clones was meticulously crafted, Pal and his team of artists roughly animated the action on paper using a typical cel animation pipeline. Since the painstaking process has not been reproduced by other studios, the look Pal achieved remains entirely original.

Hiring Harryhausen

When Pal moved to Hollywood and began working for Paramount in the early 1940s, one of his hires was a young animator named Ray Harryhausen. It was the 18-year-old's first professional job, and he spent two years working on the first 12 of the *Puppetoons* shorts, which average eight to 10 minutes in length. *King Kong* animator Willis O'Brien later came on board, but quickly became frustrated with the process. Harryhausen would later admit that he too felt the assembly-line replacement method Pal employed limited his creativity as an animator. Still, the Puppetoon factory would prove an invaluable training ground for animators who later went to work for commercial studios and special-effects companies.

Dipsy Gypsy (1941), starring the character Jim Dandy, was the first in the series of *Puppetoons* produced in the US. While this character failed to catch on with audiences, it was followed by many other puppet personalities, such as the daydreaming Rusty, teenagers Punchy and Judy and the popular *Jaspar* series. Though these films were short in length, it took a full year to complete six of them.

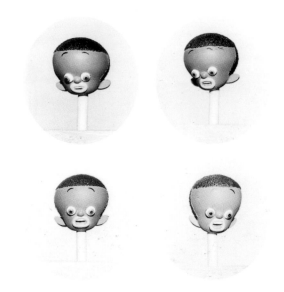

© Estate of George Pal

Puppetoons

Puppets were made for each facial expression in the painstaking task of creating the *Puppetoons*. George Pal used the money he had earned from the Philips advertisement campaign to form his own studio in order to make his *Puppetoons*, eventually employing as many as 75 artists and craftspeople, and working with glass as well as wood to build his solid sets and characters.

© Estate of George Pal

© Estate of George Pal

The snappy animation style proved a perfect companion for the popular musical numbers of the day. *Jasper in a Jam* (1946), for instance, features the music of Charlie Barnet and his orchestra and the voice of singer Peggy Lee as instruments come to life in a pawnshop.

Award Winners

Individual *Puppetoons* were nominated six times for an Academy Award, with Pal winning a special Oscar on 1943 for the techniques he developed. Of the nominated shorts, two were adaptations of *Dr Seuss* – *The 500 Hats of Bartholomew Cubbins* (1943) and *And to Think That I Saw It on Mulberry Street* (1944) – one a respectful adaptation of a black folk tale, *John Henry and the Inky Poo* (1946), and another Pal's classic adaptation of *Tubby the Tuba* (1947). The producer would achieve even greater success when he transitioned to live-action features, such as the critically and financially successful H.G. Wells adaptations *The War of the Worlds* (1953) and *The Time Machine* (1960).

After Pal's death in 1980, producer Arnold Leibovit (*The Fantasy Film World of George Pal*) compiled a number of the shorts into an 80-minute feature film titled *The Puppetoon Movie*. The 1987 theatrical release enlisted Art Clokey characters Gumby and Pokey, along with an animated vegetarian T. Rex named Arnie, to

Dimensional Cartoons

Pal's stop-motion, three-dimensional *Puppetoons* were the forerunner of today's CG cartoons from Pixar and Blue Sky Productions. Brilliant color design and art direction were employed and audiences were dazzled by the charm of the characters. Pal received an Oscar for the technique in 1943.

introduce the titles: *The Little Broadcast* (1943), *The Big Broadcast of '38* (1937), *Hoola Boola* (1938), *South Sea Sweethearts* (1938), *Sleeping Beauty* (1935), *Tulips Shall Grow* (1942), *Together in the Weather* (1946), *John Henry and the Inky Poo, Phillips Cavalcade* (1934–39), *Jasper in a Jam* (1946) and the last Puppetoon short made, *Tubby the Tuba*. The film was later released on DVD by Expanded Entertainment and contains 12 bonus *Puppetoons*.

WISE GUYS EMERGE

The early 1940s saw animation studios acting en masse to create "wise guy" cartoon characters: smart-aleck stars far less well-mannered than had previously been the trend. Some have attributed the wise guys' triumph to Americans' tensions over the coming war; it was an emotional release to watch funny animals wreak unapologetic havoc. On the other hand, one might also theorize that Donald and Daffy Duck — the prototypical wise guys of the 1930s — had struck an unexpected chord with moviegoers, and that studios in the 1940s merely ramped up their efforts to follow the ducks' lead.

© Metro-Goldwyn-Mayer

Tom and Jerry

Whatever the cause, when a blue-gray cat and brown mouse debuted in MGM's *Puss Gets the Boot* (1940), it was not the result of a conscious effort to create new star characters. Working under Rudy Ising, de facto directors William Hanna and Joseph Barbera just happened to concoct a cat and mouse story. The later sequels that followed were the result of *Boot*'s unexpected success.

Puss Gets the Boot tells the simple tale of Jasper the house cat being warned not to break chinaware — after which a mouse tries to make the cat run foul of the rule. The theme is nothing special. It is what Hanna and Barbera did with it that stood out — both in *Boot* and later on.

Hanna, a veteran of the Harman-Ising school of art, designed a cat and mouse lifelike enough that one saw them as real and felt their pain. Then Barbera, a skilled gag man, piled on the pain — putting the realistic animals through the lumps usually reserved for less believable cartoon stars. The result was a unique kind of "slapstick you could feel" — and that would have been objectionable in its sadism, had not the characters made clear that their pride alone was injured. As it shaped up, the pain level of the violence equated only to the embarrassment level of a given defeat.

Northwest Hounded Police

Created by Tex Avery, Droopy made his debut in 1943's *Dumb Hounded*. This 1946 remake, *Northwest Hounded Police*, shows how Avery really progressed as a film-maker. It is faster, funnier and more outrageous. Avery loved using Droopy as a simple foil for a gallery of bad guys, bullies and crooked characters.

Red Hot Riding Hood

Avery's sensual adaptation of the classic tale was an instant hit, although the Red cartoons were at first banned from TV for being too provocative. Red's sexy looks and demeanor, as well as making her a pinup during the war, had a lasting impact on animated characters long after her last short: in the 1980s, Jessica Rabbit was based on Red.

Tom and Jerry – golf

Tom and Jerry established themselves as a firm cartoon favorite from their first outing in 1940. With *Tom and Jerry*, Hanna and Barbera broke Disney's Oscar monopoly for cartoons: in 20 years, they won seven Oscars. Hanna was the timing director, whereas as Barbera invented the stories and worked out the gags.

It was a new way to feel for cartoon characters. Jasper and his mousy foe became Tom and Jerry in *The Midnight Snack* (1941), wherein the cat's backside takes a rough ride down a cheese grater. In *Fine Feathered Friend* (1942), a pair of shears repeatedly threatens Tom with harm. One cannot do the gags justice by describing them in print: the realistic feel gives them their bite on screen. Added bite is provided by Tom's cynical owner, whose frustration with her "no-good cat" was magnificently voiced by Lillian Randolph.

Finding Their Way

It would take Tom and Jerry several years to hit their stride. In the early days, Tom was physically over-detailed, his whiskers mimicking a stage villain's mustache in *Mouse Trouble* (1943). The early cat and mouse even spoke, using Dead End Kid voices in *The Lonesome Mouse* (1942). By the mid-1940s, Tom would be visually streamlined and both cat and mouse more typically silent, but no matter. With audiences, both had long since been going from strength to strength. *Puss Gets the Boot* garnered an Oscar nomination; *The Yankee Doodle Mouse* (1943) and *Quiet Please* (1945) won the prize. For Tom and Jerry's fans, such recognition could not come too soon.

Perhaps the most famous wise guy in cartoons was this crazy bird – quite literally crazy, for actual insanity was the original calling card of Walter Lantz's biggest star. In truth, Woody's creator – Walter Lantz story man Ben Hardaway – had been dealing with the daft for quite a while. At Warner a few years earlier, Hardaway had toiled as a story man on that darn Daffy Duck; later, with Cal Dalton, Hardaway more or less copied Daffy to create the embryonic Bugs Bunny. From proto-Bugs to Woody was just a short step. In particular, the woodpecker's celebrated call – "Ha-ha-ha-HA-ha!" – was first heard from Hardaway's version of the rabbit.

Explosive Effect

When it came to the Lantz studio, however, more important than Woody's originality was the effect he had on his surroundings. At Warner, Daffy and Bugs had been born into a cartoon environment that was already screwy: a natural home for the iconoclastic new stars. By contrast, many Lantz cartoons in 1940 still revolved around childish themes and cuddly cuteness. Even Andy Panda, the mischievous leading light, was sweeter than he was bratty. Dropping Woody into this innocent atmosphere was like detonating an atomic bomb.

The big debut came in *Knock Knock* (1940), when Woody repeatedly appeared on Andy's roof to confound Andy and his pop. If viewers had any doubt of the bird's lunacy, it was dispelled by the finale. In a scene similar to one written by Hardaway for *Daffy Duck and Egghead* (1938), woodpeckers from the nuthouse arrive to cart Woody off – but turn out to be just as crazy as their ward.

From there it was on to wackier heights for the new Lantz star; and the longer Woody persevered, the more he shook free the veneer of cuteness that had long hung over the studio. A wise guy needed stooges – and other wise guys – to do battle with, and suddenly Lantz shorts were full of them. At first, Woody dealt with the one-off likes of a fox psychiatrist in *Woody Woodpecker* (1941) and a Mexican bull in *Hollywood Matador* (1942). Soon, though, Woody found a recurring foe in Wally, the irascible Swedish walrus of *The Beach Nut* (1944). Blustery Wally was about as far from a traditional Lantz star as Woody had been, but the atmosphere had changed to make the walrus's introduction seem entirely natural.

Streamlined Success

The Beach Nut also included a version of Woody that was new to audiences of the time. The woodpecker had started life in 1940 as a long-beaked, toothy bird with a distracting red belly. Beginning with *The Barber of Seville* (1944), however, studio color stylist Art Heinemann tired of the character's grotesque look and asked Lantz's permission to draft a streamlined model. With that, the slicker, toothless, blue-and-white "classic" Woody Woodpecker was born.

Walter Lantz & Grace Stafford

Walter Lantz's wife, Grace (pictured), provided Woody Woodpecker's trademark high staccato "ha-ha-ha-HA-ha" laugh after an anonymous audition in 1952. Mel Blanc provided the original voice in 1940 when Woody first appeared in an Andy Panda short.

© Walter Lantz Studio

The Barber of Seville

Like all characters, Woody's design changed after his first few years. Most of his early films involved him trying to get food, gate-crashing an event, or heckling, and Woody's "new look" was unveiled in this short. He became one of the most popular icons of the 1940s.

Hollywood Matador

Woody was a hit during the war years with his brio and straight-talking manner. His image appeared on US aircraft and mess halls, and audiences on the home front watched Woody cope with familiar problems such as food shortages. He appeared in this short with one of his first "costars" – a bull.

© Walter Lantz Studio

The Barber of Seville also pushed the envelope in other ways. In production, the short included a scene where Woody maniacally trimmed a customer to the tune of Rossini's "Largo el Factotum". As the music got faster, however, the story crew had not reflected the speed-up in the action. Director Shamus Culhane decided to do so, matching every "Figaro!" to a new jump cut. The result was the fastest, funniest scene that had ever been in a Woody cartoon – or a Lantz cartoon. The fact that the woodpecker swung a mean razor was not lost on Culhane either.

Crazy, Wild Bird

By the mid-1940s, Culhane had become Lantz's leading director, and Culhane's own enthusiasm became that of the studio as a whole. Non-cute, fast-moving, increasingly vicious cartoons were now the norm. Andy Panda, once such a cuddly little bear, set a death trap for his own dog in *The Painter and the Pointer* (1944). And In *Fair Weather Fiends* (1946), Woody himself reached a crazy high point – forcing a hungry wolf into a meat grinder to become Woody's own meal.

Later in his career, Woody Woodpecker would evolve to incorporate some of the cuteness he had originally forsaken. Luckily for fans, though, the woodpecker most of us remember today is the wild wise guy of Hardaway, Culhane and the 1940s – a wise guy who continues to reach today's viewers on TV and DVD.

FOX AND CROW

The year 1941 found former Warner Bros. director Frank Tashlin – unhappy after a brief stint at Disney – moving over to Columbia to become production supervisor. In an effort to guide the staff, he also wrote and directed several shorts himself. *The Fox and the Grapes* (1941), the most influential of the group, had a fairly simple story: a crow tries to mooch a fox's picnic lunch by tempting the fox with some unreachable grapes (both characters voiced, in this initial appearance, by Mel Blanc). But more important than the plot was the film's storytelling style.

Innovative Techniques

As he had done earlier at Warner, Tashlin took advantage of the cartoon medium to draw viewers into the action, utilizing numerous quick cuts and imaginative camera angles. Tashlin also deployed the body of the story – the fox's determined efforts to get at the grapes – through short, snappy blackout gags. In the long run, *Grapes'* seminal blackouts would influence the style of 1950s Warner cartoons. In 1941, they made *Grapes* unique in audiences' eyes, driving them to ask for more of that fox and that crow. Columbia director Bob Wickersham obliged, initially under Tashlin's supervision, and a series was born.

The blackout gag tradition of *The Fox and the Grapes* was carried on in another early Fox and Crow short, *Toll-Bridge Troubles* (1942), but the series as it developed had less to do with gag formula and more to do with simply exploring the main characters' personalities. Blackout gags still cropped up, but so did extended mind games and sitcom-like scenarios. Crawford S. Crow was usually looking for a sucker – his "Sucker Detector" machine appeared several times – and Fauntleroy Fox was it, despite being sharp enough to outwit many of Crow's ploys.

© Columbia Pictures

Fox and Crow

Tashlin brought new life and energy to the hitherto unheralded Screen Gems unit of Columbia. The series' use of blackout gags foreshadowed the Coyote and Roadrunner series at Warner Bros., an influence readily acknowledged by Chuck Jones.

Frank Tashlin and Warner Bros. » 88

© DC Comics

The Fox and Crow Comic

The characters first appeared in DC Comics' *Real Screen Funnies* in 1945 alongside other Columbia stars like Flippy and Tito and his Burrito. They eventually became so successful in this format that they landed their own series of comics in 1951. The comic book Fox and Crow characters had very few noticeable differences from their on-screen counterparts.

Star Quality

Wickersham detailed Fauntleroy's and Crawford's relationship from both perspectives, so that audiences could see through either character's eyes – a highly novel means of storytelling. In *Room and Bored* (1943), for example, refined Fox takes in rowdy Crow as his tenant and lives to regret it. The story would normally call for us to sympathize with Crow; like Woody Woodpecker, he is the viewer's id, playfully unbalancing a culture-vulture who was asking for it. On the other hand, Wickersham makes Fox's frustration real enough – and his intelligence obvious enough, despite his gullibility – that Fauntleroy earns a viewer's sympathy too. Both characters' superb voices, now provided by Frank Graham, only enhanced their star quality.

Unfortunately, Wickersham and his writers failed to understand storytelling and pacing as well as they understood their two heroes. For every classic Fox and Crow cartoon, there is another that tells a good story badly, great characterization notwithstanding. *Way Down Yonder in the Corn* (1943) has a surefire concept at its core: Crawford disguising himself as a scarecrow to get a job "guarding" – and eating – Fox's food. But as executed by Wickersham, the cartoon's early scenes sail by too fast, while a climactic chase is much longer than necessary. Worse, the story's logic is confused: Fox learns his "scarecrow's" true identity from a radio-gossip reporter, despite there having been no moment when the reporter could have witnessed what he reports.

Past Their Sell-By Date?

The sheer likability of Fauntleroy and Crawford led to their survival over the years, despite their dilemma of often being great characters in mediocre cartoons. Their success led Screen Gems to create other wise guys, most notably the canary and cat duo Flippy and Flop. It also led to Columbia's desire to keep Fox and Crow alive after the Screen Gems studio's later demise.

Finally, Fox and Crow's success led to their appearance in comic books – where first Wickersham himself, then cartoonist Jim Davis, successfully carried them on until 1968. The two creators were often acclaimed for their work on the series, proving, if nothing else, that real wise guys can succeed in spite of the odds.

NFB: THE BEGINNINGS

In its rich, decades-long history, the National Film Board of Canada (NFB) has won hundreds of accolades for its animation films and filmmakers, including 25 Oscar nominations and four Oscar wins. One of the leading production entities in the world of animation, the NFB's influence can be seen in the work of such diverse artists as Stanley Kubrick with *2001: A Space Odyssey* (1968), David Byrne's Talking Heads videos in the 1980s and Michel Gondry with the White Stripes' 'The Hardest Button to Button' video (2003).

John Grierson

In 1938, British documentary filmmaker John Grierson was invited by the Government of Canada to prepare a report on government film activities. This report recommended the founding of a National Film Board. On 16 March 1939, the National Film Act was passed and seven months later John Grierson set about to create the National Film Board of Canada, with its mandate "to interpret Canada to Canadians and to the world".

With the outbreak of World War Two, Grierson's first priority was war-related propaganda and the commissioning of three films from the Walt Disney Studio: *The Thrifty Pig* (1941), *Seven Wise Dwarfs* (1941) and *Stop That Tank* (1942).

McLaren Comes on Board

Forming an in-house animation unit was also a priority. A phone call, a promise that he could make films his way and a salary of $40 per week brought Norman McLaren (1914–87) to the NFB's Ottawa headquarters. As soon as he arrived, McLaren was assigned the task of putting together a short Christmas-themed publicity film reminding all Canadians to *Mail Early* (1941). More importantly, his central task was to recruit young artists for this newly formed department. Among the artists McLaren enlisted were Evelyn Lambert and Grant Munro, who became McLaren's assistants and respected filmmakers in their own right; Rene Jodoin, who later became the head of French animation at the NFB; and George Dunning, who went on to direct *Yellow Submarine* (1968). The animation unit was officially formed in January 1943.

Begone Dull Care

This film was a virtual journey into the essence of a jazz selection performed by the Oscar Peterson Trio. It was made visible by the use of vivid colors, lines, and shapes, either painted directly on the film or created by the scratching off of some of the film's emulsion to reveal stark white lines and shapes.

Norman McLaren

Norman McLaren intended to specialize in set design when he entered the Glasgow School of Fine Arts in 1932, but quickly realized the relevance of animation as a means of expression, and began painting directly on film, scratching the emulsion to make the film stock transparent, unaware that Len Lye was also carrying out similar experiments.

Norman McLaren working with Evelyn Lambart

Begone Dull Care, made by McLaren and Evelyn Lambart, embodied two main characteristics of McLaren's films: the application of the colors and images directly onto the film itself, and the use of music as an integral part of the work. The technique was so effective that the viewer was able to see as well as hear the music.

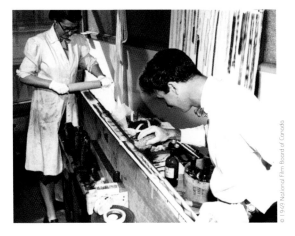

The War Effort

Much of the animation studio's early work was to service other film-making units within the Film Board, primarily titles and animated sequences for documentaries such as *Salt from the Earth* (1944). Early films made by the animation department focused mainly on wartime-related activities such as *Murder in the Milk Can* (1944) by Laurence Hyde and *Grim Pastures* (1944) by George Dunning. Both were designed to remind farmers that the well-being of their animals was key to the war effort. Jim McKay's drawn-on-film *Stitch and Save* (1943) urged Canadians to reuse clothing, and McLaren's *Keep Your Mouth Shut* (1944) reminded all that loose lips sink ships.

Some of the animation unit's most popular shorts were a series of animated sing-alongs, *Chants Popularizes* ('Let's All Sing Together', 1944–51). Intended to boost morale on the home front, these animated adaptations of popular songs were extremely inventive, very bold and graphically stylized.

In the summer of 1945, as Canada's involvement in the war effort was winding down, John Grierson left the NFB. At the same time Norman McLaren, wanting to focus on making his own films, stepped down as animation department head while remaining at the board, and the reins were passed to Jim McKay.

Norman McLaren » 102 Halas and Batchelor » 104

THE MAGIC OF NORMAN McLAREN

Norman McLaren has been called "the poet of animation". Born in Stirling, Scotland, McLaren's first encounter with film was at the age of seven when a neighbor gave him a projector and a box of film. McLaren attended the Glasgow School of Art, where he was inspired by the films of Fischinger, Cohl and Eisenstein. The way objects moved fascinated him: "I found painting and drawing not satisfying because they didn't have motion and movement in them. I saw film as a means of manipulating motion." McLaren's first experiments, consisting of stripping film of its image, applying colored dyes to the clear celluloid and playing them with jazz music, were the foundation of his use of movement and music. In 1935, McLaren's *Color Cocktail* was awarded a prize at the Glasgow Amateur Film Festival. Impressed with McLaren's talent, John Grierson of Britain's General Post Office Film Unit offered him a position.

Bold Approach

Following his first assignment to film the Spanish Civil War, McLaren returned to London where he animated two films for the General Post Office. *Many a Pickle* (1938) explored a technique (pixilation) McLaren would later return to. *Love on the Wing* (1938) demonstrated how far McLaren had advanced his drawing-on-film technique. He said, "Working constantly, directly with film at the editing table, I realized that film is but a celluloid strip, the length of which is time. So my first drive to draw directly on film without use of a camera seemed increasingly justified. To make a film, drawing straight onto film stock is not like painting a picture, where one thing goes here and another here. It is like writing a letter or telling a story, where there is a constant creative consequence related to improvisation."

The Move to America

Hearing that the Guggenheim Museum of Non-Objective Art was interested in buying abstract films, McLaren emigrated to New York where he animated *Allegro* (1939), *Dots* (1940) and *Loops* (1940) and out of necessity, as much as from a technical curiosity, McLaren composed a hand-drawn soundtrack, revealing how early in his career he had developed a level of sophistication.

A Little Phantasy

Isle of the Dead, by the nineteenth-century painter Arnold Boecklin, was the subject of this McLaren film experiment. The spectral island wakes to mysterious life, flickers in an ethereal light and fades again into the dark – the whole effect heightened by an interpretive musical score by composer Louis Applebaum.

© 1946 National Film Board of Canada

© 1968 National Film Board of Canada

Pas De Deux

In this film, Norman McLaren looked at the choreography of ballet. Two leading stars of Les Grands Ballets Canadian danced a pas de deux against a black backdrop, their silhouettes thrown into relief by rear lighting. By exposing the same frames as many as ten times, McLaren created a multiple image of the dancers.

Ballet Adagio

This was one McLaren's last major works for the NFB, and illustrated the movements of ballet to students through the use of slow-motion photography. The dancers were pictured interpreting Albinoni's *Adagio*.

© 1971 National Film Board of Canada

In 1940, McLaren collaborated with pioneer avant-garde filmmaker Mary Ellen Bute on a traditional cel-animated film *Spook Sport*. In 1941, while employed by Caravelle Films, he received an invitation from John Grierson to join the National Film Board of Canada, promising him that he could create cinema as only he understood it.

From 1941 to 1945 McLaren concentrated mainly on war propaganda films. After the war he began to experiment with animated pastel drawings. *A Little Phantasy on a 19th–Century Painting* (1946) is a very mystical, brooding film and a change from McLaren's usual lightness and visual wit.

Drawn to the Rhythm

In 1949, McLaren made one of his greatest filmsm *Begone Dull Care*. Restless lines and shapes sparkle, converge, change shape, multiply and recede to a composition by jazz composer Oscar Peterson. McLaren stated, "It's the movement in the music, not particularly the instrumentation or coloration or harmony. The movement is the common denominator between the picture and sound. We made *Begone Dull Care* in shots. We'd run them on the Moviola. Some were painted as the Moviola was moving and we'd dance the brush full of paint to the rhythm of the music in the picture gate." In the same year, McLaren was sent on behalf of UNESCO to China to teach a group of artists his animation techniques.

In 1953 McLaren returned to pixilation with the release of his most well known film *Neighbours*. McLaren, who held strong antiwar feelings, tells the story of two neighbors quarreling over a flower that has suddenly sprouted on their borders. Their civilized world grows more irate until their houses, families and finally themselves are completely destroyed. *Neighbours* won McLaren an Oscar.

The Ballet Trilogy

During the 1950s and early 1960s, McLaren continued making films using a variety of techniques. In 1967 McLaren produced what many people consider his masterpiece, *Pas De Deux*. Choreographed movements of dancers from the Les Grands Ballets Canadiens are optically treated, creating a deeply sensual, lyrical film.

In 1972 he made a sequel of sorts, titled *Ballet Adagio*. It is designed for ballet students and lovers of ballet as a means to study technique and mechanics, and to emphasize the human and aesthetic aspect of movement.

From 1976 to 1978, McLaren co-produced with Grant Munro a five-part series titled *Animated Motion Narcissus* (1981). This, McLaren's last film, retells the Greek legend. It is an optical printer tour de force and the third of McLaren's ballet trilogy.

On 26 January 1987, McLaren died, aged 72. Filmmakers the world over have enthused about the tremendous impact that McLaren and his films have had on their careers.

HALAS & BATCHELOR

Hungarian-born János Halász (John Halas) gained a universal reputation for producing animated instructional films in England for over 40 years with his wife, Joy Batchelor (1914–91). Educated in Hungary and Paris before entering the film profession, Halas became George Pal's assistant between 1928 and 1931, producing commercials. By 1935 he had inaugurated his own Hungarian studio, making animated advertising cartoons, which resulted in an invitation to England in 1936 by British Animated Films.

A Glossy Start

Joy Batchelor had been involved with design and creating fashions for glossy magazines such as *Harper's Bazaar* and *Queen*. She worked for independent animator Denis Connolly on *Robin Hood* (1935) at British Animated Films, a commercial company run by photographer Gabriel Denes. While working on a further project titled *Music Man* (1938), she met John Halas, who had just arrived from Hungary. After the completion of *Music Man*, the two of them tried to set up a studio in Hungary, but due to the political atmosphere and lack of finances they returned to England.

John Halas and Joy Batchelor formed Halas and Batchelor Cartoon Films as a division of the J. Walter Thompson Advertising Agency in May 1940. Their initial productions were two Technicolor advertisements: *Train Trouble* for Kellogg's Corn Flakes (1941) and *Carnival in the Clothes Cupboard* (1941) for Lux soap flakes.

Drawing for Victory

The General Post Office Film Unit's chief, John Grierson, steered them toward the need for films stressing wartime needs. The recently formed Ministry of Information invited Halas and Batchelor to produce propaganda films for them and the War Office. The resulting factor was an association that lasted for the next nine years. Halas and Batchelor were prompted to breathe life into mundane subjects such as victory gardens in *Digging for Victory* (1942) and "Mobilise Your Scrap" in *Dustbin Parade* (1941).

Filling the Gap

This wartime short from 1941, commissioned by the Ministry of Information, was concerned with the effective deployment of garden space for growing vegetables and other foodstuffs. Titles of other films they made during wartime included *Look Out in the Blackout*, *From Rags to Stitches* and *Blitz on Bugs*.

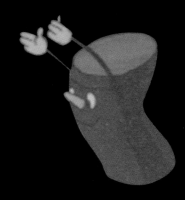

Dustbin Parade

Dustbin Parade, made in 1941, about recycling materials for munitions, was one example of the 70 artful but highly engaging cartoon films made by the studio addressing domestic, government and military needs.

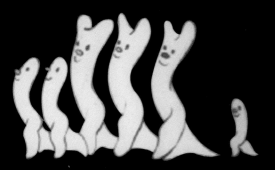

Dustbin Parade – iron

Recognizing animated films' capacity to educate as well as entertain, the Ministry of Information invited Halas and Batchelor to create wartime public information and propaganda shorts, such as *Dustbin Parade* (pictured).

Festival of Britain

In 1951 the studio embarked on its most ambitious project to date, bringing to the screen a faithful representation of George Orwell's cautionary tale *Animal Farm*, about animals revolting and taking over a farm. It was a project that dominated the studio for three years.

On the crest of the success of Britain's first feature cartoon, the team returned to the business of making animated cartoons and experimenting with paper sculpture in *The Figurehead* (1953), the three-dimensional in *The Owl and the Pussycat* (1953) and Cinerama in *Cinerama Holiday* (1955). The studio continued to make commercial, instructional, industrial and children's entertainment films, winning many awards and nominations along the way.

Commercial Success

With the advent of commercial television in 1955, Halas and Batchelor jumped straight into the medium and were the first to make TV commercials, and later children's series such as *Foo-Foo* (1959), *Snip and Snap* (1960), *Do-Do the Kid from Outer Space* (1964) and *Tales of Hoffnung* (1965), which interpreted the humor of popular British cartoonist Gerard Hoffnung. Amid their colossal output, time was somehow found for another feature, *Ruddigore or the Witch's Curse* (1967), an animated representation of Gilbert and Sullivan's libretto.

Always a little ahead of the others, Halas and Batchelor moved into the computer age before others realized that computer animation was the future.

Animal Farm » 166

DAVID HAND & BRITISH ANIMATION

July 1944 heralded the arrival of the noted animator and director David Dodd Hand (1900–86) to England's shores. He had been brought over to launch a British animation studio for the J. Arthur Rank Organization in the expectation of rivaling the American market in pure entertainment films. New Jersey-born Hand had been a veteran of the cartoon field since 1919, commencing his career by animating on the very basic *Andy Gump* series, filtering through the Bray Studios and finally settling at the Walt Disney Studios in 1930. His crowning glory came when Walt Disney asked him to direct the first full-length animated feature, *Snow White and the Seven Dwarfs* (1937).

Founding an Industry

The war was still rife in Europe when Hand first sailed to England to investigate the possibilities of creating a cartoon industry over an eight-week period, and with a budget of just $8,000. It had been decided that war-torn London would be out of the question for a studio, but then he discovered Moor Hall, a sumptuous Victorian mansion in the idyllic setting of the Berkshire village Cookham-on-Thames. This was the base that trained and housed many of the staff while London was reeling with severe war damage and housing shortages. The end product had the lengthy title of Gaumont-British Animation, Ltd. (GBA).

One of the first priorities was to start a training school, and for this he brought over three highly competent ex-Disney employees on a three-year contract: story man Ralph Wright, effects animator John Reed and animator Ray Patterson. Cameraman Bill Garity (later to become Walter Lantz's right-hand man) was also brought over to help set up the camera department. Extensive advertising encouraged many young hopefuls fresh from art school and the services to train as directors, story men, animators, paint mixers, camera operators, inkers and painters, etc., culminating in nearly 200 employees involved in a four-year training schedule.

The manor's old coach house was converted into a camera department, air-raid shelters became a review theater and recording studio, and a model stage was built on to the library. Two basic units were established: one to tend to instructional demands, and the other, captained by Bert Felstead, to produce a series of entertainment cartoons for theatrical distribution. These were essentially the *Animaland* and the *Musical Paintbox* series.

Varied Output

Throughout this duration, GBA was also responsible for many instructional cartoons on subjects as varied as blood circulation and digestion, to an account of the Magna Carta, alongside commercials ranging from Oxydol to Rowntree's Cocoa.

David Hand (center) with Ralph Wright

David Hand set up the animation studio at Moor Park with the aim of producing a regular series of cartoon films to entertain and, above all, to be British in character and humor. Sadly, the plan floundered and plans for feature-length cartoon versions of Lewis Carroll's poem 'The Hunting of the Snark' and H. G. Wells' *The First Men in the Moon* were shelved.

The Lion

Hand's *Animaland* series included *The Lion*. Hand was supervising director on Disney's *Snow White* and *Bambi*, so it is no surprise that the characters featured in these shorts bear some resemblance, although they are perhaps zanier and more adventurous, to Snow White and Bambi's woodland friends.

The Platypus

Hand and his team tried to develop a new style rather than just mimic Disney, with clever plots, strange characters and surreal settings. Most of the *Animaland* shorts had minimal dialogue, but when the characters did speak, they often had British accents. Some were introduced by an off-screen British narrator, who would give "scientific" information about the lead animal, such as the platypus (pictured).

Snow White and the Seven Dwarfs » 58 Halas and Batchelor » 104

© Gaumont-British Animation Ltd. (GBA)

The *Animaland* series featured one-offs such as *The Lion* (1948), which depicted the life span of a lion from cub through adolescence, with the lion finally devouring the narrator for his lunch. *The Platypus* (1949) exercises a similar theme, of the platypus setting up home, finding a mate, losing his mate and finally getting together and starting a family. Along with the antics of Ginger Nutt, a red squirrel, and his forest friends, these *Animaland* cartoons are far closer to Disney than Hand wanted and are chiefly aimed at the junior market.

While the *Animalands* were fully animated, another series was produced on a lesser budget and in a process that is currently known as Photomation, where the essential parts are rendered in limited animation with the camera moving around on a static piece of art. This process had been used by Hand to a greater success on Disney's wartime epic *Victory Through Air Power* (1943).

The *Musical Paintbox* series was what Hand desired: "Basically British in content", relying heavily on folklore and traditional songs. Publicity of this era indicates that both series were intended for worldwide distribution (although there is little to back this theory up: the existence of the *Musical Paintbox* series appears to be alien to anybody outside the British Isles).

© Gaumont-British Animation Ltd. (GBA)

End of a Short Era

Before GBA could really get under way, in November 1949 Rank decided to pull the plug on the whole deal; they were losing money and not able to sell the product to the US as they had initially hoped. Having spent over £500,000 ($900,000) starting up the company, by 1949 each cartoon was costing around £10,000 ($18,000) to make. Although the commercial end was helping subsidize the cash flow, it was not enough, and on 7 February 1950, Moor Hall closed its doors for good.

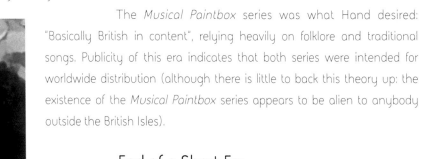

HANS FISCHERKOESEN

The award-winning cartoonist Hans Fischerkoesen (1896–1973) stands head and shoulders above the other German animators of the Nazi regime, if only for having the courage to make purely entertainment films that, in retrospect, appear to be against all fascist policies. Born Hans Fischer in Bad Koesen, Germany, and an asthmatic child, Fischer was inspired by his parents to indulge in activities such as drawing and staging puppet shows. Classified unfit for service in World War One, he worked in hospitals close to the front. His experiences with the wounded arriving from the trenches were to scar him for life mentally, and he envisioned making a film that would expose profiteering as being the real motive behind war.

First Success

With the armistice, Fischer began work on his exposé, which he named *Das Loch im Westen* ('The Hole in the West', 1919). He drew 1,600 individual images of his experiences on the front line and decided to make the film himself by building his own animation stand from an old wooden crate. The completed film was bought by a provincial distributor for DM 3,000, and Fischer was on his way to making a career out of animated cartoons.

In the 1920s, Fischer turned to making advertising films and had a moderate success with *Bummel-Petrus* ('Strolling Peter', 1921) for the Nordheimer shoe factory. This led to his union for the next two years with legendary German pioneer animator Julius Pinschewer (1883–1961), whose animated commercials had been highly regarded since 1910.

The name of "Fischer" seemed to be fairly commonplace in the motion-picture realm, so Hans attached the name of his hometown to the end of his name to set himself apart from the others. Armed with his new name, he established Fischerkoesen Studio in Leipzig, where he started producing advertising animation.

Wartime Repression

The Nazi minister for education and propaganda, Joseph Goebbels, made a decree in 1941 claiming that all non-German and abstract art was "degenerate", and therefore forbidden. The fantastic input from the American market dried up, and Germany was not producing enough of its own cartoons. Very little of the animated entertainment scene survives from the Hitler era.

The Snowman

This film established Fischerkoesen's mastery of creating the illusion of three-dimensional space. During the opening credit, layers of snowflakes fall down through the frame. As the credits finish, the viewer flies down over a snow-covered twilight village, around the steeple of a church (a stereooptical model), down to a snowman in an open space – all seen as if from a snowflake's point of view.

Hans Fischerkoesen

Hans Fischerkoesen's success with animated fairy tales and commercials resulted in an order from propaganda minister Joseph Goebbels to move his staff and studio from the Leipzig area to Potsdam to make himself available for consultations and special effects on features and documentaries.

Weather Beaten Melody

This film was technically brilliant, and Fischerkoesen used little quirky details to bring the bee to life: she uses dandelion seeds as a parachute, and wipes herself with a petal when a berry accidentally bursts over her.

Murals

Fischerkoesen worked in the kitchen at Sachsenhausen and painted murals using vegetable caricatures to represent the daily trials and terrors of prison living. These are now preserved as a national historical monument.

Fischerkoesen found that he was being pressed by the disruptive German government to front the new German animation industry, and was relocated to Potsdam, near the UFA studios. The huge state-controlled corporation functioned under the swastika, and with a governmental grant produced the type of propaganda films that the Nazis needed.

Not wishing to become involved with Goebbels or his cause, Fischerkoesen turned down an invitation to make sympathetic Nazi cartoons by claiming that he just made advertisements and did not have the imagination to create anything else. Because of this, Goebbels assigned him to work with Berlin newspaper cartoonist and "gag man" Horst von Möllendorf, whose contribution to screen cartoons was negligible despite several story credits.

Wartime Resistance

Goebbels' legacy also included a mandate that new three-dimensional effects using model backgrounds be developed to rival the process invented by the Fleischer Brothers. Their Stereoptical process had used a rotating wooden set photographed behind the drawn cel animation to produce "reality" and an impression of depth to their cartoons. However, by this time the Fleischers had just about abandoned this expensive process.

The debut cartoon to be made incorporating new German methods was *Verwitterte Melodie* ('Weather-beaten Melody', 1942). This was filmed with a newly acquired multiplane camera as well as the Stereoptical process. A bee dives from the sky and through meadows, and frolics about until she finds a record player to play music from. There do not appear to be hidden messages in this to benefit Hitler and his regime; indeed, there are many suggestions of a subtle subversion to it. Following the bee on her travels, there is a sense of freedom of movement, an affirmation of the multi-layered nature of reality that demands (even subconsciously) that viewers think for themselves – something sternly forbidden by Nazi doctrine as the most dangerous action of all.

With the war at an end, and although he had been a member of the underground resistance, Fischerkoesen was imprisoned by the invading Soviet troops as a suspected Nazi sympathizer. During his three years in Sachsenhausen concentration camp, he worked in the camp kitchen where he freely illustrated the walls with amusing, appropriate murals.

Once released, Hans and his family managed to escape from East to West Germany, and there he re-established his studio where he resumed his career by continuing to make commercials until 1969.

© Goskino/Soviet State Film Committee

In 1924, Goskino, the Soviet State Film Committee, produced the first Soviet animated film, *Soviet Toys*. It was a crudely drawn piece of propaganda celebrating the victory of the proletariat over the capitalists by the new Soviet republic. Directed by Dziga Vertov and shown in cinemas throughout the Soviet Union, the film established the stereotypes by which capitalists, workers and peasants would be portrayed in Soviet animation for the next 70 years.

First of Many

Two years after *Soviet Toys*, Ivan Ivanov-Vano (who directed many propaganda films in the 1930s) and the Bromberg Sisters – who later became acclaimed directors of animated fairy tales – were hired to work as artists on *The Interplanetary Revolution* (1926) and *China in Flames* (1926). Both films were produced to promote Communism.

Dozens of anti-capitalist and anti-American animated propaganda films followed. The movies were shown throughout the Soviet Union as shorts before feature films. For the next 60 years – until perestroika – animation would continue to serve as a primary means for delivering the state's political messages in a lucid and enjoyable manner, aimed at winning over the hearts and minds of the Soviet people.

Soviet Toys

Although made before the the World War Two era, Ivanov-Vano's ground-breaking film set the standard for the animated films that would follow. Its creator, Ivan Ivanov-Vano went on to make state propaganda films during the war.

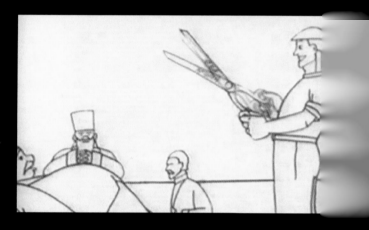

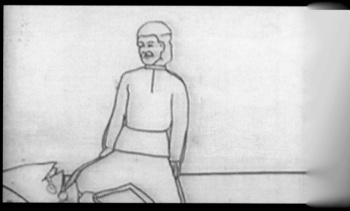

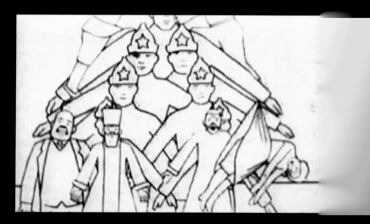

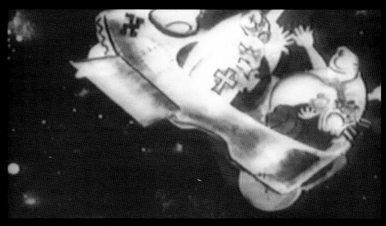

© Goskino/Soviet State Film Committee

The Interplanetary Revolution

Another Ivan Ivanov-Vano Communist propaganda short made before the war, this was a cartoon parody of the Soviet film *Aelita* in which three Soviets fly to Mars. There a love affair develops between the Martian queen, Aelita, and one of the Soviet men while a revolution takes place on the planet.

Soyuzmultfilm

For the most part, animation production in Eastern Europe and the USSR — what there was of it — came to a complete stop during World War Two. However, the Soviet State animation studio, Soyuzmultfilm (founded in 1936), continued to produce an assortment of fairy tales and propaganda films during this period.

Following the Nazi invasion of the USSR in 1941, Soyuzmultfilm made patriotic animated short films with titles like *Not to Stamp Fascist Boots on Our Homeland* (1941) by Ivan Ivanov-Vano and *Vultures* (1941) by Pantilemon Sazonov. The first is a black-and-white film highlighted by a rousing rendition of a popular patriotic marching song "Our Armor Is Strong and Our Tanks Are Fast", and the latter, *Vultures*, is about those German "fascist vultures".

These shorts and others like them — many of which have not survived — were shown in cinemas across the Soviet Union. Because of the urgency of the messages, the ideas for these films were born on the spot and created very fast. Many of the animators actually felt that they were being mobilized like soldiers, that they were obligated to make these films. And in fact they were. But the animators also tried to inject these films with ingenuity and enthusiasm.

Shortly after the war began, those not mobilized into the army were sent to Samarkand, a desert city in Uzbekistan. Work continued at the studio, but many major projects were put on hold and completed only after the war.

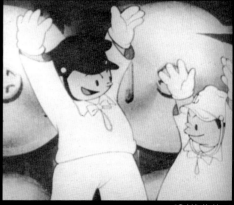

© Tadahito Mochinaga

Japanese animation from 1940 through to the end of World War Two was almost totally devoted to domestic military propaganda. The Imperial Navy fully supported this with funding and scarce production supplies, and deferral from military service for animators.

Something for Everyone

There was plenty of live-action cinematic propaganda for adults, so the animated shorts tended to be aimed at families and children. Two cartoons that glorified the Imperial Navy with heroic little boy submarine crews and fighter pilots were *Ma-bo's Paratroop Unit* (1943) by Ginjiro Sato and *Fuku-chan and the Submarine* by Tadahito Mochinaga (1919–99), released in November 1944.

After December 1941, when Japan added America and Britain to its foes, caricatures of Anglo-enemy leaders became common. Little-boy and funny animal soldiers and sailors bravely stood up to menacing giant lampoons of Roosevelt, Churchill and Chiang Kai-shek, who cravenly ran away when stood up to.

Fuku-chan and the Submarine

This 1944 film by Tadahito Mochinaga featured Fuku-chan, one of one of Japan's most popular newspaper comic-strip characters, and was intended to boost patriotism. There were severe food shortages at the time, the abundant food supply in the submarine kitchen was prepared into various dishes along with a merry, rhythmic song.

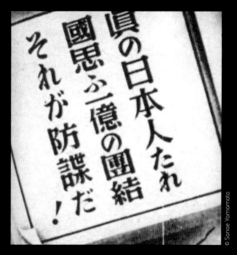

© Sanae Yamamoto

Spies Defeated

Made in order to boost morale amongst the Japanese population, Sanae Yamamoto's 1942 film saw British and American spies caught soon after they are sent to Japan.

The Spider and the Tulip

This film was made in 1942 using real flowers, and a cartoon spider and ladybird. It has been called anti-Western, and has been seen as political protest, with the tulip/ladybird representing the Japanese population and the spider symbolizing the American invaders, who gets its comeuppance when it is blown away by a storm.

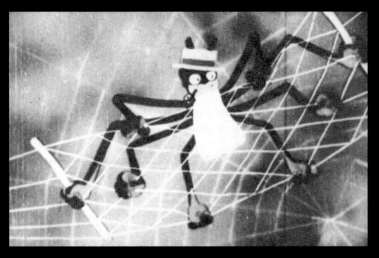

© Kenzo Masaoka

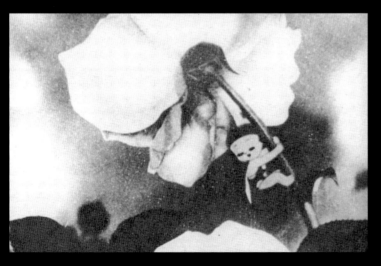

War Leaders Vilified

In Sanae Yamamoto's *Spies Defeated* (1942), Roosevelt and Churchill send spies into Japan who are quickly captured. Ryoji Mikami's *Hooray for Japan!* (1943) combines live-action exhortations to support the war effort with animated political cartoon exaggerations of the quick defeat of the British Army and Navy in December 1941 to early 1942, and a caricature of Chiang Kai-shek as an incompetent puppet of the Americans and British. Mitsuyo Seo's 1933 monkey soldier Sankichi returned, redesigned to look less humorous and more dramatic, in two films by Kotaro Kataoka: *Sankichi the Monkey's Marine Corps Air Defense* (1941) and *Sankichi the Monkey's Fighting Submarine* (July 1943).

The little fine-art animation that there was during this period was dominated by two animators, Kazugoro Arai (b. 1907) and Kenzo Masaoka (1898–1988). Kazugoro Arai was a dentist whose hobby was animation of delicate, stately silhouette cut-outs in the style of Japanese shadow puppetry. He produced two romances set in ancient Japan, *Fantasy of the Butterfly Wife* (1940) and *Princess Kaguya* (1942), and also *Jack and the Beanstalk* (1941). He was then swept up into the propaganda animation production, contributing to *Hooray for Japan!* and *Momotaro's Sea Eagles*.

The Spider and the Tulip

In 1940 Kenzo Masaoka set up a small, independent animation study programme. In 1941 he was hired by Shochiku Films to add it to its animation department. With Shochiku's resources, Masaoka produced the lovely art film *The Spider and the Tulip* during late 1942, released April 1943. A little girl ladybird playing happily in a flowery forest is menaced by a spider with a black face, wearing a Western-style straw hat. This film was not anti-Western per se, however, since such straw hats were a standard Japanese stage and movie prop for low-class buffoons and hoodlums. The spider tries to lure the ladybird, which is hidden from him by a friendly tulip. But the spider is not fooled, and is prying her out of the tulip when a violent storm breaks out. The spider's desperate attempts to keep from being swept away are so courageous that he wins the audience's sympathy, but he ultimately fails, leaving the ladybird to emerge safely when the storm ends. *The Spider and the Tulip* has a lush prerecorded score by an 80-piece orchestra. It was both a popular and a critical sensation, and is still cited by some critics as Japan's finest animated film.

THE FIRST ANIMATED FEATURES

In 1939, Mitsuyo Seo joined the Geijutsu Eigaha (Art Film Company) that produced short animated films for the Ministry of Education, with Tadahito Mochinaga as his assistant. For their *Ant Boy* (1941), Mochinaga devised Japan's first multiplane camera. In late 1942 the Imperial Navy assumed patronage of the studio and commissioned Seo to create longer and more impressive propaganda films. Seo produced the 37-minute *Momotaro's Sea Eagles* (1943) in three months. This restaged the attack on Pearl Harbor with Momotaro as a little boy commander of a monkey and rabbit naval force dive-bombing "Devil Island", despite the comically ineffectual defense of Popeye's Olive Oyl and Bluto.

© Mingaicho Film Company

Impressive Results

This was so popular that the navy ordered a sequel twice as long. Seo's 74-minute *Momotaro's Divinely-Blessed Sea Warriors*, still with Mochinaga's assistance, begins with four young animal naval cadets (bear cub, puppy, monkey and pheasant) returning to their forest home to say farewell to their families and to encourage their younger siblings to support the war effort. The action cuts to the Imperial Navy as bunny sailors build an airstrip on a hot island, with elephants and proboscis monkeys dressed as Indonesian natives looking on in awe. Admiral Momotaro and the four animal buddies as his aides-de-camp arrive with a squadron of fighter planes. After several scenes of happy naval-base life (plus a brief "why we fight" sequence in silhouette animation), the squadron flies off to attack a base of slovenly British troops shown as humans with a foreign devil's horn. The British surrender is a parody of Japanese newsreel footage of the surrender of Singapore. Released in April 1945, this would be Japan's first and only animated theatrical feature until 1958. It is still considered an impressive animation production for its time and the conditions under which it was made.

The Wan Brothers

Greatly impressed by Disney's *Snow White and the Seven Dwarfs* (1937), the Wan Brothers threw their new Xinhua United Film animation department into the production of a feature-length adaptation of an incident from the long *Monkey King* (a.k.a. *Journey to the West*) folk tale, first written in the sixteenth century by Wu Cheng-en. On their journey to India, the Buddhist priest Tripitaka and his three supernatural bodyguards – Monkey, Pigsy and Sandy – enter a region being terrorized by demons led by a cruel buffalo-headed king who controls fire, and his wife, a princess with a magic iron fan that creates freezing cold. Monkey must defeat her and steal her fan to put out the fires and liberate the villagers.

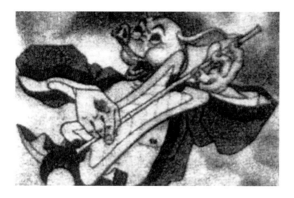

© Ryoji Mikami

Hooray for Japan!

Another propaganda film made in 1943, Ryoji Mikami caricatures Chiang Kai-shek as a puppet of the British and Americans.

Princess with the Iron Fan

Working under adverse financial and technical conditions, the Wan brothers developed an original style based on the use of clay and human models to trace movements and action. *Princess with the Iron Fan*'s plot is adapted freely from part of *Journey to the West*, an epic sixteenth-century romance that recounts the hardships and adventures of the Tang Dynasty monk Tripitaka and his disciples on their travels in search of Buddhist scriptures.

The Chinese Snow White

The 76-minute *Princess Iron Fan* (or *Princess with the Iron Fan*) was produced in 16 months by a team of 237 artists. The cartoon animation was heavily Rotoscoped to speed production and increase the quality. Advantage was taken of the protection of the French concession from the Japanese occupation of the rest of Shanghai to draw parallels between the sadistic demons and the Japanese oppression of the Chinese people. It was released in mid- or late 1941 in unoccupied China and in Chinese communities throughout Southeast Asia to great acclaim.

After the Japanese declaration of war against the Western powers in December 1941, the French concession of Shanghai was abolished. The Wan Brothers left for Hong Kong to work on artistic projects outside of animation for the rest of the war. The Japanese authorities released *Princess with the Iron Fan* in Japan (minus the obviously anti-Japanese scenes) in early 1942, where it was equally popular. It was an acknowledged influence on the Imperial Navy's decision to authorize Seo's production of the 1943 and 1945 Momotaro films. Osamu Tezuka later credited seeing *Princess with the Iron Fan* when he was 13, and the Momotaro feature when he was 16, as inspiring him to become a cartoonist and animator. Tezuka's 1950s comic-book adaptation of the Monkey King legend, produced by Toei Animation in 1960 as its third animated feature, is a remake of this same story.

Creativity Cut Off

Other Chinese animators had just begun production in 1941 before they were brutally cut short by the war. Qian Jia-jun (b. 1916), who would become prominent in the 1960s, finished his first cartoon animation that year, *The Happiness of Peasants*. In August the Chinese Cartoon Association was created in the British colony of Hong Kong. It only produced one cartoon, *The Hunger of the Old Stupid Dog*, before the Japanese occupation of Hong Kong. There was no other Chinese animation until 1947.

V

1945–49:
THE POST-WAR ERA

A return to normality, that is if you can call a Tex Avery cartoon normal. Tex, Hanna-Barbera, Shamus Culhane, Chuck Jones and Friz Freleng all strengthened their considerable skills, and Hollywood cartoons got sharper and funnier as a baby boom began. Heckle and Jeckle, Casper the Friendly Ghost, Foghorn Leghorn and the Road Runner were the new kids on the block. And a young upstart studio, United Productions of America, began to get noticed.

Disney started to make combination live-action/animation films and expanded his artistic reach with a series of animated package films – 10-part compilation movies experimenting with different animation techniques – from surreal abstractions to literal narratives all set to current popular music.

With world markets reopened, new countries joined the animation community with ambitious feature films: France's *Mr Wonderbird*, Russia's *Magic Pony* and Italy's *Rose of Baghdad*. State-sponsored animation studios were established in Iron Curtain countries. The greatest of these was the Zagreb studio, where new ideas and personal visions were realized with freedoms otherwise impossible in the land of their creation.

A new world had begun.

After the war, the Disney studio regrouped. Full-length narrative features, in particular, *Peter Pan*, *Alice In Wonderland* and *Lady and the Tramp*, had been on hold and time was needed to gear up to produce them. Government contracts ended, and money was tight. Disney's studio decided to play to its strength – the animated shorts.

Starring Donald Duck

Donald Duck was Disney's biggest star. Eight Duck cartoons joined Pluto and Goofy, and an occasional Mickey or Figaro, on the RKO release schedules every year. None of them won Oscars – but many of them were quite good.

Jack King directed a trio of classics during this period: *Cured Duck* (1945), in which Daisy uses a machine to cure Donald's bad temper; *Donald's Dilemma* (1947), where a flowerpot smashed on the head provides Donald with a superior singing voice; and *Donald's Dream Voice* (1948), in which a box of pills gives Donald a distinctive, Ronald Coleman-esque enunciation.

Jack Hannah took over the series and emerged as the leading Duck auteur during this period. He moved Donald into the suburbs and built the series around his frustrations with intruding garden pests, including twin chipmunks in *Chip and Dale* (1947) and a variety of insects, including ants in *Tea for Two Hundred* (1948), bees in *Inferior Decorator* (1948) and beetles in *Bootle Beetle* (1947).

Jack Kinney made his mark as the director of a comedic series of Goofy "how-to" shorts. This led to a post-war series of hilarious sports shorts with the Goof

Winter Storage

One of a series of Donald Duck cartoons featuring chipmunks Chip and Dale, *Winter Storage* was made in 1949. The two chipmunks are trying to find acorns for winter and take advantage of Donald's tree-planting scheme.

Donald Duck

Donald Duck made his first appearance in 1934, supporting Mickey Mouse in *The Wise Little Hen*. He finally became the star of the show in 1937 in *Donald's Ostrich*, with his distinctive squeaky voice provided for many years by Clarence "Ducky" Nash.

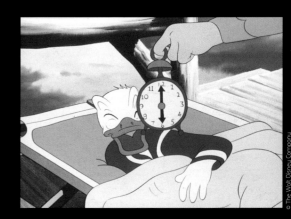

Disney's Wartime Shorts » 80 Disney Returns to Features » 150

© The Walt Disney Company

fumbling all challenges in *Hockey Homicide* (1945), *Tennis Racquet* (1949) and *Goofy Gymnastics* (1949).

Focus on Features

Walt decided to stick with entertainment films – and canceled his contracts for industrial, commercial and educational films during this period. This was a bold move, because the studio needed income from these films. *The Dawn of Better Living* (1945), commissioned by Westinghouse Electric, and *The ABC of Hand Tools* (1946) for General Motors were typical of Disney's post-war commercial films, featuring strong visual storytelling that quickly and easily explained complicated messages – a studio speciality, learned by years of producing military training films.

Disney's *The Story of Menstruation* (1946), for Kotex, was the last commercial film the studio made for some time. This short, shown in girls' high-school hygiene classes for decades, like all Disney educational and industrial films, contains the highest standards of the studio's production values in art, animation and good taste. Though it was his strong suit, Disney knew that animated shorts were on their way out. The money was in feature production, and he had to find new ideas, and new formats, for his storytelling talents.

Going Live

In an effort to push himself forward, Disney took a risk by releasing his first live-action short – a documentary, no less – and announced it as the first in a new series: *A Walt Disney True-Life Adventure*.

In *Seal Island* (1949), director James Algar cleverly assembled hours of live-action footage, detailing a family of Alaskan sea lions and their living habits into 27 entertaining minutes. It paid off, winning an Oscar and signaling a new direction for Disney's movie-making ambitions.

Disney had great plans for his studio, and this post-war period was a transitional time that allowed him to consider his past mistakes – and reinforce his skills.

Pluto's Fledgling

Pluto is the star in this Disney animated short, made in 1948, in which he teaches a young bird to fly. He is more commonly featured as Mickey Mouse's sidekick, a clumsy pet dog. In his first appearance in *The Chain Gang* in 1930 he was actually one of the dogs tracking down an escaped Mickey, only becoming his faithful pet in his third animated outing, *The Moose Hunt* in 1931.

DISNEY MOVES ON

Between 1945 and 1949, Disney released seven feature-length films – yet none of them was a traditional animated feature-length story. Most were "package films" – feature-length collections of short segments not unlike *Fantasia* (1940), only this time the music was contemporary and popular, and the narratives were somewhat traditional.

Spanish Style

The Three Caballeros, released in 1945, delayed due to restrictions on Technicolor printing, was a holdover from the South American "Good Neighbor" films Disney began during the war. This film, on the whole, is a surreal experience, with Donald Duck entering a Latin American picture book and interacting with (i.e., lusting after) a group of sexy live-action samba singers.

Surreal and Spanish also sum up Walt Disney's aborted collaboration with Salvador Dalí toward the end of 1945 and into the early part of 1946. The musical short *Destino* (abandoned, then completed in 2003) was surely an attempt to redefine what an animated film can be. But by 1946, the realities of operating a commercial studio clashed with his artistic ambitions.

© The Walt Disney Company

Fun and Fancy Free

This feature-length package cartoon from Disney consists of two sections: "Bongo" and "Mickey and the Beanstalk", joined together by various live-action scenes narrated by the character Jiminy Cricket.

The Feature Collections

Disney knew he needed to fill his feature-film pipeline quickly – at least one film per year – so various package films were developed and live-action movies were pursued. Disney had his staff work up multiple musical scenarios for a variety of short films. These would take the place *Silly Symphonies* had held a decade earlier, and prepared his crew for more ambitious feature-length cartoons to come.

Make Mine Music was the first such collection, released in 1946. A collection of 10 segments, loosely bridged together, it contains a variety of visual styles and music. Popular singers and musicians including Dinah Shore, the Andrews Sisters, Nelson Eddy and Benny Goodman tell the stories of "Willie the Operatic Whale", "The Martins and the Coys", and "Casey at the Bat", among others.

Output Increases

The same year, Disney released his first live-action narrative film *Song of the South* (1946). Bringing to life the American folk tales of Uncle Remus, this film incorporated three lengthy animated segments with B'rer Rabbit, B'rer Bear and B'rer Fox. The post-Civil War setting of this melodrama was controversial in its day for its portrayal of black plantation stereotypes, but regardless, it is one of Disney's finest films. Its success gave Disney the courage to pursue further live-action movies and grow his film output.

Next came *Fun and Fancy Free* (1947), which essentially tied together two tales of fantasy. "Bongo" is about a circus bear who finds love and danger in the forest, and "Mickey and the Beanstalk" is an epic Mickey Mouse, Donald Duck and Goofy adventure.

Melody Time (1948) was the best of the package films. Each segment is a winner: the surreal South American holdover "Blame It on the Samba" with Donald Duck; "Bumble Boogie", featuring a bee trapped in a bizarre musical landscape and set to the tune of "Flight of the Bumble Bee"; the more traditional tales of Johnny Appleseed, sung by Dennis Day; and "Pecos Bill", told by Roy Rogers.

Disney released his next live-action film *So Dear to My Heart*, in 1949 – a nostalgic tale of a boy and his pet lamb, this time with minimal (but excellent) animation segments. He ended the decade with *The Adventures of Ichabod and Mr Toad*, his last package film.

© The Walt Disney Company

B'rer Fox

Song of the South featured James Baskett, who initially auditioned for a small voice part in the film. He not only got the part of Br'er Fox, but also Uncle Remus, making him the first live-action actor to be hired by Disney. Baskett also won an honorary Oscar for his efforts.

Ichabod Crane

The Adventures of Ichabod and Mr Toad was the last of the package pictures of the 1940s. Money was saved during the production of packaged films by reusing animated sequences and basing characters on others that had already been drawn. As a result of this belt-tightening exercise, the Disney studio was able to finance animated features once again.

© The Walt Disney Company

Ichabod Crane and Mr Toad

The characters of the timid Ichabod Crane and the wild Mr Toad were two personalities the Disney crew could draw to perfection. In the feature, Kenneth Grahame's *The Wind in the Willows* is narrated by Basil Rathbone and features some of the funniest character animation the studio ever achieved. Washington Irving's *The Legend of Sleepy Hollow*, on the other hand, has one of the strongest, most unforgettable dramatic sequences in the studio's history – the spooky encounter between Ichabod and the Headless Horseman.

All of these package films experimented with animation design, and allowed Disney's character animators to explore every possible range of human emotion. Disney's team was now ready to return to full-length features.

UPA IS FORMED

The 1941 Disney strike by the Screen Cartoonist Guild was a defining moment for American animation in more ways than one. It not only ended Disney's artistic and commercial hegemony, but also indirectly led to the birth of United Productions of America (UPA), the most innovative studio of the post-war era – in fact, it was often said to have been formed on the Disney picket lines. What's more, the political activism behind the strike carried over into an aesthetic activism that proved heavily influential for years to come.

Developing Style

The company was formally established in 1944 as Industrial Films and Poster Service by Dave Hilberman, Zachary A. "Zach" Schwartz and Stephen Bosustow to produce *Hell Bent for Election* for the United Auto Workers (UAW) on behalf of Roosevelt's re-election campaign. Its production had been brokered by the union's business agent and largely utilized talent from other studios, especially from Warner Bros., which donated time to the effort and also director Chuck Jones. However, it was storyboarded by John Hubley, Phil Eastman and Bill Hurtz. In terms of design, it owed much to earlier Jones cartoons such as *The Dover Boys* (1942), which was among several films of the period that had decisively broken away from Disney and exhibited a more modern look. It was this type of stylization that was to develop way beyond what Jones had done and became the hallmark of UPA. Their films tended to use limited animation and put more emphasis on graphic elements such as design and color.

Hell Bent for Election

Many animators were keen Franklin Roosevelt be re-elected and so a number, including Chuck Jones, gave their services for free in order that the film be made on time. Roosevelt and opponent Thomas Dewey where depicted as train: the "Win the War Special" and the "Defeatist Limited" respectively. Although the result was not as technically advanced as UPA's later work would be, it was vibrant, stylish and persuasive – and very successful.

© UPA Productions/Columbia Pictures Television

Industrial Output

This distinctive style was initially seen in several non-theatrical assignments, most notably in *Flat Hatting* (1944), a flight-safety film for the US Navy by John Hubley (1914–77), and *Brotherhood of Man* (1946) by Robert A. "Bobe" Cannon (1910–64). The former, in terms of story and gag construction, was very much in the comic tradition of the army's Private Snafu cartoons, but featured flatter character designs by New Yorker cartoonist Robert Osborne.

Brotherhood of Man was a plea for racial tolerance and understanding based on the pamphlet *Races of Mankind* by anthropologists Ruth Benedict and Gene Weltfish. Commissioned as a recruiting tool for the UAW, it later received wide distribution well beyond union halls, and became widely used in classrooms. Hubley felt it was this film's character designs, which were heavily influenced by the sharp-nosed characters of Saul Steinberg, that were going to be a decisive turning point artistically for the studio.

In 1946, Schwartz and Hilberman left UPA and moved to New York, where they established Tempo Productions, a pioneer in the production of TV commercials. They sold their shares in the company to Bosustow, who, despite selling shares to some key artists, kept control of the studio. He became executive producer and, more importantly, named Hubley supervising director.

Mr Magoo

Despite UPA's growing reputation, it proved difficult to keep the studio afloat until Bosustow managed to interest Columbia Pictures into giving it a trial run of four cartoons, three starring its Fox and Crow characters, in hope of landing a contract. The first two cartoons, *Robin Hoodlum* (1949) and *The Magic Fluke* (1949), were smartly directed by John Hubley and used highly stylized backgrounds and flat patterns, which were unlike anything Columbia had ever seen. They were subsequently nominated for Academy Awards, which by themselves would have guaranteed the company an agreement with Columbia.

As successful as these films were, Hubley and others at UPA did not want to be stuck with anthropomorphic animal characters; instead, they wanted to use human characters. The result was Hubley's *Ragtime Bear* (1949), which Columbia only agreed to make because it featured a bear. It was this film that saw the birth of UPA's most popular and endearing character, the nearsighted Mr Magoo, who was inspired in part by W. C. Fields and Hubley's uncle.

The story, which had the vacationing Magoo mistaking a bear for his banjo-playing nephew, proved the perfect vehicle for a series of hilarious sight gags, which set the mold for future films in the series. Its success, both critically and especially at the box office, provided the springboard for a period of intense creativity that was fundamentally to change the face of American and international animation for years to come.

Mr Magoo

These original artworks are of Mr Magoo, the short-sighted cartoon character who, within a couple of years, was the star of half the cartoons UPA released – by the mid-1950s, the studio was doing little else. Four Magoo shorts were nominated for Oscars, and two of them – *When Magoo Flew* (1954) and *Mr Magoo's Puddle Jumper* (1956) – won.

Industrial Films and Poster Service

Pictured left are Dave Hilberman, Zachary Schwartz and Stephen Bosustow in 1942. Hilberman and Schwartz had originally rented the office to give them both space in which to paint during their spare time. The first job the three worked on was a film about air safety for Hughes Aircraft.

As World War Two abated and the United States returned to peacetime, the Warner Bros. cartoon unit entered into one of its most creative and expansive periods. These were the years that would see a deeper development of the already established Warner's characters like Bugs Bunny, Daffy Duck, Porky Pig and Elmer Fudd, as well as the rise of important and long-lasting additions to the studio stable. Most important of all is the sharpening of timing and the visual and narrative sophistication of the cartoons leading up to the 1950s, an era that saw the best of the shorts and, ironically, the beginning of the end, to all intents and purposes, of the theatrical short cartoon.

© Warner Bros.

Wise Guys Emerge

Leon Schlesinger, the legendary cartoon producer, sold his studio directly to Warner Bros. in 1944. The new studio (if in name only) was placed under the supervision of Edward Selzer. Schlesinger's almost comical brand of benign neglect had given the fledgling studio just the right lack of vision it needed in the 1930s and 1940s to help the crew begin to develop the devil-may-care, wise-guy attitude that had become a Warner Bros. hallmark. Selzer's main contribution was to annoy the animation unit so much that it inspired them to reach beyond what had been accomplished, to create new and more deliberately crafted films to spite the humorless producer.

The Stars of the Show

Things started out providentially enough with the first cartoon of 1945. Chuck Jones's *Odor-able Kitty* was the first film featuring the irrepressible Pepé le Pew, and also offered the first variation of the fundamental le Pew plot conceit: an amorous skunk mistaking a hapless cat (this time a male!) as the object of his unrequited affections. No sooner was

© Warner Bros.

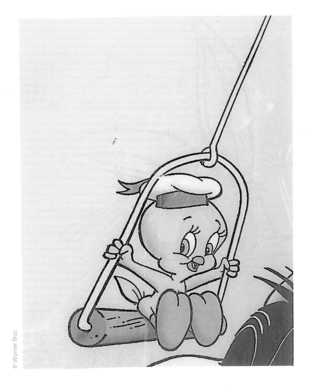

Pepé out of the box than Isadore Friz Freleng launched Sylvester the Cat in *Life with Feathers* (1945), his very first line being – what else? – "Sufferin' succotash!". Just a month later, Freleng would introduce the somewhat self-inspired Yosemite Sam as the perfect foil for Bugs Bunny in *Hare Trigger*.

By the middle of the year, Robert Clampett, perhaps the studio's most stream-of-consciousness-driven animation director, was reintroducing Tweety Pie in *A Gruesome Twosome*. Tweety had appeared in two other cartoons, *A Tale of Two Kitties* (1942) and *Birdy and the Beast* (1944), also directed by Clampett. It would not be long before Friz Freleng would develop the definitive cat-chases-bird team by casting Sylvester as the "puddy tat" fall guy in the Oscar-winning *Tweety Pie* (1947). The two would be together in Warner's cartoons, comic books and advertising from then on.

Bugs, Sylvester and Tweety

Three of the most enduringly popular cartoon creations, Bugs Bunny, Sylvester the Cat and his nemesis Tweety Pie were all created by the Warner Bros. Studio in the 1940s.

Bugs Bunny Rides Again

Set in the Old West and featuring Yosemite Sam, *Bugs Bunny Rides Again* was released in 1948 and remains one of the most popular outings for the rabbit.

Sylvester the Cat

Although Sylvester's most successful partnership was with the ever-elusive Tweety Pie, he also featured in cartoons with other sparring partners. Hippety Hopper (a baby kangaroo) and Speedy Gonzales, the Mexican mouse, both took on Tweety's role as thorn in the side of the perennially frustrated cat.

V: 1945–49: THE POST-WAR ERA NORTH AMERICA: WARNER BROS.

© Imagine-Metode-Art

La Rosa di Baghdad ('The Rose of Baghdad', 1949) marks a significant milestone for Italian animation. Not only does it have the distinction of being Italy's first feature cartoon, but it was also their first film, animated or otherwise, to be produced in Technicolor. It was created and directed by a top Italian advertising designer, Antonio Gino Domeneghini (1897–1966) at his own company, Ima-Film Productions (Imagine-Metodo-Arte). He and his artists labored away through the war years between 1942 and 1949 to complete this ambitious animation project.

La Rosa di Baghdad

First shown at the Venice Film Festival in 1949, *La Rosa di Baghdad* was one of the first Italian feature-length animations along with *I Fratelli Dinamite* ('The Dynamite Brothers') which was screened at the same time.

La Rosa di Baghdad

Producer and director Antonio Gino Domeneghini had to move his animation team from Milan to Bornato, in the countryside of Brescia, to escape the bombing during World War Two.

La Rosa di Baghdad

Despite an awkward narrative progression *La Rosa di Baghdad* has some beautiful scenes, such as Princess Zeila singing as the sun sets and the final firework celebration. The film did well at the box office but Domeneghini returned to advertising after its completion.

Surviving the War

With the market for advertising dying on its feet, the only way Domeneghini could manage to keep his team of skilled craftsmen above water through the Blitz was by creating this film for them to work on. They stayed engaged on this production for a stressful seven-year period, spanning much of the war. Milan being one of the chief targets for Nazi bombing, Domeneghini and his crew were forced to relocate the studio away from the city in the countryside at Bornato.

A key member of Domeneghini's team, illustrator and comic artist Angelo Bioletto (1906–87), was responsible for the character design, owing more than a passing debt to Disney's *Snow White and the Seven Dwarfs*. The atmospheric backgrounds were rendered by Libico Maraja and the music was provided by Riccardo Pick Mangiagalli.

Arabian Nights

The story is taken from an Arabian Nights fable featuring a young flautist named Amin, whose love for the fair Princess Zeila is put to the test. The villain of the piece, the evil chamberlain Burk, plans to do away with Amin, but the flute player finally wins the day, and the heart of the princess. Other characters involved are Oman the Caliph; the Princess's uncle, Sheikh Jafar; the three wise men, Tonko, Zirco and Zizibè; and Kalinà the magpie.

Filming in Technicolor proved to be an expensive luxury. The process used was the successive exposure system. Filmed on a single black-and-white negative, the method involves three identical frames shot through blue, red and green filters. This lengthy and expensive procedure was eventually abandoned in favor of the quicker Eastman Kodak system.

La Rosa di Baghdad did well at the box office and won first prize at the Festival dei Ragazzi in 1949 as part of the 10th Venice Film Festival. Despite this, however, Domeneghini never returned to the world of animated feature films and re-established himself with what he knew best – making commercials.

The Singing Princess

In 1952, an English speaking version was dubbed, featuring the teenage Julie Andrews who was fast making a name for herself as a radio singer. This version was later re-discovered in the USA when Julie was at her most popular, and got a new lease of life when reissued under the title of *The Singing Princess* (1967).

V: 1945–49: THE POST-WAR ERA WESTERN EUROPE: ITALY

THE ZAGREB STUDIO

Yugoslavia was always an anomaly in the Cold War battle. President Josip Broz Tito, who ruled the country from 1946 until his death in 1980, managed to maintain a unique neutrality. While his government was staunchly Communist, he rejected Stalin's policy of dictating to every Communist nation. He also accepted military and economic aid from the West while refusing to be subservient to the United States. Tito's strong personality and adept political instincts also managed to keep together the disparate elements of the Yugoslavian nation, despite the national aspirations of six nominally equal republics. The country's eventual breakup after his death into the independent nations of Croatia, Montenegro, Serbia, Slovenia, Bosnia-Herzegovina, and Macedonia is testament to Tito's political skills.

Inspirational Animation

The country's primary animation studio holds an equally rare place in animation history. Its origins can be found in the advertising industry prior to World War Two, with men like Serij Tagatz, who trained in Moscow, and the Maar brothers, who had fled Germany to escape anti-Semitism. After the war, the popular magazine editor Fadil Hadzic, who has been called the "Cocteau of Yugoslavia", almost single-handedly jump-started animation production in Zagreb, the capital of Yugoslavia's Croatian republic. He organized a group of young animators and decided that their first film would celebrate the country's unique straddling of the east-west divide. The 17-minute satirical short, *The Big Meeting*, a metaphor for Yugoslavia's split with Stalinism, inspired a generation of animators.

© Fadil Hadzic, The Big Meeting, Zagreb Film

© Fadil Hadzic, The Big Meeting, Zagreb Film

Getting Underway

With the help of the government, which was delighted with the film's success, Hadzic organized a group of about 100 artists and founded Yugoslavia's first animation studio, Duga Film. The popular comic-strip artist Walter Neugebauer became the director of one of the four production groups, and Dusan Vukotic headed another. Neugebauer was clearly influenced by Disney, but Vukotic concentrated on developing a national animation style all their own. But before the studio could really get going, the government withdrew its support, choosing to invest in schools, hospitals, and roadways rather than cartoons.

But the seeds had been planted, and former Duga artists like Vukotic, Zlatko Grgic and Aleksandar Marks, who would each later direct his own classic shorts, were not about to stop animating. They found commercial work and began to implement a limited animation style that would soon become the group's trademark. Partly this style was due to necessity, since supplies were scarce, and funds even scarcer. By reducing the number of drawings by a third, they began rudimentary yet highly stylized films that delighted their commercial clients. They were clearly influenced by the UPA Studio in America, but also by the award-winning animated films coming out of Czechoslovakia. This limited style forced the animators to rely on personality and story, and on a meticulous rendering of each drawing. Viewed today, the style seems quite modern, as it is utilized in many commercials and even some television series. At the time, however, it was a ground-breaking departure from the much more realistically vivid Disney cartoons.

The Big Meeting

Fadil Hadzic, publisher of the popular review *Kerempuh*, was the pioneer of animated film in Yugoslavia. Hadzic backed a team of animators to create the country's first animated cartoon. Completed in 1949, it told the story of some frogs that were plagued by midges, in short: the story of Yugoslavia's break with Stalinism.

The Big Meeting

Bordo Dovnikovic, a cartoonist and illustrator for *Kerempuh*, was one of the animators who worked on this film. Production was initially scheduled to take two months but ended up being in taking a year. Bordo and his colleagues had underestimated the production process since they had never produced an animated film.

RUSSIAN DELIGHTS

Following World War Two, Soviet animation continued to be dominated by children's productions that were made in the vein of Walt Disney.

Social Realism

While cut-out and puppet animation did exist, for the most part, Soviet animation (at least in Russia) was drawn on cels. Furthermore, genre and style were completely hindered by the "social realism" mandate. As such, all creative talent and technologies at Soyuzmultfilm during the 1940s and 1950s were used solely for the creation of moralistic fables and fairy tales. These films – Soyuzmultfilm was making about 30 films a year during this time – were, like Disney's, made in a "realistic vein" and were adored by Soviet audiences.

While the content of many of the films leaves little to the imagination, they were all technically proficient and displayed an excellent knowledge of drama and narrative. In addition to short films, Soyuzmultfilm also made full animated features.

Among the experienced directors at the studio were Ivan-Ivanov Vano, the Brumberg sisters and Lev Atamanov. If Alexander Ptushko was the Soviet Spielberg, then Ivan Ivanov-Vano was its Disney. Throughout the late 1940s and 1950s, Ivanov-Vano produced a number of well-made and entertaining films that were immensely popular with children.

Ivan Ivanov-Vano

Invano-Vano became something of a household name in the Soviet Union with the feature film *Ivan and his Magic Pony* (1947). In order to become a prince and marry the princess, a peasant boy named Ivan – accompanied by his humpbacked horse – must overcome three obstacles and defeat an evil king.

Ivanov-Vano was a relatively prolific and eclectic director. After *Ivan*, he made *The Story of the Prince, the Swan and the Czar Saltam* (1951), co-directed by L. Milchin and an interpretation of Alexander Pushkin's re-telling of *Snow White*; a re-telling of Pinocchio, called *The Adventures of a Puppet* co-directed by Dmitri Babichenko; and *The Twelve Months* (1956).

The Twelve Months is a charming and beautifully animated film about an arrogant and rude young queen who thinks she can change the laws of nature. To prove her point, she demands that someone in her kingdom find flowers in the middle of

The Twelve Months

This film's creator, Ivan Ivanov-Vano, is often dubbed the Russian Disney. Telling the story of the 12 spirits of the year who save a little girl from certain death in the forest, this is classic good-triumphing-over-evil fairy tale from Soyuzmultfilm that was so popular at that time.

© Soyuzmultfilm

winter. If flowers are not found, people will lose their heads. With echoes of Cinderella, a greedy mother sends her stepdaughter into the harsh winter to find the impossible. In the forest the girl meets the 12 months of the year, who help her find the flowers.

The Brumberg Sisters

The Brumberg sisters (Valentina and Zinaida) made many feature films, including *The Missing Diploma* (1945), *Christmas Eve* (1951), *Flight to the Moon* (1953) and *Wishes Come True* (1957), about a lumberjack who performs a good deed and suddenly receives whatever he wishes for.

The sisters also made many moral films in which idleness and poor behavior are criticized. In the film *I Drew the Little Man* (1948), for example, a boy draws a picture on the school wall and lets another classmate take the blame. Eventually, overwhelmed by guilt, he confesses in front of the whole class.

Lev Atamanov

Lev Atamanov left Soyuzmultfilm in 1937 and returned to his native Armenia. After making a couple of films there, he later returned to Moscow and made a number of films for Soyuzmultfilm. His work was not particularly imaginative and often overly sentimental. One of his best feature films was *The Golden Antelope* (1954), which was based on an Indian tale. In the film, a greedy man exploits an antelope that can produce gold coins from his hooves. In 1957, Atamanov made a popular adaptation of Hans Christian Andersen's *The Snow Queen* about a boy who is imprisoned in the ice palace of an evil queen (note that Japanese animator Hayao Miyazaki listed *The Snow Queen* as one of his influences). While Atamanov's output consisted primarily of children's films, he made a number of more adult-oriented films in the 1960s and 1970s, including the charming film *Ballerina on a Boat* (1969).

Boris Dioskin

Mention should also be made of Boris Dioskin, who worked as an art director for many years at Soyuzmultfilm before co-directing the award-winning *An Unusual Match* (1956). In the 1960s, Dioskin would make a series of impressive sports animations, including the warm and humorous hockey film *Goal! Goal!* (1964).

© Soyuzmultfilm

The Golden Antelope

Released in 1954 and based on a traditional Indian tale, *The Golden Antelope* is about a greedy rajah who tries to exploit an antelope that can produce gold coins from its hooves.

The Golden Antelope

Both *The Golden Antelope* and *The Snow Queen* were loved by audiences and festival juries, winning several awards.

STARTING AGAIN

By 1945, production materials in wartime Japan were in such short supply that virtually no animation was produced in the final year of the war. In late 1945, as soon as the military government was no longer in power, the three influential animators Sanae Yamamoto, Yasuji Murata and Kenzo Masaoka proposed the creation of a professional animation studio. Around 100 animators supported their foundation of the Shin Nihon Doga Sha (New Japan Animation Company). However, due to the devastated Japanese economy, production was slow in starting both for the new company and for individual animators. One of the first post-war films was *The Magic Crayon* (1946) by Masao Nogawa.

The Nihon Doga Company

Difficulties led Yamamoto and Masaoka to leave and start a different company in January 1948, the similarly named Nihon Doga (a.k.a. Nichido) Company. Their impressive early film was Masaoka's *Tora-chan, the Abandoned Kitten* (1947). This 24-minute cartoon animation was followed by *Tora-chan and the Bride* (1948).

Another notable short film under the Nihon Doga label was Seo's *The King's Tail*. A funny-animal version of *The Emperor's New Clothes* featuring a tail-less fox king, this is one of the earliest examples of Japanese anthropomorphized animals shown as humans, but with animal ears and tail. It was started in January 1948 with the goal of being a 46-minute featurette, and was released in October 1949. Despite having a running time of only 33 minutes, it was still a beautifully elaborate musical production. It was suppressed by the authorities, however, on the charge that its ridiculing of authority made it Communist propaganda. Seo abandoned animation to become an author and

animation that was pouring into Japan, along with the latest American movies that the occupation authorities brought in. The entire Japanese cinematic industry was aware that it had to modernize — and fast. This they would do in the next decade.

China

China's wartime devastation, followed immediately by the Nationalist–Communist civil war, hampered the renaissance of Chinese animation. The first encouragement came in 1947 from Communist-controlled Northern China/Manchuria, where the Party-subsidized Tong Pei Film Studio was instructed to make animated films satirising Chiang Kai-shek's nationalist government. The puppet-animated *The Emperor's Dream* was directed by Chen Bo-er (b. 1907) and animated by Fang Ming that year, and the cartoon-animated *The Turtle Caught in the Jar* was directed and animated by Fang Ming the next year.

Tadahito Mochinaga

© Shin Nihon Doga Sha

Fang Ming was actually the Chinese name of Tadahito Mochinaga, Mitsuyo Seo's former assistant. He was born in Tokyo but had spent his youth in Manchuria where his father worked. Due to the increasing bombing of Japan in 1945, Mochinaga returned in June to Changchun in the puppet-nation of Manchuko to join the art department of the Manchuria Film Studio. The studio's Manchurian employees were treated as peons by the Japanese staff, and Mochinaga started a movement to demand that they all be treated equally. This won him the friendship of the Chinese, and when most of the Japanese were pressured to return to Japan after the war's end, Mochinaga was asked to remain at the renamed Tong Pei (Northeast) studio. As Fang Ming, Mochinaga became an enthusiast of Chinese-style puppet animation. After the Communist government won control over all mainland China in 1949, the cultural division assigned Te Wei (b. 1915), a print cartoonist from Shanghai, and Fang Ming to produce educational and morally uplifting animation for China's youth.

Animation also began a shaky rebirth in Hong Kong with Tan Xin Feng's 1948 puppet-animation *Prince of the Big Tree*, now lost.

V: 1945–49: THE POST-WAR ERA ASIA: JAPAN & CHINA

1950–55:
CARTOONS MATURE

United Productions of America (UPA) challenged Disney's long-held animation philosophies. With imaginative use of limited animation, modern graphics and new ideas, this small studio gained worldwide influence over the way people perceived and produced animated films.

UPA made popular modern fables, with contemporary characters, pushing the envelope artistically and creatively. And they won three Academy Awards. But Hollywood itself was undergoing a change. Widescreen CinemaScope and 3D movies were in vogue – and animation had to stretch to stay apace. At the same time, traditional animation found its greatest success. Chuck Jones made his Daffy Duck masterpieces – *Duck Dodgers*, *Duck Amuck* and *The Scarlet Pumpernickle* – and Disney returned to making feature-length fairy tales, including *Cinderella* and *Peter Pan*.

Disney may have had the feature-film arena to himself in the US, but in Europe new film-makers decided to compete vigorously, with ambitious productions of *Animal Farm* (Great Britain), *Mr Wonderbird* (France), and *The Snow Queen* (Russia).

Animation had found its place, and was now evolving in new directions.

It is often implied that United Productions of America (UPA) was born out of the Disney Studio strike of 1941. That event probably had something to do with bonding the original members of UPA together in some sort of alliance, but the studio would not actually come into its own until after World War Two, and the driving force would not be a strike, but a vision of animation as a modern-art form.

First Successes

Initially, Steve Bosustow, Zack Schwartz, Dave Hilberman, John McLeish, Ted Parmelee, Phil Eastman, and especially John Hubley, formed a company called United Film Productions and found work in the burgeoning wartime animation industry. After making several films for the government, they teamed up with Warner Bros. director Chuck Jones and produced a film for Franklin Delano Roosevelt's 1944 re-election campaign, *Hell Bent for Election*. It was an immediate hit and brought a lot of attention to the small studio, now re-named United Productions of America. UPA continued to do government work, and also produced the first film that would feature the flat, graphic style that would become the studio's hallmark. *The Brotherhood of Man* (1945) was produced for the United Auto Workers to help prepare the southern states for union organization that would include racial integration. It was another success and was widely distributed beyond union meetings and community halls because of its message of tolerance and equality.

Hollywood Under Scrutiny

World War Two ended, and the Cold War began. The FBI turned their suspicious attention to Hollywood. The UPA crew was ripe for this kind of scrutiny. Many had, after all, been instrumental in union activities and were not at all shy about their left-of-center politics. No one at UPA was charged with anything, but as the Red Scare escalated, UPA's government projects dried up.

Mr Magoo Arrives on the Scene

The studio began to look for theatrical work to keep busy. It was at precisely this time that Columbia was searching for a new group to replace its moribund Screen Gems animation division. Bosustow, who had become UPA's executive producer, worked out a contract and the studio completed a couple of films featuring Columbia's Fox and Crow characters. They also had in mind a new character and produced a short, *Ragtime Bear* (1949), to introduce him to the public. His name was Mr Magoo, and he and his first cartoon were an immediate hit.

  Ragtime Bear was an eye-opener for the animation industry. Daring to use bold graphics and limited animation techniques, not to save money but rather to

© UPA Productions/Columbia Pictures

Christopher Crumpet's Playmate
This 1953 short demonstrates other aspects of limited animation: distorted perspectives; only the essential elements of the scene being present; and outlined, transparent characters. This simplified, stylized style of animation influenced the advertising industry and also the newborn medium of television.

© UPA Productions/Columbia Pictures

Mr Magoo – sketches and cel
The creation of Quincy Magoo was inspired by a number of real-life people: the director, John Hubley's bullheaded uncle; screen comedian W. C. Fields; and Jim Backus used observations of his father when devising the voice.

Mr Magoo – Hotsy Footsy

UPA's limited animation style was characterized by flattened perspective, abstract backgrounds and strong primary colors. Instead of filling in backgrounds with lifelike detail, broad fields of color were used, with small squiggles to suggest clouds and trees. Rather than vary the shades and hues of colors as in the natural world, UPA's cartoons used bold, bright, saturated colors.

make an artistic statement, this initial Magoo short and other UPA productions of the era stood in sharp contrast to the efforts of other animation studios, particularly Disney, for increasingly heavily articulated realism.

Limited Animation Style

UPA's approach to limited animation relied on graphic technique, color and stylized motion to caricature the world rather than imitate it. Animation was structured into recognizable, often repeated action, with heavy emphasis placed on clear, diagrammatic design and voice performance – Magoo's success was in no small part also due to the brilliant, ad-libbed vocals of Jim Backus. To this day, no one else seems to be able to capture the befuddled, ornery confidence of his performances. The designers at UPA used this bold graphic style to its best advantage, furthering the vision best expressed by John Hubley of animation as an art form. In many ways, the artists at UPA proved architect Ludwig Mies van der Rohe's famous adage that "less is more".

Unicorn and Fudget's Budget

UPA's highly stylized look is exemplified in these two shorts, *Unicorn in the Garden* (1953) and *Fudget's Budget* (1954) short.

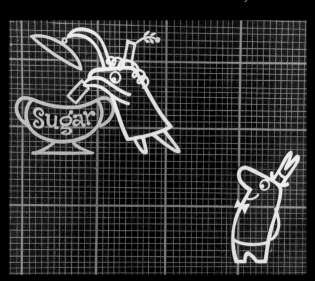

JAMES THURBER'S
BATTLE OF THE SEXES!
The masterwork of
America's master humorist... now the greatest
of all UPA miracle cartoons!

PROUDLY PRESENTED BY COLUMBIA PICTURES

color by TECHNICOLOR

A **UNICORN IN THE GARDEN**

A UPA CARTOON HIT!

UPA: THE MAGOO YEARS

In the early 1950s, UPA's style, a departure from the traditional realistic design approach, was so influential that nearly all of the other studios began to move in this direction. Warner Bros. began to stylize their backgrounds, which was problematic in the early stages because their established characters did not particularly match. Nevertheless, films like Freleng's *Pizzicato Pussycat* (1955) and *Three Little Bops* (1957), and Chuck Jones's two Ralph Philips shorts, *From A to Z-Z-Z-Z* (1954) and *Boyhood Daze* (1957), began to reflect the new look. This continued until the studio closed.

New Faces

Terrytoons' lackluster product went completely UPA with their designs for new characters like Flebus, designed by Ernest Pintof,f fresh from a stint at UPA, and Clint Clobber and Sidney the Elephant, created by Gene Deitch (b. 1924), also from UPA. Deitch's most important contribution was the wonderfully inspired television series *Tom Terrific* (1957–59). Even Disney got on board with such stylized special projects as *Melody* (1953), the Oscar-winning *Toot, Whistle, Plunk and Boom* (1953) and *Pigs Is Pigs* (1954).

Award Winning

The Magoo series won two Academy Awards: *When Magoo Flew* (1954) and *Mr Magoo's Puddle Jumper* (1956). Magoo's success paved the way for other progressive cartoons, notably *Gerald McBoing-Boing* (1951). The first McBoing-Boing film, based on a story by Theodore Geisel (Dr Seuss), about a boy who can speak only in sound effects, also went on to win an Oscar. The studio did not just rely solely on these popular characters, however. One-off films such as John Hubley's *Rooty Toot Toot* (1952), a stylized retelling of the Frankie and Johnnie blues saga; Edgar Allan Poe's psychological thriller *The Tell Tale Heart* (1953); and the delightful James Thurber-inspired *Unicorn in the Garden* (1953) all added to the studio's reputation as an influential trendsetter and a force to be reckoned with.

Troubled Times

In 1952, at the height of the Red Scare and the McCarthy hearings, UPA again became a target. This time John Hubley, perhaps the major creative force at the studio, was blacklisted. Along with Phil Eastman, Hubley left to avoid bringing unwanted governmental scrutiny onto the studio. With Hubley went a good deal of the vision the studio needed to maintain their originality. Other members of the crew, such as Bill Scott, Bobe Cannon, Abe Levitow, Jules Engel, Bill Melendez and Bill Hurtz, tried to keep the

Gerald McBoing-Boing

Gerald McBoing-Boing saw UPA make further of use non-realistic animation. They won an Oscar for it, and it provided the impetus for limited animation to be accepted at the major Hollywood cartoon studios, including Warner Bros. and MGM.

The Tell Tale Heart – producer and director

Based on an Edgar Allan Poe story,this limited animation cartoon relied more upon suspension of belief than on realistic depiction of events, and the animators used artistic styles that were not bound to the limitations of the real world to achieve this goal. Pictured are producer Steve Bosustow (left) and director Ted Parmelee.

© UPA Productions/Columbia Pictures

© UPA Productions/Columbia Pictures

Widescreen and 3D » 154 John Hubley » 214

© UPA Productions/Columbia Pictures

1001 Arabian Nights

This was UPA's first full-length feature, and during production Magoo's chief animator, Pete Burness, left the studio. Although the final result lacked the charm of the Magoo shorts, the design and color were very stylized, reflecting the studio's influential animation techniques.

momentum going, and the studio did manage to continue making some terrific films. However, a failed first feature, *1001 Arabian Nights* (1959), diminishing budgets and attrition in the creative ranks took a heavy toll. Soon, Steve Bosustow was the only one left of the original crew. He sold UPA to Henry Saperstein in 1960.

Moving to TV

Saperstein wanted to expand the studio's product base and began focusing on television. UPA had done one television project, *The Gerald McBoing-Boing Show* (1956–58), which was not a success. But now limited animation, the studio's stylistic calling card, was used to cut costs rather than as a tool for artistic expression. Under Saperstein, two Mr Magoo television series were produced, as well as a Dick Tracy show, but they all suffered either from artistic or creative shortcomings. The one bright spot was the pilot for the otherwise offbeat *The Famous Adventures of Mr Magoo*.

Magoo's Christmas Carol (1962) was a wonderful project in all aspects. A musical adaptation of the Charles Dickens tale with songs by Jule Stein, this episode remains a classic piece of work. The rest of the series was forgettable at best – as was almost everything else produced by UPA during this period. A final feature, *Gay Purr-ee*, released by Warner Bros. in 1962, stumbled at the box office and, to all intents and purposes, was the death knell for UPA as an animation studio.

Heyday Is Over

UPA still existed as an entity, and later Saperstein contracted with DePatie-Freleng for additional Magoo television properties. It also became the distribution arm for a number of Japan's Toho Studios "giant monster" films, including many Godzilla titles. UPA still holds the rights to its library of animated films and characters, but the days of the original studio vision and the unbridled, idealistic creativity that UPA happily brought to the public and the animation industry, while still influential, are long gone.

Mr Magoo

In Magoo's earliest cartoons, he is like a grizzled, old man; by 1952 his appearance had become rounder and cuter; in 1954 he was stubbier and shorter; and by 1955 he had become what he is like today.

© UPA Productions/Columbia Pictures

DISNEY RETURNS TO FEATURES

When Disney released *Bambi* in 1942, few would have guessed that it would be the studio's last true feature-length cartoon for eight years. But the demands of World War Two – and then post-war economic doldrums – prevented the company from tackling another one. The drought was finally broken by *Cinderella* in 1950, followed quickly by *Alice in Wonderland* (1951) and *Peter Pan* (1953).

The Nine Old Men

But much had changed since the *Snow White* era. The Disney-trained artists who would be known as "The Nine Old Men" were starting to dominate animation; star animators of the earlier features were gone from the studio (Art Babbitt, Bill Tytla) or relegated to lesser contributions (Norm Ferguson, Fred Moore). And Walt Disney himself was increasingly preoccupied with other pursuits, from live-action movie-making to the creation of Disneyland.

The conservative products of a conservative time, *Cinderella*, *Alice* and *Peter* – all of which were directed by Clyde Geronimi (1901–89), Wilfred Jackson (1906–88) and Hamilton Luske (1903–68) – do not rival the innovation and depth of the early features. But to give these movies their due, they are polished, tuneful entertainments that remain popular five decades later.

Return of the Princess

Each of Disney's first five animated features was distinctly different in story, setting and approach. The sixth, *Cinderella*, intentionally returned to *Snow White*'s world of fairy-tale princesses and storybook endings. Disney had seen animation potential in Charles Perrault's 1697 tale of the servant girl and the glass slipper as early as 1922, when he adapted the story into his final *Laugh-O-Gram* short.

By the late 1930s, inspirational artist Bianca Majolie was doing early sketches for a *Cinderella* feature. When Disney resumed feature production in 1947, the story was the first to enter production, apparently at Roy Disney's behest, as Walt preferred *Alice in Wonderland*. Still strapped for cash, the studio

At The Ball

Disney was determined that *Cinderella* would be a success, and was involved in all aspects of its creation, attending story meetings and commenting on how to improve small details that would add polish to the film.

Snow White and the Seven Dwarfs » 58 *Alice* and *Peter Pan* » 152

© The Walt Disney Company

Cinderella

Because of the cost of animating a feature-length cartoon, Disney wanted to ensure that all of the scenes that involved humans would work, before they were transferred to cel so live actors were photographed performing some of the key scenes. Some of this footage was traced – the animators were not so keen on this process, as they felt it detracted from their ability to develop characters.

Gus and Jacques

Rather than be incidental to the action, as in other Disney features, the animals played key roles. Supervising animator Ward Kimball was largely responsible for the creation of the two main mice, Jacques and Gus, and it is rumored that Lucifer (the cat) was modeled on his pet.

shot a bare-bones live-action version of the movie. The animators, including Marc Davis (1913–2000), Milt Kahl (1909–87) and Eric Larson (1905–88), who were responsible for Cinderella, used photostats of this footage to help plan their drawings. That shortcut led to work that sometimes felt stagier and less soulful than earlier Disney animation had, but the technique was repeated for *Alice* and *Peter Pan*.

True Cartoon Moments

Ward Kimball (1914–2002) was fortunate enough to get a truly animated assignment: the chase scenes involving Cinderella's mouse friends, Gus and Jacques, and the greedy cat Lucifer. While these sequences were hardly central to the story, they were some of the most confident visual comedy in any Disney feature. Michael Barrier has described them as being "like brilliant short cartoons inserted into this live-action film".

Early Disney soundtracks relied on a mix of character actors, newcomers and homegrown talent. *Cinderella* was dominated by radio veterans, including Ilene Woods (b. 1929) as Cinderella, Eleanor Audley (1905–91) as the stepmother, Verna Felton (1890–1966) as the fairy godmother and Luis Van Rooten (1906–73) as both the king and the grand duke. The songs, by Mack David, Jerry Livingston and Al Hoffman, included such Disney standards-to-be as "A Dream Is a Wish Your Heart Makes" and the Oscar-nominated "Bibbidi-Bobbidi-Boo".

Critics and film-goers in 1950 seemed content to embrace *Cinderella* for what it was: an entertaining return to pleasantly familiar Disney territory. On those terms, it still holds its own today.

© The Walt Disney Company

ALICE & PETER PAN

Deeply original and quirky, Lewis Carroll's *Alice's Adventures in Wonderland* (1865) seems to defy satisfying adaptation. But that has never stopped movie-makers from trying. At least half-a-dozen film versions preceded the Disney film; Walt Disney's first nod to the British classic had come in 1923 with *Alice's Wonderland*, the first of his *Alice Comedies* about a real girl in an animated world.

Disney's Brave New World

Sporadic work on Disney's *Alice* feature began as early as 1939–40, when British illustrator David Hall (1905–64) turned out approximately 400 striking, inspirational drawings. Then in 1945, Disney hired *Brave New World* author Aldous Huxley (1894–1963) to work on a story for a live-action/animated version.

When the film finally arrived in 1951 – drawing material from both Alice and its sequel, *Through the Looking Glass* – it owed little to Hall's or Huxley's visions. It also bore scant resemblance to John Tenniel's original illustrations. Rather, it was dominated by the brashly American, unapologetically cartoony style of animator Ward Kimball's work. In fact, Kimball was responsible for some of the most memorable moments: the Mad Tea Party scene and the appearances of the Cheshire Cat and Tweedledum and Tweedledee. Also influential was designer Mary Blair (1911–78), whose love of vivid colors and flat shapes helped determine the film's look.

Disney Down the Rabbit Hole

Like most adapters of *Alice*, Disney gave in to the temptation to cast well-known performers: radio comedians Ed Wynn (1886–1966) and Jerry Colonna (1904–86) played the Mad Hatter and the March Hare. Alice herself was a British girl, Kathryn Beaumont (b. 1938); she promoted the film by appearing in *One Hour in Wonderland*, the first Disney TV special in the 1950s.

Ultimately, Disney's *Alice* retained Carroll's episodic structure but little of his verbal ingenuity. The movie compensated to some degree with its own visual inventiveness, but offered almost no depth of character or story. Neither the press nor movie-goers gave it a warm welcome, and even Disney's own artists seemed eager to disown it: "Alice herself gave us nothing to work with," complained Marc Davis, quoted in Bob Thomas's *Disney's Art of Animation* (1991). Only upon re-release, to theatres and on video, has Alice's reputation modestly improved.

Peter Pan

Unique among Disney animated features, *Peter Pan* was based on a play: the 1904 British classic by J.M. Barrie (1860–1937), which Barrie turned into the

Alice

Disney always had a strong interest in Lewis Carroll's *Alice* books. Sir John Tenniel's original illustraions were freely adapted by Disney's animation team, Months of rough sketches preceded the final model sheets.

© The Walt Disney Company

novel *Peter and Wendy* in 1911. In 1939 Disney obtained film rights to the tale of the boy who would not grow up. On the stage, Peter is typically played by a woman and Tinker Bell is portrayed by a silent beam of light; the audience is encouraged to revive Tink by applauding during the play's climax. Disney abandoned most of these customs. For instance, he found his Peter Pan in studio child star Bobby Driscoll (1937–68), whose most recent role had been Jim Hawkins in *Treasure Island* (1950).

Tinker Bell became a tiny, but shapely, humanized character. She remained speechless, but Marc Davis's superlative animation made the petulant fairy an endlessly expressive character. Disney cast Hans Conried (1917–82) as both Captain Hook and the Darling children's father, following another stage tradition.

Bringing Peter to Life

In many other ways, the studio put its own imprint on the story. Kathryn Beaumont, who had played Alice, returned as the prim but courageous Wendy, and her brother John was voiced by British actor Paul Collins. But most major vocal characterizations were American, although Conried's foppish Hook at least sounded British, more or less.

Hook's genially dim-witted sidekick Mr Smee sounded like Tex Avery's Droopy – perhaps because he was voiced by the same actor, Bill Thompson (1913–71). Conried and Thompson gave bravura comic performances, and the accompanying animation, by artists such as Frank Thomas and Wolfgang Reitherman (Hook) and Oliver Johnston (Smee) was highly refined slapstick. Some of the Smee footage was by one-time Disney great Fred Moore, in one of his final assignments; he died aged 41 after an accident in November 1952, less than three months before *Pan*'s release.

Comedy Genius

The heavy dose of pratfall comedy had a profound effect. Unlike earlier Disney villains such as *Snow White*'s Queen or *Pinocchio*'s Stromboli, Hook is hard to take seriously as a threat. That and other elements of the film – flirty mermaids, wacky Indians, cheery songs – made this movie into a light-hearted, somewhat superficial romp. But what a well-executed romp it is. When Peter, Tinker Bell and the Darling children soar over Edwardian London to Sammy Cahn and Sammy Fain's "You Can Fly, You Can Fly", *Peter Pan* is post-war Disney animation at its best.

© The Walt Disney Company

Peter Pan

As in previous animated Disney films, actors performed the whole production in live-action so that the animators could capture their actions, movements, poses and facial expressions on paper. The actors used props and were properly dressed in costumes.

Wendy and Tinker Bell

In the original play, Tinker Bell was never shown except as a projected beam of light. Marc Davis created the feminine pixie seen in the Disney version, her shapely form originating from the "pin-up girls" of World War Two.

The Little Mermaid » 276

WIDESCREEN & 3D

One thing television could not offer home viewers of the early 1950s was a gigantic, panoramic visual experience. Thus, out of competition for audiences, was born Cinemascope. Although the theater owners, and audiences, may have loved the new widescreen format, it did present some new challenges to animated film producers.

Cinemascope

Gene Deitch was hired as the creative head of Terrytoons when the Columbia Broadcasting System bought the venerable animation studio in 1957. "We had a release schedule of 12 animated films a year — all to be made in Cinemascope," Deitch said. "Now 'Cinemascope' sounds great, but for animation production it was terrible! And our films had to be widescreen because our distributor, Twentieth Century Fox, owned Cinemascope." One problem that he found artistically vexing was the inability to use camera tilts. "Think of it. You tilt the camera just a little in Cinemascope and you start to see the edge of the paper." Another creative limitation was brought on by the fact that CBS, being the owners of a major American television network, naturally wanted their cartoons designed for ultimate broadcast use. "So all the main action had to occur in the middle section of the screen," recalls Deitch. Despite the obstacles, Deitch managed to do an impressive job of Cinemascope layout and design on films such as *The Juggler of Our Lady* (1957), based on the R. O. Blechman book.

Walt Disney Productions faced the aspect ratio problem by shooting their first Cinemascope feature, *Lady and the Tramp* (1955), twice; once for Cinemascope, and once, with altered layouts, for standard screen dimensions. The studio's Donald Duck visited a widescreen Grand Canyon in 1954's *Grand Canyonscope* (wherein Ranger Woodlore advises a crowd to "Spread out, folks. This is Cinemascope!"), while the Disney Oscar-winning short *Toot, Whistle, Plunk and Boom* remains a tour de force in Cinemascope design. Not to be outdone, MGM provided its stars Tom and Jerry, Spike and Tyke and Droopy with widescreen backdrops for nearly 30 cartoons.

© The Walt Disney Company

Lady and the Tramp

It took over four years and 200,000 individual drawings to create this feature. Cinemascope, with its superior storytelling potential and dramatic widescreen effects, sometimes quadrupled the work on each scene and increased the overall expense by about 30 per cent.

© The Walt Disney Company

Rotoscope » 38 UPA » 148 *Tron* » 268

© Famous Studios/Paramount

3D Animation Pioneers

Much has been made in recent years of "3D animation", in which the term has incorrectly been used to describe computer-generated (CG) animation, which aims for a naturalistic dimensional representation of images. But "real 3D" animated films go back to the very first presentation to mass audiences of a film using polarizing 3D glasses (the colorless lenses – not the inferior red and green lenses). The ground-breaking film was called *Motor Rhythm* (1939). It featured stop-motion animation with a synchronized score and was shown at the 1939 New York World's Fair. It may have helped inspire the 1950s 3D craze; four short 3D films, two of them animated, were produced for the Festival of Britain in 1951. When the subsequent Hollywood-made 3D feature *Bwana Devil* opened to a big box office in late 1952, the movie business went mad for 3D.

Popeye

The Ace of Space was the only 3D Popeye cartoon that was made, and was dubbed "a stereotoon". Casper the Ghost, Woody Woodpecker and Bugs Bunny also appeared in 3D during this era.

Toot, Whistle, Plunk and Boom

Pictured is a character from this Oscar-winning short.

© The Walt Disney Company

Toot, Whistle, Plunk and Boom

This was Disney's first cartoon filmed in Cinemascope. This new technique allowed the characters to move about in a larger proscenium, and gave the animators more opportunity for visual development.

Crazy for It

From early 1953 through the first six months or so of 1954, American audiences could go to their neighborhood theaters, don a pair of glasses with polarizing lenses and watch their favorite stars in what actually appeared to be three dimensions.

Audiences enjoying watching Edward G. Robinson and John Forsythe vie for the attentions of Kathleen Hughes in Universal's 3D feature *The Glass Web* (1953) might also discover Woody Woodpecker and Buzz Buzzard cavorting on skyscrapers in *Hypnotic Hick* (1953). Crowds flocking to see comedy team Dean Martin and Jerry Lewis tangle with Pat Crowley and Richard Haydn in Paramount's 3D flick *Money from Home* (1953) might also encounter a friendly ghost named Casper starring in the outer space 3D cartoon *Boo Moon* (1954) or the spinach-eating sailor in *Popeye, The Ace of Space* (1953). The RKO 3D release *Dangerous Mission* (1954), starring Victor Mature, Piper Laurie and Vincent Price might also offer its audience the Walt Disney 3D short *Working for Peanuts* (1953), featuring the somewhat less intense trio of Donald Duck and Chip and Dale.

But the 3D craze ran its course. An occasional animated 3D cartoon may be announced nowadays, but the films, few and far between, are usually made for specialized venues. The 2003 feature *Spy Kids 3D* featured up-to-date computer animation, but used the inferior red and green lenses. However, for one shining moment in the 1950s, all Hollywood – and Cartoonland – was in 3D.

CHUCK JONES IN HIS PRIME

Charles M. "Chuck" Jones grew up in a family where attention to literature and a freewheeling appreciation for any kind of creative expression were evident. While Jones's mother probably had more impact on his artistic sensibilities, it was, in fact, his father who pulled him out of high school in his junior year and sent him to Chouinard Art Institute (now CalArts), to avail himself of a "marketable skill".

From the Bottom to the Top

During the Great Depression, Jones managed to find work at a string of animation studios, starting at the bottom and working his way up to assistant animator by the time he had signed with the Schlesinger unit in 1936. There he watched and learned from the most creative animation directors of the era: Tex Avery, Bob Clampett, Frank Tashlin and Friz Freleng. In 1938, Chuck was assigned to direct his first cartoon, *The Night Watchman*.

Jones' early films were mostly sentimental, rather "Disneyfied" creations: nicely animated, but with little of the snap or wit that would become his trademark. Films like *The Curious Puppy* (1939), *Bedtime for Sniffles* (1940) or *The Brave Little Bat* (1941) were always clever, but rarely seemed spontaneous or much different from what many other animation directors were doing. Then, in 1942, he directed the almost experimental *The Dover Boys*. Jones admitted that this film, with its lively blend of animation and satiric style, became a benchmark for him – a departure from his storytelling approach, both graphically and narratively. It is possible that Jones's raucous work on the Private Snafu series (1942–45), made for the army during World War Two, may have had some effect on his style as well.

Developing Personalities

Jones had worked with the Warner Bros. stock characters – Bugs Bunny, Daffy Duck, Porky Pig and Elmer Fudd – from the start, but now he was beginning to codify their personalities, bringing them into sharp relief and contrasting one against the other. Their personalities began to run deeper than just a wise guy, hyperactive wacko or comic foil. Over the next few years, we would come to recognize in Jones's cartoons a deeper psychology and motivation for all of these personalities, except perhaps for Elmer, who remained a doofus throughout. The cartoons became more brisk and willing to let the audience draw its own inferences from an increasingly clever emphasis on character and

Bully for Bugs

Chuck Jones employed slapstick comedy and timing to an ever-precise degree in his animation. His experiments, at first unpopular with management, later became legendary. *Bully for Bugs* was created immediately after he had been forbidden to make a cartoon about bullfighting.

Pepé le Pew

Pepé le Pew was a malodorous, amorous skunk, whose object of affection was Penelope the cat. Pepé is said to be a parody of Pepé le Moko, the character played by the legendary actor Charles Boyer in the 1937 movie *Algiers*.

© Warner Bros.

Avery, Jones and Clampett » 86 Freleng and Tashlin » 88

"PEPÉ LE PEW"
© 1960   WARNER BROS. PICTURES INC

© Warner Bros.

expression. Two cartoons from 1944, *Tom Turk and Daffy* and *Bugs Bunny and the Three Bears* are good examples of this developing style.

Soon Jones would add more characters to the Warner stable. In 1945, he unleashed Pepé le Pew, a skunk with an insatiable romantic streak in *Odor-able Kitty*. He paired Hubie and Bertie and the neurotic Claude Cat in *Mouse Wreckers* in 1948, and Bugs went in for opera in *Long Haired Hare* in 1949. That was the same year that Jones and his longtime writer Michael Maltese came up with *Fast and Furry-ous*, the first in an ever-escalating series of hysterically plotted commentaries on the nature of fanaticism, featuring the hapless Wile E. Coyote and his nemesis, Roadrunner.

© Warner Bros.

Duck Dodgers

Duck Dodgers in the 24 1/2th Century was a spoof of the popular *Buck Rogers in the 25th Century AD* pulp fiction. The cartoon includes highly stylized backgrounds, one of creator Jones's and creator Maurice Noble's trademarks.

One Froggy Evening

Only one six-minute cartoon was ever made featuring Michigan J. Frog. The cartoon, complete with spectacular song-and-dance routines, was written by Michael Maltese, and the frog went on to become Warner Bros. TV network's official logo in the 1990s.

Golden Era

The 1950s were undoubtedly the banner years for Jones. His characters were fully realized, his humor was fearless and his team had worked so long and well together that they could very nearly finish each other's sentences. These were the years of *The Scarlet Pumpernickel* (1950), *The Rabbit of Seville* (1950), *Rabbit Seasoning* (1952), the nearly perfect cartoon about cartoons *Duck Amuck* (1953), and perhaps Jones's crowning achievement of the era, *What's Opera, Doc?* (1957).

There were many other wonderful films of the period. Jones would be nominated for three Academy Awards – *The High Note* in 1960, *Beep Prepared* a year later and *Now Hear This* in 1963. He won an Oscar in 1965 for *The Dot and the Line*, ironically not for Warner Bros., but for MGM. Jones would also become successful in making animated films for television, especially his adaptation of Dr Seuss's *How the Grinch Stole Christmas* (1966) and a terrific series of Rudyard Kipling stories. But is was those years from the mid-1940s through to the late-1950s that seemed to be the real golden age for Chuck Jones: a time for fully realized characters in ideally told tales so brief and ingenious in their structure it could take the breath away, and yet so disarmingly simple that even adults could understand them.

© Warner Bros.

RAY HARRYHAUSEN

In any career there is usually one major defining moment. For Ray Harryhausen (b. 1920), it came at the impressionable age of 13 when he walked into Grauman's Chinese Theater in Hollywood to see some "ape picture" he knew little about. That movie was the 1933 smash-hit *King Kong* and it would set Harryhausen on the path to becoming the "father of modern visual effects".

Monster Influence

If Harryhausen is the patriarch of stop-motion-effects animation, then the title of grandfather most certainly goes to Willis O'Brien, the man who breathed life into the great Kong and the other prehistoric inhabitants of Skull Island. Years earlier, O'Brien had astonished audiences with the dinosaur animation he performed for the 1925 screen adaptation of Sir Arthur Conan Doyle's *The Lost World* (1912). But it was *King Kong* that fueled young Harryhausen's insatiable thirst for knowledge about the process that allowed human actors to share the screen with towering monsters from another time.

© Warner Bros.

The Golden Voyage of Sinbad

This is the second film in the Sinbad trilogy from 1974. The others were *The Seventh Voyage of Sinbad* (1958) and *Sinbad and the Eye of the Tiger* (1977).

Early Lessons

Harryhausen was lucky to have parents who not only encouraged his creative pursuits, but also contributed to his projects. His father was a machinist and constructed the metal ball-and-socket armatures for his puppets, while his mother sewed the costumes. She even let Ray cut up her fur coat to cover his first stop-motion model, a man-eating cave bear. Throughout his high-school years, Harryhausen continued to experiment, and he was eventually granted the opportunity to show some of his puppets to his idol, O'Brien. O'Brien was impressed, but told the budding animator that his stegosaurus's legs looked like sausages and suggested he take anatomy and art courses. This advice would prove invaluable to Harryhausen and his ability to push the lifelike qualities of his creations.

At the age of 18, Harryhausen landed his first professional job, working on the *Puppetoons* shorts George Pal was producing for Paramount. His two-year tenure there ended when Pearl Harbor was bombed and he enlisted in the army, where his stop-motion training film *How to Bridge a Gorge* got him assigned to Colonel Frank Capra's Special Service Division.

The Valley of Gwangi

Gwangi was a pet project of Harryhausen's since the 1940s. His Dynamation technique allowed a stop-motion model to be animated directly in front of a screen showing live-action footage with human actors.

George Pal and Puppetoons » 92 *Jurassic Park* » 306

© Warner Bros.

Forging His Style

Returning from the war with a load of discarded 16 mm Kodachrome film, Harryhausen began producing a series of fairy tales for children. Combining his own style with what he learned from working with Pal, he animated the fables using articulated models with a series of replaceable heads. The last of the shorts, *The Tortoise and the Hare*, had just gone into production when he was called by O'Brien to serve as lead animator on the 1949 feature *Mighty Joe Young*. The opportunity would lead to a long and lucrative career creating awe-inspiring visual effects for such indelible classics as *The Beast From 20,000 Fathoms* (1953), *It Came From Beneath the Sea* (1955), *20 Million Miles to Earth* (1957), *The Seventh Voyage of Sinbad* (1958), *Jason and the Argonauts* (1963) and *The Valley of Gwangi* (1969).

While Mighty Joe Young was another giant ape picture produced to capitalize on the popularity of King Kong, the differences in the animation are striking. Harryhausen was already showing that he was improving the art form O'Brien originated. While O'Brien masterfully infused Kong with personality, he often applied broad strokes in his increments, which lent a degree of jerkiness to the animation and made the great ape move a bit too fast on-screen. Harryhausen handled Joe with more subtlety, and slowed the animation down to convey a sense of scale and help make the small model appear huge to audiences.

The Valley of Gwangi – sketch

Before starting work on a film, Harryhausen would draw in charcoal the most exciting scenes he wanted to do. From the drawings came 300 to 400 pen-and-ink sketches used to flesh out the sequences, so as to clarify the action during filming.

Dynamation

Harryhausen's signature innovation is something he dubbed "Dynamation". The process involved elaborate setups that sandwiched the stop-motion animation models between glass matte paintings or optically matted foreground elements and rear-screen-projected background plates. The effect produced more convincing composites as giant monsters rampaged through city streets and humans battled sword-wielding skeletons.

Having witnessed the birth of a new era in special effects with the arrival of *Star Wars* (1977), Harryhausen put his surface gauges away after finishing the 1981 *Clash of the Titans*. He briefly came out of retirement in 2002 to help animators Mark Caballero and Seamus Walsh complete *The Tortoise and the Hare*, the short he had abandoned 50 years earlier. A year later he received his long-deserved star on the Hollywood Walk of Fame, yet another testament to his enduring influence on the motion-picture industry and the impact his films will continue to have on generations of creature-feature fans.

© Warner Bros.

Aardman Animation » 322   CGI Victorious » 338

With the Red Scare of the late 1940s, the Canadian government began cleaning its house of "Communist sympathizers" working within the public sector. Several artists at the National Film Board (NFB) suspected of having ties to Communism were asked to leave. Norman McLaren, a one-time member of the Communist Party, was spared. In 1949, Jim McKay, head of the animation unit, wanted a change and left along with George Dunning to set up a commercial studio in Toronto. Colin Low, a man who would later go on to be one of the creators of IMAX, was named department head.

The Romance of Transportation in Canada

Setting NFB's trademark style, this Oscar-nominated short took a whimsical look at how Canadians solved the problem of covering their country's vast distances with transport options from carts and horses to trains and planes.

© 1952 National Film Board of Canada

Early Successes

The film board had begun moving beyond the more experimental techniques they had pioneered. Although there were a few earlier attempts, *Teamwork – Past and Present* (1951) is considered the NFB's first traditional cel-animated production. Their second cel-animated film, *The Romance of Transportation in Canada* (1953), not only set the template for the cartoony-style the NFB became known for, but was also nominated for an Academy Award.

Bob Verrall and Wolf Koenig, along with Low, were responsible for *Teamwork* and *Romance of Transportation*. They would be key film-makers in the NFB's development not only in animation, but also as documentarians, directing two of the Film Board's finest documentaries: *City of Gold* (1957) and *Lonely Boy* (1961). Their immense influence is still felt at the NFB today.

Huff and Puff

Co-directed by Gerald Potterton and Grant Munro, *Huff and Puff* was made for air force crews informing them of the dangers of hyperventilation in high altitudes, and gave advice as to how to recover with appropriate respiration.

© 1955 National Film Board of Canada

NFB: The Beginnings » 100 Norman McLaren » 102 *Animal Farm* » 166

© 1952 National Film Board of Canada

Neighbours

In this film, a parable about two people who come to blows over the possesion of a flower, Norman McLaren animated live actors, changing their positions 24 times a second, using the same techniques employed in puppet animation. It won him one Oscar and a nomination for another in 1952.

NORTH AMERICA: CANADA

VI: 1950–55: CARTOONS MATURE

Educating and Entertaining

With the arrival of British animator Gerald Potterton, the NFB strengthened its cartoon animation team. Trained on Halas and Batchelor's *Animal Farm* (1954), Potterton's first film at the NFB was an instructional film (co-directed with Grant Munro) for the Royal Canadian Air Force titled *Huff and Puff* (1954). Potterton had a keen understanding of cartoon timing – and would go on to direct the master of comedic-timing Buster Keaton in *The Railrodder* (1965). One of his gifts was to take didactic educational films and make them entertaining and amusing. His second film for the NFB, *Fish Spoilage Control* (1955), was the film board's second lip-sync cartoon and not only featured Potterton's wit, but also a wonderful jazz score by Eldon Rathburn.

The 1950s was also a rich period for the NFB's experimental filmmakers. As part of the 3D craze, Norman McLaren produced two 3D films, *Around Is Around* (1951) and *Now Is the Time* (1951), for the British Film Institute's Festival of Britain. In 1952 McLaren created what many consider his greatest work, *Neighbours*, which featured animators Grant Munro and Jean Paul Ladouceur. This pixilated anti-war analogy not only won an Academy Award for Best Documentary Short Subject, but it is alleged that after viewing the film, two tribes from Central Africa decided to put an end to their long-standing strife – perhaps the film's greatest achievement. In the late 1950s, McLaren returned to pixilation with *A Chair Tale* (1957), co-directed with Claude Jutra, a film which has influenced many music video directors, including Michael Gondry in his Beck video for 'Deadweight' (1998).

In April 1956, the National Film Board of Canada moved from its cramped, and at times dank, offices on John Street in Ottawa to a new facility in Montreal. It was the start of a new era for the NFB.

TELECOMICS

Telecomics has to be considered one of the first cartoon series produced for television. However, there was virtually no animation on the show. It is just as its title suggests: a series of comic-strip-style drawings filmed sequentially, with an occasional animated effect.

Early Days

Telecomics, Inc. was first formed in 1942 by a pair of Disney animators, Dick Moores and Jack Boyd. In 1945 they filmed a pilot, "Case of the Missing Finger, Chapter 4, The Belt of Doom" starring Peril Pinkerton. This led to a syndicated 15-minute television program in 1949, which consisted of four three-minute stories. The original show contained "Brother Goose" by Cal Howard; "Joey and Jug", a clown story by Arnold Gillespie; "Rick Rack

Secret Agent", by Miles Pike and Pete Burness; and "Sa-Lah", an Arabian nights fantasy drawn by A. J. Metcalf. Jack Kirkwood, Lillien Leigh and Bill Grey provided the voice-over narration. The syndicated series was distributed by Vallee Video (owned by singer Rudy Vallee), but unfortunately these early broadcasts have been lost.

Danny March

Pre-production sketches show sequential scenes in an episode of "Danny March", one of the segments on *Telecomics*. There was very little animation on this series — mostly just narration and dialogue over static scenes like these.

Made-for-TV Animation

The NBC network optioned the property in 1950, re-packaging the program and hiring cartoonists Moores and Boyd to produce it. The re-named *NBC Comics* now earned a place in history as the first made-for-TV network cartoon program.

The NBC show contained serialized adventures of a new group of adventure comic stars. Episodes would begin with the opening of a comic book, the first page showing a silhouette of the lead character and indicating it was either part one, part two or part three of the day's episodes. The page then was turned to show a full-screen character opening title. Each episode was approximately three-and-a-half minutes long. "Space Barton" was the most interesting of the lot. Horace "Space" Barton, Jr. is an

all-American college football star who enlists in the Army Air Corps and is chosen to test the first US jet plane. He then blasts off to Mars with his brother Jackie as a stowaway in a rocket ship built by Professor Dinehart, an astronomer. The adventures have them engaged in a civil war on the red planet, pitted against a faction led by a deranged Earth scientist who had preceded them to Mars.

Colorful Characters

Other *Telecomics* stars include Danny March and Kid Champion. Danny March was the orphaned son of a Yale man who was raised by his uncle to be one of the toughest kids in Metro City. Danny turned to detective work when he was unable to become a police officer because of his short stature. Building a reputation as a tenacious private eye, he is hired by the mayor as his personal detective to stop crime in Metro City.

"Kid Champion" is the story of Eddie Hale, a musician who was urged by his former boxing-champ father to become a boxer. When Eddie mistakenly believes that he killed a gas-station attendant during a holdup, he teams up with a hard-luck fight manager, Lucky Skinner; changes his identity to Kid Champion; and refuses to talk about his past to anyone.

The humorous "Johnny & Mr Do-Right" followed the exploits of a young boy and his zany dog.

One hundred and sixty-five episodes ran on NBC-TV from 18 September 1950 until 30 March 1951. Voices included Robert C. Bruce, Pat McGeeham, Howard McNear, Lurene Tuttle, Tony Barret and Paul DeVall. The individual adventures were not titled, and after their network run, they again entered syndication as *Telecomics*. It left TV screens in the early 1960s, due mainly to the onslaught of the Hanna-Barbera-led color cartoons, and the fact that the *Telecomics* had been filmed in black and white.

Telecomics sequence

The *Telecomics* series was filmed in black and white, and was one of the first cartoons made for TV.

© NBC Comics

INDUSTRIAL-STRENGTH ANIMATION

© Western Electric Company, Inc./Fleischer Studios

The value of film as an educational and propaganda tool was demonstrated during World War Two, when animation helped to motivate and unite in the common cause of victory. During the post-war years, this victorious spirit shifted to mainstream America with the presence of information films known as "industrials".

The Industrials

With the dark days of the Depression and wartime rationing over, the Eisenhower administration suggested an exciting future with economic stimulation. Many new goods and services were for sale, and the most dynamic medium for selling was the industrial film. Many of these films embraced the positive aspects of government, community and consumerism. Animation in particular was applied to dress up all manner of subjects, from the virtues of drinking milk to the workings of consumer finance.

Origins

Industrial animation evolved in the silent era along with the first theatrically produced cartoons. Some of the earliest of these were used as insert sequences in demonstration or "training" films produced to teach salesmen about the workings of electrical devices, cream separators, tractors and automobiles. The Bray Studio was one of the earliest commercial animation studios to produce films for industry and the military. With the outbreak of World War One, animation was used for the rapid training of troops in areas such as auto mechanics, firearms and contour map reading.

The 1920s saw established New York cartoon producers such as Max Fleischer producing scientific films that taught the theories of evolution and relativity using animated diagrams and effects animation. Fleischer produced various industrial films for Western Electric, such as *That Little Big Fellow* (1926) and *Now You're Talking* (1927), as well as the sound demonstration film *Finding His Voice* (1929), which explained the sound recording and reproduction process for audio engineers and theater managers.

Into the 1930s, New York studios such as Fleischer, Terry and Van Beuren continued to produce commercial films for Texaco, Lysol and Borden's Dairy. But these were incidental productions for these studios since the majority of their work was geared toward theatrical entertainment.

Finding His Voice – sequence

This 1929 short is this an excellent example of Fleischer's work, and gives a helpful overview of how sound on film works, a technology that remained basically the same until the advent of multi-channel stereo on film in the early 1990s.

Finding His Voice

This film features Talkie, the talking filmstrip and his silent filmstrip friend, the latter of whom wants to know how he can get a voice. The pair go to Mr Western, who gives them the scientific background of how sound is produced.

© Western Electric Company, Inc./Fleischer Studios

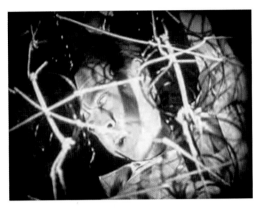

Jam Handy

To meet demand, specialized industrial film studios developed in major advertising and manufacturing centers. In Chicago, Illinois, the Wilding Company was a major producer for clients such as Chrysler. But the Jam Handy Organization in Detroit, Michigan, was one of the foremost producers of industrial films in the United States. Jam Handy had an animation department consisting of two divisions: technical and cartoon. The technical division concentrated on animated diagrams and working details of mechanisms. The cartoon division produced animated short subjects for theaters, road-show conventions and department stores.

A Coach for Cinderella (1938) was another Jam Handy Technicolor cartoon produced for the promotion of the 1939 Chevrolet that used both cartoon and technical animation. *Rudolph the Red-Nosed Reindeer* was produced by Max Fleischer in 1944.

The Modern Era

With the outbreak of World War Two, Hollywood cartoon studios such as Disney, MGM and Warner Bros. produced various training and motivational films. But this was not enough. Specialized military units were created to maintain the security of classified information.

The navy set up an animation unit in 1942 at the Naval Photographic Center in Washington, D.C. and the army established an animation unit under the Signal Corps in Culver City, California. Many credited animators of draft age were assigned to these units, and their experience moved the mission forward with great efficiency, as they came in with the necessary training.

Wartime requirements demanded rapid production methods, with new approaches emphasizing strong design and art direction called limited animation. One notable production was *Hell Bent for Election*, directed by Chuck Jones. The United Auto Workers commissioned this cleverly executed film for the re-election of Franklin D. Roosevelt with a "win the war" theme. But UPA's navy film, *Flat Hatting* (1944), became the benchmark for the next decade.

The post-war period saw some of the greatest advances through Gene Deitch at Jam Handy. His UPA influence moved industrial animation into the modern era with films like *Wings for Roger Windsock* (1947) and *Building Friends for Business* (1950) using sophisticated writing to motivate audiences.

A Case of Spring Fever

Spring Fever is an early example of live-action being combined with animation. Made by Jam Handy in 1940 for Chevrolet, it is the tale of Coily, an obnoxious sprite, who grants an exasperated man his wish for all springs to disappear while he is encountering difficulty mending a sofa. Coily shows him what everyday life would be like without springs and emphasizes their importance in many mechanical objects, especially the Chevrolet car.

CREATING ANIMAL FARM

George Orwell's stark satire about a group of animals taking over the running of their farm was a best-seller in the mid-1940s. With an overlaying theme of the Russian Revolution, it is a somber fable of totalitarianism, humanitarianism, power and corruption. Napoleon, the tyrannical pig, was likened to the despot Soviet leader Stalin; Snowball, his opposition leader, was envisioned as a combination of Lenin and Trotsky (whom Stalin had killed); and Old Major, who instigates the initial revolt, was similar to Karl Marx.

Two Legs, Four Legs

The story concerns some ill-treated livestock who revolt due to their growing antagonism toward the cruel Farmer Jones, overthrowing their oppressor and attempting to run the farm by themselves. They first set down some ground rules: "Whatever goes on two legs is an enemy"; "Whatever goes on four legs is a friend"; "No animal shall wear clothes"; "No animal shall sleep in a bed"; "No animal shall drink alcohol"; "No animal shall kill any other"; and, above all, "All animals are equal".

The pigs, fronted by Old Major, soon have delusions of grandeur and oust Major in favor of the Stalin-esque Napoleon. With the voice of reason out of the way, the pigs move from the barn into the comfort of Jones's farmhouse and live as the corrupt humans did before them. Napoleon trains a pair of vicious hounds to dispose of Snowball, the rational pig, and continues to take over leadership, backed up by his henchmen, a pig named Squealer, and the two dogs. The other creatures are forced by the pigs to carry on slaving at their farm work and, when Boxer the cart horse is injured while building a windmill, Napoleon sells him for horse meat. With the pigs in power, the animal commandments are all but worthless, although one condition is added to "All animals are equal": "But some are more equal than others".

The pigs are now no better than the humans and the other animals retaliate to eradicate them.

From Book to Big Screen

American producer Louis de Rochemont brought this austere fable to the screen. Two years after Orwell's death, he decided to take advantage of the resulting popularity of Orwell's book. Rumor also had it that backing came from the CIA, which reportedly wanted this parable to be used as future propaganda ammunition for the Cold War. This theory has yet to be proved, though.

Producing feature cartoons was a departure from the norm for de Rochemont, as he had previously only been involved with the production of Movietone newsreels. To get his film made, he went straight to the largest established British animation studio, Halas & Batchelor, run by the husband and wife team of John Halas and Joy Batchelor. Halas & Batchelor was the only studio that could be considered large

© The Halas and Batchelor Collection Limited

John Halas and Joy Batchelor viewing sketches

Before the husband and wife team began to make Animal Farm, Britain's first animated feature, their creative team numbered 20; within a year of starting production on the film it had grown to 70.

Benjamin – sketch

A pre-production sketch of Benjamin the donkey, who, together with Boxer the cart-horse and Snowball the pig band together with the other animals to overthrow the farmer and create a new society.

© The Halas and Batchelor Collection Limited

Boxer

The animals' reaction to their beloved Boxer's fate is typical of this film: resigned stoicism rather than righteous anger. Halas and Batchelor's version of Orwell's novel was not sentimental and was aimed at adults, rather than children.

Animal Chorus

The animals, having been so badly treated by Farmer Jones, join in a barnyard rebellion and run the farm themselves. At first all is well, until some of the pigs begin to assume more of the power.

enough to handle the job; other studios such as Larkins and George Moreno's were decidedly minor in comparison.

This was also a new venture for Halas & Batchelor. Up to then, they had only been producing industrial, promotional and informational shorts for the Ministry of Information, and they were by no means certain that they could produce something that would carry as much dramatic impact as Orwell's tale.

HALAS & BATCHELOR'S FEATURE

The idea of a feature cartoon that dealt with such a serious subject as anti-Communism and contained little or no laughs was a challenge to the Halas & Batchelor team, but they proceeded and started production in 1951.

Starting Work

In an interview for *Animator* magazine in 1989, John Halas revealed that the making of *Animal Farm* was not without its problems: "From its commencement it was like travelling down a long dark tunnel with no light at the end, and when at last a faint flicker could be seen, I raced to emerge into the light of a new day." Halas was against taking a strong anti-Stalin stand and insisted that it had to be a universal film for all audiences. His opinions were overruled, resulting in the overlaying theme being one of a specifically adult nature – a fight for freedom. In retrospect, Halas's personal view of the film's basic flaw was that far too much attention had been paid to "unnecessary" details rather than to the overall flow of the film.

Disneyfication

Ex-Disney animator John Reed was called in to handle the animation direction. Reed had recently been involved with David Hand's GBA studio and was responsible for the "Disney-esque" appearance of *Animal Farm*. In most cases the Disney style jars with the story, seen, for instance, with the annoying intrusion of a "cute" duckling that is constantly pushed aside by its peers. The other main animators involved were Eddie Radage, Arthur Humberstone, Ralph Ayres, Harold Whitaker and Frank Moysey. The final storyboard for 75 minutes of action consisted of fewer than 2,000 sketches used from an original collection of 10,000. The original storyboard followed the novel and included three confrontations between animals and humans but, in film terms, three fights proved too cumbersome and the number was reduced to just two.

    While production on *Animal Farm* was forging ahead in London's Soho Square, a second unit was formed at Halas's other studio 120 miles away in Stroud to help carry some of the load. In addition to all this, the studio still carried on with their normal scheduled workload.

Sound and Music

Hungarian composer Matyas Seiber was brought in to compose the imposing atmospheric music. His greatest musical problem was a "battle hymn" for the animals when about to overthrow Farmer Jones. This had to be written as a parody of all revolutionary music and sung without words by the animals. After singers who could sing in "animal" tones had been found, the final mixing of music and animals amounted to as many as eight separate recording tracks.

© The Halas and Batchelor Collection Limited

Storyboard

The bleak atmosphere portrayed in the film suits the subject-matter. The backgrounds are darkly colored and broadly textured, with smoothly illustrated figures shrugging off the yoke of oppression.

Pigs –sketches

The pigs in Orwell's allegory, and Halas and Batchelor's adaptation, were direct counterparts of figures in the Russian Revolution: Old Major is Karl Marx; Napoleon is Joseph Stalin; and Snowball is Lenin and Trotsky.

The narration was handled by radio announcer Gordon Heath and the multi-voiced radio actor, Maurice Denham. Denham proved a godsend in supplying all of the animals' voices, which ranged from the rantings of Napoleon down to the most minor characters. Denham studied pig sounds for months before the actual recording sessions, and even based the pompous Old Major's gruntings on some of Winston Churchill's orations to give him a suitably authoritative air.

Critical Success

The concluding passage of the novel had the depressing reality of Napoleon, the oppressor, and his cohorts remaining in power, but the American financiers preferred an upbeat ending and the finale was altered to suit public taste. This involved all of the other creatures rebelling with the intent of subjugating the pigs.

The film took an exhausting three years to complete, employed over 70 people and finally got its British release in April 1954. The pre-publicity – stating that "Pig Brother Is Watching You!" – wryly linked *Animal Farm* with Orwell's other best seller, *1984*, which had recently enjoyed much success as a controversial television play.

The finished film adaptation surprised Louis de Rochemont, who, aware only of the written word and the effect this had on him, was unprepared for someone else's visual interpretation of the novel. He confessed to being delighted with the end product, however.

On the film's initial release, some critics claimed the Disney-esque styling of the farm animals took the raw edge off Orwell's satire, but overall the reception was favorable, earning it an Oscar as the Best Film of 1954.

Pig Comrades

The original ending was changed to give the film a more upbeat conclusion. In the book the animals conduct a second revolution that overthrows Napoleon and the pigs, but even then it can be seen that the entire cycle is going to repeat itself over again; in the animated version the second revolution is a success.

MR WONDERBIRD

The complicated history of *The Curious Adventures of Mr Wonderbird* begins in 1936 when animator André Sarrut formed his studio, Les Gémeaux, with business partner Paul Grimault. Here, they produced animated advertising cartoons until the war intervened and Grimault was called up. Sarrut had been planning to form a European school of animation to make feature cartoons since the inception of his studio but had little money to exercise such a monumental project.

Le Bergère et la Ramoneur

After World War One, Jacques Prévert, screenwriter of the classic live-action *Les Enfants du Paradis*, came to Sarrut with his screenplay for *Le Bergère et la Ramoneur* ('The Shepherdess and the Chimney-Sweep'), based on a Hans Christian Andersen story about two china figurines who fall in love. The English-dubbed version of this would eventually become *The Curious Adventures of Mr Wonderbird*. Prévert had collaborated with Sarrut and Grimault on the highly successful *Le Petit Soldat* ('The Little Soldier', 1947), another Hans Christian Andersen tale concerning a villainous jack-in-the-box who tries to come between the love of a toy soldier and a doll: a plot not far from *The Shepherdess*.

Envisioning this as the answer to Disney's feature cartoons, Sarrut showed the story to Dimitri de Grunwald, a British producer, and together they managed to obtain financial backing from a bank. A crumbling mansion on the outskirts of Paris was purchased, transformed into a studio and then stocked with young talent from local art schools and commercial studios. French composer and Sarrut's longtime associate Joseph Kosma was also brought in to help provide the atmospheric music for the presentation.

Production Fallout

The whole production experienced a particularly turbulent journey. This was due to many factors: pre-completion hype, spiraling production costs, delays and a court case declaring that the director, Paul Grimault, who had worked on the film for three years, be removed from the project. As a result, Sarrut was left to supervise the final stages on his own.

An English-language edition entitled *The Curious Adventures of Mr Wonderbird* was prepared with dialogue by Dimitri de Grunwald's brother Anatole. The technicalities for this version were handled in Britain by veteran animator Anson Dyer at Stroud studios in Gloucestershire. He became ill halfway through the production schedule and, when work on the film was finished, resolved never to be involved with film-making again. He kept to his word and retired soon after completion.

After over 200 artists had labored for four years, the final production cost amounted to £500,000 ($900,000) – a large sum of money in those days. When *Le Bergère* finally saw the light of day in 1952, it had been harshly edited to a fragmented 63-minutes running time and additional scenes had been added. It was given a cool

© Les Gémeaux

Le Bergère et la Ramoneur

Paul Grimault hoped to produce France's first animated full-length feature in the late 1940s, but was not able to complete his masterpiece until 20 years later.

Paul Grimault

Paul Grimault, the French animation master, has influenced countless others, including Japanese animator Hayao Miyazaki. Grimault's animation is full of magic, wit, personality and imagination.

© Jacques Prévert/Paul Grimault

© Jacques Prévert/Paul Grimault

Roi et l'Oiseau

When restoring and completing the film, Grimault retained the look and feel of the original. Although released in 1980, the film has the authentic look of a late-1940s animated feature, which is when work began on the original, *Le Bergère et la Ramoneur*.

Roi et l'Oiseau – sketch

The film was a labor of love, and includes beautifully designed sets and backgrounds, caverns, towers, arches, Venetian canals and squares, and vast palaces with Escher-like staircases. Each of the animators worked on their own characters, giving each their own personality and characteristics.

© Jacques Prévert/Paul Grimault

reception by the critics. This version incensed Paul Grimault and Jacques Prévert enough to bring court actions against Sarrut and have their names removed from the credits.

The Metamorphosis of Mr Wonderbird

Mr Wonderbird had been a bone of contention with Grimault since his ousting in 1950. Then, in 1967, he managed to acquire the rights to it along with control over all of the negative stock. With help from Jacques Prévert, Grimault hoped to put matters right by reconstructing the film in a different way. They managed to round up the surviving animators who had worked on the original, as well as many new artists and the one surviving actor of the initial French voice cast, Roger Blin. Work began on re-creating the whole project.

As no original artwork remained, the artists had to retain the original hand-drawn 1940s style to match the remaining animation on-screen. This was certainly a laborious task, as styles had moved on since 1947 and the artists only had the film as a reference.

Production was finally completed by 1980, this time titled *Le Roi et l'Oiseau* ('The King and the Mockingbird'), and an English-language version was dubbed using American actors. It now stands, 33 years after the original concept, as a monument to Jacques Prévert, who sadly died three years before completion and was never able to see his labor of love in its final form.

BULGARIA & POLAND

An animation division of the state-run Bulgarian film industry was established in 1948. It was created on the advice of Dimitar Todorov-Jarava. Jarava studied painting at the Academy of Arts in Sofia and worked as a teacher until he took over the animation division. Jarava was also an inventor of sorts. In 1938, he received a patent for a phenakistascope-like device that he made for children.

Bulgarian Pioneers

In 1950, Todorov-Jarava made the first real Bulgarian animation film *It's His Own Fault* (1949), followed by *Wolf and Lamb* (1953) and the first color film in Bulgaria, *Woodland Republic* (1954). The first Bulgarian puppet animators, Aron Aronov and Dimo Lingurski also

Monsieur Tete

This film was made by Jan Lenica in 1959, who had been inspired by the 1955 Warsaw fine arts exhibition in Warsaw. It demonstrates his characteristic graphic style, which favored thick outlines and heavily stylized design, cut-out figures and collage all set to simply choreographed movement.

A

Surrealist in conception and tragicomic in tone, Lenica's films often represent states of mind and the urban experience. This was made in 1964, a time when Polish artists would cloak their indictments of Stalinism, power politics and repression in allegorical storytelling and ironical wit.

Labyrinth

This is a self-consciously Kafka-esque tale of a winged lonely man literally devoured by totalitarian rule, and is considered to be one of the finest political animations ever made.

started in the 1950s, and Lingurski made his first film, *The Terrible Bomb* in 1951. These early films are important in that they established roots for future Bulgarian animators, but due to poor funding and inexperience, many of these early films are technically crude.

Things begin to brighten in 1955 with the emergence of Todor Dinov. Dinov, considered the father of Bulgarian animation, had studied under legendary Russian animator Ivan Ivanov-Vano. He became an important teacher and promoter of Bulgarian animation and earned acclaim for his first film, *Marko the Hero* (1955).

Jarava's animation career was short-lived, however. Because of conflicts with management, who favored USSR or Czechoslovakian-trained animators over the self-educated Jarava, he was forced to resign.

Poland

Aside from Wladyslav Starewicz, a handful of men – including Franziska and Stefan Thermerson, who made experimental collages including the brilliant *Europe* (1931–32) – tried their hand at animation in Poland from 1917–39. However, Polish animation as an organized entity did not begin until after World War Two.

Following the war, the new Communist regime in Poland invested heavily in cinema. Animation, however, was not taken so seriously. Despite this, Zenon Wasilewski, a prominent pre-war animator, was intent on finishing a film he had shot in 1939. To do this he moved to Lodz, where he started a production and distribution company, which later became the famous puppet studio Semafor. A drawn animation studio was also established in Katowice in 1947. During this time the Polish Communists kept animation, like all of Polish cinema, on a short leash. Following the Soviet model, animation was dominated by propaganda and folk tales, espousing the concept "national in form – socialist in content". Nevertheless, a structure was in place that provided training for future Polish animators like Witold Giersz, who would make his debut in 1956 with *The Mystery of the Old Castle*, followed by what many consider his finest film, *Little Western* (1960).

Sparks of Creativiy

The most notable productions from this period come from Wlodimierz Haupe and Halina Bielinska. In 1954, the duo made the first Polish animated feature, a puppet film called *Janosik*. They followed this with an innovative film created with matchboxes called *Changing of the Guard* (1959), which won the Golden Palm at the Cannes Film Festival.

In 1955, an event took place that would drastically change the direction of Polish animation: the Arsenal Art Exhibition held in Warsaw. The exhibition featured an array of Polish fine arts, all of them very different from the prescribed "social realism". The exhibition stimulated two young artists in particular, Jan Lenica (b. 1928) and Walerian Borowczyk (b. 1923), who, a year later, would translate what they saw to animation.

The first half of the 1950s was the eve of the establishment of Japan's professional animation industry. Theatrical animated shorts started out in black and white, but they looked more like the competing modern American color cartoons in art style and quality of motion – Iwao Roda's *The Forest Concert* (1953), for instance, seems to show a Tex Avery influence. They also averaged twice as long as the six- to eight-minute American shorts.

© Kihachiro Kawamoto/Tadahita Machinaga

Changing to Color

Notable titles of this period include *The Gnome and the Green Caterpillar* by Hideo Furasawa (1950), *The Ant and the Pigeon* by Hajime Yuhara (1953), *Story of the Little Rabbit* (1954) written by Taiji Yabushita and directed by Yasuji Mori, *Kawataro the Kappa* (1954) by Taiji Yabushita, and in 1955 came Japan's first color theatrical releases, *The Happy Violin* by Taiji Yabushita and *Onbu, the Little Goblin* by Ryuichi Yokoyama. Nihon Doga, with Sanae Yamamoto as president/executive producer, remained the largest studio, producing one or two films per year.

Aladdin and a Magic Lamp

Tadahito Mochinaga, who together with Kihachiro Kawamoto produced this 1953 puppet animation, holds a unique position in the history of both Japanese and Chinese animated films. He was the first animator to use the multi-plane camera in Japan, and he also made the first stop-motion puppet animations in China and Japan. Mochinaga was among the founding members who built the Shanghai Animation Film Studio.

Fine-Art Animation

This was also the beginning of the division between popular animation made for commercial theatrical or TV release, and more artistic animation made for international film festivals. Noburo Ofuji became the first Japanese animator to gain international acclaim when his *The Great Buddha* (1951) and *The Whale* (1952) were shown at the 1952 and 1953 Cannes Film Festivals, and his 1955 *The Ghost Ship* at the 1956 Venice Film Festival.

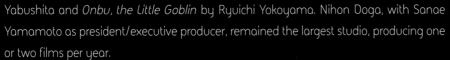

© Tezuka Productions Co., Ltd

    The Whale, a remake of his 1927 cut-paper film, substituting colored translucent cellophane for the solid-black silhouettes, was praised by Pablo Picasso. This prestige was recognized in Japan in 1963 when the annual Mainichi Film Festival created the Noburo Ofuji Award for innovative excellence in animation. Its first winner was Osamu Tezuka for his *Stories on a Street Corner* (1962). In 1953 Tadahito Mochinaga returned from China to Japan, where he soon put his experience with Chinese-style stop-motion animation to use in both fine-art and commercial puppet animation.

Stories on a Street Corner

Although Osamu Tezuka is internationally renowned for his manga, such as Astro Boy, his experimental animation should not be forgotten. There was a limited budget for stories, and to reduce the number of moving pictures, posters and other non-moving objects were used as characters, which gave an innovative impression.

Tei Wei

Pictured here at the 1995 Annecy Animation Festival is the Chinese master animator Tei Wei, with his ASIFA award which was presented to him in recognition of his life's work. He is accompanied by his friend, the Swiss animator Georges Schwizgebel.

Disney of the East

In March 1951, Toei Company, Ltd. was founded. Within a couple of years, it grew to be one of Japan's largest live-action motion-picture production studios and distributors, with a chain of theatres throughout the nation.

In 1955, one of its executives, Hiroshi Okawa (1896–1971), decided that Toei should add an animation department to make the studio "the Disney of the East". After studying Japan's animation industry and being impressed by Nihon Doga's director Taiji Yabushita and key animator Yasuji Mori, Toei bought the Nihon Doga studio outright.

On 31 July 1956, Nihon Doga metamorphosed into Toei Doga (Toei Animation Co., Ltd.), a subsidiary of Toei Co., with Okawa as its first president. Yamamoto remained as its supervising producer. With Toei's funding, Japan's first major animation studio was born.

China: The Shanghai Studio

In February 1950, the Chinese government transferred Tong Pei's animation department under director Te Wei and assistant Fang Ming from Changchun in Manchuria to the much larger Shanghai Film Studios. The greater resources and talent pool of artists and ex-animators in cosmopolitan Shanghai ("the Hollywood of China") gradually led to what is referred to as "the first Golden Age of Chinese animation", from around 1956 to the Cultural Revolution in 1965.

Pressed to show what they could do, the expanded animation studio produced the short cartoon animation *Thank You, Kitty*, directed by Fang Ming (Mochinaga), by the end of 1950. The years 1950 to 1955 were a period of setup and experimentation. Foreign animation, particularly that of China's political friend the Soviet Union, was studied.

Striving for a Distinctive Look

Mochinaga completed the first color animation tests before returning to Japan. Wan Chao-chen returned from America, where he had been studying animation, to direct the puppet animation *The Little Heroes* in 1953; and in 1954 Wan Lai-ming and Gu-chan returned from Hong Kong. Although Chinese cartoons created during this period were made primarily for domestic audiences (especially children) some, including *Why Crows Are Black* and the 1955 *The Magic Paintbrush* by Jin Xi (1919–97), were also designed as art films to be shown at Cannes, Venice and other European film festivals to bring international attention to Chinese animation. But after *Why Crows Are Black* was mistaken at the 1955 Venice Festival for Soviet animation, Te Wei was determined that Chinese animation should have a distinctive Chinese look.

1956–60:
TO THE TUBE

Television animation adapted to lower budgets, faster schedules and a new medium. Hanna-Barbera lead the way with Huckleberry Hound, Yogi Bear and The Flintstones. TV commercials became a lucrative new industry for animators – with powerful art direction as important as the sponsored message. Theatrical shorts began to peter out, though Disney produced his most expensive production, *Sleeping Beauty*, and UPA created a low budget *Mr Magoo* feature film.

Animation artists emerged outside the US – Zagreb produced the first non-Hollywood cartoon short to win an Oscar, Canadian Richard Williams made his mark in London, Osamu Tezuka tried his hand at animation, and Karel Zamen and Jiri Trinka offered unique stop-motion films from Eastern Europe. This was the time when animation was first seriously considered as a varied art form, and international festivals rose to celebrate the field and the film-makers.

It is television, however, which had the greatest impact at this time, expanding creative possibilities and creating new jobs – but sacrificing certain artistic qualities, and beginning to target children as its core audience.

TV OR NOT TV

Prior to 1956, original animation on American television was simple, low-budget and crudely made. Viewers had their choice: old theatrical shorts, Disney cartoons that aired on *Disneyland* (1954) and *The Mickey Mouse Club* (1955), or animated television commercials, such as the popular "Bert and Harry Piels" campaign for Piels Beer. Conventional wisdom held that creating cartoons that captured the appeal of full theatrical animation on television budgets and schedules was virtually impossible.

Crusader Rabbit

The first to attempt the "impossible" were Alex Anderson, the nephew of Terrytoons' founder Paul Terry, and Jay Ward, a young real-estate man with artistic aspirations. Together they created *Crusader Rabbit*, the first cartoon series made specifically for television, which over the next two years popped up on a handful of NBC affiliates. Sporting animation so rudimentary as to resemble a story reel, the adventures of Crusader and his tiger sidekick Rags (also known as Ragland T. Tiger) were presented in serialized form before leaving the airwaves in 1951. Jay Ward, of course, would be heard from again.

The gimmick of serializing short animated segments would be used by virtually every producer who entered television in the 1950s. It was the format for Terrytoons' *Tom Terrific* (1957), which aired on the daily children's show *Captain Kangaroo*; Cambria Productions' adventure series *Clutch Cargo* (1959), which employed the bizarre and creepy technique of superimposing live-action mouths over drawn faces; Q.T. Hush (1960) a comedy/mystery cartoon with a noirish veneer produced by a company called Animation Associates; and Joe Oriolo's revitalized *Felix the Cat* (1960) from Trans-Lux Productions. But the greatest and most lasting impact on animation would come from another serialized cartoon: Hanna-Barbera's *The Ruff and Reddy Show* (1957).

Distinguished Reputation

By the mid-1950s, William Hanna and Joseph Barbera were already cartoon royalty. Their Tom and Jerry shorts for MGM had won a record seven Academy Awards out of 13 nominations, most recently for *Johann Mouse* (1953). With the retirement in 1955 of Fred Quimby, the nominal and non-creative corporate head of the MGM animation division, they had become the studio's official producers, with control over every cartoon unit. In 1957, though, MGM decided to shut down its entire cartoon operation, citing high production costs and diminished returns in a changing marketplace as the reasons. Hanna and Barbera were left with few options since the short theatrical cartoon business was in decline throughout Hollywood.

Colonel Bleep

Colonel Bleep was another low-budget, early TV cartoon series. It was the first made-for-TV cartoon produced in color, but as its production values were also not high, it did not stand the test of time and by the late 1960s was rarely seen.

© Soundac Studios

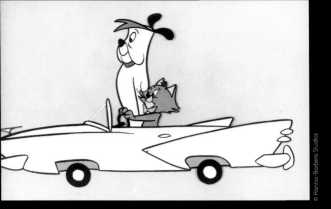

© Hanna-Barbera Studios

Ruff and Reddy

This series demonstrated that Hanna-Barbera's planned animation technique could be successful. Animation sequences, such as walking cycles, could be mass-produced and were transferred from one character to another. Although it resulted in a certain repetition of movement, it saved them a great deal of money.

Hanna, Barbera and Huckleberry Hound

Hanna and Barbera worked out a system of "planned animation". Rather than animating an entire figure, only those body parts that moved were animated, with the rest held steady – that way, most of the body could be treated as background, with one drawing sufficing for an entire scene.

© Hanna-Barbera Studios

Transition to Television

Television was the only door left open to Hanna and Barbera, who had actually dabbled in television animation a few years earlier, quietly producing a few commercials and the original animated opening to *I Love Lucy* (1951–57). With the help of director George Sidney, an old friend from MGM, they secured a deal through Screen Gems, the television subsidiary of Columbia Pictures, to produce new cartoons specifically for the growing television market.

Nothing, however, prepared them for the shock of going from the $50,000 they typically spent on one seven-minute short at MGM to the $2,700 they were being offered by Screen Gems to produce a cartoon of equivalent length. In order to survive in the new medium, Bill Hanna and Joe Barbera would have to completely redesign the process of animation.

CHANGING THE FACE OF ANIMATION

Now that they were working for television, Hanna and Barbera quickly realize animation was governed by different rules. On the one hand, the small home was more forgiving of flaws than a 40-ft high movie-theater screen. But it was al that the silent comedy and sight gags of their Tom and Jerry cartoons were exp luxuries in television, where dialogue was what carried the stories. Fortunately, th was able to lure experienced cartoon storymen and writers such as Michael Ma Warren Foster, Dan Gordon and Charlie Shows to provide the necessary dialogu along with the talented voice actors Daws Butler and Don Messick to deliver it. But the bar would also have to be raised on the artwork, certainly above the primitive level of animation seen in *Crusader Rabbit* and *Tom Terrific*.

Limited Animation

One key artist that Hanna and Barbera brought with them from MGM was layout artist and character designer Ed Benedict (b. 1912), whose crisp, attractive, deceptively simple-looking designs were a major factor in ensuring the success what came to be called limited animation. Since the economics of limited anir demanded that absolutely nothing moved that did not have to, key poses were I long as possible. Not only were the designs crucial for that, but the animators' exe of the key poses also had to be as pleasing and funny as possible.

Ironically, the animation industry's overall slump in the late 1950s proved an advantage to Hanna-Barbera, since many of the animators who were talented and experienced enough to achieve those demandingly funny key poses were then looking for work – even work in television. Veteran animators such as Carlo Vinci, Jerry Hathcock, Dick Lundy, Grant Simmons, and Don and Ray Patterson were there for the asking, and adapted to the new style of animation with relative ease.

Kid's Stuff

Technique aside, Ruff and Reddy also offered new kinds of animated character. The cat and dog protagonists were not combatants like Tom and Jerry, but rather best pals. Whether this was a deliberate attempt at a more child-friendly approach for a new audience or whether Tom and Jerry-style mayhem was simply too expensive to animate for television, it signalled the beginning of animation's descent into the realm of "kid's stuff" within the American psyche – it has yet to re-emerge.

© Hanna-Barbera Studios

Huckleberry Hound

The Huckleberry Hound Show was the first series produced and controlled entirely by the studio. It consisted of three segments, one featuring Huckleberry, the other two featuring Yogi Bear and Pixie & Dixie. A favorite with both adults and children, it won an Emmy for Best Children's Program in 1959, the first cartoon series ever to be bestowed that honor.

© Hanna-Barbera Studios

HOKEY   DING A LING   HUCKLEBERRY HOUND   PIXIE   DIXIE   JINKS

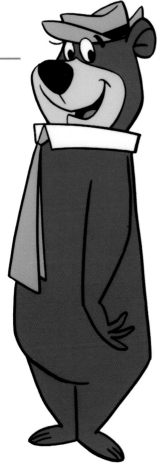

© Hanna-Barbera Studios

Yogi Bear

Yogi Bear's voice was supplied by the voice actor Daws Butler, who based it one used by Art Carney for his character Ed Norton, one of the stars of the sitcom *The Honeymooners*. He also provided Huckleberry Hound's voice, and had worked with Hanna and Barbera in their Tom and Jerry days.

Huckleberry Hound Characters

After Yogi's own show began in the early 1960s, he "left" and was replaced by Hokey Wolf and his side-kick, Ding a Ling. Pixie & Dixie and menacing cat Jinks the were essentially low-budget versions of Hanna-Barbera's old Tom and Jerry cartoons.

Yogi Bear Characters

Yogi and his co-stars provide another example of the studio's planned animation style. When a character spoke, only his mouth moved; when he walked, only his legs walked, saving hundreds of drawings. Stories were chosen which emphasized character and dialogue. The result was a seven-minute cartoon which needed only 2,000 drawings, but still resembled full animation.

Prime-Time Success

With *The Ruff and Reddy Show* a success on NBC, and sponsors such as Kellogg's Cereals becoming interested in the new style of animation, Hanna-Barbera had proven the "impossible" could be done. Their next series, *The Huckleberry Hound Show* (1958), starring a laconic, everyman Southern hound dog, was an immediate hit in syndication and would go on to win the first Emmy ever awarded to an animated programme. This was followed by *Quick Draw McGraw* (1959), a consistently funny spoof of the Western shows that were then dominating prime-time television, which proved equally popular.

In 1960, though, the studio was issued a challenge: a sponsor was interested in supporting a half-hour animated situation comedy, a format that had never been done before – the earlier half-hour shows had always been a combination of three short cartoons featuring different character groups. Even Hanna and Barbera themselves were uncertain it could be done, though the studio accepted the challenge and began to develop a series based on the structure of Jackie Gleason's *The Honeymooners* (1955–56), but set in a comically anachronistic version of the stone age.

The Flintstones

The new show was originally dubbed *The Flagstones* until it was realized that the comic strip couple "Hi and Lois" went by that last name. It was then changed to *The Gladstones*, which was the name of the Hollywood telephone exchange. But the third name change was the right one, and animation history leapt forward with the premiere on ABC of *The Flintstones* (1960).

The first animated series went to air on network prime-time and was the first to attract celebrity guest voices, including Tony Curtis, Ann-Margaret, heart-throb James Darren and songwriter Hoagy Carmichael. *The Flintstones* was written with more sophistication than the likes of Huckleberry Hound or Yogi Bear, and it appealed equally to adults and children.

While Hanna-Barbera would make rare forays back into theatrical animation, chiefly *Loopy de Loop* (1959–65), a Columbia cartoon series featuring a courtly French wolf, it was really television that became the team's home base for the next three decades.

© Hanna-Barbera Studios

YOGI BEAR   YAKKY DOODLE   BOO BOO   SNAGGLEPUSS

The Simpsons » 312

One of the most radical makeovers in the history of animation occurred in 1956. CBS had purchased the Terrytoons studio in New Rochelle, New York, and had placed an innovative animation director from the award-winning UPA studio to be its new creative head. Paul Terry's ancient studio was quickly married to one of the most talented young creators in animation, Gene Deitch (b. 1924). Practically overnight, clunky cartoons about mechanical horses, radio crooners and hundreds of cartoon mice, gave way to sharp animated satire featuring henpecked suburbanites, neurotic elephants and characters designed in cubist shapes.

© Terrytoon Cartoons, CBS Productions

It's A Living

Deitch's Terrytoon theatricals were some of the classiest-looking animated shorts of the late 1950s. His new approach to Terrytoons is best demonstrated in the cartoon *It's A Living* (1958). The film has venerable Terrytoon star Dinky Duck jumping through the theater screen – in classic Buster Keaton style – into a Cinemascope UPA-stylized universe of modern-art cartooning. There, he becomes an object for Madison Avenue executives who attempt to commercialize the duck. *It's A Living* would be Deitch's one and only use of a classic Terrytoon character.

Tom Terrific and Manfred Man

Deitch's shape-shifting Tom Terrific and his ever-faithful Mighty Manfred.

New Characters

Deitch dumped the rest (Mighty Mouse, Heckle and Jeckel, et al.) and quickly came up with contemporary characters which he could better relate to: Sidney, a maladjusted elephant who sucked his trunk in the way a child would suck a thumb; John Doormat, the typical 1950s suburbanite who is king at the office but henpecked at home; Gaston Le Crayon, a zany French artiste; Clint Clobber, the burly superintendent and sanitary engineer of the Flamboyant Arms apartments in the Bronx; and Foofle, a hapless clown.

In addition, Deitch took the opportunity to experiment with some abstract ideas. He hired his old UPA team-mate Ernest Pintoff to create an acclaimed film, *Flebus*, and encouraged Al Kouzel to adapt R.O. Blechman's *The Juggler of Our Lady* and James Flora's *The Fabulous Fireworks Family*. Talented young Turks such as Jules Feiffer and Ralph Bakshi got their start under Deitch at the New Rochelle studio.

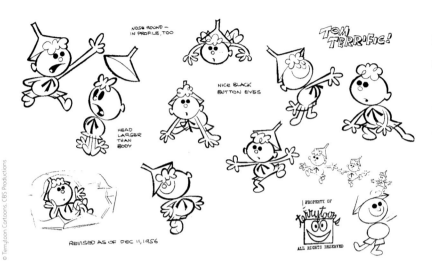

Tom Terrific – model Sheet

In creating *Tom Terrific*, Deitch was influenced by UPA's limited animation style. Imaginative, tongue-in-cheek scripts and stylized designs disguised the fact that the budget for children's TV animation was so low. The voices were generally done by Lionel Wilson, and the music provided by a harmonica.

Tom Terrific

Deitch wanted in to include as much real animation in *Tom Terrific* as possible, and avoid shortcuts such as paper cut-outs. He made use of Terrytoons' large staff of animators, and by eliminating much of the traditional process of cel animation and keeping the backgrounds extremely simple, he achieved his aim.

The History of Deitch

Deitch began his career in cartooning as the chief cover and cartoon artist of the jazz magazine *The Record Changer*. He joined UPA in 1947 as a layout assistant for Bill Hurtz and Bobe Cannon on the Fox & Crow Columbia cartoons and the early Mr Magoo films. He then joined the Jam Handy organization in Detroit directing many industrial and commercial cartoon films, but UPA called him back in 1951 where he became creative director of its newly established New York studio. During his four-year tenure, Deitch directed the celebrated Bert & Harry Piels Beer commercials and was first to animate the drawings of Saul Steinberg, working personally with the artist.

Deitch was writing and drawing a comic strip, *Terr'ble Thompson*, for United Features Syndicate (1955–56), when CBS called him about the Terrytoons position. It was not an easy role to take on. Thirty-one-year-old Deitch was disliked by many old-timers at the studio, but he saw a golden opportunity to revitalize a floundering operation and, at the time, a dying art form: the animated short. As a measure of his success, Terrytoons earned its first Academy Award nomination in 12 years (for *Sidney's Family Tree* in 1958), and the studio was no longer the joke of the industry. By 1958, CBS-Terrytoons was out-UPA-ing UPA! Deitch picked up the ball and kept running, fulfillng the promise of UPA by producing contemporary cartoons that reflected modern life using modern art.

Advantage Deitch

Deitch's sole TV effort used the limitations of television to "terrific" advantage. *Tom Terrific*, produced in black and white and broadcast as a daily serial on CBS's morning kids show *Captain Kangaroo*, was an animated rewrite of Deitch's comic strip *Terr'ble Thompson*. Shape-shifting Tom Terrific and Mighty Manfred (his "wonder dog") would save the world each week from various evildoers. The characters were animated as line drawings, without opaque centers, allowing the backgrounds to be visible through them.

End of an Era

After two years of feuds with the old guard, Deitch left Terrytoons in 1958 and producer Bill Weiss took over. Practically everything Deitch began was left abandoned. Lariat Sam soon replaced Tom Terrific, Deputy Dawg replaced Clint Clobber, and Terrytoon mainstays Heckle & Jeckle and Mighty Mouse returned. Weiss made a small group of Silly Sidney cartoons for TV, but essentially the creative bubble of the Deitch era had burst.

"Snap, Crackle, Pop!"; "Sorry Charlie"; "How about a nice Hawaiian Punch?". These are just a few of the popular expressions made famous through animated television commercials. In the 1950s, as demand for the theatrical shorts began to subside, American animators began to find work at small animation studios devoted to making 60-second cartoon advertisements for the growing medium of television.

Origins of a Golden Age

Animated TV commercials date back to 1941, when Otto Messmer (Felix the Cat) animated a lamb for sponsor Botany Mills for its long-running series of NBC weather-report broadcasts. Post-war, with television sales exploding in the late 1940s, full-scale production of cartoon commercials began to develop. Experienced studios such as UPA and veteran animators such as Shamus Culhane quickly established themselves as specialists in this new field.

By the mid-1950s, two-dozen animation shops had emerged into what was quickly becoming a golden age for the animated commercial. Much of the creative work at this time – including design, dialogue and direction – was left in the skilled hands at the various studios. Characters like Tony the Tiger, Speedy Alka-Seltzer, Chiquita Banana and Bert & Harry Piels were developed by the same artists who crafted Mr Magoo, Popeye and Woody Woodpecker.

New Talent

In fact, by 1956, Terrytoons, Walter Lantz, Warner Bros., Paramount and even Disney were all actively producing animated television commercials for various clients. New studios, started by enterprising Hollywood animators, dominated the scene. These included Tempo, founded by UPA's Dave Hilberman and Zack Schwartz; Fletcher-Smith, which employed many former Fleischer animators; as well as Jack Zander's Pelican Films, and Lee Blair's Film Graphics. They were joined by a dozen more smaller, but no less talented, units, including TV Spots, Bill Strum Inc., Swift-Chaplin, Ray Patin Productions, Animation Inc., Academy Pictures and Five Star, who specialized in stop-motion Speedy Alka-Seltzer spots.

Playhouse Pictures, founded in 1952 by UPA's production manager Ade Woolery, is still around today. Most notably, they adapted Charles Schulz's Peanuts characters to animation for a successful series of advertising spots for Ford. John and Faith Hubley established Storyboard Inc. and made a series of artistically interesting commercials – particularly memorable is their spot for Maypo, a children's breakfast food. This commercial work helped fund their Academy Award-winning personal short films *Moonbird* (1959) and *The Hole* (1962).

© General Foods

Sugar Bear

General Foods' Sugar Bear was the muscular mascot for Post Sugar Crisp cereal, who attributed his strength to eating a good breakfast which included his sponsor's "vitamin-packed" product.

© Playhouse Pictures

The superstars of cartoon pitch men in the 1950s included Gene Deitch's Bert & Harry Piels, voiced by the comedy duo Bob & Ray (for Piels Beer), Sharpie the Gillette Parrot (Gillette razor blades), Wally, a champagne-sipping bird ("It's the oonly way to fly!") for Western Airlines, The Campbell Soup twins, Fresh-Up Freddy (for 7-Up), Sugar Pops Pete (for Kelloggs) and Hubley's Marky Maypo (for Maypo maple-syrup flavored cereal).

Success Stories

Some of animation's greatest talents have devoted themselves to TV commercial production. Tex Avery joined Cascade Pictures in 1955 and spent virtually the rest of his career directing commercials for the likes of Pepsodent Toothpaste and Kool-Aid. Along the way he created the Frito Bandito and a very successful series of Raid insect repellent spots.

R. O. Blechman's 1971 commercial for Alka Seltzer, "Man vs. Stomach", popularized his squiggly line style, won numerous advertising awards and compelled him to open his own advertising studio, The Ink Tank. Richard Williams (*Who Framed Roger Rabbit*, 1988) ran London's biggest animation studio throughout the 1970s and 1980s. In subsequent years many popular independent animators, including Bill Plympton, Joanna Quinn, John Kricfalusi, Chris Hinton and Peter Chung, have lent their distinctive animation styles to TV commercials.

Superstar Appeal

Cartoon superstars including Popeye, Mr Magoo, Foghorn Leghorn, Pink Panther and The Simpsons have appeared as company pitch men for a variety of products and services. And the commercials themselves have spawned their own animated celebrities: Charlie the Tuna, the Pillsbury Doughboy, and cereal stars Cap'n Crunch, Franken Berry, Quisp and Toucan Sam leading the pack.

Animated commercials have never lost their appeal. The best ones are literally unforgettable – they were run repeatedly and have become ingrained in our minds. There are no archives for classic commercials, yet this work is a significant part of animation's evolving history. The high calibre of the artists involved and ground-breaking visuals and storytelling make this one of the most important creative outlets for animation art.

Carnation Milk/Friskies Cat Food/Falstaff Beer

Typical of 1950s animated commercials, each one used used humor and a variety of character designs. The animators had more control over the overall sell of the product during this period – by the 1960s advertising agencies would take over the creative reigns – and the commercial spots were 60 seconds long (compared to today's standard 30-second spot). This allowed for greater innovation which shaped TV advertising's future.

DeSoto Spaceman

This model sheet shows character designs for a DeSoto automobile commercial from Playhouse Pictures. Ade Woolery's Playhouse Pictures, employing many veterans of the UPA studio, combined appealing design and outstanding character animation to create classic animated commercials for five decades.

Charlie Tuna

Charlie Tuna was typical of the cartoon characters from the 1950s who became famous for being in commercials.

ANIMATION FESTIVALS

For animation film-makers, film festivals provide much-needed exposure and recognition; they are a venue in which to screen films and meet with peers. Artists and studios, such as Bill Plympton of *Your Face* (1987), Aardman Animation with *Creature Comforts* (1989), Pixar with *Tin Toy* (1988) and Mike Judge of *Frog Baseball* (1991), have all benefited from the exposure of having their work presented at festivals.

Annecy International and the World Festival

The oldest film festival devoted exclusively to animated films is the Annecy International Animation Festival. Founded in 1960, the first event took place in June in the town of Annecy, France. A who's who of animation attended the inaugural event: Alexandre Alexieff, Paul Grimault, Jiri Trnka, George Dunning, John Halas, John Hubley, Grant Munro, Bretislav Pojar, Karel Zeman, and many more. The festival was held again in 1962, and in 1963 it went bi-yearly (skipping 1969 due to political unrest) until 1998 when it went annual. Recent Grand Prize winners include *The Old Man and the Sea*, Alexander Petrov (1999); *Mt Head*, Koji Yamamura (2002); *Barcode*, Adriaan Lokman (2002); and *Hamilton Mattress*, Barry J. C. Purves (2002).

In June 1972, the World Festival of Animated Films debuted in Zagreb, Yugoslavia (now Croatia). At the first festival, Walter Lantz, Friz Freleng, William Hanna, Joseph Barbera, Stephen Bosustow and Chuck Jones took part. Despite all the political trouble in Yugoslavia/Croatia, the Zagreb Festival as been held every other year (except 1976) in years with an even number. Recent Grand Prize winners include *When the Day Breaks*, Wendy Tilby and Amanda Forbis (1999; and *Father and Daughter*, Michaël Dudok de Wit (2000).

Ottawa International and Hiroshima

With animation festivals popping throughout Europe, the Canadian Film Institute put together North America's first major film festival dedicated to animation. Debuting in August 1976, the Ottawa International Animation Festival featured tributes and retrospectives to Oskar Fischinger, the Fleischer Brothers and the National Film Board of Canada. The Festival has been held (currently in late September) in even-number years in Ottawa, except for in 1994 when it was held in Toronto, and in 1996 in Hamilton. With the 2004 event, the festival announced it would go annual. The Canadian Film Institute also produces the Student Animation Festival of Ottawa, which debuted in 1977. Recent Grand Prize winners include *The Night of the Carrots*, Pritt Pärn (1998); *Ring of Fire*, Andreas Hykade (2000); and *Home Road Movies*, Robert Bradbrook (2001).

In Japan, the International Animation Festival of Hiroshima was first held in 1985. Originally held every other year in the odd years, it switched, after skipping 1989, to being held in the even years. Recent Grand Prize winners include

Koji Yamamura

Founded in 1960, the Annecy festival is the top-ranking competitive international festival entirely dedicated to animation. Koji Yamamura won the Grand Prix in 2003 for his short *Atama Yama*.

© Koji Yamamura

Atama Yama

Atama Yama ('Mt Head') by Koji Yamamura won the 2003 short-film prize. Other categories at the festival include commissioned films, school and graduation films, and shorts and series made for the internet. The festival has established itself as a forum to promote animation in all its different forms, and attracts animation professionals from all round the world.

© Koji Yamamura

Father and Daughter

The Hiroshima International Animation Festival (which Michaël Dudok de Wit's *Father and Daughter* won the 2000 Grand Prize at) consists of the competition, special screenings, workshop, seminar, exhibits and more. Its centerpiece is the competition, but there are also screenings of the latest works from specific countries, retrospectives and thematic collections of works.

When the Day Breaks

This film won the Grand Prix at the 2000 Zagreb Animation Festival, as well as scooping awards at many other festivals, including Annecy, Cannes and Chicago.

The Old Lady and the Pigeons, Sylvain Chomet (1998); and *Father and Daughter*, Michaël Dudok de Wit (2000).

Celebrating Animation

From 1985 to 2001, Los Angeles played host to the World Animation Celebration (formally the Los Angeles Animation Celebration), held at various times, in various venues, throughout the Los Angeles area.

Other current animation festivals of note are Anima Mundi, held in Rio de Janerio and Sao Paulo, Brazil every July; the Brussels Cartoon and Animation Festival, held every February in Brussels, Belgium; the Holland Animation Festival held in November, even-number years in Utrecht, the Netherlands; Cartoons on the Bay, held every April in Positano, Italy; Fantoche International Animation Festival held in September, odd-numbered years in Zürich, Switzerland; Cinanima – International Animated Film Festival, held each November in Espinho, Portugal; Stuttgart International Festival of Animated Film held in March, even-numbered years in Stuttgart, Germany; and Turku International Animated Film Festival held in May, even-numbered years in Turku, Finland.

Coming to a Town Near You ...

Since the 1970s, a number of touring film festivals whose focus is bringing animation to an ever-increasing audience have travelled across North America. The granddaddy of these festivals, the International Tournee of Animation, began in the early 1970s. Originally run by Prescott Wright, it was taken over by Expanded Entertainment in the mid-1980s and ran until the early 1990s when it folded. The most popular of the touring festivals, Spike and Mike's Festival of Animation, began in 1977. In recent years they have become more known for their "Sick and Twisted" animation program. In 2003, Mike Judge and Don Hertzfeldt began a new touring program, "The Animation Show". These touring film festivals are a great way to see the latest animated shorts without leaving the comfort of your own city.

RICHARD WILLIAMS

At the relatively late age of 20, a Toronto-born artist named Richard Williams (b. 1933) was just coming to realize all the possibilities that animation had to offer. Disney had already cornered the market with short cartoons and spectacular features, but there were others who were still experimenting with the medium, such as John Hubley and Robert Cannon, as well as Canada's own George Dunning (1920–79) and Norman McLaren. Richard wanted to contribute his two-cents-worth to this comparatively new medium, having been attracted to animation on his initial viewing of Disney's *Snow White and the Seven Dwarfs*.

Emerging Talent

Born of artistic parents and encouraged to draw since the age of two, he was fast getting a reputation as the boy whose greatest ambition was to be Walt Disney's "top idea man". So, at the tender age of 15, Dick withdrew all his savings and invested them in a journey to the Walt Disney Studios in Burbank. Whilst visiting the studios he was advised by veteran art director Dick Kelsey to first receive a good training at art school before even attempting to enter into the world of animation. This he dutifully did, putting himself through Ontario College of Art and supplemented his income by moonlighting for various sponsors.

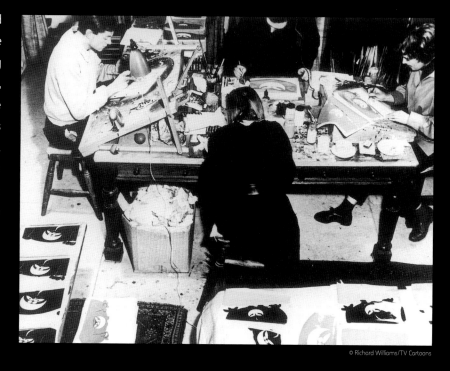

© Richard Williams/TV Cartoons

Richard Williams

Williams and team hard at work on *The Little Island*. After a lifetime spent in animation, Williams was voted "The Animator's Animator" in 1990.

© Richard Williams/TV Cartoons

The Little Island

Richard Williams worked for both Disney and UPA studios, and in 1955 he began work on the 33-minute animated film *The Little Island*, which won the BAFTA Award for Best Animated Film in 1959. This piece gained him immediate recognition as a professional and highly talented animator.

Truth, Beauty & Good

Richard Williams' ground-breaking, experimental film, completed at TVC studios in the late 1950s, was the result of hours of painstaking work by him and his team of animators.

Having earned enough money to see him through art school, he had enough cash left over to buy a car to transport himself back to the Disney Studios with classmate Carl Bell. However, Williams was quickly to become disenchanted by the whole Disney system.

The Little Island

Disillusioned by animation in general, next on the agenda was a two-year stopgap in Ibiza; his "beach bum" period where he painted, sunbathed, swam in the ocean and played jazz. It was during this idyllic interlude that the idea of his first film, *The Little Island* (1958), was born.

The changing scene of British television that occurred in the mid-1950s all happened with the coming of commercial TV in 1955. Suddenly London was the place to be, so Dick loaded himself up with an armful of drawings of *The Little Island* and set off,

arriving at the door of George Dunning's newly formed TV Cartoons studio. He supplemented the cost of Island by working on commercials for dog food, Guinness and Mother's Pride sliced bread during the day, and his own project by night.

The *Little Island* took three years of late nights and weekends to complete, with assistance from George Dunning, his staff and equipment. Made in color and widescreen Cinemascope, the film presents a parable concerning three characters representing Truth, Beauty and Good who live together on a desert isle — and certainly do not live up to their image. They ultimately exterminate themselves through a war. This half-hour epic was well received by critics and festival-goers, enabling Williams to continue pursuing his dream.

© Richard Williams/TV Cartoons

In 1956, both the national and Croatian governments completely withdrew their financial support of both Duga Film and its short-lived successor, Zora Film. But the animators in the Croatian capital were not to be denied. They now turned to another company, Zagreb Film, which at the time was working exclusively on documentaries. The studio agreed to distribute anything the local animators produced, and they jumped at the opportunity. When Dusan Vukotic's (1927–98) *The Playful Robot* (1956) won an award at the Pula Film Festival on the Istrian peninsula in Croatia, the new Zagreb Film was off and running as an animation studio, soon to be one of the most influential in the world. *The Playful Robot* was directed

by Vukotic, who would later win the studio an Oscar. The film also marked the debut of other animators who would go on to have successful careers at the studio. The drawings were by Aleksandar Marks and Boris Kolar, the design by Zlatko Bourek, and the animation by Vladimir Jutrisa.

The Zagreb School

Unified by a commitment to animation and to giving artists free reign, as well as a distinctive white horse as its new logo, the new studio began producing animation at a rapid clip. Its animation style soon became known as "the Zagreb School". In addition to limiting the number of drawings against rudimentary or abstract backgrounds, in the early days another of the studio's pioneering distinctions was the interchangeability of the artists working on direction, design, drawing and story. Ironically, in just a few years the Zagreb School also became known for the film-makers' propensity towards writing, designing and directing their own films. Somehow the two philosophies were not contradictory, as the most talented artists all worked on each other's films. The result was bold cartoons unified in design, tone and message.

Critical Success

The new studio had a breakthrough in the spring of 1958 when it began screening some of its films at the Oberhausen Film Festival in Germany. The following year, a program of films from the studio at the Cannes Festival in France received rave reviews from both

The Playful Robot

The Playful Robot was the first animated film to be produced by the new Zagreb film studio. This scene is an example of Dusan Vukotic's fondness for using simple caricature drawings dancing across a neutral background.

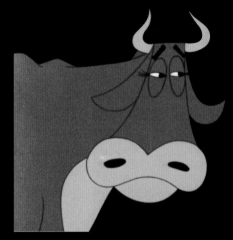

Ersatz

Ersatz shows the Zagreb style of reduced animation at its bes. The focus on the crucial elements of the graphics, direction sound, character and movement, as well as the idea and humor all helped this to be such a critically acclaimed film.

© Dusan Vukotic, Cow on the Moon, Zagreb Film

Cow on the Moon

The reduced animation style at the Zagreb Studio meant that the number of drawings had to be limited to an absolute minimum, without losing any quality from the movement. Whilst other studios like Duga would typically produce 12,000 to 15,000 drawings per film, Zagreb's was more like 4,000 to 5,000.

© Dusan Vukotic, Ersatz, Zagreb Film

critics and fellow animators. When *The Lonely*, directed by Aleksandar Marks and Vatroslav Mimica, won an award for best animated film at the Venice Festival, the studio began to receive international recognition. Many more international awards were to follow. Indeed, during the next four decades, Zagreb Film would produce about 600 animated films, winning more than 400 international awards, including three Academy Award nominations and an Oscar.

Vukotic and Erzatz

The children's film *Cow on the Moon* (1959), is an enduring short by Vokotic about a young girl who tricks a boy into thinking that the rocket ship she has built has taken them to the moon.

In 1962 *Ersatz*, sometimes known by its Croatian title *Surogat* ('Substitute'), became the first film from outside the United States to win an Academy Award for Best Animated Short. Directed by Vukotic, it tells the story of a tourist on a beach who "inflates" an entire village. A passionate love develops between the tourist and a villager, provoking jealousy, vengeance, and finally tragedy. In the end, a small nail reminds everyone of the artificiality of the world that has been created.

A crucial step in the theory and history of animation, the unique and influential style of Vukotic and the Zagreb School can still be seen in animation today.

JIRI TRNKA & KAREL ZEMAN

The son of a plumber, Jiri Trnka (1912–70) was born in Bohemia. He learned the puppet trade at an early age, helping his grandmother make toy horses and dolls and his mother make dresses. By the age of 11, he was working at the local theater, owned by famed puppeteer Joseph Skupa. In 1928 he enrolled in the prestigious School of Applied Arts in Prague. After graduation, Trnka earned a living drawing illustrations for newspapers. He directed a few theatrical plays, and had some success as a painter and illustrator of children's books.

The Czech Puppeteer

Trnka did not make his first short film, the cel-animated *Grandpa Planted a Beet* (1945), until he was 33. It immediately marked him as someone to watch, partly because his human characters made him one of the first animators to rebel against the Disney formula. After four more cel cartoons, in 1947 Trnka directed his first puppet-animation film, *The Czech Year*, depicting the six divisions of a year in the Czech countryside. Finally Trnka was able to express himself the way he wanted, and he was well on his way to becoming the world's premiere puppet animator.

International Success

In 1948 Trnka directed his first feature film, *Emperor's Nightingale*, which won him instant international acclaim. In 1951 Rembrandt Films added an English narration by Boris Karloff and released the film in US theaters, further expanding Trnka's growing reputation in the West.

In 1949 Trnka made *Song of the Prairie*, a parody of the American western, and the Chekhov tale *Story of the Bass Cello*, about a bass player whose clothes are stolen while he's bathing in a river. The following year he made the epic *Prince Bayaya*, about the heroic exploits of a poor country boy who becomes a prince.

Trnka was particularly adept at translating literature into puppet animation, for example, his interpretation of *The Good Soldier Schweik*, the comic Czech novel by Jaroslav Hasek. Private Schweik celebrates the unconquerable spirit of the common man, eternally at war to preserve his individuality against the modern military machine, or any system that treats the individual as a number.

Karel Zeman

Trnka inspired a generation of puppet animators in Prague, most notably Karel Zeman, who was actually two years older than Trnka. Zeman gained popularity with a series of puppet animation shorts starring Mr Prokouk. His most groundbreaking short was *Inspiration*, an exquisitely beautiful film depicting glass figures skating over a shimmering sheet of ice. But his most ambitious works were his feature films, like

Jiri Trnka

Trnka was the Czech master of stop-motion puppet animation. His talent lay in creating the illusion that the puppets were acting out of their own will rather than being controlled by a puppeteer. Here he is creating his 1949 film *Song of the Prairie*.

© Studio Jiri Trnka/Rembrandt Films

Song of the Prairie

Song of the Prairie simultaneously praised and ridiculed the American Western, down to the well-dressed singing cowboy, the stagecoach ride threatened by highway bandits and the villain absconding the heroine with the hero (who always has a moment to comb his hair) in hot pursuit.

Emperor's Nightingale

This is Trnka's version of the Hans Christian Anderson tale about the Emperor of China, a boy king who is caged by his life of ritual and rule, and who is eventually liberated by the song of a nightingale. This fairy tale fantasy was enhanced by the intricately designed sets and puppets, and as with many other of his films, drew the viewer in to his world.

The Treasure of Bird Island (1952), *A Journey into Prehistory* (1954), *The Diabolic Invention* (1958), and what most critics consider his masterpiece, *Baron Munchhausen* (1961).

Meanwhile, Trnka remained the master. He took control of the entire puppet-animation process, from set design, to construction of the puppets, to the meticulous frame-by-frame filming. He was a driven artist, capable of profound subtlety and beauty. He was a sculptor, painter and illustrator, but as a puppet animator he set standards for an entirely new and independent screen genre, rivaling Disney in its freshness and wonder. In 18 years he made 20 puppet-animation films and eight traditional cel films, as well as *Merry Circus*. Neither a puppet film nor a cartoon, this was an entirely unique means of expression and technique made with stop-action photography of paper cut-outs.

Dark Humor

Yet Trnka also had a dark, melancholy side. His large, foreboding presence, accentuated by the dark scar across his cheek, only added to his mystery. Part of his torment was no doubt due to his mixed feelings about the special place he held in Czech society. While he was at odds with the Communist government, he also enjoyed the extraordinary privileges it bestowed upon him. His last film, *The Hand* (1965), was banned in Communist Czechoslovakia, despite winning the top prize at the Annecy International Animation Festival. It is a darkly humorous allegory on totalitarianism. An artist, happy in his life, devotes his time making a pot for his favorite flower. But a giant hand appears and orders him to create a statue of a hand instead. He resists at first, but the hand is all-powerful and he is forced to submit, at the cost of his liberty and ultimately his life.

Trnka's legacy lies in his films' ability to entertain — to delight children and adults alike. In 1966, four years before his death, Newsday lauded Trnka as "second to Chaplin as a film artist because his work inaugurated a new stage in a medium long dominated by Disney".

"Trnka," said Jean Cocteau, "The very name conjures up childhood and poetry."

BULGARIA, POLAND & ESTONIA

Following the arrival of Todor Dinov, Bulgarian animation soon developed into one of the most creative studios in Europe. Dinov was joined by a strong group of animators including Zdenka Doycheva, Pencho Bogdanov, Radka Buchvarova and Roman Meitzov. Buchvarova specialized in children's films, ranging from folklore to social commentary. She made her most acclaimed film, *The Snowman*, in 1960. Before that Buchvarova collaborated with Doycheva on his 1958 debut, *The Mouse and the Pencil*.

Donev and Dukov

In the early 1960s, the Sofia Animation Studio (as it was now known) was divided into two branches under the direction, respectively, of Donio Donev and Stoyan Dukov, a student of Todor Dinov. Following the lead of Dinov, they injected Bulgarian animation with a strong sense of humor and morality. Donev's notable films include *Duel* (1961) and the very popular *Three Fools* series. Donev was a caricaturist of sorts who loved to expose human foolishness. On the other hand, Dukov who made his debut in 1967 with *The Fortified House*, showed more concern with graphic form in films like *The Blackest Mouse* (1971).

Poland

In 1956, the Animated Film Studio of Bielsko-Biala was established in Warsaw under the charge of Witold Giersz. In 1958, the studio separated to become Studio Miniatur Filmowych.

Thanks to a slight loosening of state restrictions, Miniatur encouraged the creation of personal short films by young artists. Two of the most notable new talents – who would change the course of Polish animation – were Jan Lenica and Walerian Borowczyk. The duo made five animated films together in the late 1950s: *Once Upon A Time* (1957), *Love Rewarded* (1957), *Striptease* (1957), *Banner of Youth* (1957) and *House* (1958). The duo's films, made in cut-out, focused primarily on individuals caught up in an absurd world.

By this time, Lenica was already a famous graphic artist. Borowczwk studied graphic art before turning to cinema. He began making live-action films in 1950. The duo stopped working together in 1958, but alone they continued to produce innovative and well-received works. Lenica made a brilliant series of films in the 1960s

© Nukufilm

© Sofia Animation Studio

Little Peter's Dream

This was Estonia's first puppet film, made by Elbert Tuganov, the founding father of the puppet genre in the country. Although it was the fledgling studio's first film, and the animation is occasionally awkward and jumpy, the character rendering and set design are accomplished and original.

The Three Fools

The Three Fools were the Sofia Animation Studio's most comic creation. The characters have been described as a concoction of elements from *Laurel and Hardy*, *The Three Stooges* and *Dumb and Dumber*.

Kõps the Cameraman

With the exception of two unsuccessful attempts at recruitment in the early 1970s, Tuganov and Pars (creator of *Kõps the Cameraman*, which is pictured here) were Nukufilm's only directors between 1958 and 1975. Tuganov retired in 1982 and Pars went on making films until 1990.

Polish Animation » 174 Eastern European Animation in the 2000s » 362

Kõps the Cameraman – in car

Heino Pars created Estonia's first animated series, which featured the recurring character Kõps the Cameraman. There were four films in the series, and in each one viewers were taken to various places, such as Mushroom Land, Berry Forest and Uninhabited Island.

including *Monsieur Tete* (1962), *Labyrinth* (1962), *Rhinoceros* (1963) and *A* (1964), while Borowczwk, who emigrated to France in 1958, made *The Game of Angels* (1963) and the strange and difficult animated feature, *Theater of Mr and Mrs Kabal* (1967). Together, Lenica and Borowczwk changed the course of Polish animation, infusing it with a dark and surreal existentialist tone, along with a strong sense of graphic design.

Estonia

Elbert Tuganov (b. 1920), the father of Estonian animation, was born in Baku, Azerbaijan, but he began his animation career in Germany working for a couple of commercial studios including the Döhring Film Company. After his discharge from the Estonian army in 1946, Tuganov sought employment at Tallinnfilm, the state film studio. For 11 years, Tuganov shot, drew and painted titles and credit sequences. During this time he also modernized the studio's primitive technical apparatus. In order to shoot credits more adequately and fashion trick-shots, Tuganov built an animation stand that would allow the studio to do frame-by-frame shooting. A visiting Moscow official was impressed by the new apparatus and suggested that the studio make animation films.

Tuganov immediately set out to find scripts and stories that would be suitable for production. He landed a Danish story called *Palle Alone in the World*. This became the basis for the first Nukufilm production, *Little Peter's Dream* (1957). In the film, a troublesome little boy, a playground bully, endures an evening of nightmares in which he wanders through a deserted city. In the end, the boy awakes fearful, but with a new awareness of the importance of being kind to others. Consequently, he returns to the playground with a much better attitude.

Laying the Foundations

For the next four years, the film-making process mimicked that of the first production – six or seven people worked on the film alongside artists from the Estonian puppet theater. After the fourth film, *Mina and Murri* (1961), animation production received a budgetary blessing from Tallinnfilm. The division's staff grew to 20, and it was decided that the puppets would then be fashioned in the studio.

By 1961, it became clear that Tuganov alone could not maintain enough of a workload to keep everyone employed. He decided to find a second director. Heino Pars, who worked as cinematographer at Nukufilm, was always approaching Tuganov with ideas for films, and in 1961 he was finally given his first opportunity to direct. He made his first film, *Little Motor Scooter* in 1962.

The years 1956 (when Nihon Doga became Toei Doga), 1957 (when its first short film was released), or 1958 (when its first theatrical feature was released) are each often cited as the year that the Japanese animation industry began. It was about a year after Toei's makeover of the studio before its first film was released in 1957: the 13-minute, black and white *Doodling Kitty* by the director/key animator team of Taiji Yabushita and Yasuji Mori. It was a major success, leading to a slightly longer color sequel, *Kitty's Studio*, in 1959, and the adoption of the young kitten as Toei's corporate logo-mascot for the next decade.

© Toei Doga

Feature Success

But Toei was more interested in theatrical features than shorts. Under Yabushita and Mori, Toei began in 1958 to produce one color feature per year: *Panda and the Magic Serpent* (1958), *Magic Boy* (1959) and *Alakazam the Great* (1960). All three exemplified Okawa's goal of making the studio "the Disney of the East": they followed the Disney feature formula of being (or looking like) adaptations of ancient Chinese or Japanese folk tales, with lots of fantasy and magic, and cute funny-animal companions frolicking around the humans. All three were released in the US in June and July 1961.

Ryuichi Yokoyama

Japan briefly had a second prestigious studio at this time. Today, Osamu Tezuka is famous as Japan's leading manga cartoonist who started his own animation studio, but he was preceded by Ryuichi Yokoyama (1909–2001). Yokoyama was the creator of *Fuku-chan*, one of Japan's most popular newspaper comic strips from 1938 to 1971. Mochinaga's 1944 *Fuku-chan and the Submarine* featured Yokoyama's little boy character, and Tezuka acknowledged Yokoyama's strip as one of his inspirations.

In the 1950s Yokoyama decided to expand into animation. After his 1955 *Onbu, the Little Goblin* proved a hit, he founded the Otogi Production Co. studio in 1956. Its first film, *Fukusuke* (1957), won two awards. Its second, *The Sparrow in the Empty Gourd* (1959), was a 55-minute featurette, while its third, *Otogi's World Tour* (1962) was a 76-minute feature. All featured beautiful color and an imaginative, modernistic art

Kitty's Studio

Yasuji Mori helped to form the Toei Doga style by creating exceptional, memorable characters and some of Japan's most impressive full animation sequences. As senior animator at the studio, he has influenced the next generation of talented animators, like Yasuo Otsuka, Hayao Miyazaki, Isao Takahata and Yoichi Kotabe.

© Otogi Production Co.

© Toei Doga

Panda and the Magic Serpent

This was the first Japanese animated feature film in color. It is based on a Chinese legend and tells the story of Xu-Xian, a young boy who is forced to free his pet snake. The snake is actually a young snake-goddess, Bai-Niang, who searches for and is eventually re-united with Xu-Xian.

Fukusuke

Fukusuke's creator Ryuichi Yokoyama, has received many awards and honors throughout his career. His hometown Kochi City awarded him as the first "Honored Citizen" in 1996 and has built the Yokoyama Gallery within a new museum, which it is hoped will become a national center for animation.

style. Otogi also produced a short art film, *More Than 50,000*, in 1961 as well as Japan's first animated TV series and several animated TV commercials. Then, without explanation, Otogi disappeared and Yokoyama abandoned animation. After retiring as a cartoonist in the early 1970s, he became a fine-art painter and sculptor, winning many national cultural awards and cartoonist societies' awards into his nineties.

Puppet Animation

Tadahito Mochinaga's return to Japan in 1953 coincided with the birth of the Japanese TV industry. He was hired to produce two one-minute beer commercials, which he did in stop-motion puppet animation with assistant Kihachiro Kawamoto (b. 1924). In 1955 Mochinaga created the Puppet Animation Film Studio to make films for screening at elementary schools, producing nine from *The Little Devil and Princess Uriko* (1956) to *The Fox Who Became King* (1960). He also took in commercial commissions, using them for experimentation, such as the 1957 beer commercial *Once Upon a Time There Was Beer*, directed by Tadasu Iizawa, which combined puppet animation by Kawamoto with colored cellophane animation by Ofuji.

In 1958, Mochinaga's *Little Black Sambo Conquers the Tigers* (1956) won the Best Film Award in the Films for Children category at the first Vancouver International Film Festival. This led to a contract two years later for Mochinaga to produce stop-motion animation for US television for Arthur Rankin Jr.'s Videocraft International, soon to become Rankin/Bass.

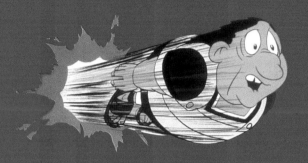

1961–70:
INTERNATIONAL EXPLOSION

By the 1960s, animation production was a global industry – and distinctive artists of all stripes had emerged. There was an explosion of frame-by-frame talent, studios and production. From Zagreb in Yugoslavia and the Pannonia Studio in Hungary, to Bruno Bozetto in Italy and Osamu Tezuka in Japan, they were joined by exciting animated films from China, France and Great Britain.

Britain had the most exciting project in the 1960s, *Yellow Submarine*. With the Beatles' blessing, this animated masterpiece fits into the style of the times – one-part pop art, two-parts psychedelia, with a dash of rock'n'roll. Along with a good story, plenty of gags and cutting-edge art direction, *Yellow Submarine* was a cartoon classic, which proved that an animated feature did not have to be pseudo-Disney.

Walt Disney himself died during this decade, while TV animation grew to new financial heights – and creative depths. *The Flintstones* led to *The Jetsons*, *Jonny Quest*, *Scooby-Doo* and a whole slew of Hanna-Barbarians. Jay Ward brought forth *Rocky & Bullwinkle* and Filmation churned out *The Archies*. The Pink Panther was born – and brought some life to the theatrical short. Underground independent animation grew as movie cameras and film equipment got cheaper and easier to access.

A new generation was beginning.

To some, the television cartoon-factory system established by Hanna-Barbera in the early 1960s signaled the ruination of the American animation industry. The phrase "illustrated radio" was coined by purists to describe it. But strictly from an industry standpoint, without Hanna-Barbera and their ability to keep producing animation at a previously unheard-of level, the American animation business might be very different today. In fact, it might not even exist.

Animation Takes Over the Airwaves

The immediate success and influence of Hanna-Barbera on television in general can be measured by glancing at the network prime-time television schedule of fall 1961, which contained three hours of animation every week – four hours if *Walt Disney's Wonderful World of Color* (formerly *Disneyland*) aired an animated program on the Sunday. In addition to *The Flintstones* and Hanna-Barbera's *Top Cat* (1961), there was Jay Ward's *The Bullwinkle Show*, a revamping of his ground-breaking *Rocky and his Friends* (1959); *Beany and Cecil* (1960), the signature show of animation's gonzo genius, Bob Clampett; *The Bugs Bunny Show* (1960), which repackaged vintage Warner Bros. cartoons inside new linking footage created by the studio's senior directors, Chuck Jones, Friz Freleng and Robert McKimson; *The Alvin Show* (1961), an animated rendition of the popular "singing chipmunk" novelty records of Ross Bagdasarian; and the forgettable *Calvin and the Colonel* (1961), an animated derivation of the radio chestnut *Amos and Andy*, featuring the original actors Freeman Gosden and Charles Correll.

All this was in addition to the series that sprung up for the syndication market, including Art Clokey's clay-animated *Davey and Goliath* financed by the Lutheran Council of Churches; Terrytoons' cornpone-flavored *Deputy Dawg* (1960); and UPA's rather appalling *The Dick Tracy Show* (1961), in which the square-jawed police detective supervised such jokey, racially insulting assistant detectives as "Jo Jitsu" and "Go Go Gomez". Animation was also creeping into the burgeoning Saturday morning marketplace, with such shows as *King Leonardo and His Short Subjects* (1960), a regal comedy starring a lion king.

© Hanna-Babera Studios

Fred and Wilma

The Flintstones was based on the sitcom, *The Honeymooners*, which ran during the late 1950s. *The Flintstones'* success saw the release of other prime-time animated shows also based on sitcoms: *Top Cat* was almost identical to *Sgt Bilko*, and *Calvin & the Colonel* was extremely similar to *Amos and Andy*.

Building the Factory

Within their rapidly growing studio, Hanna's and Barbera's personal roles remained roughly the same as they had been at MGM, at least at first. Barbera, one of the most adept storymen in animation, would work on developing the story and characters for each cartoon, and more often than not supervise the voice-recording sessions. Hanna, a master of animation timing, would take the storyboards and tracks, time them, and oversee the actual animation process. With time, though, Barbera's duties increasingly included pitching and selling shows to networks and sponsors, while Hanna's role became more supervisory.

Two former Disney artists, Charles A. "Nick" Nichols and Iwao Takamoto, joined the staff in the early 1960s, and both were to become key creative forces in the studio. Nichols, who had won an Oscar for co-directing (with Ward Kimball) Disney's *Toot, Whistle, Plunk and Boom*, became animation director for virtually all of Hanna-Barbera's early shows, while Takamoto would soon replace Ed Benedict as the studio's principal character designer.

Even so, it was unquestionably Hanna and Barbera themselves who double-handedly battered down the walls that had been holding back the flood of animation on television.

Flintstones voice cast

The list of actors who provided the voices for the cast included Mel Blanc, who was a one-man who's who of animation. In *The Flintstones* he was Barney Rubble; previously he had been the voice of Bugs Bunny, Daffy Duck, Mr Magoo, Pepé le Pew, and countless others. He would go on being the voice behind the toon into the 1980s. The rest of the cast included Alan Reed (Fred), Jean Vander Pyl (Wilma) and Bea Benederet (Betty).

Jonny Quest

Thelong-running newspaper comic strip *Terry and the Pirates* is credited by Joseph Barbera as being the main inspiration for *Jonny Quest*, not only for some of the characters but also in the sharp, angular look of the artwork, the emphasis on scientific gadgets and high-tech hardware, and the far-flung, exotic locations for the action.

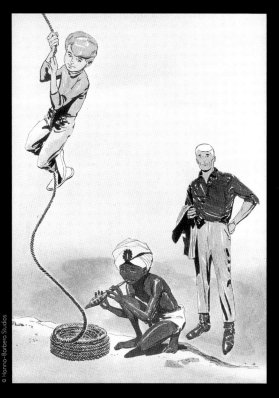

1961 was the last relatively calm year for the Hanna-Barbera studio. Only two new series premiered that year: *The Yogi Bear Show*, which took the popular picnic basket-stealing bear from *The Huckleberry Hound Show* and gave him his own series; and *Top Cat*, a prime-time half-hour situation comedy about a feline con man and his gang of New York alley cats. This latter show was one part Damon Runyon and two parts *The Phil Silvers Show* (1955–59) (otherwise known as *Sgt. Bilko*).

Top Cat

Top Cat lasted only one season on ABC, though even before its last episode had aired, a new prime-time animated series, *The Jetsons* (1962), was launched on the same network. In contrast to the "modern Stone Age family" heralded in *The Flintstones*, *The Jetsons* presented the ultra-modern, space-age family, and as such was able to capitalize on the same kind of visual gags. Whereas in *The Flintstones* all modern conveniences were operated by quirky prehistoric creatures, much of the comedy in *The Jetsons* came from man's frustrating attempts to live in a world of robotics. Without the same kind of visual gags and conceits to offset its dialogue, it could be said that *Top Cat* had occasionally earned the "illustrated radio" designation.

The real inspiration for *The Jetsons* came from Chick Young's *Blondie*, particularly in the relationship that hapless George Jetson had with his domineering boss, Mr Spacely. Also — reinforcing the connection — Penny Singleton, who had played Blondie in 28 feature films, provided the voice for Jane Jetson. *The Jetsons* lasted for only one season as well, though the voice cast was reassembled in 1987 for a series of new episodes.

Animated Action

Even though more and more Hanna-Barbera cartoons were appearing on television, the studio's first real attempt at brand-name marketing came through the Hanna-Barbera *New Cartoon Series* (1962), which promoted the tacit message that it did not really matter what the cartoons were (in this case they were *Wally*

George Jetson

The Jetsons was a reversal of *The Flintstones'* formula; the family lived at Skypad Apartments, which were raised and lowered according to the weather, in 3000 AD. While most space shows contained scary aliens, *The Jetsons* was a reassuring fantasy of the future.

Top Cat

Top Cat was another successful Hanna-Barbera prime-time series. The show was a take-off of Phil Silvers' Sgt Bilko comedies, with Top Cat himself voiced by Arnold Stang.

© Hanna-Barbera Studios

Betty Rubble

The Flintstones broke new ground in that each episode contained one story that lasted a full half-hour. Until the 1960s, cartoons were generally only a few minutes long. Half-hour programs used three or four shorts and a live-action wrap-around, usually presented by a friendly "host", to complete the show.

Peter Potamus

Peter was a friendly hippo who, with his sidekick So So the monkey, traveled back in time. Peter's voice was provided by Daws Butler, who was also the voice of other H-B characters, including Yogi Bear, Huckleberry Hound, QuickDraw McGraw and Snagglepuss.

© Hanna-Barbera Studios

Gator, Lippy the Lion and *Touché Turtle*) as long as they were from Hanna-Barbera. More child-oriented shows followed, such as *Magilla Gorilla* (1963) and *Peter Potamus* (1964). But with its next prime-time series for ABC, the studio broke completely new ground.

Jonny Quest (1964) was the first half-hour action adventure ever attempted in animation. Because of the realistically drawn characters and settings (it was developed by Doug Wildey, a comic-book artist), it was a tough and expensive show to animate, running about $64,000 per half-hour episode. But pre-teen Jonny, who traveled the globe with his scientist father, his friend Hadji and his guardian Race Bannon, was an appealing character. The settings were exotic, the villains were suitably outré, and, in addition, the driving, jazzy theme song by composer Hoyt Curtin was one of the best on television.

Despite its cancellation after one season, *Jonny Quest* encouraged Hanna-Barbera to create more action adventure shows, notably the Saturday morning series *Space Ghost and Dino Boy* (1966), which boasted character designs by comic-book artist Alex Toth, and *The Herculoids* (1967), a science fantasy/adventure.

Weekends Are Made for Cartoons

With the exception of *Ruff and Reddy*, all of Hanna-Barbera's shows prior to 1965 had been made either for prime-time or the syndication marketplace. With *The Atom Ant/Secret Squirrel Show* (1965), however, the studio began to concentrate on making series for Saturday morning, and by the decade's end they dominated the marketplace. To keep up with the increasing workload, the studio (for better or worse) pioneered the practice of employing overseas studios, first in Latin America in the late 1960s, and later in Australia, the Philippines and Taiwan.

Then, in 1969, responding to a request from CBS children's entertainment programmer Fred Silverman for a non-violent comedy mystery show, Hanna-Barbera responded with one of its all-time biggest hits, *Scooby-Doo, Where Are You?* (1969), a franchise that continues to this day.

Despite the rise of such competitors as DePatie-Freleng and Filmation, Hanna-Barbera remained the dominant force on Saturday mornings through the early 1990s, becoming the busiest animation studio in the world. At its peak period during the early 1980s, the studio turned out an incredible 10,000 feet (305 meters) of animation every week. If some of it was derivative and reflected marketing considerations more than genuine artistic inspiration, or if it lacked the fresh, pleasing look of Hanna-Barbera's early television work, at least the young audiences for whom it was made did not complain.

FIlmation » 205 DePatie Freleng » 208 Scooby-Doo » 246

TV PLAYERS

Saturday-morning children's animation exploded in the 1960s. And while Hanna-Barbera led the pack with a large array of bona fide star characters and numerous hit shows, they were unable to fill all the slots available for TV cartoons. A large number of other studios quickly emerged to feed the programing frenzy.

Veteran Animators

Jay Ward, who pioneered TV animation with *Crusader Rabbit* back in 1949, had created a sensation with his hilarious adult-skewed *Rocky & Bullwinkle* cartoons in 1959. This led to a string of hit shows from Ward Productions, all of which now have a richly deserved cult following: *Dudley Do-Right of the Mounties* (1962), *Hoppity Hooper* (1965) and *George of the Jungle* (1967).

Total Television was run by Jay Ward associate Peter Piech, a man who shared with Ward the use of a Mexican animation studio, Gamma Productions. This led to the creation of the popular *Tennessee Tuxedo* (1963) and *Go-Go Gophers* (1968) for CBS, and *King Leonardo and His Short Subjects* (1960) and *Underdog* (1964) for NBC. While not as clever as Ward's shows, these were nonetheless fun, offbeat programs that garnered big audiences.

Veteran *Looney Tunes* director Bob Clampett transformed his Emmy-winning puppet show *Time for Beany* (1950) into a popular animated show for ABC, *Beany & Cecil* in 1962. Clampett's fondness for puns and his jabs at Disney and Madison Avenue made this a must-see for cartoon fans of any age.

Producers Arthur Rankin Jr. and Jules Bass hit the big time in the early 1960s with their stop-motion special (animated in Japan) *Rudolph the Red Nosed Reindeer* (1964). However, they had been in the animation business for a few years by then, producing various series for TV including the stop-motion *New Adventures of Pinocchio* (syndicated 1960) and the cel-animated *Tales of the Wizard of Oz* (syndicated 1961). Later Rankin-Bass cartoon series included *King Kong* (1967) and *Smokey the Bear* (1969), both for ABC.

Former Fleischer animators Joe Oriolo and Hal Seeger set up separate shops in New York City to fill the seemingly unlimited demand for new TV cartoons. Oriolo had great success with a revival of *Felix the Cat* (1960) and his original take on *The Mighty Hercules* (1963). Seeger revived Max Fleischer's *Out of the Inkwell* (1962) with Koko the Clown, and kept busy with *Milton the Monster* (ABC, 1965) and *Bat Fink* (syndicated 1967).

© Jay Ward Productions Inc.

George of the Jungle

This was a parody of Tarzan, and through it, like all Ward's animation, he strove to reach three audiences – pre-school children, who would enjoy the sounds and colors; older children, who would appreciate a storyline packed with fast-moving events; and adults, for whom the clever wordplay and wry commentary were intended.

© Bob Clampett Productions

Beany and Cecil

This was Bob Clampett's one and only successful foray into TV animation. Clampett, one of the most popular cartoon directors at Warner Bros. in the 1930s and 1940s, sucessfully adapted his satirical wit and zany visual style to TV's gruelling production schedule.

© UPA Productions/Tribune Media Services

The Studios Join the Fight

It was not just veteran animators who filled the demand for programing – established studios themselves jumped into the fray. UPA took advantage of the new TV market with a series of Mr Magoo specials and short cartoons made directly for TV, and they also adapted *Dick Tracy* (syndicated 1961) into a popular comedy cartoon series.

Terrytoons entered the TV field with *Tom Terrific* (CBS, 1957), *Deputy Dawg* (syndicated 1960) and found success with *Hector Heathcoate* (NBC, 1963) and *The Mighty Heroes* (CBS, 1966).

There were some one-shot wonders among the TV hopefuls. Ed Graham Productions found success adapting General Foods' Post cereal characters into an ABC series called *Linus the Lionhearted* (1964). This series caused outrage among parent groups who protested to the FCC and won a ruling to disassociate such commercial pitchmen from entertainment programing aimed at kids.

Format Films, headed by UPA's Herb Klynn, produced a couple of noteworthy shows. *The Alvin Show* (1961) was a prime-time series for CBS based on the singing chipmunks of recording fame – and established the singing trio as cartoon stars. Format's highly stylized *The Lone Ranger* (1966) boasted the enormous talents of Disney legends Bill Tytla and Art Babbit. Unfortunately, rushed TV schedules did not allow any of their genius to shine through.

Hanna-Barbera's greatest competitor, Filmation, emerged in the mid-1960s. Lou Scheimer and Norman Prescott, who joined Filmation Associates in 1962 – creating commercials, movie titles and an ambitious self-produced feature film, *Journey Back to Oz* (not completed until 1974) – got a big break in 1965. Fred Silverman, then head of children's programing for CBS, asked them to make *Superman* cartoons for the Saturday-morning schedule in 1966.

The superhero show was a smash hit and led to continuous work for Filmation for over 20 years, rivaling Hanna-Barbera as the leading provider of American children's programming. Filmation's *The Archies* (1968), based on the long-time comic book characters, even produced something Hanna-Barbera never achieved – "Sugar Sugar", one of the very few number-one hit songs to come from an animated TV show.

Dick Tracy

This began life as a comic strip. The animated version consisted of five-minute segments featuring detective Tracy assisted by unlikely sounding supporting characters: Heap O'Calory, Joe Jitsu, Go-Go Gomez, Hemlock Holmes and the Retouchables.

Rocky and Bullwinkle

The verbal interplay between the voice actors is what really stood out with this show. The scripts were cleverly written, often sly and subversive, and made up for the animation, which was often referred to as "illustrated radio", being extremely limited.

© Jay Ward Productions Inc.

TV SUPERHEROES

The turbulent 1960s saw a plethora of superheroes arrive in animated form on the small screen. Setting the decade's tongue-in-cheek tone, *Batman* creator Bob Kane's *Courageous Cat* and *Minute Mouse* debuted in 1960. The obvious satire of Kane's earlier creation had Courageous Cat living in the Catcave, driving the Catmobile and using the Catgun, which shot anything needed for any given situation (except bullets). Through 130 episodes, the duo fought various anthropomorphic adversaries, notably the Frog, a cigar-chomping, Edgar G. Robinson-esque amphibian.

Japanese Imports

The early 1960s saw many futuristic heroes like Cambria Studios' *Space Angel*, featuring drawn characters with human mouths. However, a profound TV milestone arrived in 1963 with *Astroboy* whose popularity in US syndication was a surprise. Due to the stellar success of this Japanese import, others soon came, including *The 8th Man*, *Gigantor* and *Speed Racer*.

An Unlikely Hero

In 1964, television viewers were introduced to the phrase "There's no need to fear, Underdog is here!" Produced by Leonardo TV Productions and Total Television and created by Joe Harris, the long-running *Underdog Show* starred a mild-mannered beagle and shoeshine boy, who emerged from telephone booths as the rhyming caped canine (voiced by Wally Cox) whenever star TV reporter Polly Purebred (voiced by Norma MacMillan) fell into the clutches of various villains, including Riff-Raff and Simon Bar-Sinister (both voiced by UPA legend Allen Swift). Geared toward a younger audience, the series was an epitome of the unlikely hero.

In 1966, Hanna-Barbera started churning out superhero-themed cartoons, beginning with *Sinbad Jr.*, *Atom Ant*, *Secret Squirrel* and *Space Ghost*. This was followed by other short-lived series like *Frankenstein Jr. and the Impossibles*, *Birdman*, *The Herculoids* and *Samson and Goliath*. These were third-rate superheroes at best, but the shows featured voice actors like *Jonny Quest*'s Tim Matheson, *Looney Tunes* master Mel Blanc and *Scooby-Doo*'s Don Messick.

Super Superheroes

Snyder-Koren Productions debuted *Roger Ramjet* in 1965, featuring broadcaster Gary Owens as the mock-heroic Roger. Like Underdog, Ramjet received

Marvel Comics

The animation in *The Marvel Superheroes* cannot claim to be very advanced, but it did stick closely to the comic book original. In *Captain America*, most scenes are direct lifts from artist Jack Kirby's unique, bold artwork with the characters cut out and shifted back and forth on the frame.

The Mighty Heroes

Ralph Bakshi was asked to put together a superhero TV cartoon series in 1965 by CBS. Full of disdain for this commission, he created Tornado Man, Cuckoo Man, Rope Man, Strong Man, James Hound and Diaper Man. Incredibly, CBS loved it, and thus was born the short-lived but energetic series *The Mighty Heroes*.

Japanese TV Animation » 236   TV Toons » 316

© Marvel Comics Group

his powers from taking pills – an irony not lost in the counter-culture. In 1966, King Features Syndicate Television and Bob Kane created *Cool McCool*, a James Bond spoof featuring a gadget-wielding spy whose good looks covered up his bumbling ways. Terrytoons brought 28-year-old Ralph Bakshi into the world of superheroes with *The Mighty Heroes*, a comic book satire featuring six inept heroes – Strong Man, Diaper Man, Tornado Man, Cuckoo Man, Rope Man and James Hound – who often saved the day by sheer luck. *Tom of T.H.U.M.B.*, produced by Rankin-Bass and animated by Toei Company, had shrunken secret agents battling the schemes of M.A.D. (Maladjusted, Anti-social and Darn Mean). *Rocky & Bullwinkle* creators Jay Ward and Bill Scott launched *Super Chicken* in 1967, starring a Super Sauce-drinking chicken and his trusted feline butler Fred. Former Fleischer animator and *Milton the Monster* creator Hal Seeger created *Batfink*, a *Batman* satire featuring the hero with "wings of steel" and his sidekick Karate, a take on *Green Hornet*'s Kato. Before premiering *Pink Panther*, DePatie-Freleng produced *Super President*, where the US leader could change into any element.

DC Comics and Marvel Comics

In 1966, influenced by the success of the campy live-action *Batman* series, other DC Comics characters soon arrived in animated form. Filmation's *The Adventures of Superman* featured highly dramatic Superman adventures, often featuring guests like the Atom and Green Arrow. With long-time *Superman* comic book editor Mort Weisinger serving as script supervisor, the series reunited the voice cast of the radio series – Bud Collyer (Superman), Joan Alexander (Lois Lane) and Jackson Beck (narrator). In the second season, the series was renamed *The Superman-Aquaman Hour of Adventure* and renamed again as *The Batman-Superman Hour* in 1967 when Aquaman received his own series. However, these shows were soon canceled partly due to the "violence on television" protests of advocacy group Action for Children's Television.

Marvel Comics heroes Ironman, Sub-Mariner, Captain America, The Hulk and Thor all arrived in the anthology series *The Marvel Superheroes*, produced by Grantray/Lawrence Animation. The series' limited-animation techniques often led to unintentional humor. In 1967, Grantray/Lawrence produced *Spider-Man*, featuring the famous jazzy theme song and script consulting by *Spider-Man* creator Stan Lee. Notably, Disney legend Shamus Culhane and Ralph Bakshi served as producers on the Grantray/Lawrence production. That same year, Hanna-Barbera premiered *The Fantastic Four*, whose animation now looks dated, but stands as the most accurate adaptation yet of the comic-book quartet.

Many of the 1960s superheroes have been forgotten, due to silly story lines and low production values, yet the "it's so bad, it's good" factor has influenced many postmodern cartoon makers.

Spider-Man

The superhero began life as a Marvel comic strip and the character was animated by Grantray/Lawrence Animation in Toronto, Canada. The results were a crudely animated show which today are considered a kitsch classic.

© Marvel Comics Group

By the 1960s, most of the major animation studios had shut down their divisions or were severely curtailing production. However, theatrical animation continued to thrive in features and even more often through engaging main credit sequences for live-action films. This practice, which dates at least as far back as the 1940s, led to the birth of the Pink Panther.

New Directions

By the time Warner Bros. had closed its in-house studio in 1963, director Friz Freleng had joined with Warner Bros. executive David DePatie (b. 1935) to form DePatie-Freleng Enterprises. They retained many of Freleng's old co-workers, including director Robert McKimson (1910–77), layout man Hawley Pratt (1911–99) and animator Norm McCabe (b. 1911). The new studio would eventually be hired by Warner to produce a series of rather crude new cartoons featuring Daffy Duck, Road Runner and other established characters.

However, DePatie-Freleng soon became active in producing and/or designing animated film titles and other graphics, mostly for United Artists, which would subsequently distribute the team's original theatrical series. For their first assignment in this regard, live-action comedy director Blake Edwards (b. 1922) hired the firm to produce animation for the caper comedy *The Pink Panther* (released in the US in March 1964). The film's title was derived from a famous diamond with a flaw resembling a limping panther.

Classic Credits

For the opening and closing, Freleng, Hawley Pratt and others created a distinctively suave and debonair panther character, accompanying an equally distinctive theme by Henry Mancini. The character engagingly cavorted through the credits and was pursued

The Pink Panther

Friz Freleng had trouble finding the perfect voice for the pink cat and decided to leave him silent (except for *Pink Ice* and *Sink Pink*). When a third series was made, his voice was provided by Matt Frewer.

The Pink Panther – model sheet

The cool, contemporary style of the design and graphics, Henry Mancini's distinctive theme music and the pantomime comedy were a complete departure from the cheaply made theatrical cartoons created by competitors. Rather than being targeted at children, these sophisticated shorts appealed more to adults.

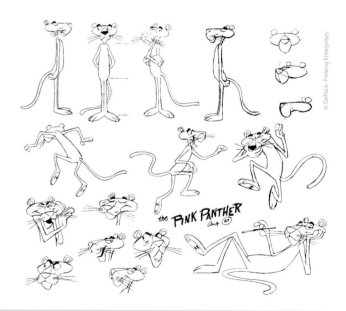

by both a glove (representing David Niven's Phantom character) and a mustachioed detective, the first animated incarnation of Peter Sellers' soon-to-be immortal Inspector Clouseau. The credits were as widely praised as the film itself, if not more so, and on December 18 of the same year, the Panther debuted in his first solo cartoon, *The Pink Phink*. Thus what was arguably the last significant theatrical cartoon series had begun.

Blake Edwards' role was acknowledged — his name would appear above the title throughout the 1960s. The Henry Mancini score was also retained, with arrangements by Bill Lava or Walter Greene.

The most engaging aspect of the Panther cartoons, in fact, is their return to animation's roots in pantomimed movement accompanied by music. In *The Pink Phink*, the panther continually disrupts the efforts of an architect to build and paint a blue home, repainting the walls, floors, etc., with his trademark pink. The architect is depicted as a drab, shapeless, pale white little man with a beaky nose and bushy mustache. In a variety of guises and with the occasional slight design change, he would return as the panther's foil or nemesis and was the only other recurring character in the series.

An International Cat and Film Icon

Though far less lush than Freleng's earlier work, the short's colorful design and simple pantomime, along with Freleng's reputation, may have contributed to an Academy Award for Best Short Subject for that year, an excellent start to the series. Though dialogue would surface in eight subsequent cartoons (including two with Rich Little giving the Panther a Rex Harrison-esque voice), the series in the main relied on the jazz music and the Panther's suave, laid-back walking movements. This allowed for greater success internationally.

The year 1964 also saw the release of the second Clouseau film, *A Shot in the Dark*, which again featured jazzy Mancini music and an animated star, a redesigned Sellers/Clouseau caricature designed by DePatie-Freleng but animated by the crew of George Dunning (1920–79), director of *Yellow Submarine*. Again, a spin-off was born; the Clouseau character, now known only as the Inspector, voiced by Pat Harrington Jr. and accompanied by the Mancini theme, would feature in over 20 shorts between 1965 and 1969. As in the film, he was often at odds with his increasingly harried and near-homicidal superior.

Concurrently with the Panther series, MGM tried to resurrect pantomime on their own, with Chuck Jones directing new Tom and Jerry shorts, but these cartoons were oddly reliant on vocal effects over pantomime. Though the *Panther* series soon went into television, new shorts continued to be released theatrically, outlasting Walter Lantz's declining *Woody Woodpecker* which ended in 1972. After the series folded in 1980, the panther would resurface in various TV incarnations and paint advertisements, and still remains a distinctive film icon.

The Inspector

This series of shorts featured the Inspector character (who was not as clumsy as his live-action counterpart), Sergeant Deux-Deux (inspired by Clouseau's taciturn sidekick) and the Commissioner. Their humor derives mainly from the injuries they all receive from the bizarre villains that are featured.

The Ant and the Aardvark

Seen on segments of *The New Pink Panther Show*, *The Ant and the Aardvark* was concerned with a hungry purple aardvark who spent the duration of the show trying to catch a diminutive red ant.

As Disney's restlessness moved the company into new fields in the 1950s, he had less time to devote to animation. *Sleeping Beauty* was supposed to be released in 1955, but due to the work that the animation studio did for Disneyland and for television, the film was not ready until 1959. The long production schedule added to the film's costs; it was the studio's most expensive animated feature up to that time, and it was a box office disappointment. As a result, there were significant layoffs in the animation department.

A Break from Tradition

The next film, *101 Dalmatians* (1961), was a break from the past in several ways. It was the first feature to use the Xerox process to transfer the animators' drawings onto acetate instead of tracing them by hand. Art director Ken Anderson exploited the look of xerography by designing a feature that relied heavily on lines, even in the backgrounds. The film also marked the directorial debut of Wolfgang Reitherman, who co-directed with veterans Ham Luske and Gerry Geronimi.

Starting with *The Sword and the Stone* (1963), Reitherman became the sole director of the Disney animated features. Unfortunately, Reitherman was not an ambitious storyteller; his films lacked narrative drive and shied away from large emotions. *The Sword in the Stone* was the weakest Disney animated feature up to that time. It contained some excellent animation by Milt Kahl and Frank Thomas, but the story was episodic and the climax was woefully under-developed.

After working on *Mary Poppins* (1964), the animation crew began work on *The Jungle Book* (1967). Disney's hand was still present in various ways. He was responsible for the casting of Phil Harris as the voice of Baloo. He also eliminated a sequence with a rhino that he felt was too active after the sequence with King Louie.

Walt Disney died during the production, and the crew finished the film without him. While one is tempted to think of it as Walt Disney's last animated feature, animation historian Michael Barrier has pointed out how much *The Jungle Book* has in common with the other films that Reitherman directed. While Disney's influence was there, it did not dominate the film the way it had in the past.

Robin Hood

This was the first Disney feature to be conceived, written and directed entirely without Walt Disney's input. Disney had been looking to do an all-animal animated feature based on the legend of Robin Hood since the early 1930s. His live-action *The Story of Robin Hood and His Merrie Men* from 1954 served as narrative inspiration for the animated version, although it was more dramatic.

Cruella De Vil

The Xerox process, used on *101 Dalmatians*, meant that the drawings used in the film retained much of the vigor of the animator's original drawing. Rather than being traced by an inker, a cleaned-up copy of the animator's artwork was copied directly by a photocopying process.

101 Dalmatians

This was the first Disney feature film in which the Xerox process was used, making possible the complex animation it contains. It also set the visual style of Disney animation – a scratchy, hard outline – for years until the technology advanced enough to allow a softer look.

© The Walt Disney Company

The Wilderness Years

The villains of Disney films like *101 Dalmatians* and *The Jungle Book* were ruthless would-be killers. Once Walt Disney was gone, Reitherman's villains in *The Aristocats* (1970) and *Robin Hood* (1973) were a disgruntled butler and a thumb-sucking mommy's boy, an indication of how lightweight the films had become. The animators, though still great performers, were stuck with weak material.

There was also pressure from upper management to control costs. This led to re-using animation from earlier films. In *The Jungle Book*, there were scenes of Mowgli that were re-drawn scenes of Wart from *The Sword in the Stone*. The chase after King Louie's song in *The Jungle Book* was lifted from *Ichabod and Mr Toad*. *The Aristocats* used animation pinched from *101 Dalmatians*, and in *Robin Hood*, Maid Marian's dancing was animation taken from *Snow White*.

Few new artists were hired in the years after *Sleeping Beauty*. At the same time, the crew was losing artists to death and retirement. At the time of Disney's death, the remaining crew was only able to produce a new feature every three years.

The artists realized that if they did not train a new generation, then Disney animation would die with them. The studio started recruiting from art schools, and  veteran animator Eric Larsen took charge of the training program within the studio.

The New Generation

The Rescuers (1977) was the last hurrah of Disney's artists and the freshman effort for many of the new recruits. For the first time since *101 Dalmatians*, Reitherman shared directing credit (with John Lounsbery and Art Stevens), and the results were much improved. The film contained stronger emotions and more excitement than any film since *101 Dalmatians*. The veterans had rallied for their last effort and were able to go out with their heads held high.

The Rescuers marked the end of an era. Walt Disney was dead and his key animation personnel were no longer at the studio. Now, it was up to a new management and a new generation of artists to continue the Disney legacy.

© The Walt Disney Company

WALT DISNEY'S LEGACY

When Walt Disney died in 1966, the whole world mourned. Two generations of people around the globe had grown up watching his films. People saw him on television every week in shows like *Disneyland* and *The Wonderful World of Color*. Children read books or comic books featuring the Disney characters and listened to recordings of Disney songs. Their parents read Disney comic strips in newspapers and thought about taking the family for a holiday at Disneyland.

A Visionary Leader

While Walt Disney Productions was a publicly owned company, it still revolved around the creative leadership of Walt Disney. He was the visionary who drove the company forward. He had brought sound and color to animation and expanded it from short subjects to feature-length cartoons. He increased the studio's output by moving into live action. After the war, when other movie studios were afraid of television, Disney embraced it. He understood the concept of marketing synergy before the term had been coined and used television to promote his films. He re-imagined the amusement park and invented the theme-park industry.

In the years before his death, Walt Disney was not resting on his laurels. If anything, he was busier than ever. In 1964, *Mary Poppins* became the studio's biggest live-action success, garnering 13 Academy Award nominations. Now that Disneyland was up and running, Disney starting planning another theme park for Florida, one that would be larger and benefit from the knowledge gained in building Disneyland. Disney saw the 1964 New York World's Fair as a laboratory for Disneyland and contributed several attractions. One exhibit crossed animation with robotics: an audio-animatronic figure of Abraham Lincoln reciting the Gettysburg Address.

At the time of his death, Disney was planning EPCOT, which stood for "experimental prototype community of tomorrow". Over the course of his life he had gone from doodling cartoon characters to designing cities.

© The Walt Disney Company

Walt and Mickey

Walt Disney's legacy to the animation industry has been profound. His studio set the standard for personality character animation, he made early use of Technicolor and he explored the relationship between visuals and music. He was also the first to make an animated feature in the US.

© The Walt Disney Company

The Jungle Book

This was the last feature Disney supervised, but it was also the first Disney animated feature to base the major characters on the voice artists' personalities. They were allowed to ad-lib and alter their lines to suit their own personas and speech rhythms, and the story was altered as they worked.

Guiding Force

Walt Disney had gathered an army of creative talent around him – artists, film-makers, designers and engineers – but he was the general who gave the orders. As animator and storyman Dick Huemer recalled, "We all went to work for Disney as dedicated people who appreciated what he was trying to do and felt we were in on something historic. Like disciples who might have worked with Michelangelo, we were part of a thing that was maybe going to last and that had a chance to be remembered".

With Walt Disney's death, the company lost its creative engine. His brother Roy had worked miracles to finance Walt's ideas, but while Roy took charge of the company, he was no match for Walt as an innovator. Everywhere in the company, the question was "What would Walt do?" Unfortunately, Walt was not there to answer.

In all of the years since his death, there has been no one to replace Walt Disney. He remains the single-most important person in the history of animation, as well as a major figure in twentieth-century popular culture.

JOHN & FAITH HUBLEY

John Hubley began his animation career at Disney in 1935 and left after the 1941 strike for Screen Gems, where he became a director. This was followed by a stint with the Army Air Force's First Motion Picture Unit. In 1944 he joined UPA, where he directed some of its most important films, including *Rooty Toot Toot* (1952). After being forced to leave because of the Hollywood blacklist, he became involved in an unsuccessful attempt to make an animated version of *Finian's Rainbow*. Faith Elliot Hubley (1924–2001), John's second wife, entered the film industry at 18 as a messenger at Columbia Pictures. She eventually worked herself up to becoming script supervisor on James Wong Howe's *Go Man Go* (1954) and Sidney Lumet's *12 Angry Men* (1957), which she also edited.

© The Hubley Studio, Inc.

A Fruitful Partnership

When they got married in 1955, the Hubleys promised to always eat dinner with their children and make one independent film a year. To do the latter, they established Storyboard Productions in New York to produce commercials and educational films. Their resulting collaboration proved to be one of the most fruitful of the post-war era, and helped define the nature and scope of independent animation in the United States. It also helped inspire a renaissance of theatrical animation in New York.

Though they made a series of popular TV commercials for such clients as Ford, Maypo and Bank of America, they are better known for their highly personal shorts, which began with the *The Adventures of* * (1955), a film that created something of a sensation. The story is of a baby, represented by a "*" symbol, and how his appreciation of the visual world changes as he grows up.

All About the Music

In this and other films, they explored a whole new visual vocabulary, often inspired by their soundtracks; this resulted in a free-form visual style, where graphic elements often seemed to float in the air. In particular, this style essentially illustrated improvised dialogue and/or music from jazz greats such as Dizzy Gillespie, Oscar Peterson and Quincy Jones. The jazz element was clearly seen in their second film, *Harlem Wednesday* (1957), which featured the music of Benny Carter, and *Tender Game* (1958), which used Ella Fitzgerald's version of 'Tenderly'.

More important was the Oscar-winning *Moonbird* (1959), a loosely told tale of two children chasing a bird at night, which had dialogue improvised by their young children. John's interest in such dialogue probably dates back to *Ragtime Bear* (1949) at UPA, when he had Jim Backus, the voice of Mr Magoo, improvise many of his

The Hubleys

Through their films, the Hubleys' ultimate goal was "to increase awareness, to warn, to humanize, to elevate vision, to suggest goals, to deepen our understanding of ourselves and our relationship to one another".

The Hat

This depicted the absurdity of war and the arms race, and employed the Hubleys' non-traditional techniques, using a blend of watercolor, wax crayons, multiple exposures and lighting from beneath the camera, which resulted in a spontaneous appearance and emphasized their characteristic free-form graphic approach.

Windy Day

A central thread that ran through the Hubleys' films was the importance of children as people. This film used the musings of John and Faith's daughters and attempted to capture the real world of children on film rather than what children do that adults think is cute.

Northern Ice, Golden Sun

Faith Hubley's last film displayed her trademarks: the lyrical nature of her work and the influence of the art of primitive cultures, as well as the more sophisticated glyph languages of modern painters like Paul Klee and Joan Miró.

Cartoons Go to War » 90   UPA and Limited Animation » 146

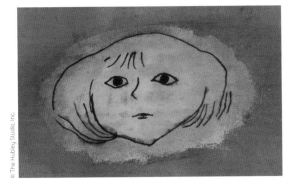

lines. This type of dialogue was later seen in films such as the Oscar-winning *The Hole* (1962), about a conversation between two construction workers about nuclear war, voiced by Dizzy Gillespie and actor George Matthews; *The Hat* (1964), which deals with the problems of national borders; and *Windy Day* (1968), which explores the world of childhood using the voices of the Hubleys' two daughters.

Their other films include two educational features, *Of Stars and Men* (1961), in collaboration with Harlow Shapley, and *Everybody Rides the Carousel* (1976). Faith finished production of *A Doonesbury Special* (1977), based on the Gary Trudeau comic strip, after John died, and it became their seventh film to be nominated for an Oscar.

Going It Alone

After John's death, Faith continued making films, bringing her own sensibility to the fore and inspiring a whole new generation of women film-makers, including her daughter Emily. If anything, her films were more personal than those made with John, being more meditative than narrative in structure; they also frequently used visual imagery from different cultures and employed a vibrant color palette. Although she continued to use jazz, Faith's films did not feature much in the way of dialogue.

Her first solo effort was *W.O.W. (Women of the World*, 1975) – made after she was diagnosed with cancer – which presents "a creative history of the earth from a feminist point of view". Other films include *Sky Dance* (1980), which featured animated versions of prehistoric and primitive art; *The Big Bang and Other Creation Myths* (1981), a self-styled new-age presentation of creation myths from around the world; *Yes, We Can* (1988), an environmental plea to save the Earth; the autobiographical *My Universe Inside Out* (1996); and *Northern Ice, Golden Sun* (2001), a poetic look at the Inuits' attachment to their environment, finished just before she died.

JOHN & JAMES WHITNEY

The Whitney brothers, John (1917–95) and James (1921–82), pioneers in American independent animation, are noted not only for their abstract films, but also for laying the groundwork for the whole field of computer animation and digital special effects.

Myriad Techniques

While in Paris in 1937–38, John studied 12-tone music and animation of abstract designs. Upon returning to the US in 1939, he joined with James, a painter, to make their first film, *Twenty-Four Variations* (1940), an 8 mm abstract film using circles and triangles. Production of this was made possible by an optical printer that John built. Their next and final collaboration comprised five abstract film exercises (1940–45), considered masterpieces of abstract animation, in which they photographed light rather than illuminated images. In addition, John created sound directly on film – a technique later developed by Norman McLaren.

Also anticipating McLaren's paint-on-film techniques were a series of films John made by photographing drawn images on an oil-coated luminous surface, then adding colors during printing; these included *Mozart Rondo* (1949), *Hot House* (1949) and *Celery Stalks at Midnight* (1951). In 1952, he founded Motion Graphics, Inc. to produce commercial films, moving to UPA as a director in 1955 before working as a film specialist at the Charles and Ray Eames Studio; he also designed the title sequence for Alfred Hitchcock's *Vertigo* (1958).

Beginning in 1959, he began to use a World War Two gun sight, essentially a simple analog computer, to produce visual effects. They were assembled in *Catalog 1961*, designed to demonstrate the commercial viability of the process. These and other experiments led to IBM in 1966, resulting in such pioneering computer/optical printer films as *Permutations* (1966), the *Matrix* series during the early 1970s and *Arabesque* (1975). In 1986, he helped develop a computer program designed to combine computer graphics and music composition, which aimed to match "tonal action with graphic action".

A Spiritual Experience

After collaborating with his brother, James Whitney devoted himself to "poetic research", including the study of oriental philosophy, Jungian psychology and quantum physics. From the time he returned to film-making in the 1950s until his death, he made only five films, which are considered among the finest non-objective cinematic

Catalog

This became a popular classic of 1960s psychedelia, and featured a curve, multiplied dozens of time, appearing in a twisting wave, reminiscent of a blossoming flower.

© and courtesy of the estate of John & James Whitney

© and courtesy of the estate of John & James Whitney

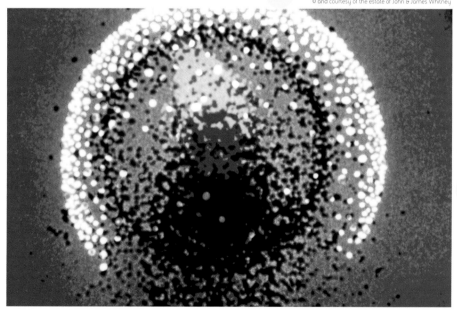

Lapis

Lapis was made with John Whitney's prototype motion-control camera. Motion-control meant that a camera could be programmed to shoot an image over and over with subtle variations. In *Lapis* a configuration of 250 dots, via calibrated camera rotations and color filters, cascade and dance kaleidoscopically.

Yantra

Painstakingly drawn by hand, this film takes its title from a Sanskrit word for "machine" or prayer wheel, and melds ancient mysticism to the sublime visual effects of ultrasmooth mathematical motion.

works ever made. *Yantra* (1955) is described as a series of "quasi-musical variations of implosions and explosions" and, like his other films, is conceived as a visual/spiritual experience. He returned to painting before finishing *Lapis* (1965), which again used images derived from a series of points; while he did use his brother's computer-guided camera equipment during production, the images themselves were handcrafted.

James's last project, left unfinished when he died, was a tetralogy representing the four primary elements: fire, water, air and earth. The first, *Dwija* (1976) uses images of a bird being reborn, bathed in liquid light, while the climatic image in *Wu Ming* (1977) is of a black circle gradually shrinking until it disappears, creating a feeling of grandiosity. *Kang Jing Xiang* (1982) is perhaps best described by translating the title as "what is seen during a lustrous religious ecstasy", and features contrasts between misty and bright, pulsing images. Unfortunately, James died before completing the last film in the project, but the three that exist offer fascinating viewing.

YELLOW SUBMARINE

Although not actually the first animated cartoon to jump on the Beatles' bandwagon, *Yellow Submarine* still stands out as a landmark in cult-animation history.

What's It All About?

The prolog takes place in the mythical region of Pepperland, where everything is tranquil and echoes to the sound of laughter and the music of Sgt Pepper's band. A hostile sneak attack by the music-loathing Blue Meanies leaves the band encased in a bubble and the inhabitants frozen in time. Old Fred is the only one who manages to escape the wrath

© Subafilms Ltd.

of the Blue Meanies and goes to find help, making his exit in the very vehicle that had brought their forefathers to Pepperland, a flying yellow submarine. Fred successfully takes the sub to the rain-sodden streets of Liverpool, where he encounters Ringo and begs his assistance. Soon John, George and Paul are rounded up and they set off in the yellow submarine on a journey to Pepperland, a land lying firmly beneath the jackboot of the despotic Blue Meanies.

Finally disembarking at their destination, the foursome prepare for the battle by first freeing the trapped band with a rousing chorus of 'All You Need Is Love', which brings the life back into the populace of Pepperland. This takes the Meanies by surprise and a battle ensues. The outcome has the villains and their cohorts being finally routed and the Chief Meanie's views drastically altered as he realizes that love and music are not really the demons he imagined them to be. With the return of serenity in Pepperland, a celebration in music and song takes place with the Fab Four and their counterparts joining in with 'All Too Much'.

In a filmed epilogue, the Beatles appear and comment on the film. John claims that "newer and bluer Meanies have been sighted" and that the best reply is to go out on a song... 'All Together Now!'

© Subafilms Ltd.

The Fab Four – heads

Chief artist Heinz Edelmann brought his unique vision to the pacing of the film to infuse it with a heightened sense of excitement and vibrant immediacy. He thought that the film should be a series of interconnected shorts, as it would keep the interest going until the end. It was an effective approach, and a technique that broadened the visual imagination of animated films.

Animal Farm » 166

'Eleanor Rigby' sequence

One of *Yellow Submarine*'s signature innovations was its unique method of merging live-action photography with animation. This process was showcased in the 'Eleanor Rigby' sequence, where realistic images from newsreel footage, cut-out figures and photographs of Liverpool were blended, rather than just superimposed, to give striking perspective to the scenes and fantastic effects to the story.

Pilot

Poster artist Heinz Edelmann's highly stylized drawing characterized this feature. Director George Dunning did not want the artwork to be too cartoon in style, or too realistic. Edelmann's drawings were neither. His images were bold, not cuddly, his colors were bright, not pastel, and his characters were rectangular, not circular.

Small-Screen Beginnings

The Beatles' widespread popularity in the 1960s captured the public's imagination on both sides of the Atlantic. Apart from enjoying their music, one could also read special magazines about them, buy their merchandise and watch their antics in live-action films such as *A Hard Day's Night* and *Help!* Another spin-off of their success was an animated television series featuring the band. This premiered in 1965, and was engineered by Al Brodax, King Features Syndicate's producer, and made in part at TV Cartoons (TVC) in London. Around this time, the Beatles were under contract to supply three feature films to United Artists, but found themselves too busy with other projects to complete the deal. It was not long before entrepreneur Brodax heard of this situation and, based on the success of the television series, convinced Brian Epstein that the third film could be animated. So was born *Yellow Submarine* (1968).

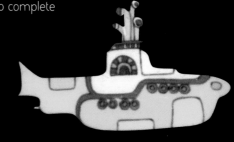

TVC's MASTERPIECE

A plot for *Yellow Submarine* was structured around the lyrics of the Beatles' eponymous song. King Features fronted the money, George Dunning was asked to direct the feature at his London-based studio, TVC, and the project got off the ground.

Teething Problems

Although several top writers were brought in to provide story treatment, they also had to gain the approval of the Beatles' manager, Brian Epstein, who was notoriously difficult. Tom Stoppard, Ian la Frenais and Joe Orton were considered to help construct a story; even *Catch 22* author Joseph Heller had a stab at scripting it, only to be met by Epstein's indifference. Finally the writing settled on a Yale academic, Erich Segal. He was asked to provide a screenplay, but even then, Liverpool poet Roger McGough was later called in to help iron it out.

Although the Beatles supplied four new songs for the voyage, they maintained their lack of enthusiasm for the project. This complacency was founded on their disappointment with the television series which, although popular with the viewers, fell short of expectations. They imagined the feature to be a prolonged version of what they had seen on the TV screen and were keen to keep their distance. After seeing the completed film, however, the Beatles changed their opinions and have regarded it with fond affection ever since.

Swinging Sixties Style

The illustrator Heinz Edelmann was brought in to lend his kaleidoscopic graphic designs to help capture the essential "flower power" spirit of the Swinging Sixties. Apart from his design of the Beatles themselves, Edelmann created an extraordinary and bizarre collection of monsters and villains, such as the Dreadful Flying Glove; the Snapping Turtle Turk, whose stomach becomes the jaws of a shark; the huge, furry Butterfly Stomper; and the 40-foot-tall Apple Bonkers, who disarm their enemies by dropping huge apples on them from a great height.

The direction, credited to George Dunning, but carried out chiefly by Bob Balser and Jack Stokes, was stylish and experimental. They used everything from traditional animation to photographic montages in the 'Eleanor Rigby' section, plus a sparkling combination of Rotoscope and watercolors for the 'Lucy in the Sky with Diamonds' sequence.

"A Magnificent Pop Trifle"

As the Beatles were busy elsewhere, three Liverpool actors were brought in to supply their voices. Paul Angelis played Ringo, John Clive was John Lennon, Geoff Hughes was Paul and a non-actor, Peter Batten, was heard as George. Al Brodax had tried to get the actors

© George Dunning/TVC London

Flying Man

Flying Man was a witty and technically innovative film made by George Dunning in 1962. Using his experimental impulses, he delineated characters and props – a man who can fly, a man who cannot, a coat, a dog – through loose watercolour brushstrokes floating in space without any defining lines. The film won the Grand Prix at Annecy's International Animation Festival.

George Dunning and the National Film Board of Canada » 160 Richard Williams » 188

© Subafilms Ltd.

Yellow Submarine

Yellow Submarine was the first animated feature to star real people in animated form. It famously went into production without a final script, or a final storyboard. Pre-production and development lasted 13 months, running through 14 different script drafts and utilizing 40 animators and 140 technical staff. The actual shooting period was then condensed into a frantic 11-month schedule.

to moderate their Liverpool accents to a "transatlantic" sound, as he was under the impression that no American would be able to understand them. The actors stuck to their guns, however, and remained determinedly Liverpudlian.

To help the fun along there are many in-jokes to spot along the way: the US Cavalry riding to the rescue, guest appearances by King Features' own comic-strip characters, Frankenstein's monster, King Kong, Albert Einstein, reference to the Hamlet cigar commercials and even mention of the Rolling Stones, who were considered as rivals in those days. The Chief Meanie's accomplice is called Blue Max after a coveted World War One medal and a recent award-winning movie.

The whole production was completed within a year in London and the US and within a budget of one million dollars, far less than the normal cost at that time for such an immense project. Once described as "a magnificent pop trifle", *Yellow Submarine*'s vivid colors, psychedelic designs and use of the Beatles' popular melodies amounted to a sure-fire success, and outshone anything else that was on on the screens in that era.

BRUNO BOZZETTO

When the award-winning Italian animator Bruno Bozzetto (b. 1938) first decided to venture into the world of animated films, the "home-grown" cartoon was practically unheard of in Italy. Inspired by the simple graphics of the Disney short *Toot, Whistle, Plunk and Boom*, the amateur film-maker sat down to make his own creations with homemade equipment constructed by his father.

Critical Success

With his first experimental film completed, *Tapum! La Storia Delle Armi* ('Tapum! The Story of Weapons', 1958), he considered it worthwhile enough to have it entered at the Cannes Film Festival. Greeted by a favorable review from the Italian critic Pietro Bianchi, this was encouragement enough for the young Bruno to make more shorts for his own enjoyment.

Tapum! was followed by *The History of Inventions* (1959) and *Alpha-Omega* (1960), all accomplished in his spare time while concurrently pursuing an education in law and later in geology, with Bozzetto displaying little interest in either. When his schooling was over, Bozzetto plunged headlong into the world of advertising, which allowed him to indulge in a sideline of making funny entertainment shorts.

A Foray into Features

Attracted by the unknown territory of feature-films, he soon completed his first hand-drawn feature, *West and Soda* (1965), which simultaneously satirized and paid homage to American Westerns. Acquiring a taste for feature cartoons, Bozzetto soon completed another, *VIP, Mio Fratello Superuomo* ('VIP, My Superhuman Brother', 1968), which envisioned a whole household of comic strip superheroes.

Along the way, the Milanese film-maker also found the time to craft a series of amusing and entertaining shorts for Italian television, centered around the ill-fated Mr Rossi, the luckless protagonist. The resourceful bourgeois is for ever seen as an innocent battling against the elements, whether it be on a camping trip, at the seaside, on a trip to Venice, with a new car or even in the Milan traffic. Whatever the situation, Rossi just cannot win.

Often taken with a pinch of bitter irony, Bozzetto's product can usually make us look at ourselves, and *Sottaceti* ('Pickles', 1971) was no exception, presenting a collection of themes as disparate as hunger, electricity, war and military victories. Made with Bozzetto's constant right-hand man Guido Manuli (b. 1939), *Opera* (1973) mercilessly knocks down the age-old traditions by poking fun at Italian lyric opera, resulting in an uproarious string of high-class musical blackout gags. This won him the prize for films for youth at the Annecy Animation Festival.

Tapum!

Made when Bozzetto was 20, this short brought him to international recognition. To make it, he used rudimentary equipment, propping his camera up on an ironing-board while he worked.

Mr Rossi

Bozzetto's hapless middle-aged character brought him great success: Mr Rossi is a man in whom most of the audience regonizes itself. Bozzetto made numerous shorts and three feature films chronicling the mishaps, small triumphs and adventures of Mr Rossi and his dog Harold,

© Bruno Bozzetto

A Talented Team

Bozzetto's films have always been loyally supported by an equally valuable production staff, including storyman Guido Manuli; scene designers Giovanni Mulazzani and Giancarlo Cereda; animators Giuseppe Laganà, Sergio Chesani and Franco Martelli; film editor Giancarlo Rossi; and cinematographer Luciano Marzetti, among countless other talents.

By the late 1970s he had completed the third of his animated features, *Allegro Non Troppo* (1977). This film embodies much irony and a dash of violence, allowing Bozzetto to vent his own particular brand of quirky outrage by touching the untouchable with this parody of Disney's *Fantasia*. *Allegro* contains half-a-dozen musical fables of modern-day Italy set to the music of Debussy, Dvorák, Ravel, Sibelius, Vivaldi and Stravinsky.

A Varied Output

Soon to follow was the much cherished *Striptease* (1977) in which a live-action striptease artiste shows the effect she can have on an animated audience. *La Piscina* ('The Swimming Pool', 1978) involves fragmented blackout gags with swimmers.

Helping to boost the Olympic Games, Bozzetto's *Sigmund* (1985) conveys the imagination of a small boy watching the Olympics on television. With each event, he becomes the athlete he sees, until his mother tells him to turn it off... and from that point, Sigmund (Freud) begins his fascination with psychoanalysis.

Although his foundation lies in slapstick, Bruno Bozzetto's humor also carries an edge of bitter irony to it, revealing a pointed wit that seems even more prevalent in the twenty-first century. Still involved with cartoon production, Bozzetto's output has lessened in recent years – but his work still retains a satirical bite.

West and Soda

In this film, Bozzetto both satirized and paid homage to the American Western. A sleepy desert town, a nasty local land-baron, a damsel in distress and a lonesome cow-poke all feature in this perennial struggle over the territories of the land and the heart.

© Bruno Bozzetto

Allegro Non Troppo » 254

ASTÉRIX

In the late 1950s, René Goscinny and Albert Underzo founded *Pilote*, a new magazine that appeared on the newsstands for the first time on October 29, 1959. Notably this issue featured the first appearance of a powerful little mustachioed character whose popularity was soon to sweep the country: Astérix, Champion of the Gauls.

René Goscinny

Writer René Goscinny (1926–77) was born in Paris, although his parents soon moved to Argentina where he was educated in Buenos Aires. At the age of 17 he secured a job as an assistant book-keeper but, dissatisfied with that, he moved to New York in 1945 and spent three years working for an import and export firm.

Finally realizing what he wanted to do, Goscinny managed to get a job in an art studio, where he rubbed shoulders with cartoonists Harvey Kurtzman, Will Elder and John Severin. Here he also met Belgian artists Jijé (Joseph Gillian) and Morris (Maurice de Bevère), who asked him if he would like to be the scriptwriter for the new cowboy comic strip *Lucky Luke*.

Albert Underzo

Albert Underzo (b. 1927), a Frenchman of Italian parentage, started creating comics for fashionable magazines at the age of 19. Interrupted by his military service, Underzo continued his artistic career for International Press. It was in this position that, in 1951, he became acquainted with Jean-Michel Charlier and René Goscinny, and he and René combined their talents by producing several series of comic strips together.

After a struggling start at *Pilote*, Georges Dargaud, the French representative for *Kuifje*, took over the running of the magazine. He appointed Goscinny as editor-in-chief and never looked back. The publication of the stories in albums proved more of a financial success than the magazine, and a turning point came in 1965 with *Astérix et Cléopâtre* ('Astérix and Cleopatra'). The combination of Goscinny's fun, visual jokes and outrageous puns,

Astérix et Cleopâtre

In the 1960s, Belvision, which made this film, was one of Europe's largest animation studios, and transformed many comic strips to feature-length animation, including this one. This delicate transformation was not always made without a clash, and while they were too literal and graphically hybrid, they had a certain charm and garnered remarkable success.

© Belvision

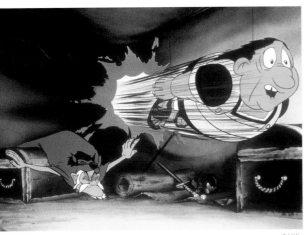

The Big Fight: flying man

This was based on two popular Astérix comic books: *Astérix and the Big Fight* and *Astérix and the Soothsayer*.

The Big Fight: Astérix

Numerous versions of this film were made for the different language markets (French, English and German) and featured different voice artists accordingly.

coupled with Underzo's meticulous attention to detail on subjects such as history, architecture and uniforms, amounted to a hit.

Gallic Strength

The character of Astérix is a feisty Frenchman living in Roman France. He is the Gallic counterpart of Popeye the Sailor, inasmuch as he is strong and lives on his wits, but with a little bit of extra strength courtesy of a Druid's magic potion. The Gauls' community is centered around a meager village where they try to live in peaceful harmony, but are forever being pestered by the invading Roman legions. Julius Caesar is the chief thorn in the side of the villagers and vice versa. Caesar wants to conquer Gaul, and this tiny village and its inhabitants are the only things that stand in his way of making the country part of the Roman Empire.

Astérix's oversized buddy, Obelix, is rumored to have fallen into the Druid's pot of magic potion as a child, thus providing him with an immutable strength. Together, these two set out with Obelix's dog, Dogmatix, to travel the world and prevent the Romans from taking it for themselves.

Big-Screen Success

In the late 1960s, an animated feature was produced by Belvision, a production company dedicated to cinema and television production. Their first adaptation was *Astérix le Gaulois* ('Astérix the Gaul', 1967). Originally intended for television viewing but finally released theatrically, it introduced Astérix and his loyal, lumbering companion Obelix, who began sorting out the Romans for the first time on screen. A year later there was another adaptation of a story first published in 1965, *Astérix et Cléopâtre* ('Astérix and Cleopatra', 1968) in which our heroes voyage to Egypt to assist in the building of the queen's desert palace.

In 1973, publisher Dargaud left Belvision to form the animation studio Idéfix under the direction of Henri Gruel and Pierre Watrin. This resulted in a third feature, an adaptation of *Les Douze Travaux d' Astérix* ('The Twelve Labours of Astérix', 1975), enlarging on the original story. More features were to follow including *Astérix in Britain* (1986) and *Le Coup de Menhir* ('Astérix and the Big Fight', 1989).

Although the animated versions were faithful to the stories and captured the art style, they had nowhere near as much vibrancy as Goscinny's and Underzo's originals. With Goscinny's death in 1977, Underzo took on the dual tasks of writing and drawing and has been doing so ever since.

Raymond Briggs and *The Snowman* » 280

The late 1950s to 1970s was a golden age for Zagreb animation, a combination of outstanding animators and highly original storylines, with Dusan Vukotic winning an Oscar for his short *Ersatz* (a.k.a. *Substitute*) in 1962.

Sharp Shorts

In their message, many of the animated shorts from Zagreb Film had a dark, comic edge to them, often with a less than happy ending. In Borivoj Dovnikovic's (b. 1930) *The Ceremony* (1965), six people are grouped and regrouped in front of a wall as if for a photograph. The punch line is that they are being lined up for execution. Ante Zaninovic's *The Wall* (1965) is a take on the Sisyphus story of the mythical king condemned in Hades to roll a heavy stone endlessly uphill that constantly rolls down again; in this version, instead of rocks up a hill, wall after wall blocks the man's way. The struggle to get past the wall costs the man his life, only to reveal another wall blocking the path of the next person to appear.

In *Holes and Corks* (1966), Zaninovic's story of a man's persistent battle with the forces of nature, success only breeds further failure. In *Mask of the Red Death* (1970), based on the Edgar Allan Poe story, a plague devastates the world. Inside the castle, Count Prospero and his decadent court continue their orgies, but the plague then takes a mysterious form to do its evil work inside the court as well.

Even many buoyantly comic films from Zagreb had an ironic, if not downright pessimistic, conclusion. In *The Fifth One* (1964), for example, Pavao Stalter takes a humorous look at human stubbornness. A harmonious quartet confronts an indestructible pest – the trumpet player.

Bordo Dovnikovic

Borivoj Dovnikovic, or "Bordo", became the studio's premier creator of the gag cartoon. Bordo perfected the art of using a limited-animation style to illustrate the humanity of everyday people going about their everyday lives. Perhaps his best-known work was *Curiosity* (1966), about a group of people, each with his or her own idea about what might be inside a paper bag held by a man on a park bench. It turns out the bag is empty, of course. In his 1968 military satire *Krek*, a soldier, hounded by his superior, has the last laugh by taking a stroll around the world. Other classics include *The Flower Lovers* (1970), about the invention of explosive flowers that start out as a fad but ultimately blow up everything and everyone, and the surreal *Second Class Passenger* (1974), part

© Pavao Stalter, The Fifth One, Zagreb Film

The Fifth One

One of the studio's pioneering distinctions was that its film-makers wrote, designed and directed their own films, as Pavao Stalter did with *The Fifth One*, pictured. The studio's unique animation style which became known as "the Zagreb school" developed as film-makers were allowed to pursue their own visions and maintain control over their work.

© Borivoj Dovnikovic, Curiosity, Zagreb Film

Curiosity

Director Bordo Dovnikovic was known for combining humor with an acute understanding of human psychology. *Curiosity* is about human curiosity – an affliction for which no cure has ever been found. This short won the First Prize for Animated Film in Leipzig in 1967.

Foundation of the Zagreb Studio » 138

The Flower Lovers

Common to many of Bordo's films is the theme of survival in impossible situations. The protagonist is usually an ordinary person trying to enjoy a life with privacy and respect in a society that is continually harassing her or him, for example surviving in a city gone mad through an obsession with exploding flowers in *The Flower Lovers*.

The Bird and the Worm

A scene from Grgic's series for children, one of many that he produced.

slapstick, part philosophy. Some of his later work includes *Learning to Walk* (1978), which tells the story of a man whose countrymen each try to teach him their own style of walking, although he already knows how to walk just fine, and *Exciting Love Story* (1989), in which a man is in search of his sweetheart, Gloria.

Zlatko Grgic

Another of Zagreb's comic masters was Zlatko Grgic (1931–88), whose debut film in 1965 at the age of 20 was *The Devil's Work*. It demonstrated his comedic talents at their best, as a well-meaning fellow learns to appreciate the benefits of "devilish" behavior. His other films included *Little and Big* (1966), his take on the classic cartoon chase; *Musical Pig* (1966), a comical story of an operatic pig that finally finds a friend but at a steep price (he's eaten); and *The Bird and the Worm*, a *Pink Panther*-like series for children. Other animated characters for children included Grgic's whimsical canine, MaxiCat, and the popular Professor Balthazar series. In the late 1960s, Grgic moved to Canada and switched to advertising films and university teaching.

ZAGREB IN THE 1960s: MOVING ON

The Zagreb studio gave its animators a remarkable degree of independence, which in the hands of many artists resulted in very personal films. Nedeljko Dragic was a well-known cartoonist and became one of Zagreb Film's most acclaimed artists. He made widely divergent films, but always with a very distinctive voice. His first film, *Elegy* (1965), was based on one of his comic strips. A prisoner stares sadly into a courtyard from behind the bars of his cell's small window. As the years go by, the growth of a single red flower gives him hope. In a later film, *Way to Your Neighbor* (1981), Dragic perfectly set up his punch line as a man dresses for just another day at the office, only to climb into a tank at the end of the film.

Animation for Adults

Many of the animated films from Zagreb were decidedly not for children. *The Fly* (1967), for example, by the successful team of Aleksandar Marks and Vladimir Jutrisa, was a Kafka-like tale about a man and a fly butting heads, but ending up as equals. Some later films, like *Plop* (1987), directed by one of Zagreb's zaniest animators, Zlatko Pavlinic, use nudity as part of the element of surprise. In this one a man picks up a girl in a bar and takes her home, expecting her to do his housework: he's in for a big surprise. In *Dream Doll* (1979), a remarkable collaboration between Zlatko Grgic and the British animator Bob Godfrey, a man falls in love with a blow-up doll.

International Hits

Other films, like *Satiemania* (1978) by Zdenko Gasparovic, and later *Album* (1983), by Kresimir Zimonic, are sophisticated renditions of the artist's personal musings. Based on the music of Eric Satie, *Satiemania* remains one of Zagreb's most internationally acclaimed films. It portrays the jungle of the big city – the supermarket, brothels and bars, and the ripple of water in simultaneous harmony and conflict – all moving to the mocking but lyrical music of Eric Satie. In *Album*, a young girl's childhood memories come to life as she thumbs through her family photograph album. Both *Satiemania* and *Dream Doll* were nominated for Oscars. Oscar-winning Dusan Vukotic also collaborated on other animators' films. For example, he wrote *Last Waltz in Old Mill* (1995), which was drawn and directed by Darko Krec.

While a limited-animation style was Zagreb Film's trademark, the fact that the films were artist-driven meant that animators were also free to break this convention. Films like *Satiemania*, *Album*, and *Diary* (1974) by Nedeljko Dragic, for example, are notable for their bold colors, full animation and lack of subtlety.

End of an Era

The studio began to decline in the 1980s for a variety of reasons. First of all, there was a loss of talent. Vlado Kristl left for Germany in the 1960s. Vatroslav Mimica went back to

Elegy

Nedeljko Dragic's touching short about a prisoner who regards the growth of a red flower beneath his window as a ray of hope won numerous prizes, including a Diploma in Venice, 1966.

© Nedeljko Dragic. Elegy. Zagreb Film

© Zdenko Gasparovic, Satiemania, Zagreb Film

making feature films, while Dusan Vukotic became increasingly interested in making feature films. Dragutin Vunak also left the studio. In an attempt to take advantage of its international reputation, the studio also began concentrating on more commercial work, including television series co-productions with Germany and Canada. The result was that independent films were not given as much priority and the new generation of animators simply could not maintain the high standards of their predecessors.

Nevertheless, a number of award-winning films were made during this period, including *Skyscraper* (1981) by Josko Marusi, two films by Bordo Dovnikovic: *One Day of Life* (1982) and *Exciting Love Story*, and three films by Nedeljko Dragic: *Way to Your Neighbor*, *The Day I Stopped Smoking* (1982) and *Pictures from Memory* (1989).

What Does the Future Hold?

Like all the animation studios of Eastern Europe, Zagreb Film had trouble adjusting to a market economy after the fall of Communism. It also had its own unique problems, of course, due to the violent break up of Yugoslavia in the early 1990s. One of the few young animators during these years to create distinctive cartoons with ties to the old school was Josko Marusic. *Fisheye* (1980) is his metaphor of how the normal order of things sometimes goes awry, as one night the fish take control of a village.

In recent years Zagreb Film has gone through a series of studio directors, but remains intent on restoring some of its past luster as it continues its attempts to attract co-productions with the West. The studio is also looking to its past, successfully beginning to distribute its significant library of animation shorts.

© Kresimir Zimonic, Album, Zagreb Film

Satiemania

This is a fireworks of techniques and moods accompanied by the piano music of Eric Satie. Each frame could easily stand on its own as a drawing or a painting. Film-makers, such as Zdenko Gasparovi, were deeply rooted in the fine arts, having attended the Zagreb Academy of Fine Arts. This influence, together with an interest in expressionism, pop art and surrealism, and writers such as Freud, Kafka, Camus, that produced animated films of this nature.

Album

Drawn in the style of Frence adult cartoons, Kresimir Zimonic's film about a young girl's childhood memories coming to life as she leafs through her family photograph album won the Best Debut Film award at Annecy in 1983.

PANNONIA FILM STUDIO

In 1948, after the Hungarian film industry was nationalized, animation slowly began to emerge. Even so, until around 1959 the output was limited to about one animated film every one or two years. The few films that were made — including Hungary's first color film in 1951, *The Little Cock's Diamond Halfpenny* by Gyula Macskássy and Edit Fekete — were aimed solely at children. These generic films used folk tales to teach children lessons about morality.

New Directions

Until the mid-1950s, Mafilm Newsreel and Documentary Studio controlled Hungarian animation production. In 1954, Mafilm was incorporated into Hungarian Synchronisation Co., and in 1959, the animation department became the Pannonia Film Studio.

As with many countries, the 1960s signaled a new direction for Hungarian animation in both form and content. Under the guidance of Gyorgy Matolcsy, Pannonia Film produced an assortment of quality children's productions, but more importantly, they also began to create films dealing with larger philosophical, intellectual and social ideas.

International Acclaim

Pannonia first captured international attention in 1960 with award-winning productions *Pencil and India Rubber* (1960) and *Duel* (1960), by Gyula Macskássy. *Duel* — which tells the story of the long struggle between war and peace through the figures of a Greek warrior and a scientist — was awarded the jury's special prize at Cannes. In 1961, Tibor Csermák's *The Ball with White Dots* won the Golden Lion Prize in Venice. The real turning point, however, was József Nepp's *Passion* (1961), which, by using caricature, was the first Hungarian animation to steer away from folk tales and deal with the challenges and issues of contemporary Hungary.

Mézga Family

This funny series was created by József Nepp in 1968, and was widely acclaimed.

© Pannonia Film

Hugarian Animation in the 1930s » 50 John Halas » 104

Passion

This short helped change the face of Hungarian animation. No longer just concerned with retelling old stories, absurd, morbid or black-humored animation explored the everyday issues facing the individual. In *Passion*, a passionate smoker sees the world differently a few hours after the doctor warns him sternly not to smoke anymore.

Doctor Bubó

This wise owl, Doctor Bubó from the series *Next, Please!*, created by József Nepp, cured his patients' ailments on a psychological basis, assisted by Ursula the bear-nurse. The ailments were mostly neuroses, such as kleptomania and megalomania.

József Nepp

József Nepp followed in the footsteps of animator Gyula Macskássy, who helped found Pannonia Studios. Macskássy set up his own studio in Budapest in 1932 where he worked with John Halas and George Pal, among others. After Pannonia was established in 1959, the next generation of animators, including Nepp, continued the work begun by Macskássy and his peers.

During the 1960s, Pannonia also excelled in the creation of cartoon series. Their first attempt was an eight-episode series called *Arthur* (1961) for an American production company. *Arthur* encouraged the studio to produce a Hungarian-based series, and in 1962 they made *Peter and the Robot*, which led to a series called *Peter's Adventures*, which ran from 1963–67. In each episode, Peter battled with a new technology.

Gustavus

Along with a puppet series called *Memoirs of a World Famous Hunter* (1968) by Ottó Foky and István Imre, Pannonia produced the highly popular *Gustavus* series. *Gustavus*, based on József Nepp's *Passion*, followed the misadventures of an ambitious and lovable loser. *Gustavus* was a huge success and became known in more than 70 countries. From 1964 through to the 1970s, Pannonia produced over 160 episodes. Most significantly, *Gustavus* debuted the next generation of Hungarian animators, including Attila Dargay, József Nepp, József Gémes, Tamás Szabó Sípos, Béla Ternovszky and Marcell Jankovics.

The studio also continued to produce an array of technically and conceptually ambitious short films, including György Kovásznai's animated oil-paint film *Double Portrait*, an unusual film showing the heads of a man and woman changing and developing. They also produced Sándor Reisenbüchler's highly original collage debut *Kidnapping of the Sun and the Moon*, based on Hungarian folk art and a poem by Ferenc Juhász. The works of Reisenbüchler and Kovásznai injected Hungarian animation with an element of lyricism and graphic complexity that had not been explored before.

A Dark Side

If there is a dominating tendency or characteristic of Pannonia's output of this era it is the use – not unlike that of Zagreb or Estonia – of a dark, sarcastic and often absurd humor to examine and criticize individual life in modern Hungary. Films of this genre include *Five Minutes of Murder* (1966) by József Nepp, *Ten Dekagrams of Immortality* (1966) by Gyula Macskássy and György Várnai, *Concertissimo* (1968) by József Gémes and *A Ceremonial Opening of a Bridge* (1969) by Marcell Jankovics (b. 1941).

In 1968, Hungary underwent a series of economic reforms that put an end to Stalin's rigid state-planning system and gave businesses more independence. With these new reforms, Pannonia now not only had to worry about the quality of their work, but they also had to find a market for it.

Pannonia and Marcell Jankovics » 258

GENE DEITCH

One day in October 1959, William L. Snyder, the one-man Rembrandt Films, walked into the office of Gene Deitch. Puffing on his signature Cuban cigar, Snyder proceeded to deliver one of the great sales jobs of the Cold War. "I'm told you're the best animation director in New York," Snyder told him. "I want you to go to my studios in Prague to take care of a few things for me."

Deitch laughed, wondering how someone could have an animation studio in Prague, Oklahoma. He was remembering his basic training days in Muskogee, Oklahoma, when he and his army buddies would go to a bar in a nearby hick town named Prague.

"No, not Prague, Oklahoma," said Snyder. "Prague, Czechoslovakia."

On the Move

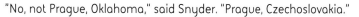

Deitch had recently started his own independent animation company. He had never even had a passport before. The last thing he wanted to do was travel to a Communist country on someone else's lark. But Snyder, who had begun importing films from Prague in the early 1950s and had just begun making cartoons there, made Deitch an irresistible offer. Snyder could not help noticing the storyboards for *Munro*, based on a book by Jules Feiffer, that lined the walls of Deitch's office. If Deitch would travel to Prague to help him to sort out his current problems, Snyder promised to fund the production of *Munro*. Deitch agreed, but only after adding four words to their contract, "for ten days only".

Ten days turned into almost half a century, because Deitch fell in love with Zdena Najmanova, a producer at the Czech animation studio. They married, and Deitch has been living in Prague ever since, directing animated children's films exclusively for American clients.

Rising Talent

Deitch already had an impressive résumé even before Snyder sent him to Prague. In 1951 he had been named creative director of the newly established UPA New York studio, where he was responsible for animating the first NBC color peacock. In 1956, he became creative director at CBS-Terrytoons, where he brought in young talent such as Jules Feiffer, R.O. Blechman, Ralph Bakshi and Ernest Pintoff. Under his supervision,

Munro

Munro won Deitch an Oscar in 1960. It was based a cartoon by satirist and cartoonist Jules Feiffer, who developed the character of Munro, a four-year-old-boy drafted into the army by mistake, during his free time while serving in the Signal Corps.

Munro with General

Munro was created in New York at Deitch's studio and animated in Prague. The voice of four-year-old Munro was that of Seth, Deitch's son, who was three at the time the short was made.

© Rembrandt Films

Nudnik

Nudnik was based on a character called Foofle that Gene Deitch first created while at Terrytoons. Foofle was an inept clown who embodied Deitch's own physical clumsiness, but he did not develop the character fully until he arrived in Prague.

Terrytoons created a host of innovative cartoon characters like John Doormat, Clint Clobber, Foofle, Gaston Le Crayon – and, of course, Tom Terrific, who, with Mighty Manfred the Wonder Dog, starred in the first animated series for American network television.

With Rembrandt Films, from 1961 to 1968, Deitch directed films for MGM, Paramount Pictures and King Features, including 13 episodes of *Tom & Jerry*, 26 episodes of *Popeye*, and 52 episodes of *Krazy Kat*. Snyder and Deitch also produced their own cartoons in Prague. Between 1960 and 1964 they received four Academy Award nominations and an Oscar for *Munro*, about a four-year-old boy mistakenly drafted into the United States army. Deitch and Rembrandt Films also pioneered the animation of classic children's books, including Ludwig Bemelmans' *Madeline* series, James Thurber's *Many Moons* and Eve Titus' *Anatole*.

Most of these films were distributed as theatrical shorts by Paramount. They included 12 cartoons starring the irrepressible Nudnik, Deitch's best-known creation during these years. A Yiddish word, *nudnik* literally means "bore", but in American vernacular it means someone who can do nothing right – a nut, a bumbler. Indeed, Deitch's Nudnik is a rubbery-faced hero who tries his best to compete against the overwhelming problems of everyday life.

From Books to Films

Beginning in 1969, Deitch began an ongoing relationship with the Connecticut-based Weston Woods Studios, which adapts high-quality children's picture books into animated films. Included among the long list of prizewinning films Deitch has directed for Weston Woods are those adapted from books by Maurice Sendak (*Where the Wild Things Are* and *In the Night Kitchen*), Tomi Ungere (*The Three Robbers* and others) and Crockett Johnson (*Harold and the Purple Crayon*). More recently, he directed two films adapted from books by his old colleague Jules Feiffer, *Bark, George* and *I Lost My Bear*.

In between films for Weston Woods, Deitch has worked for other producers, including Palm Plus Multimedia, for whom he directed 53 short films adapted from Dick Bruna's Miffy bunny character, and 26 episodes of *Anton*, created by the Danish animator Borge Ring. All of the films by Deitch during these years in Prague were made with his wife Zdena (now Zdena Deitchova), who in 2000 was named head of the Kratky Animation Studio.

Tom Terrific and Manfred Man » 182 Gene Deitch and Czech Aniamation in the 1990s » 328

SOVIET EXPANSION & MATURITY

The return to maturity and experimentation in Russian animation took place in the early 1960s when, thanks in part to the period of liberalism in the Soviet Union known as the "Khrushev spring" or "thaw", Soviet animation broke with the Disney influence of previous generations. More experimental and artistic personal works were created by a new generation of animators, including Fyodor Khitruk, Andrei Khrjanovsky and, later, Yuri Norstein.

Fyodor Khitruk

Fyodor Khitruk (b. 1917) was the major Russian animator of the 1960s, and is perhaps the greatest ever. He started working at Soyuzmultfilm in 1924, where he spent almost 25 years as an animator. He did not make his first film, *Story of One Crime*, until 1961.

Story of One Crime triggered a new era of Soviet animation by dealing with issues of modern life with an innovative graphic style that had more in common with the American studio UPA than with any previous Soviet animation film. The film, about a man who cannot sleep because of his noisy neighbors, was critical of Soviet society and, as such, caused some controversy. However, because of the international recognition being attracted by Soviet animation, largely due to Khitruk's work, animators were given a little more artistic freedom than in other mediums. Khitruk's other satires of this period include *Man in the Frame* (1966) and the widely lauded *Film Film Film* (1968), a hilarious parody of the film-making process in the Soviet Union. Khitruk also made several accomplished children's films, including *Boniface's Vacation* (1965), *Teddy Bear* (1964) and *Winnie the Pooh* (1968).

Andrei Khrjanovsky and Yuri Norstein

A graduate of the Soviet State Film School (VGIK), Andrei Khrjanovsky (b. 1939) began his career at Soyuzmultfilm working for Fyodor Khitruk. It was here that he made his first animation film, *There Lived Kozyavin*, in 1966. As with Khitruk's intention in *Man in the Frame*, Kozyavin offered a critical look at Soviet bureaucracy. The film was shown throughout the Soviet Union to great response, but was not screened abroad. Khrjanovsky's next film, *Glass Harmonica* (1968), a tale about the repression of artistic ambition and freedoms, was banned by Soviet censors, who found the film's ideological message disturbing.

Yuri Norstein (b. 1941) joined Soyuzmultfilm at the age of 20. He worked as an artist and art director on a number of short films and features before making his powerful directorial debut in 1968 with *The 25th: The First Day* (co-directed by Arkady Tiurin). Using previously banned formalistic Russian art and music, Norstein celebrates the first day of the October Revolution. Ironically, Norstein's film was banned for being

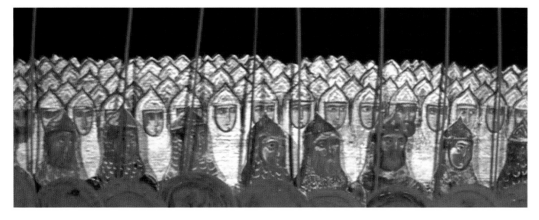

"too formalistic".

In 1970, Norstein collaborated with Ivan Ivanov-Vano on *The Battle of Kerjenets*, made in 70 mm film. Kerjenets uses frescoes and icons to describe Russia's victorious resistance against Tartar invaders. Among the film's many awards was the Grand Prix at the Zagreb Animation Festival in 1972.

In the 1970s Norstein would go on to make a number of outstanding films including *The Heron and the Crane* (1974), *The Hedgehog in the Fog* (1975) and, for some the greatest animation film ever made, *The Tale of Tales* (1979). Dreamlike and transitory images flow throughout the film, representing a mixture of fragmented memories, dreams and visions. *The Tale of Tales* is an astonishing tribute to the imagination, innocence and pain of childhood.

Russian Talent

Other notable contributors of this period include Boris Stepantsev, who made a delightful version of *The Nutcracker* and an award-winning children's film *Petia and Little Red Riding Hood*. Vadim Kurchevsky, who began at Soyuzmultfilm in 1957 as an art director of stop-motion films, made his debut in 1966 with *My Green Crocodile*, a film about the problems of modern love.

Roman Katsanov, who collaborated with Anatoly Karanovich on *The Cloud in Love* (1959), made the award-winning puppet film *The Mitten* (1967) and *Ghena the Crocodile* (1969). Anatoly Petrov was already an established artist and animator when he made his directorial debut with *Singing Teacher* (1968), a film about bureaucrats who stole the ideas of others for their own benefit. It was very popular with Soviet audiences.

In 1969, Viacheslav Kotenochkin, who was an apprentice at Soyuzmultfilm for many years, achieved wild popularity in the Soviet Union with the Road Runner- and Coyote-influenced series *Just You Wait*, which featured a wolf and rabbit involved in much more gentle activities than their American predecessors.

Film Film Film

Fydor Khitruk's first films, from 1961 onward, created films with serious messages, despite the strict censorship of the arts. With a revolutionary new graphic style and dark social criticism, his films, including *Film Film Film*, garnered him great success.

The Battle of Kerjenets

This film uses traditional fresco and icon painting to tell the story of the Russian people's struggle against foreign invaders. Music from Rimsky-Korsakov's opera *The Legend of the Invisible City of Kitezh and the Maiden* gives it a great momentum, with poignant, energetic color to match.

Russian Animation in the 1980s » 290

Toei Doga produced a dozen features between 1960 and 1970. At first these continued the policy of adapting traditional Japanese legends like *The Littlest Warrior* (1961) and *The Little Prince and the Eight-Headed Dragon* (1963). But as Oriental fairy-tale themes failed to win international sales, Toei switched to feature adaptations of European folk tales for foreign sales, and adapting popular sci-fi manga for the domestic market. *Sinbad the Sailor* (1962), *Gulliver's Adventures Beyond the Moon* (1965), *The World of Hans Christian Anderson* (1968) and *Puss in Boots* (1969) are examples of the former. *The Little Norse Prince* (1968) was an original story in the style of Norse mythology.

An experiment with Japanese sci-fi manga was a big success. *Cyborg 009* by Shotaro Ishinomori (1938–98) was made into a theatrical feature in 1966.

It was so popular that a sequel, *Cyborg 009: Fighting Monsters* followed in 1967, and then a 26-episode *Cyborg 009* TV series in 1968. In 1969 and 1970 Toei produced features of Ishinomori's *The Flying Phantom Ship* and *30,000 Miles Under the Sea*.

Television Animation

Japan's first TV animation was Otogi Pro's *Otogi Cartoon Calendar*, a daily series of 312 three-minute educational cartoons from 1962 to1964. Its first significant entertainment animation was Mushi Production Co.'s *Astro Boy* (193 episodes, 1963–67). Osamu Tezuka created Mushi Pro in 1962 to produce TV animation based upon his own popular 1950s manga.

Other notable 1960s TV animation included *Gigantor* (1963), the first sci-fi with a giant robot; *8th Man* (1963) and *Cyborg 009* (1968), on the sci-fi theme of humans bio-engineered into semi-robotic supermen; *Treasure Island Revisited* (1965), the first made-for-TV animated feature (a New Year's Day special); *Kimba the White Lion* (1965), which was the first color TV animation and the first funny animal TV series; *Sally the Little Witch* (1966), the first girls' TV series and the first in a "magical little girls" genre; *Princess Knight* (1967), the first *shojo* (girls' romance)

Speed Racer

Speed Racer was a 1966 creation of Tatsuo Yoshida, the founder of the Tatsunoko Productions studios in 1962. Yoshida had previously been a manga cartoonist, and one of his works was a licensed Japanese version of *Superman*. Yoshida used his American *Superman* art-style for his *Speed Racer* character designs.

Gigantor

Gigantor was a 1963 adaptation of a popular 1950s and 1960s manga and was Japan's first giant-robot animation. Unlike most of his giant-robot successors, Gigantor did not have a human pilot who rode inside him; he was guided instead by a control-box in the hands of boy detective Jimmy Sparks.

The Little Prince and the Eight-Headed Dragon

This was the sixth of Toei Doga's feature-length films. An action-adventure story, it drew on Japanese myth of a young god/prince named Susanoo, who embarks on an adventurous journey to the Underworld to find his dead mother Izanami. Along the way he fights off the Eight-Headed Dragon.

© Toei Doga

series; *Kitaro's* (*Scary Ghost Moan*) (1968), the first series on the theme of traditional Japanese supernatural-horror fantasy (although a comedy); *Sasuke* and *The Detective Stories of Sabu and Ichi* (1968), the first two significant series in the sixteenth–nineteenth century "samurai-ninja" historical-adventure genre; *Mrs Sazae* (1969), the first domestic comedy for housewives (still in production; it is the longest running animated TV series in the world); *Attack No. 1* (1969), the first sports-themed series (girls' school volleyball); and *Tomorrow's Joe* (1970), the first boys' sports series (boxing).

Many later prominent animators and animation directors began their careers during this decade, including Gisaburo Sugii (b. 1940), Rintaro (Shigeyuki Hayashi, b. 1941), Yoshiyuki Tomino (b. 1941) and Osamu Dezaki (b. 1943).

Independent and Art Animation

In 1960 Tadahito Mochinaga created the M.O.M. Production Co. to produce puppet animation for America's Rankin/Bass. These ranged from TV series such as *The New Adventures of Pinocchio* (1960) and TV specials like *Rudolph the Red-Nosed Reindeer* (1964) to the theatrical feature *Mad Monster Party* (1967).

After Mochinaga's retirement in 1967, his staff (Takeo Nakamura, Koichi Oikawa and Tadanari Okamoto) kept together as Video Tokyo Productions, producing puppet and cut-paper animation. Many of their puppet-art films in the traditional Japanese *bunraku* style, such as Nakamura's *Torayan on the Boat* (1970), won international film-festival awards.

Japan's second animator to gain international acclaim through frequent worldwide festival screenings was Yoji Kuri (b. 1928). His cartoon shorts such as *The Human Zoo* (1962), *The Chair* (1962), *Samurai* (1965), *The Maniac Age* (1967) and *Flower* (1967) were short (often less than five minutes), sardonic line-art squiggles that influenced such animators as Canada's Richard Condie.

Two more notable animators were Sadao Tsukioka (b. 1939) and Tatsuo Shimamura (b. 1934). Tsukioka was the director of Toei's first TV animated series, *Ken the Wolf Boy* (1963–65); then he moved to Osamu Tezuka's Mushi Pro, where he worked on many TV series. Tezuka encouraged him to make his own art films, using Mushi's facilities, such as *Cigarettes and Ashes* and *The Story of Man*.

Shimamura also began as a Toei animator in 1958, but soon left to work independently. His films include *A Moonlit Night and Eyeglasses* (1966), *Fantasy City* (1967), *Love* (1970) and *A Fantasy of Flames* (1989).

It was during the late 1960s that the word "anime" (from the American and European words for animation) began to replace the Japanese word "doga" (moving drawings) in common usage.

Osamu Tezuka (1928–89), honored with such titles as "the God of Comics" *(Manga no Kamisama)* and "the Disney of Japan", was born in Osaka to a medical family. It was assumed that he would become a doctor (and he did obtain his doctorate in medicine in 1961, although he never practiced), but while at Osaka University he began his first published comic strip in 1946. In 1947 his *New Treasure Island* became a best-selling manga and revolutionized the Japanese manga industry by its use of cinematic art direction, such as dramatic camera angles, pans and close-ups instead of static imagery. Tezuka acknowledged the influence of American animation by Disney and the Fleischers, as well as Wan Bros.' *Princess with the Iron Fan* and Seo's wartime *Momotaro* films.

A Multitude of Influences

Beginning in the 1950s Tezuka became Japan's leading comic-book creator, in both popularity and influence. He was incredibly prolific, creating an estimated 150,000 pages of manga art during his lifetime. He created for all genres throughout the 1980s, including comics (and picture books) for infants; boys' adventure; girls' romantic fantasy; adult drama, including political thrillers; adult erotic humor and drama; cartoon adaptations of classic literature, such as Dostoyevsky's *Crime and Punishment*, and biography, such as the lives of Beethoven and the Buddha; and sci-fi as social satire. He actively promoted the concept that cartoon art is not a medium merely for children's entertainment. Tezuka became a celebrity by the mid-1950s, appearing in magazine articles and on TV as Japan's highest-earning artist of the decade.

In 1959 Toei Doga began a theatrical feature adaptation of Tezuka's *My Son Goku* (manga serialization, 1952–59), his take on the Chinese Monkey King legend. Tezuka was named a co-director, and although he later said his association with *Alakazam the Great* (1960) was more for publicity than actual production, it did inspire him to create his own animation studio. He felt that he could match the quality of the American new limited-animation TV cartoons, and he had his own 10-year backlog of popular manga to draw upon.

Mushi Production Company

Tezuka's Mushi Production Co., Ltd. was created during 1962. Its first work was the arty *Stories on a Street Corner* (1962) for the Mainichi Film Festival. Its next was the New Year's Day 1963 premiere of the TV cartoon animated *Astro Boy* (syndicated in the US beginning September 1963). It was an immense success, running for four years with

Pictures at an Exhibition

Tezuka's response to Disney's *Fantasia* used the 10 musical sequences of Mussorgsky's *Pictures at an Exhibition* as accompaniment to artistic satires of modern themes such as "War", "Politics", "Capitalism", and "Vapid Media Personalities".

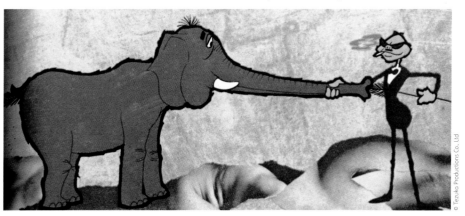

Astro Boy

Created by Dr Tenma (Dr Boynton) to replace his dead son, Astro Boy was sold to a robot circus when the inventor realized he could never grow up like a real boy. He was rescued from abuse by Ringmaster Hamegg (Cacciatore) by kindly Dr Ochanomizu (Elefun), who helped Astro Boy develop his human characteristics and use his powers against evil and for humankind, but also to stand up for "robot rights" against anti-robot prejudice. Tezuka was a pioneer in using his popular cartoons to advocate equal rights for all humanity. The original 1963–66 *Astro Boy* TV series was remade in 1980–81 and again in 2003–04.

© Tezuka Productions Co., Ltd

The Thousand and One Nights

This was Tezuka's first theatrical, feature-length animated movie. It was intended to bring anime to international attention, and was a major undertaking for the studio. 70,000 drawings were used in its creation and thousands of staff were involved. The soundtrack was mostly rock music, another ploy to guarantee its success on the world market.

© Tezuka Productions Co., Ltd

193 weekly episodes, and jump-starting Japan's TV-animation industry.

Mushi Production Co. was a major animation studio throughout the 1960s. In addition to animating adaptations of his own manga, Tezuka produced TV cartoon series of several other cartoonists' works. He also experimented with puppet animation, like *Boys' Space Patrol* (1963), and combined live-action with cartoon animation, as in *Vampire* (1968). His *Kimba the White Lion*, Japan's first color TV animation, was partly subsidized by the US's NBC. Mushi's most prominent director was Eiichi Yamamoto (b. 1936), who Tezuka had hired away from Otogi Pro because of his expertise in high-quality animation.

Tezuka was interested in exploring animation as an art form. He wrote and produced several experimental films, from *Memory* and *Mermaid* (five minutes each, both 1964) to the 34-minute *Pictures at an Exhibition* (1966). Tezuka was determined to produce sophisticated, feature-length animated films for theatrical release, again to emphasize that animation was not just for children.

New Directions

The Thousand and One Nights (1969) and *Cleopatra* (1970), both directed by Yamamoto, were brilliantly innovative and erotic, but they bewildered the critics and bankrupted Mushi Pro. Tezuka left in 1971 to start Tezuka Production Co., while Mushi staggered on until 1973, with Yamamoto completing its final art film, *The Tragedy of Belladonna*.

Tezuka had no regrets. His Tezuka Production Co. produced an annual cartoon TV movie for NTV from the late 1970s to the late 1980s, as well as the 1980 theatrical feature *Phoenix 2772* and a 1980–81 color remake of his *Astro Boy* TV series.

Tezuka did not keep it a secret that he considered these primarily as commercial works. He was proud of the independent animated shorts that he wrote, storyboarded and co-directed for personal presentation at international film festivals. Notable among these were *Jumping* (1984), *Broken Down Film* (1985) and *Legend of the Forest* (1987). Tezuka's final appearance, three months before his death, was at the November 1988 first Shanghai International Animation Festival, where he was one of the judges.

Miyazaki and Otomo » 296

HAVOC IN HEAVEN

The artistic development of the Shanghai Animation Studio continued from 1961 until 1964. Overshadowing all else was China's second animated feature, *Havoc in Heaven*. This was directed by Wan Lai-ming as a follow-up to *Princess with the Iron Fan*, although it is from an earlier section of Wu Cheng-en's sixteenth-century novelization of the Monkey King legend.

Retelling a Legend

Sun Wu Kong, the Monkey King, causes so much mischief on Earth that the Heavenly Court decides to sidetrack him by offering him a supposedly prestigious but actually demeaning job in heaven. Monkey discovers that he has been tricked and goes on a rampage, defeating several heavenly generals before returning to his Earthly home at Flower and Fruit Mountain. Wan directed this 106-minute cel animation feature in the stylized yet energetic manner of the Beijing Opera Company's gymnastic performances

Havoc in Heaven – fighting

Based on a well-known episode from the classic, *Journey to the West*, *Havoc in Heaven* is an 11,000 foot-long animation, containing beautiful drawings and supernatural feats. Sun Wu Kong, the Monkey King, an enduring symbol of intelligence, courage and free will in Chinese culture, travels between Heaven and Earth, causing much uproar along the way.

© Shanghai Animation Film Studio

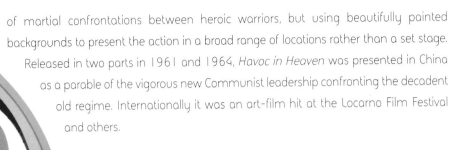

of martial confrontations between heroic warriors, but using beautifully painted backgrounds to present the action in a broad range of locations rather than a set stage. Released in two parts in 1961 and 1964, *Havoc in Heaven* was presented in China as a parable of the vigorous new Communist leadership confronting the decadent old regime. Internationally it was an art-film hit at the Locarno Film Festival and others.

Beginnings of the Cultural Revolution

Other notable cel animated films included *A Golden Dream* (1963) by Wang Shu-chen (1931–91), which heralded the Cultural Revolution by presenting Chinese peasants being oppressed by a haughty general, a tax collector and an intellectual; and *Two Heroic Sisters of the Grasslands* (1964), by Qian Yun-da (b. 1929) and Tang Chen, about little shepherd girls in northern China who save their flock in a blizzard. Te Wei and Qian Jia-jun continued their animation of watercolor brush painting (in the style of famous traditional landscape artist Li Keran, 1907–89) in *Buffalo Boy and the Flute* (1963).

Traditional puppet animation was seen in the feature-length *The Peacock Princess* (1963) by Jin Xi, and *The Cock Crows at Midnight* (1964) by Yiou Lei. Cut-paper animation was represented by Wan Gu-chan's *The Spirit of Ginseng* (1961); by *Wait for Tomorrow* (1962) and *More or Less* (1964), both by Hu Xiong-hua (1931–83); and by *Red Army Bridge* (1964) by Qian Yun-da. The Shanghai studio's first experiment in animating folded-paper figures (best known in the West under its Japanese name, *origami*) was *A Clever Duckling* (1960) by Yu Zhen-guang (1906–91).

Havoc in Heaven – face

This film has broken export records for Chinese animation. In June 1983, nearly 100,000 people saw the film after it premiered in 12 Paris theaters; by 1984, it had been distributed to 44 countries and regions.

© Shanghai Animation Film Studio

Studio Closes Down

All this was brought to a halt in 1964 by the beginnings of the Cultural Revolution. A major new enemy of the Chinese people was revealed to be effete intellectuals out of touch with the masses. Winning prizes at international film festivals was an undeniable sign of intellectualism. Art films such as *Buffalo Boy and the Flute* were denounced as irrelevant to the class struggle. In 1965 the Shanghai Animation Studio was closed and its officers and leading animators sent to re-education camps and peasant villages to experience hard manual labor.

Havoc in Heaven – musical instrument

The completion of *Havoc in Heaven* was all the more satisfactory for Wan Lai-ming because he had been forced to abandon his initial plans for it in the early 1940s. The film won a number of international prizes, including one at the 1978 London Film Festival.

1971–79:

ANIMATION FOR GROWN-UPS

The outrageous Ralph Bakshi made his mark with a string of notorious animated features during this decade. From *Fritz the Cat* and *Heavy Traffic* to the controversial *Coonskin*, the cult-fantasy *Wizards* and his adaptation of *Lord of the Rings*, Bakshi defined adult animation with an audacious grown-up use of the medium. His was a lone voice during this decade as television cartoons became the scapegoat of parent groups, and were stripped of any intelligence, art and fun. Independent animators, such as claymation master Will Vinton and the artists commissioned by the National Film Board of Canada, kept the art form alive in an explosion of inventive and important short subjects.

Bakshi's X- and R-rated features strove to remind the public that animation was not just a medium for children. Others followed his lead, like Charles Swenson's *Dirty Duck*, Martin Rosen's *Watership Down*, René Laloux's *Fantastic Planet* and Bruno Bozzetto's *Allegro Non Troppo*. An audience was found among the college crowd and literate adults, who understood that animation art could be used to challenge conventional thinking, and could take the viewer on a journey no live-action film could challenge.

Picture above: Great © Bob Godfrey. **Pictures clockwise from top left:** Every Child © 1979 National Film Board of Canada; Le Planète Sauvage © Krátký Film Praha, Les Films Armorial, Service de la Recherche ORTF, Ceskoslovensky Filmexport; Hugo the Hippo © Pannonia Film; Great © Bob Godfrey; California Raisins © Will Vinton Studios; Allegro Non Troppo © Bozzetto Film; Bob Godfrey © Bob Godfrey; The Archies © Filmation Associates. **Centre picture:** The Nine Lives of Fritz the Cat © Steve Krantz Productions

RALPH BAKSHI & FRITZ THE CAT

© Aurica Finance Company, Black Ink, Fritz Productions, Steve Krantz Productions

Brooklyn-born Ralph Bakshi (b. 1938) gained international notoriety for the first X-rated animated feature, *Fritz the Cat* (1972), which was based on Robert Crumb's underground comic-book character. It not only established the viability of adult animation, but also was a reminder that feature animation could also be an outlet for personal expression.

Fritz the Cat

Starting life as a character in comics, *Fritz the Cat* only made it to the big screen in 1972 in the first ever X-rated animation feature of the same name. It was only a modest commercial success.

Beginnings

Bakshi began his career in animation at Terrytoons, where he directed such TV series as *Deputy Dawg* and became its creative director when he created *The Mighty Heroes* (1966) series. He then became head of Paramount Cartoon Studios during its final days, where he directed such shorts as *Marvin Digs* (1967) and *Mini Squirts* (1968). He was then hired by Steve Krantz Productions to take over direction and production of the *Rocket Robin Hood* and *Spider-Man* TV series.

Perhaps inspired by the success of George Dunning's *Yellow Submarine*, Krantz produced Bakshi's *Fritz the Cat*, his take on the 1960s counter-culture. Its huge financial success, combined with the controversy over its depiction of sex and drugs, woke people up to the possibilities of an animated film. Critics and moviegoers took it seriously. As Bakshi told Mike Barrier, "They treat it like film."

© Steve Krantz Productions

The Nine Lives of Fritz the Cat

This follow-up to *Fritz the Cat* was released in 1974, but original director Ralph Bakshi was no longer involved. This was the last film to feature Fritz.

Heavy Traffic

Mixing live action with animation, *Heavy Traffic* was released in 1973 to considerable acclaim. Originally X-rated, the film follows a Jewish-Italian man as he grows up in a tough area of New York.

American Pop

Following several generations of a troubled but musically talented family, *American Pop* is an animated guide through music from the pre-jazz age through soul, 1950s rock, drug-laden psychedelia and punk, finally ending with the onset of new wave in the early 1980s.

Mixed Fortunes

Bakshi next made *Heavy Traffic* (1973), which many consider his finest film. In it, he uses the tale of a struggling white cartoonist-animator to depict the underside of life in New York. Enjoying his new-found celebrity, he formed Bakshi Productions and spoke frequently of the expanding possibilities offered to the animation film-maker. However, his next film, *Hey Good Lookin'* (1975), was shelved after some disastrous previews, only to be unsuccessfully revised for release in 1982.

Accusations of racism regarding *Coonskin* (a.k.a. *Street Fight*) (1975), which had its premiere at New York's Museum of Modern Art, caused Paramount Pictures to drop the film, and subsequent distribution was limited.

Bakshi tackled fantasy with *Wizards* (1977), a post-apocalyptic sci-fi fantasy that failed at the box office, he had one of his biggest financial successes with *Lord of the Rings* (1978), which capitalized on the popularity of author J. R. R. Tolkien. However, it was criticized for its extensive use of Rotoscoping, which seemed to rob the visuals of the vitality of his earlier films.

American Pop (1981) was an unsuccessful attempt to provide a picture of American popular music in the twentieth century through the story of a Russian-Jewish family. And the failure of *Fire and Ice* (1983), created with famed fantasy illustrator Frank Frazetta, made Bakshi turn his attention to TV.

Return to Form

It was with the live-action/animated Rolling Stones' 'Harlem Shuffle' music video in 1986 that Bakshi seemed to find himself again. He went on to produce *Mighty Mouse: The New Adventures* (1987–88), the groundbreaking TV series that jump-started the career of John Kricfalusi and laid the groundwork for a renaissance in television animation.

He briefly returned to movies with the poorly received live-action/animated *Cool World* (1992), before returning to TV with the live-action movie *The Cool and the Crazy* (1994). After the short-lived animated sci-fi detective series *Spicy City* (1997), Bakshi left animation and devoted himself to painting.

SATURDAY MORNING BLUES

TV animation in the US was essentially relegated to a Saturday-morning ghetto during the 1970s. Adding to the medium's misery was the development of overseas production – American studios were farming production work mainly to Japan or Australia – and the triumph of various parent groups in their efforts to strip all of the fun from cartoons, essentially removing all slapstick action and comic violence, and injecting educational and pro-social messages into the narratives. Animation was now widely perceived as a children's medium. The poor reputation of Saturday-morning cartoons comes from the programming created during this decade: cheap productions, poor animation and weak writing were aimed at an undiscriminating audience. And on top of all that: Action for Children's Television (ACT).

Imposing Restrictions

ACT grew out of the suburban Boston living room of housewife and mother Peggy Charren, who used her organization to lobby Washington to impose new rules on kids' programming – cartoons in particular. Their voice grew louder as the decade wore on, and their campaign for change was very effective. Soon, network executives began dictating the content of the programming they chose to air. Independent thinking and artistic genius were no longer welcome – Jay Ward, Bob Clampett and other top talents left the field to the remaining cartoon factories: Hanna-Barbera, Filmation, DePatie-Freleng and Rankin-Bass.

Hanna-Barbera's *Scooby-Doo, Where Are You?* premiered in 1969, and became a staple of Saturday-morning TV for the subsequent decade. The program, about a quartet of teenage mystery solvers and their mascot – a fearful, lumbering Great Dane named Scooby-Doo – had the right combination of suspense, laughs and character types to appeal to children at the time.

Scooby-Doo's success led to a succession of similar ideas and derivative series: *Amazing Chan & the Chan Clan* (1972), *Goober and the Ghost Chasers* (1973), *Butch Cassidy and the Sundance Kids* (1973) and *Clue Club* (1976), to name but a few.

Competition

Hanna-Barbera's chief rival at this time was Filmation, which had scored a hit with their rock'n'roll revision of *The Archies* (1968–78). Typical American teenagers Archie Andrews, Veronica Lodge, Betty Cooper and Jughead Jones had been comic book stars for over 20 years when the Filmation series propelled them into even greater fame – a cartoon show that spawned one of the biggest-selling records of 1969, 'Sugar Sugar'.

Hanna-Barbera fought back by adapting another group of Archie Comics stars, *Josie and the Pussy Cats* (1970), which combined rock'n'roll music with *Scooby-*

The Archies

Originally appearing in comic-book form in 1941, *The Archies* featured red-headed Archie Andrews as a "typical" American teenager along with his friends at Riverdale High.

Jughead and Big Ethel

Archie made the transition to the small screen in 1968 in a cartoon series that ran in various incarnations for about 10 years. Popular supporting characters included Jughead Jones and his nemesis, Big Ethel.

Peak of Prime-Time TV » 202 Saturday Morning TV » 204 Animation in Australia » 262

© Filmation Associates

Doo-like mystery – creating the ultimate hybrid cartoon show of the 1970s. For the rest of the decade, the studios took their cues from those elements: a pre-sold character or celebrity teamed with rock music and mystery. The results: *Partridge Family 2200 AD* (1974), *The Brady Kids* (1972), *The Jackson Five* (1971), *The Osmonds* (1972), *Sabrina and the Groovie Goolies* (1970), *The New Adventures of Gilligan* (1974) and *Will the Real Jerry Lewis Please Sit Down?* (1970). Saturday-morning cartoons were at their emptiest, most soulless extreme.

There were some exceptions. *Fat Albert and the Cosby Kids* (Filmation, 1972) was a cartoon with an educational message – but it was inspired by a talented creator, comedian Bill Cosby. With characters you could relate to and strong entertainment values, this series delighted ACT members because it proved that pro-social animation could compete commercially.

Superheroes Return

Superheroes had not lost their appeal, however. Hanna-Barbera picked up DC's costumed characters and refashioned the Justice League as the educator-approved, family-friendly Super Friends. Now, instead of fighting criminal jokers and madmen intent on destroying the world, Superman, Batman, Robin, Aquaman and Wonder Woman would solve mysteries created by well-meaning scientists whose experiments have run amok.

Other 1970s superheroics were performed by the funny animals in *Hong Kong Fooey* (1974), real-life celebrities in *The Harlem Globetrotters* (1970) and *I Am The Greatest: The Adventures of Muhammad Ali* (1977), or other comic-book rivals like *The New Fantastic Four* (1978).

American TV animation lost its promise and sank to new depths during this dark decade. And it would get a lot worse before a new wave in the late 1980s would return its potential. But 1970s series like *Fat Albert* and *Scooby-Doo* – even the Super Friends – have endured the test of time to become kitsch classics to a generation who were raised on them.

The Groovie Goolies

A cartoon series about a group of ghouls and their various adventures at Horrible Hall, *The Groovie Goolies* combined with *Sabrina the Teenage Witch* for a brief series in 1970. Following the demise of *Sabrina and the Goolies*, the two strands became individual programs. The characters of Count Drac, Missy and Wolfie are shown here.

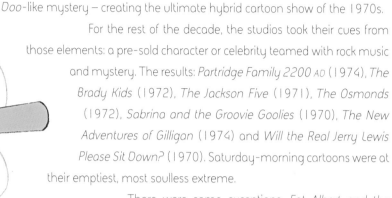

By the early 1960s, the NFB had become known as much for its cartoons as for its experimental films. These cartoons, equal to those of Hollywood's Golden Age, include *The Great Toy Robbery* (1964); Gerald Potterton's *My Financial Career* (1962) and *Christmas Cracker* (1963); Kaj Pindal's comic masterpieces *I Know an Old Lady who Swallowed a Fly* (1964) and *What On Earth!* (1966); *Evolution* (1971); *Propaganda Message* (1974); and Zlatko Grgic's *Hot Stuff* (1971).

An International Flavour

In 1966, the NFB set up a separate French animation studio. Favoring individual expression, by the 1970s the studio had become home to Jacques Drouin, master of pinscreen animation (*Mindscape*, 1976); puppet animator Co Hoedeman (Oscar winner for *Sand Castle*, 1977); Pierre Hebert (*Memories of War*, 1982); Paul Driessen (*An Old Box*, 1975); and Peter Foldes (*The Hunger*, 1974, an early computer animated film).

Born in Seattle, Washington, in 1946, Caroline Leaf joined the French animation studio to direct *The Owl Who Married a Goose* (1974), and also directed *The Street* (1976) for the English studio. Based on Mordecai Richler's short story, Leaf used the technique of animating colored oil on glass directly under the camera. Animating colored sand, Leaf adapted Franz Kafka's *The Metamorphosis of Mr Samsa* in 1977.

Ishu Patel arrived at the NFB in 1970 from India. Working with various techniques directly under the camera, Patel was nominated for two Academy Awards for *Bead Game* (1977) and *Paradise* (1984).

Special Delivery (1978) won directors John Weldon and Eunice Macaulay an Academy Award. The following year the NFB again won an Oscar for *Every Child* (1979), directed by Eugene Fedorenko. The most beloved animated film in Canada is *The Sweater* (1976), directed by Sheldon Cohen and based on Roch Carrier's short story of a young Montreal Canadiens fan forced to wear a Toronto Maple Leafs jersey.

Frederic Back

The NFB was not the only government agency producing animation. Société Radio-Canada had formed an animation department in 1968.

Born in Saarbrucken, Germany, in 1924, Frederic Back joined Société Radio-Canada as a graphic artist in 1952. In 1970 Back directed his first film (with Graeme Ross), *Abracadabra*. He followed this up with *Inon, or the Conquest of Fire* (1972), *The Creation of the Birds* (1973), *Illusion* (1974) and *Taratata* (1976).

With *All-Nothing* (1978) Back began using the technique of animating with colored pencils directly on frosted cels – essentially creating moving paintings. *All-Nothing* received an Oscar nomination, the first of four for Back.

© 1974 National Film Board of Canada

The Owl Who Married a Goose

In this film Caroline Leaf interprets an Inuit legend about an owl who falls in love with a goose and meets a tragic end. The film is animated using sand and the soundtrack features Inuit Indian voices imitating bird sounds.

National Film Board of Canada » 160 Paul Driessen » 256

© 1979 National Film Board of Canada

Every Child

This six-minute animation was made for the United Nations to celebrate UNICEF's Declaration of Children's Rights and the International Year of the Child. One of the ten principles of the Declaration is illustrated in the film, namely that every child is entitled to a name and a nationality.

A hymn to the traditions and culture of Quebec, *Crac!* (1981) tells the story of a rocking chair that has been passed through a family, but when discarded finds itself again the center of attention at an art museum. Influenced by the painters Degas and Monet, and by Quebec folklore, *Crac!* won Back his first Academy Award.

The Man Who Planted Trees (1987) is Back's masterpiece. The story by Jean Giono is of Elzear Bouffier, a shepherd from the Maritime Alps who tirelessly plants thousands of oak trees and transforms a barren plain into a paradise. If *Crac!* is a hymn, then *The Man Who Planted Trees* is a poem. It won Back his second Oscar. *The Mighty River* (1993) continued Back's environmental concerns, visually documenting the development of the St Lawrence Seaway.

Successful Decade

Commercial animation in Canada bloomed in the 1970s. Contract work for American broadcasters had been performed in Canada since the early 1960s. After leaving the NFB, Gerald Potterton set up his own studio in the late 1960s to create both live-action and animation projects. After producing a number of TV specials, Potterton directed the feature film *Heavy Metal* (1980). With a very short production schedule, sequences were subcontracted to studios across Canada and around the world.

In the early 1970s Michael Hirsch, Patrick Loubert and Clive Smith formed Nelvana. Their first successes, *Cosmic Christmas* (1977) and *The Devil and Daniel Mouse* (1978), led to the feature film *Rock and Rule* (1983). Involving one of the greatest staffs in animation, mostly homegrown talent, *Rock and Rule* (a.k.a. *Ring of Power*) featured some outstanding animation and design. Unfortunately, the film went way over budget and took so long to finish that by the time it was released much of the film's music was passé. It brought Nelvana to the brink of bankruptcy. The studio turned to series work to survive, and would go on to be a major force in TV animation during the 1980s.

TV Co-Production » 378

INDEPENDENTS GROW

During the 1970s and 1980s, Will Vinton (b. 1948) almost single-handedly revitalized stop-motion animation with his trademarked claymation shorts and helped establish the viability of regional animation in the US. While studying architecture and film, he came under the influence of the visionary Spanish architecture of Antonio Gaudi's organic forms. After working in live-action, he experimented with clay animation, which eventually resulted in his collaborating with Bob Gardiner on the Oscar-winning short *Closed Mondays* (1974).

Will Vinton Productions

He then set up Will Vinton Productions in Portland, Oregon, where over the next decade he made a series of shorts that made his reputation and earned him Oscar nominations for *Martin the Cobbler* (1976), *Rip Van Winkle* (1978) and *The Great Cognito* (1982). The latter, which became his signature film, is a *tour de force* in which the title character undergoes a series of rapid metamorphoses as he delivers a comic monologue.

Among his other short films were *Mountain Music* (1975), a version of Antoine de Saint Exupéry's *The Little Prince* (1979) and *Dinosaur* (1980). The failure of his sole feature effort, *The Adventures of Mark Twain* (1984), essentially a collection of short films, was eclipsed by the acclaim for his John Fogerty 'Vanz Kant Danz' (1985) music video and the 'Speed Demon' sequence in Michael Jackson's *Moonwalker* feature (1988).

Commercial Success

Toward the end of this period, Vinton began leaving directing chores to others and eventually concentrated on the creative aspects of running the studio. As he did this, the company achieved great popularity for its California Raisins commercials, which led to two prime-time TV specials: *Meet the Raisins* (1988) and *The Raisins Sold Out!* (1990). In 1987, he won Emmys for *A Claymation Christmas Celebration* and for the animated/live-action sequence in the popular *Moonlighting* TV show.

Will Vinton Studios eventually expanded into digital animation, especially for TV commercials, and had moderate success with *The PJs*, a prime-time TV series co-produced with Eddie Murphy using traditional puppet animation. However, the failure of a subsequent prime-time series, *Gary and Mike*, and the collapse of the market for TV commercials led to Vinton losing control of the studio in 2003.

Bob Godfrey

Bob Godfrey (b. 1921) has been one of Britain's most distinctive comic talents, emerging from the same irreverent spirit that energized the free cinema movement of the 1960s.

© Will Vinton Studios

California Raisins

The California Raisins were created from different colors of Van Aken clay, including yellow, blue and white, resulting in Raisin Purple. The Raisins had a trademark song 'I Heard It Through The Grapevine', (a Marvin Gaye classic), and were animated with the help of reference footage of actors dancing.

© Bob Godfrey

Bob Godfrey

Specializing in hand-drawn media, Bob Godfrey is famous for his distinctive "wobbling" cartoons, which are created using a technique called boiling. His witty, fast-paced animations have included several popular series for children, including *Henry's Cat* and *Roobarb and Custard*.

Richard Williams » 188 Music and TV Animation » 280 Aardman Animation » 322

Great

As well as highly successful children's cartoons, Godfrey also did a number of more adult-themed animations. *Great* (1975) is a breakneck sprint through Isambard Kingdom Brunel's life and achievements. Using hand-drawn, mixed-media animation, it won an Academy Award in 1975 and a BAFTA in 1976.

Roobarb and Custard

The first animated television series ever to be made in the UK was *Roobarb and Custard*, a series of cartoons featuring a cat and dog that has achieved cult status since its first airing in 1974. The characters in the Roobarb cartoons were colored in with nothing more sophisticated than Magic Markers.

He has proved himself equally adept at adult-oriented shorts – lampooning British attitudes, especially sexual attitudes – and children's TV series.

Born in Australia, Godfrey came to the UK as a baby. He began his animation career in 1949 as a background artist for the W.M. Larkin Studio on promotional and technical films, and directed his first film, *The Big Parade*, in 1952 with Keith Learner. In 1954, he joined up with Jeff Hale to form Biographic Films, which made some of the first commercials for Britain's ITV, as well as many cinema advertisements. This allowed him the freedom to do a series of personal films that he became identified with, including *Polygamous Polonius* (1959) and *Do-It-Yourself Cartoon Kit* (1961). These films showed the influence of *The Goons*, along with his interest in political satire and British morals, sexual and otherwise. While visually rather crude, their quintessential British humor put them very much outside the dominant American mode so prevalent at the time; as such, they helped establish a uniquely British school of animation.

Variety of Subjects

In 1964, he formed Bob Godfrey Films to gain more control over his work, which included such mock-erotic films as *Henry 'Til 5* (1970), *Kama Sutra Rides Again* (1971) and *Dream Doll* (1979), made with Zagreb Studio's Zlatko Grgic. His most ambitious film was *Great* (1975), the Oscar-winning half-hour satirical biography of British engineer Isambard Kingdom Brunel.

In addition to his theatrical efforts, Godfrey was also active in TV. He directed four episodes of *The Beatles'* TV series in 1966, and in 1974 wrote and narrated the highly influential *The Do-It-Yourself Film Animation Kit* TV series, which Aardman's Nick Park said was instrumental in getting him into animation. More recently, he made *Millennium – the Musical* (1999), a satirical TV special profiling Margaret Thatcher. He has also produced several popular children's series, including *Roobarb and Custard* (1974), which was based on the stories of Grange Calveley and has become a cult classic; *Henry's Cat* (1983); and *Kevin Saves the World* (2002).

RENÉ LALOUX

French artist René Laloux (1929–2004) had already determined he would dedicate his life to painting when he was invited to create an experimental workshop at Cheverny Court, a private psychiatric clinic. Here, with the assistance of the inmates, he produced a jarring 14-minute film, *Les Dents du Singe* ('The Monkey's Teeth', 1960), involving a primate having his teeth forcibly extracted.

Clinical Experiment

By adapting a number of the patients' drawings, Laloux and his students managed to construct a 16 mm (0.6 in) animated cut-out film as a clinical experiment. The end product was seen and bought by Fréderic Rossif and, spurred on by his success at making animated films, Laloux took the money for *The Monkey's Teeth* and sank it into a second project.

His next film, *Temps Morts* ('Dead Times', 1964), conveyed another somber message and was described as "a visual perception of death and its consequences". In collaboration with post-surrealist painter and writer Roland Topor (b. 1938), he next presented a bizarre gothic-horror tale concerning a town overrun with colossal snails entitled *Les Escargots* ('The Snails', 1965).

Adventures in Science Fiction

By the early 1970s, he was embarking on his most challenging project to date, lending his distinctive style of art to an adaptation of Stefan Wul's popular 1957 science-fiction parable *Ome en Serie*. Retitled *La Planète Sauvage* (a.k.a *Fantastic Planet, The Savage Planet* or *Planet of Incredible Creatures*, 1973), the story deals with existence on the planet Ygam. The Oms, a race of humanoid creatures (the name "Ome" is derived from "homme", the French word for man), struggle to rid themselves of domination from the 39-ft- (12-m-) high, blue-skinned "Draags" who treat them as domestic pets.

The Draags are higher beings who dedicate their leisure time to meditation and keeping the population of the Oms down by culling them every so often.

La Planète Sauvage

Released in 1973, *La Planète Sauvage* is a surreal tale that takes place on a faraway planet where giants rule and tiny humans must fight for equality and their lives. It depicts the eternal human struggle for freedom, showing what happens when the human capacity to think and learn is suppressed.

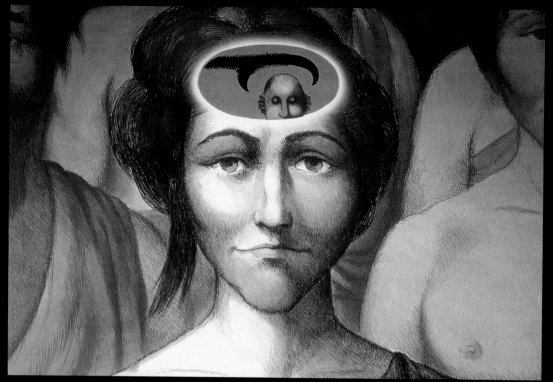

© Kratky Film Praha, Les Films Armorial, Service de la Recherche ORTF, Ceskoslovensky Filmexport

Terr, one of the Oms belonging to the chief Draag's daughter, manages to escape and, inciting the others to rebel, guides them to a "wild planet" where they discover the secret of the Draags' energy source. Armed with this information, they return and finally manage to get their oppressors to recognize them as their equivalent.

The whole production took Laloux and Topor over three years to complete, but it was certainly worth it because *La Planète Sauvage* won international acclaim, including the Special Critic's Award at the 1973 Cannes Film Festival. Laloux then collaborated with the celebrated comic-strip artist Moebius (Jean Giraud) to produce his next project, *Les Maîtres du Temps* ('Time Masters'), in 1982. Moebius provided the visually striking original animation sketches for the story of a mercenary who races across the cosmos to save a young boy from an extraterrestrial force of evil.

La Planète Sauvage

This film was one of the first feature-length animations dedicated to adults and science fiction. It won a prize at the Cannes Film Festival when it was shown there in 1973, and it has been something of a cult classic ever since.

La Planète Sauvage

A joint production by French and Czechoslovakian film-makers, this film was seen as a metaphor for Soviet oppression of what was then Czechoslovakia. Pressure from the Communist government forced the production to move to France, where it was completed in 1973.

IX: 1971–79: ANIMATION FOR GROWN-UPS   WESTERN EUROPE: FRANCE

ALLEGRO NON TROPPO

Filmed in monochrome and Technicolor, Bruno Bozzetto's high-spirited 1977 film *Allegro Non Troppo* (a musical term meaning "lively, but not too much") has been described as a parody of Disney's *Fantasia*. In many ways, however, it is not comparable in either parody or style to the Disney masterpiece. *Allegro Non Troppo* stands on its own by expanding the technique of blending music perfectly with the animated art.

© Bozzetto Film

Classical Influence

Featuring half a dozen unrelated segments set to a selection of classical-music themes, the performance starts in live-action with the arrival of a conductor who prepares himself to conduct his orchestra. A live-action comedy scene with the musicians is shown in between each animated sequence.

The first in line is Debussy's *Prélude a l'après-midi d'un faune*. Set against a tasteful background of pastels and watercolors, a bespectacled satyr appears on the trail of a pretty wood nymph. His pursuit of her lasts until the realization hits him that there is no need to seek her because many such beautiful creatures surround him.

The second sequence is set to the music of Dvorák's *Slavonic Dance No. 7*. A firing squad is about to put an end to a "non-conformist" when they drop their pants and "moon" at the offender.

Next is an interpretation of man's evolution set to Ravel's *Bolero*. An American rocket departs from an unnamed planet, leaving behind an empty bottle of Coca-Cola. From the bottle springs life: a procession of monsters who go past battlegrounds, ending up at a statue. The statue splits open to reveal an ape inside.

Vivaldi's Concerto in C Major features a bee settling down for a picnic. His enjoyment is soon disrupted by the arrival of a pair of lovers who start to make love on the picnic ground. The bee puts matters right by stinging them.

Sibelius' *Valse Triste* pictures a wide-eyed cat reminiscing as he wanders around a derelict tenement building. He recalls various events as he journeys from room to room, and it is only at the end that we discover that the building is about to be demolished and the cat is, in fact, a ghost spending his final moments in a home he once loved. The orchestra is seen weeping for the cat's demise. The brilliant design and clever animation of the cat make this one of the most haunting and memorable sequences.

© Bozzetto Film

Allegro Non Troppo - cat

A humorous tribute to Disney's *Fantasia*, *Allegro Non Troppo* consists of six sequences set to music by Debussy, Dvorák, Ravel, Vivaldi, Sibelius and Stravinsky. The cat pictured here is from the haunting Sibelius section, *Valse Triste*.

Bruno Bozzetto » 222

Allegro Non Troppo – dinosaurs

Set to Ravel's *Bolero*, the section featuring dinosaurs has various creatures evolving from the remains of a discarded bottle. These different forms of life are finally defeated by man in the form of an ape.

Allegro Non Troppo

Exuberant and imaginative, *Allegro Non Troppo* uses free-form animation and understated use of color to great effect. A theme common to all Bozzetto's work – and also seen in this film – is the lament for a society based on consumerism and machines.

Stravinsky's *The Firebird* concerns the Garden of Eden and the snake that tries to tempt Adam and Eve with an apple. The snake is shown the present day by Satan and is pictured as a white-collar worker in a chaotic world of noise, clutter and bombs. He returns to his original status.

Happy Ever After?

An epilogue shows an apartment superintendent taking a miniature theater to the basement to show a succession of parodies of the musical form. He smashes the theaters and departs, only to be stopped in his tracks by a block of cement bearing the inscription "Happy End" hurtling down to squash him. The orchestra leader, having got what he can from his musicians, then disposes of the players by shooting them all.

Satire or Homage?

Allegro Non Troppo has been called a satire of *Fantasia*, but the only entry that can really be likened to the Disney classic is the visually stunning *Bolero*. In this placement Bozzetto definitely pays homage to the *Firebird* sequence of *Fantasia* and the dinosaurs' trek across the burning desert in search of sustenance.

Another gentle reminder of *Fantasia* is the presence of a live-action orchestra that passes comments on the proceedings. The live-action photography is handled by comedian Maurizio Nichetti, who is also seen as the symphony conductor preparing his musicians to play, even though the music throughout the film is pre-recorded.

Bozzetto's trademark anti-war sentiments are visible throughout the film: the threat of a firing squad, the war-torn battlegrounds in *Bolero*, the cat who is already a ghost, the superintendent being crushed and the conductor who shoots his players at the end. Sex is also a recurring theme, seen in the predatory satyr, the copulating lovers and Adam and Eve's temptation. Bizarre surrealism abounds, but this weird and wonderful film remains a testament to Bozzetto's animation genius.

© Bozzetto Film

Yuri Norstein and *The Battle of Kerjnets* » 235

MULTITUDE OF TALENT

Dutch animator Paul Driessen (b. 1940) is a rich example of an independent animator formulating his own style of art and humor purely from within, without any influence from other sources. Driessen trained in graphic design and illustration at Utrecht Academy of Fine Arts, where he ultimately disregarded all he had learned in favor of following his own path.

Driessen's Early Years

A longtime admirer of the wonderful work of Dutch cartoonist Marten Toonder (b. 1912) and puppet animator "Joop" Geesink (1913–84), Driessen dreamed of one day animating his own films. His ambitions came to fruition when, in his early twenties, Driessen secured a job creating his own commercials in the Dutch advertising company Cinecentrum. It was there he learned his film-making craft under the guidance of American Jim Hiltz, and the young Dutchman was let loose to write, draw and direct his own work.

Moving On

As chance would have it, George Dunning happened to be visiting the studio when he saw Driessen's work and invited him to come to his TVC studio in London. The young Driessen arrived there just in time to embark on TVC's most adventurous project, *Yellow Submarine*, where he was kept busy for months among the storyboards and animation.

After working on *Yellow Submarine*, he returned home where he obtained a grant to make *Het Verhaal von Klein Yoghurt* ('The Story of Little John Bailey', 1970) about a boy who is rescued by his elephant friend after accidentally starting a forest fire. In 1972, he emigrated to Canada where he joined up with the NFB. He was shunted into the NFB's French section, whose main concerns lay with ecological issues. His debut films, therefore, dealt with the horrors of pollution.

The turning point came in 1974 with *Au Bout du Fil* ('Cat's Cradle') where Driessen's willowy, spidery graphics help illustrate a spider's web spinning an abstract yarn involving various Gothic characters who all exist in a hungry, natural world. On the crest of that wave, he next produced *Une Vieille Boîte* ('An Old Box'), featuring a character who finds an old box full of wonders to behold, but decides to exploit it on the street.

After a string of hits – and winning more than 50 international prizes – Paul Driessen is now on the faculty of Kassell University in Germany.

Terry Gilliam

Terry Gilliam's (b. 1940) anarchic cut-out animation is completely different, and is best-known as the material used to link sketches in *Monty Python's Flying Circus* (1969–74).

An Old Box

The French Department at Canada's NFB encouraged animators to work without dialogue in their films. For Paul Driessen this meant that the films had to be more creative and he often used fairy tales, legends and Biblical stories to communicate his message, adding a special twist to surprise his audience.

© 1975 National Film Board of Canada

Cat's Cradle

Cat's Cradle shows Driessen's skill in connecting disparate stories to form a consistent whole. He uses a single black line to link different situations, from funny to frightening to surreal. The tale stars Gothic characters, witches and cloaked riders, and has no dialogue but a concoction of sound effects.

© 1974 National Film Board of Canada

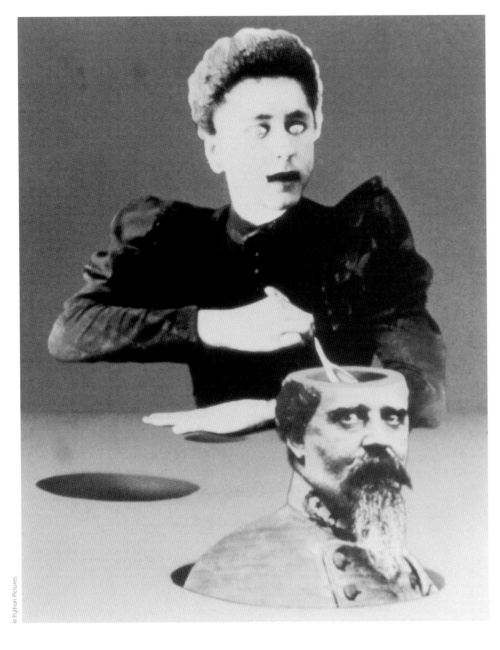

© Python Pictures

Minneapolis-born Gilliam studied political science before immersing himself in a variety of jobs, finally becoming a writer, illustrator, cartoonist and editor on Harvey Kurtzman's *Help!* magazine. When work dried up in the States, he descended on an unsuspecting London and, via John Cleese, managed to get some sketches accepted for the children's comedy show *Do Not Adjust Your Set* (1967–69), where he also became acquainted with Eric Idle, Michael Palin and Terry Jones.

A Laugh-a-Minute

His quirky animation was first seen by television viewers when producer Humphrey Barclay invited him to provide cartoons and caricatures for the newly formed London Weekend Television comedy show *We Have Ways of Making You Laugh* (1968). Gilliam was asked to animate a short sequence to illustrate a ragbag of Jimmy Young's radio-show recipes and, with very little cash up front, he figured that the only way it could be done was with cut-out animation. The formula was a hit and stayed. Gilliam is not one to let a skimpy budget get in the way of making a funny cartoon. The following year was to set his name in stone when the initial series of *Monty Python's Flying Circus* went on the air, fascinating television audiences with Gilliam's own particular brand of frantic humor.

Expect the Unexpected

The essence of Gilliam's work is full of bizarre Kafka-esque fantasies, such as a man-eating baby carriage, elephantine chickens descending from above and squashing an unsuspecting onlooker, flying houses and an unhealthy obsession with dismembered feet. Even the opening sequence of *Python* finishes with Bronzino's painting of Cupid and Venus, where Cupid's foot crashes down to stomp the title to a pulp.

Relying heavily on an element of shock and the unexpected, Gilliam's animation could be described as the stuff nightmares are made of, although you are helpless with laughter at the same time. The cheapness of it all adds to the charm.

Monty Python's Flying Circus

The animation Gilliam produced to link the live-action sections of *Flying Circus* was typical of his animation style in that he frequently used recognizable images in unpredictable and outrageous ways. There is a sense of the macabre in much of his work (his use of skulls and monsters, etc.), which gives the viewer a sense of uneasiness, and heightens any disorientation the animation might have created.

During the 1970s, the Pannonia studio continued to excel in the production of artistic shorts and television series. In fact, Pannonia had achieved such a high level of success that they even established two branches. One of them was founded in Kecskemét, the other in Pécs. The studio also ventured into the international co-production arena.

Features and TV

In 1973, the studio moved into feature animation production with *Johnny Corncob* by Marcell Jankovics. The success of their first feature encouraged the studio to set up a feature-animation division. By the end of the 1970s, they had produced three more animated features: *Hugo the Hippo* (1973), by Bill Feigenbaum and József Gémes, which strangely enough, was commissioned by the US company Fabergé; *Matty the Gooseboy* (1976), by Attila Dargay; and the ambitious avant-garde musical *Foam Bath* (1979) by György Kovásznai.

Television productions remained the main mode of production for Pannonia. The first TV productions were two highly successful series: József Nepp's *Mézga Family* – aimed primarily at children – was about a family's comic adventures;

Hugo the Hippo

Surreal and psychedelic, *Hugo the Hippo* tells the story of 12 hippos imported to Zanzibar to rid the harbor from sharks. After a jetty is built, the hippos are massacred, with Hugo being the only survivor.

Hugo the Hippo

Hugo is put on trial for causing damage to a village, but the Sultan denounces his persecutor, Aban Khan, and reminds the court of the hippos' invaluable past service. A dark and often bizarre film, Hugo the Hippo has nonetheless become a cult classic of sorts.

Fight

Winner of the Palme d'Or for best short film at the 1977 Cannes Film Festival, Fight was one of several very successful animations to come from Hungarian animator Marcell Jankovics.

Tamás Szabó Sípos's *Let Me Explain* took on a more educational function. In each episode, a character named Dr Brain set out to explain the world. In one episode, for example, Dr Brain, in a jovial and ironic manner, explains the basics of economics.

The 1970s also saw other TV productions, including *Tails the Cat-Chaser*, which used a cut-out technique; *Kukori and Kotkoda*; *Mirr-Murr the Tom-Cat*; *Elek Mekk — Jack-of-All-Trades*; and *Tales from Crow Hill*. In 1978, Marcell Jankovics launched a new adult series called *Hungarian Folk Tales*.

Not Short on Shorts

Despite the increasingly commercial nature of the studio, Pannonia continued to encourage and support the production of short animation films. While the older generation concerned themselves primarily with ethical and philosophical questions, the younger generation turned their attentions to modern challenges and realities. Among the highlights of this period are *Moon Flight* (1975) and *Panic* (1978), both by Sándor Reisenbüchler; *Wave Length* (1971) by György Kovásznai; *Modern Sports Coaching* (1970) by Bela Ternovsky; and two films that won prestigious Golden Palm awards at the Cannes Film Festival, Sándor Reisenbüchler's *1812* (1973) and Marcell Jankovic's *Fight* (1977).

A new generation of animators emerged during the 1970s, notably Kati Macskássy, daughter of Hungarian animation pioneer Gyula Macskássy, who made quality children's films including the acclaimed *Push Button* (1973) and *I Think Life's Great Fun* (1976). Péter Szoboszlay made the humorous *Hey, You* (1976), Csaba Szórády produced *Rondino* (1977) and Csaba Varga took a group of amateur film-makers from Pécs and formed the animation studio IXILON in 1974. Varga was commissioned by Pannonia to produce films and to establish a studio in Pécs. The studio became known for its bold graphic style and adult-tailored films. In 1988, the studio would become the famous Varga Studio.

Marcell Jankovics

One of the most successful and interesting Hungarian animators of this period was Marcell Jankovics. Born in Budapest, he made his first film, *The Legend of Saint Silvester* in 1964. Since then, Jankovics has alternated with great ease between children's films, television series, feature films and his own personal short films. His short films have garnered wide international acclaim and have themselves been diverse in tone, ranging from satire in *Deep Water* (1971) to heavier, existentialist films like *SOS* (1970), *Sisyphus* (1973) and *The Fight* (1977).

TV animation was dominant during the 1970s, with most theatrical features being big-screen spin-offs. Some did not even present new stories, but merely summarized the TV story line. The most notable exceptions to this standard were the two *Lupin III* features produced by TMS Entertainment Ltd (a.k.a. Tokyo Movie Shinsha): *Lupin III: The Secret of Mamo* (1978), directed by Soji Yoshikawa, and *The Castle of Cagliostro* (1979), written and directed by Hayao Miyazaki. The most significant advance in TV animation was the upgrading of its target audience from children to adolescents and young adults. The distinctive art styles of manga cartoonists Go Nagai (b. 1945), Leiji Matsumoto (b. 1938) and "Monkey Punch" (Kazuhiko Kato, 1937) became familiar fixtures on the small screen.

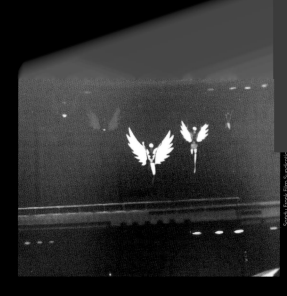

Space-Age Animation

Nagai created the concept of heroic teenagers who donned mechanical battle armor or piloted transformable vehicles and fought as giant robots to protect the world (Japan) from ruthless conquering outer-space armies. The first was *Mazinger Z*, produced by Toei Doga in 222 episodes under three titles from 1972 until 1977. By the end of the decade, there were 40 giant-robot cartoon series created by practically every TV animation studio.

A major variant was introduced by Nippon Sunrise studio writer/director Yoshiyuki Tomino in 1979 with *Mobile Suit Gundam*, which recast the giant robots from unique superhero suits to more realistic futuristic military combat vehicles, and the adversaries from humans versus demonic aliens to warring human space nations.

Nagai also pioneered TV animation with supernatural horror, with *Devilman* (1972), and the first risqué-humor adventure series, *Cutey Honey* (1973), featuring a buxom teen girl (actually an android) whose clothing briefly disappeared when she changed from one costumed disguise to another.

Small-Screen Adventures

Leiji Matsumoto specialised in interstellar sci-fi adventure series, notably the long-running *Space Battleship Yamato* (1974), plus several sequels, *Space Pirate Captain Harlock* (1978) and *Galaxy Express 999* (1978). Monkey Punch was known primarily for his long-running manga *Lupin III* about a charismatic international jewel thief. Designed for adults rather than for children, its TV animated series ran for over 200 episodes throughout the 1970s and mid-1980s, evolving into a series of annual animated features that continue today.

Other major TV animation included Tatsuo Yoshida's sci-fi superhero team in *Battle of the Planets* (1972); the adolescent tear-jerker romance *Candy Candy* (1976–79); *The Rose of Versailles* (a.k.a. *Lady Oscar*, 1979), based upon Ryoko Ikeda's historical romance set at the court of Louis XVI; and a TV cartoon series of Fujio Fujiko's manga for children about the time-travelling robot toy cat *Doraemon* (1979).

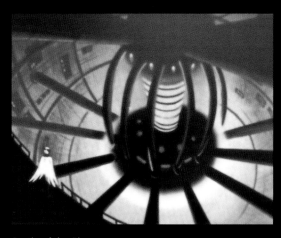

Battle of the Planets

This began as the Japanese 1972 TV cartoon series *Science Ninja Team Gatchaman* (first and third images). It was transformed for American TV in 1978 by a team led by Disney/Hanna-Barbera veteran Jameson Brewer and *Flintstones* director Alan Dinehart (second image: robot 7-Zark-7, an American addition to the cast).

© Renzo Kinoshita/Studio Lotus

Independent Shorts and Puppet Animation

In art animation, Renzo Kinoshita (1936–97) began as a TV animator in the 1960s, but under the influence of Tezuka and Kuri he switched to making independent short films for festival screenings. His masterpiece is the anti-nuclear warfare *Pika-Don* (1978); others include *What on Earth is He?* (1971), *Made In Japan* (1972), *Invitation to Death* (1973), *The Calculating Machine* (1973) and *The Japanese* (1977). He was a co-founder in 1985 of the bi-annual Hiroshima International Animation Festival, which he directed with his wife Sayoko until his death.

Kihachiro Kawamoto, "the Magician of Puppet Animation", began at Tadahito Mochinaga's puppet studio in the 1950s. In 1962 he went to Czechoslovakia to study under puppet animator Jiri Trnka. His first film, *Breaking Branches is Forbidden* (1968), was the first of his many films to win international-festival prizes. In 1972, Kawamoto and fellow Mochinaga veteran Tadanari Okamoto began an annual show touring major Japanese cities, featuring both puppet and cut-paper animated films and live-puppet plays of Japanese folk tales and classic drama. Kawamoto's films included *The Devil* (1972), *The Journey* (1973), *The Life of a Poet* (1974), *Dojoji Temple* (1976) and *House of Flames* (1979). In the 1980s and 1990s the governmental NHK station funded his puppet dramatizations of classic Japanese and Chinese literature.

Tadanari Okamoto's first puppet film, *Strange Medicine*, won the 1965 Ofuji Award. He was not as prolific as Kawamoto, but his puppet and cut-paper works include such international festival favorites as *Home My Home* (1970), *The Flowers and the Mole* (1971), *The Mochi-Mochi Tree* (1971), *The Crab's Vengeance on the Monkey* (1972), *Praise Be to Small Ills* (1973), *Water Seed* (1975), *The Bridge of Strength* (1976), *The Magic Fox* (1982) and *A Well-Ordered Restaurant* (1991), which was completed posthumously by his assistants.

Made in Japan

Made In Japan won the Grand Prix at the New York International Animation Festival in 1972. Renzo Kinoshita began working as an independent animator in 1967 making films with powerful messages to contemporary society. Kinoshita's wife Sayoko worked with him on his films often helping with in-betweening, coloring and making puppets.

© Kihachiro Kawamoto

Dojoji Temple

Dojoji Temple is a traditionally inspired Japanese story about a woman's passion. The woman's emotional state is cleverly communicated by changes in the lighting of her face. The style of the watercolour backdrops resembles the narrative picture scrolls of traditional Japanese art.

Two Australian animators are having lunch. The eager, younger one states, "Animation is imagination!" His companion – older, more pragmatic – replies, "Yes, but is it local imagination or imported imagination?"

The Influence of TV

Australian animation took a long time to become a viable, substantial industry. Before the modern telecommunications age, Australian animation suffered from entrenched national problems: a tiny population (and consequently a too-limited market), a lack of the centrally concentrated resources of Hollywood and the ever-present "tyranny of distance". Despite attempts by pioneers like Eric Porter (1910–83) and Melbourne's Owen Brothers (Will and Harrie) to make indigenous theatrical cartoons, little of major animation consequence happened until the advent of television in 1956.

Suddenly, TV commercials and a constant supply of flashy promos and animated network logos were required, and the business began to benefit from regular work. Very quickly, that work matched international standards, employing a wide variety of graphic styles, ranging from traditional character animation to more UPA-inspired modeling, to outright experimental design work.

Meanwhile, in America the TV cartoon business mushroomed following the huge success of Hanna-Barbera's *Ruff and Reddy* and *Huckleberry Hound* shows. By the end of the 1950s the demand for episodic cartoon product was rapidly outstripping the supply of American animation talent.

Slice of the American Pie

To solve this dilemma, producers like Al Brodax in New York and Jay Ward on the West Coast began subcontracting animation of their shows to outfits in Mexico, Canada and Holland. Storyboards and soundtracks were prepared in the States, but the labor-intensive drawing process was executed overseas under American supervision. Wanting a piece of this lucrative pie, Australia established its credentials as another cost-effective outsourcing center. Artist Gus McLaren recalled, "It wasn't just a matter of us being cheaper; there was a dearth of animators in America."

In the early 1960s the first examples of Down Under "runaway production" occurred when the animation wing of Artransa Park Studios (busy with

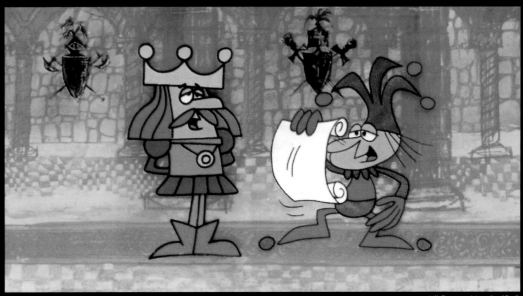

© Air Programus International Studio

King Arthur and the Square Knights of the Round Table

In 1966, 39 half-hour episodes were made of this all-Australian production. This was API's most successful series and was syndicated in the US by Twentieth Century Fox and sold to 14 countries. Zoran Janjic, an animator originally from the Zagreb Studios, directed the series.

advertising assignments) took on the animation of various cartoon series for Al Brodax, and TV cartoons like *Beetle Bailey*, *Krazy Kat* and *Snuffy Smith* were soon being churned out. Artransa's animation department was originally set up and trained by veteran animator Eric Porter; veterans recalled it fondly as a stimulating place to work and learn. Porter, who set up his own production house in 1958, also began subcontracting on animated American series, like *Cool McCool* and *The Lone Ranger*, although his studio was more noted for its slick cartoon work on many TV commercials.

Air Programs International (API) was set up by Walter Hucker in the late 1950s. By 1966, API had overseas TV deals, and had sold the first cartoon series fully created and produced in Australia, *King Arthur & the Square Knights of the Round Table*. API also sold a series of prime-time animated specials, consisting of classics like *A Christmas Carol*, to America's giant CBS network.

Marco Polo Jr vs. the Red Dragon

Marco Polo Jr sets sail for Xanadu to reunite two halves of Kubla Khan's magical golden medallion. This scene from Eric Porter's very popular feature film shows *Princess Shining Moon*, the rightful heir to Xanadu's throne, surrounded by the evil ruler Red Dragon and other villainous characters.

Hanna-Barbera Australia

In 1970, API commenced work on a Hanna-Barbera TV cartoon series, *The Funky Phantom*, and veteran producer William Hanna flew to Australia to oversee. Hanna's presence was soon being viewed with concern by several API staffers, who sniffed a possible takeover. Watler Hucker's wife, Wendy, said, "An ideological difference with H-B developed. We had battled to build an Australian industry – it was a long, hard road to hoe."

Hanna-Barbera Australia, one of the earliest examples of cartoon globalization, opened in early 1972. H-B was taken to court when API accused them of poaching API's staff. Hanna-Barbera successfully defended the case. William Hanna stated, "We won our point: that we were not here to damage API." But many artists did defect to Hanna-Barbera, including Peter Luschwitz, Don McKinnon and Gwyn Perkins who became top artists in the field. Perkins recalled, "It was like this great white god of animation – Bill Hanna – arrived, and suddenly we had real American model sheets to work from!" Some supervising American animators made the trip Down Under to help train local talent to Hollywood standards, including Disney veteran Volus Jones.

H-B Australia animated various American TV series, like *Wait 'Til Your Father Gets Home*, as well as prime-time cartoon specials like *The Flintstones Meet Count Rockula*, before setting up a dedicated commercials division in 1974.

CARTOONS DOWN UNDER

In the early 1970s Australian animation was dominated by the presence of farmed-out American TV shows. This new work certainly provided welcome and regular employment; at Hanna-Barbera Australia, many young people were well trained, at least in TV cartoon techniques. But inevitably, the essentially "sausage machine" quality of H-B's TV cartoons palled after time. A group of creative designers and animators found themselves churning out product that was formulaic and uninspiring. Animator Anne Jolliffe said, "As it developed, after they set up, it seemed to us like time-serving: (eventually) it was like bottling pickles."

A New Era Dawns

By the end of the decade, a new maturity and confidence in Australia's national identity (due to a change of government after 23 years) ensured that animation was far more capable of sustaining a homegrown industry. The Australian cartoon pioneer Eric Porter again led the way. Less than a year after Hanna-Barbera was set up, Porter released his feature-length cartoon *Marco Polo Jr vs. the Red Dragon* (1972). The well-crafted film had its share of flaws, but it proved highly popular on initial release, and was noted for a new sophistication and overall Australian achievement.

Ultimately, though, the *Red Dragon* feature proved a financial drain and Porter was finally forced to close his studio. In 1983, shortly before his death, he was honored at the Australian Film Institute awards, receiving the prestigious Raymond Longford Award for a life devoted to the cartoon medium. He was popularly hailed as the "father of Australian animation".

Yoram Gross and Dot the Kangaroo

After Porter's death in 1983, the next successful producer of Australian feature cartoons was Polish émigré Yoram Gross (b. 1926), who said, "I knew that I could never compete with Disney - the magnificent job he had done. Instead, I chose to put animated cartoon characters on live-action backgrounds. (The technique) is nothing new in the film industry, but it is quite rare." (In fact, Eric Porter had employed some live backgrounds years earlier in his 1937 color short, *Waste Not, Want Not*, starring his character Willie the Wombat in an Australian version of Disney's earlier Silly Symphony, *The Grasshopper and the Ants*.) Desiring to make specifically "Australian films about Australian life", Gross produced *Dot and the Kangaroo* (1977). This feature-length cartoon was successfully exhibited at the Cannes Film Festival, resulting in immediate sales to 17 countries. Somewhat surprisingly to its makers, this uniquely "Oz" feature was being translated into languages like Chinese and Russian.

Gross made several more Dot movies over the next eight years, including *Dot and the Smugglers* (a.k.a *Dot and the Bunyip*, 1986) and *Dot and the Whale*

Yoram Gross Film Studios

Yoram Gross and his wife formed an animation studio in Sydney in 1968. Their first feature *Dot & The Kangaroo* became one of Australia's most popular animated features and won the first prize at the first Television Children's Film Festival in Teheran, 1977.

Dot & The Kangaroo

In this film Dot, the daughter of settlers in the Australian outback, loses her way in the bush. She is saved from the terrifying strange sounds and dark shadows by a kangaroo, who carries Dot in its pouch. With the help of many bush creatures including a koala, a platypus and a kookaburra she finally finds her way home.

Dot & The Kangaroo © Yoram Gross Film Studios PTY LTD

Lip-Sync Drawings

These lip-sync drawings of Dot and the Kangaroo are used to help make the characters talk. The different poses are used to animate the lips and mouth and are fitted to a pre-recorded dialogue track which has been broken down to work out the timings of the speech.

(1987), before scoring an even bigger success in animated TV cartoon shows, starting with *Blinky Bill*, the adventures of a mischievous but endearing koala, from a beloved Australian literary property. While commercially successful, Gross remains an enthusiastic proponent of animation's capacity to surprise and its limitless potential. Today Gross, partnered with the European EM-TV, is producing a raft of highly individual TV cartoon series. These multi-episode properties include *Tabaluga*, *Flipper and Lopaka*, *Old Tom* and *Fairy Tale Police Department*, all of which have been favorably received in foreign countries.

Bruce Petty

The final figure to loom large in 1970s animation was the independent cartoonist and satirist Bruce Petty (b. 1929). His distinctive, highly caricatured finished art was akin to most animators' "roughs", and he was able to use the cartoon medium as a powerful engine for biting social comment.

"I think my animation style — like everybody else's — derives from the drawing technique, and my technique suggests very quick, jumpy sort of movements. It does allow (for) a certain amount of information to happen," said Petty. He felt that history was too often dryly presented as a mere catalogue of names and dates, noting, "There's a lot more substructure we ought to know about — it's very hard to teach, a little boring, but it's terribly important; anything that can convey this level of economic and commercial structures is important, and I think animation (is) a good way to teach".

One of Petty's most interesting films was *Leisure* (1976), produced by Film Graphics. He described that project as "an interesting puzzle — there were abstract notions about human values, and we tried to turn them into graphic images. There was a big experimental component (to) *Leisure*, and I think that's a good direction for animation to go in". The film won an Oscar, and capped a turbulent decade by putting Australia firmly on the road to international animation credibility.

1980–89:
NEW DIRECTIONS

This was an exciting decade for animation. Shifts in corporate management, the retiring of an old guard and a new breed of upstart cartoonists all conspired to cause change in the mainstream perceptions of animation.

In feature-films, the decade began with *Heavy Metal* and *Tron* – and ended with *The Little Mermaid* and *Akira*. Television went from *Pac-Man* to *He-Man* to *Pee-Wee Herman* – and introduced us to a dysfunctional family: *The Simpsons*. Hayao Miyazaki came into his own as a master of anime; Richard Williams proved himself with *Who Framed Roger Rabbit?*; and Don Bluth took a group of Disney renegades and raised the bar with *The Secret of NIMH*. Steven Spielberg joined the fray with *An American Tail* and *Tiny Toon Adventures*.

Animators experimented with new ideas, new styles and new techniques. One technique in particular was very intriguing, computer animation. Former Disney animator John Lasseter began making short experiments at Pixar, marrying his traditional character-animation training to computer graphics. The result: an Academy Award for *Tin Toy* – and a glimpse of things to come.

The world was alive with the new possibilities of animation art and the directions in which it could go.

TRON

Tron, released by Disney in 1982, was the movie that introduced computer animation to the masses. Directed by Steven Lisberger, the film was a visual delight, and featured ground-breaking computer-generated imagery (CGI) combined with live-action.

The Story

Tron is about a brash young computer hacker named Flynn (Jeff Bridges) who owns a video arcade. Flynn was a star programmer at Encom, a stereotypical faceless corporation. A co-worker of Flynn's, named Dillenger (David Warner), stole Flynn's work and used it to get promoted. In the process, Dillenger also managed to get Flynn fired. Flynn enlists Alan and Lora (Bruce Boxleitner and Cindy Morgan), two friends and ex-colleagues, to help him break into Encom so he can prove Dillenger stole his work. While attempting to de-activate his stolen program, Flynn is beamed into the computer itself. There, he enters a computer-generated world where he must battle other programs in video-game-like combat in order to defeat the Master Control Program.

Computer-Generated Magic

Unlike modern CGI films, which promise total realism, *Tron* saturated the audience in bright colors and unabashedly computer-generated visuals. The production design by Syd Mead, Dean Edward Mitzner and Jean "Moebius" Giraud gave a beautiful look of the inside of a computer that pre-dated such movies as *The Matrix* (1999) by decades. Some of the production design was dictated by the primitive state of computer animation at the time, which could only handle simple shapes and textures. The resulting film showed how good design could overcome any technical limitations.

The most successful parts of the film were those that took place within the computer itself. One of the most memorable scenes is the light-cycle sequence, where Flynn must pilot a CG motorcycle at breakneck speeds. The animation was truly stunning, and for the first time immersed theater audiences in the world of the video game.

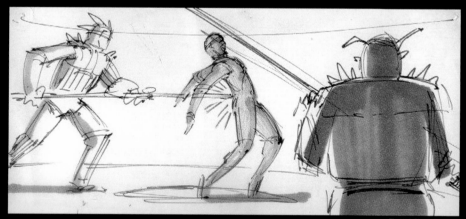

© The Walt Disney Company

Tron – storyboard

In order for the production team to determine what would be required by way of computer-generated backgrounds, storyboards were drawn up to provide a blueprint for the action.

Tron's characters

The actors' costumes were decorated with black and white outlines and patterns designed to resemble circuits on electronic boards. Once filming had taken place, each frame was then enlarged and separated out into layers of high-contrast images (one containing the outlines, one containing the background, etc.). These images were then individually backlit and re-photographed with colored filters, combined with CGI and composed together with the help of mattes.

Almost 20 minutes of the film consisted of moving images generated entirely by computer. There were also over 200 scenes using computer-generated sets intertwined with live-action actors, a Hollywood first. In the computer-animated sequences, the live actors were photographed in black and white. The resulting images were selectively colorized using backlight compositing to make circuits in the actors' suits glow, giving them a very unique look.

Computer-Animation Pioneers

Because of the amount of computer-generated imagery necessary for *Tron*, Disney divided the work among four pioneering computer graphics companies: Digital Effects, Robert Abel & Associates, Mathematical Applications Group Incorporated (MAGI) and Information International Incorporated (Triple-I). These companies went on to produce further computer animation in the 1980s, but all of them went out of business within a few years. The employees of these companies went on to found many of today's top studios, including Blue Sky, Metrolight, Keiser/Walczak and Rhythm & Hues.

In addition to giving a number of computer-animation pioneers their start, *Tron* had a huge influence on everyone involved with computer graphics at the time. While it was a pioneering moment for animation, the movie itself did only moderate business at the box office. Some of that may be due to the script, but it was also because the film went up against the blockbuster *ET* in the summer of 1982. The failure of *Tron* to attract a mass audience may have set back computer animation in Hollywood by as much as a decade.

PIXAR

No studio has done more for the advancement of computer character animation than Pixar. The studio developed the technology alongside an artistic sensibility that made computer animation work on the big screen.

Beginnings

The roots of Pixar go back to the very roots of computer graphics, which originated during the 1960s and 1970s. Over the course of a decade, researchers and mathematicians from a number of institutions, including the University of Utah and the New York Institute of Technology, invented methods for creating and rendering images on computers, and developed many of the techniques used today. Most of these researchers were scientists, not artists, however, and while they may have dreamed of making feature-films, they were by no means skilled film-makers or animators.

The Genesis Effect

In 1979, several of these researchers, including Ed Catmull, Ralph Guggenheim and Alvy Ray Smith, were hired by George Lucas to start a computer-research division for Lucasfilm, bringing them out of academia and into a real movie studio. The small organization developed and refined a number of important technologies, most of which were geared toward special effects. In 1982, the division produced the "Genesis Effect" for the movie *Star Trek, the Wrath of Khan*, in which a missile, tipped with a life-creating warhead called Genesis, hits a dead planet and turns it into a one flourishing with life, a sequence that was entirely computer-generated.

In 1984, a young animator named John Lasseter joined the team and directed his first CG short for Lucasfilm, titled *André and Wally B*. The plot was fairly simple, with André, a simplified version of a rubber-hose character, getting chased by Wally, a small bumblebee. This was one of the very first examples of CG character animation, and showed off new techniques such as motion blur, as well as using the more traditional "squash and stretch" technique.

In 1986 George Lucas sold the LucasFilm computer division to Steve Jobs, who renamed the company Pixar. Jobs wanted to turn Pixar into a computer company that would sell a graphic workstation called the Pixar Image Computer, but these expensive computers never really got off the ground. Pixar did, however, branch off into the software business with the release of Renderman, a rendering application used on most feature-films to this day.

© Pixar Animation Studios

Geri's Game

Having started out making CG shorts in the 1980s, Pixar went on to hone their skills, creating *Geri's Game* in 1997. Using it as a research and development exercise to help them improve their animation of humans and also to better their cloth simulations, it won the Oscar for Best Short in 1997.

For The Birds

At just three-and-a-half minutes, *For the Birds* (2000) was a very short short, but continued the Pixar tradition of creating films that explored the creative and technical possibilities of computer animation. This time the aim was to develop a way to make feathers and to ruffle them both as a group and individually.

Tin Toy

This won an Oscar in 1988, the first computer animated film to do so. To create a digitally animated character, the animator designs a computer model of the object using points and lines connected together and oriented in 3D virtual space. This is what makes computer-generated images look so real. Like an object in the physical world, an object in 3D virtual space can be moved, rotated, twisted and bent.

© Pixar Animation Studios

© Pixar Animation Studios

The Shorts

Throughout the 1980s, Pixar continued to do research and make short films. The short films were largely done as demonstrations of the studio's advancing technology, but under the direction of John Lasseter, they became enjoyable films in their own right.

Luxo Jr. (1986) astonished the computer-graphics and animation communities with its terrific character animation and a level of visual realism never before seen in computer animation. This was honored by an Academy Award nomination, the first ever for a computer-animated short.

Red's Dream (1987) explored the mind of a small unicycle named Red, who dreamed of juggling in the circus. The film marks one of the first attempts at representing human characters, with the introduction of a clown named Lumpy. It also showed off some of Pixar's developments in special effects like rain and naturalistic lighting.

Tin Toy (1988) truly put Pixar on the map. Tinny, a tin toy fresh out of the box, wants to play with his new owner – a baby with a penchant for eating and destroying toys. When he realizes his fate involves copious amounts of drool, Tinny runs for his life. *Tin Toy* was a large advance in digital character animation, and the film won the 1988 Oscar for Best Animated Short.

KnickKnack (1989) stars a lonely snowman that tries to escape his fortress-like snow globe. Very cartoony with a number of *Looney Tunes* moments, it was a huge leap from *Tin Toy* in terms of movement and acting.

Making It Big

Pixar's success in the late 1980s generated considerable business for the company. Disney offered them a contract to create a digital ink and paint system called CAPS (Computer Animation and Production System), which was first used in *Beauty and the Beast* in 1991. Pixar also picked up a lot of production work, mostly in the form of television commercials for clients such as Lifesavers, Listerine and Trident. The additional business allowed the studio to hire more artists, including Pete Docter and Andrew Stanton among others.

Beauty and the Beast » 302

TV WAKES UP

The early 1980s was a time of despair for American animators as TV producers started exporting work in wholesale lots to less expensive overseas studios, especially following the disastrous 1982 strike against runaway production. However, the following year, Filmation – which was headed by Lou Scheimer and resisted subcontracting work overseas – made an end run around the major networks and produced *He-Man and the Masters of the Universe* for daily syndication at the rate of 65 episodes a year for two years, instead of the usual 13 for a Saturday-morning show. In 1985, it followed suit with 65 half hours of *She-Ra: Princess of Power*. DIC Entertainment also came out with its own set of first-run syndicated series, *Inspector Gadget* (1983) and *Heathcliff* (1984). As a result, Filmation effectively broke the monopoly of the three major TV networks and provided new opportunities for independent studios. And because of its actions, Filmation effectively prevented a large-scale exodus of talent from the animation industry.

© Filmation Associates

Pee-Wee's Playhouse

During the 1980s, independent animators had few outlets for their work on television, aside from selling their films for fillers on cable and soliciting commissions from *Sesame Street* and MTV. But a surprising opportunity emerged with the success on CBS of *Pee-Wee's Playhouse* (1986–91). Hosted by Pee-Wee Herman (Paul Reubens), this live-action Saturday-morning series had its origins in a comedy review by Reubens. *The Pee-Wee Herman Show* was skewed toward baby boomers and their early memories of kiddie-show hosts.

The television series, which appealed to children and adults, included clips from vintage cartoons and original animation from independent film-makers and Aardman Animations. The program's animation directors included Prudence Fenton, as well as Aardman's Peter Lord and David Sproxton, with Nick Park and Craig Bartlett (later the creator of *Hey, Arnold!*) among the animators. As such, the series provided a quality of animation considerably different from what was usually seen on network TV and included such ongoing features as *Penny*, *The Dinosaur Family* and *Ants*, plus the popular 'A Life in the Fridge' segments.

© DiC Entertainment

© DiC Entertainment

Care Bears

The Care Bears' origins lie in greetings cards, and after their first foray onto the big screen in 1985, a TV show began later that year. As well as being successful as animated characters, Care Bears' coloring, activity and comic books were published, and 40 million Care Bear toys were sold between 1983 and 1987.

He-Man

For He-Man's first season, Filmation Rotoscoped live-action footage to create a library of stock character movements. Their background artists created some stunning and surreal settings for the action, and the incidental music was haunting and lyrical. As a result, it had a look and feel that was startlingly different from other cartoons of the time.

Heathcliff

Running for 65 episodes, beginning in 1984, Heathcliff (also featuring the Catillac Cats) was based on George Gately's comic strips. Heathcliff's voice was provided by Mel Blanc, who also was the voice of Bugs Bunny and thousands of other cartoon characters in a career that spanned over 60 years. Heathcliff was one of his last roles.

CBS canceled Pee-Wee's Playhouse in 1991. Reubens became involved in a minor scandal, prematurely ending what was one of the more endearing chapters of American TV animation.

Mighty Mouse: The New Adventures

Also significant was Mighty Mouse: The New Adventures (1987–88), the short-lived CBS Saturday-morning TV series using the famed Terrytoons character produced by Ralph Bakshi. As senior director, he picked John Kricfalusi, a Canadian animator who had previously worked for Bakshi on the popular Rolling Stones' 'Harlem Shuffle' music video.

Kricfalusi, a big fan of the films of Chuck Jones and Bob Clampett, had the then-radical idea of reorganizing production using the unit system employed during the heyday of Hollywood cartoons. In essence, this provided for the same director and crew to work on an episode from beginning to end, a method that had been seen by many as too inefficient and costly to be used for TV.

Kricfalusi's Limited Animation

He was also determined not to allow the economics of limited animation to prevent him from making strong visual statements. In an interview with Harry McCracken, Kricfalusi explained, "We just wanted to prove to people that it is possible to make a real cartoon, and keep it on a cheap budget... Everybody told us: 'The reason you can't do expressions and strong poses is because it's limited animation. It won't work.' And I always had the theory: 'Why not? Limited animation needs strong poses even more than full animation'." This had the advantage of providing directors with more control over what overseas studios were doing and giving the artists a greater sense of satisfaction.

All this plus Kricfalusi's irreverent sense of humor revolutionized the production of TV animation and provided a model for creator-driven shows subsequently made by Warner Bros., Nickelodeon and Cartoon Network.

While Mighty Mouse: The New Adventures did not attract a big audience, it became something of a cause célèbre when CBS refused to renew the show when one episode was said to show Mighty Mouse getting his super powers from snorting cocaine. This controversy presaged the later controversy that would surround Kricfalusi's Ren & Stimpy Show for Nickelodeon, which in a way helped bring animation into the mainstream of popular culture.

Don Bluth (b. 1937) is one of the key figures in the feature-animation revival of the 1980s. His early films, including the half-hour TV special *Banjo the Woodpile Cat* (1982), and especially the feature-length *The Secret of NIMH* (1982), helped revive the almost-forgotten art of classic Disney animation. As such, they helped pave the way for the more ballyhooed revival of Disney's own feature-animation program years later.

Bluth's Mission

While attending Brigham Young University, Bluth was hired by Disney as an assistant animator on *Sleeping Beauty*; bored with the work, he soon left to become a Mormon missionary in Argentina. He returned to animation at Filmation in 1967 after running a theater with a younger brother in Los Angeles, then returned to Disney in 1971. There he animated on *Robin Hood* (1973), *The Many Adventures of Winnie the Pooh* (1977) and *The Rescuers* (1977), and was animation director on the live-action/animated *Pete's Dragon* (1977).

In terms of feature animation, the 1970s was a period initially galvanized by the work of Ralph Bakshi, whose promise seemed increasingly to diminish as the decade wore on. In England, Richard Williams was starting his own effort to revive the classic Disney tradition, but with the exception of *The Rescuers*, the Disney studio seemed to have lost direction.

New Recruits

It was also a period in which graduates of the new character-animation program at the Disney-funded California Institute of the Arts (CalArts) and Canada's Sheridan College started entering the industry in force. Full of energy and ideas, they were increasingly frustrated and unhappy by what they found. It was in this atmosphere that Bluth persuaded a group of animators to work on *Banjo the Woodpile Cat* in their spare time.

One purpose of working on the film was to learn the process of film-making, rather than just doing animation by itself. In the process, they also rediscovered some of the techniques used in classic Hollywood films, techniques that were no longer being used at Disney. When Disney management ignored his efforts on *Banjo*, Bluth, along with Gary Goldman and John Pomeroy, rather defiantly and publicly quit to form Don Bluth Productions. The next day, they were followed by 11 other animators, a move that caused delays in the production of Disney's *The Fox and the Hound* (1981).

The Secret of NIMH

Diverted only by a slick animated sequence in the Olivia Newton-John fantasy musical *Xanadu* (1980), Bluth concentrated his efforts on his first feature, *The Secret of NIMH*, based on Robert O'Brien's popular children's novel *Mrs Frisby and the Rats of NIMH*. The

© Mrs. Brisby Ltd. Don Bluth Productions

Don Bluth

Don Bluth left Disney and vowed to make a return to their classical style of animation. He wanted to make a visually ravishing film that harked back to Disney's pre-World War Two glory days, which he did with *The Secret of NIMH*.

Mouse falling

Don Bluth brought back the multiplane camera, a Disney invention of the 1930s, in *NIMH*. It gives hand-drawn animation a live-action depth by arranging different parts of a scene on glass plates set at staggered levels.

Mouse running

In *NIMH*, Bluth wanted to avoid the graphic look that had crept into animation, so the background artists used special brushes to create a soft look without hard edges. He paid great attention to detail: when an animal stepped on a fallen branch, it gave way with a crunch, and the characters cast shadows.

The Disney Studio: After Walt » 210 Disney Strikes Back » 304

Dragon's Lair

Dragon's Lair was 22 minutes of full animation, and cost $1.3 m. It was successful from the start; a *Dragon's Lair* feature film that was planned, storyboarded and written, but never put into production. Called *Dragon's Lair: The Legend*, it was to be a darker, more developed story than the light-hearted, thrill ride *Dragon's Lair* was.

film was greatly admired for the quality of its animation and *mise-en-scène*, but it nevertheless failed at the box office. In order to keep busy, Bluth and company briefly went into the production of video games. Taking advantage of the possibilities offered by new laser-disc technology, he introduced feature-quality animation to video gaming in *Dragon's Lair* (1983) and *Space Ace* (1983), which are considered landmarks in the field.

Moving On

Bluth then joined forces with Steven Spielberg to produce *An American Tail* (1986), the tale of a young Jewish mouse that emigrates to America in the hope of finding a land without cats. Though the film's striking animation could not entirely compensate for a weak story, its financial success finally proved someone could compete head-to-head with Disney in its own market and still remain standing.

George Lucas joined Spielberg to help produce Bluth's next film, the equally successful *The Land Before Time* (1988), about an orphaned brontosaurus's quest for the legendary Great Valley. After production began in Los Angeles, Bluth abruptly shifted operations to Dublin in order to save costs. Bluth's relationship with Spielberg and Lucas was not a happy one, and he subsequently went off on his own. There followed a series of movies, beginning with *All Dogs Go to Heaven* (1989), which saw his star rapidly decline. With the exception of his version of Hans Christian Andersen's *Thumbelina* (1994), films such as *Rock-A-Doodle* (1991), *A Troll in Central Park* (1994) and *The Pebble and the Penguin* (1995) lacked the box office appeal of his early work, and he seemed to become a marginal figure. Bluth left the production of the latter, which was released without a director credit. But the bigger budgets and more ambitious productions were yet to come.

THE NEW DISNEY

In the 1980s, the Disney animation department slowly rebuilt itself and began to produce popular features again. *The Fox and the Hound* was the first animated feature done primarily by the new generation of artists at the Disney studio. While it was made by new blood, the film seemed old and tired. Only the climax, a battle with a bear animated by Glen Keane, gave a hint of things to come. It was followed by *The Black Cauldron* (1985), a film where the studio's ambition outstripped its abilities. An attempt to create animated sword and sorcery, the film's dark tone and unappealing main characters failed to interest audiences. It was a major failure, costing more and grossing less than *The Fox and the Hound*.

All Change

During the production of *The Black Cauldron*, in a financial battle that was widely covered in the business press, the studio changed management. Ron Miller, Walt Disney's son-in-law, was ousted as company CEO and replaced by Michael Eisner. Shortly afterwards, the animation department was taken out of the building that Walt Disney had constructed for it in 1940 and moved off the studio lot. The animators were forced to recognize that the new management might shut them down completely.

But slowly the animation department battled back. *The Great Mouse Detective* (1986) was a solid adventure tale highlighted by some excellent character animation. The climax inside the workings of Big Ben took place among computer-animated gears and machine parts. John Musker and Ron Clements cut their directing teeth on this film, which they co-directed with Ted Michener and Burny Mattinson.

A Rabbit Named Roger

Who Framed Roger Rabbit? (1988) was a co-production between Disney and Steven Spielberg's Amblin' Entertainment. Robert Zemeckis was the director of the live-action and Richard Williams directed the animation. The film was a major box-office success. It capitalized on nostalgia for old cartoon characters, and its combination of live-action and animation was extremely ambitious.

Normally in films that combined live-action and animation, the live-action camera was kept stationary in order to make it easier to register the animation to the live-

Roger Rabbit – Roger

During the making of this film, over 85,000 hand-inked and painted cels were created and composited with the live-action backdrops and characters; some scenes involved up to 100 individual film elements. Shading and shadows were produced using optical film printers.

Roger Rabbit – Jessica

Jessica Rabbit was a "new" cartoon character in a film that was packed with cameos from most of the classic characters from Hollywood's cartoon roster. The crowd scenes might also be familiar, as they were packed with many of the obscure players from Disney's earlier history.

© Touchstone Pictures, Amblin' Entertainment, Silver Screen Partners III

action. Williams told Zemeckis to shoot the live-action however he wanted, and that he would make the animation match.

The character of Roger Rabbit was popular enough to be featured in several short cartoons for theaters. However, disagreements between Disney and Amblin' left Roger consigned to corporate limbo.

Oliver and Company (1988), directed by George Scribner, was a conscious attempt to make the Disney cartoons feel more contemporary, though it was loosely based on Charles Dickens' *Oliver Twist*. The story was transposed to animals and set in New York City, and the soundtrack was filled with pop songs composed for the film by Barry Manilow, with vocals by Billy Joel and Bette Midler.

The Little Mermaid

This was the last Disney animated feature in which hand-painted cels and analog camera and film work were used. The final sequence was made using a computer system (CAPS). The artists' drawings were scanned into a computer, digitally colored and combined with scans of the background painting on a computer screen.

Recipe for Success

The Little Mermaid (1989) was the first Disney cartoon since *Sleeping Beauty* to be built around a princess in love. Everything seemed to come together for this film. The artists' skills had matured. Musker and Clements directed with a sure hand. Even demographics worked in the film's favor. By 1989, the post-war baby boomers had children of their own, providing this film with a sizeable audience.

The film's music also contributed to its success. Howard Ashman and Alan Mencken, the lyricist and composer, provided the best songs in a Disney feature since the 1960s. They had a romantic sensibility that worked beautifully with the story. More importantly, they greatly enhanced the film's theatrical smarts.

By the end of the decade, the new artists at Disney had mastered their craft and regained their audience. The animation department was now poised to go from success to success in the early 1990s.

© The Walt Disney Company

1980s INDEPENDENTS

Influenced not only by the Hollywood cartoons of the golden age, but also by the films of independent film-makers and artists the world over, a new generation of artists embraced animation as an art form, bringing a freshness to the medium.

Bill Plympton

Bill Plympton moved to New York City from Portland, Oregon, in 1968. He served a long tenure as an illustrator and cartoonist for newspapers and magazines such as *The New York Times*, *Vogue*, *The Village Voice*, *Vanity Fair*, *Penthouse*, *Rolling Stone* and *National Lampoon*. In 1983 he animated an adaptation of Jules Feiffer's *Boom Town*. After a series of successful shorts – *Your Face* (1987), which was nominated for an Oscar; *One of Those Days* (1988); *How to Kiss* (1989); and *25 Ways to Quit Smoking* (1989) – Plympton, almost single-handedly, animated his first feature, *The Tune* (1992). Features and shorts continued to flow from his pen, including *I Married a Strange Person* (1997), *Mutant Aliens* (2001) and *Hair High* (2004).

Marv Newland

Needing a film to graduate from the Los Angeles Art Center College of Design, Marv Newland put pencil to paper and, in the course of several late nights, created the 30-second masterpiece *Bambi Meets Godzilla* (1969). After a short stint in Toronto animating commercials and segments for *Sesame Street*, he moved to Vancouver, setting up International Rocketship. In addition to commercials Newland and International Rocketship have produced a number of outstanding short films: *Sing Beast Sing* (1980), *Anijam* (1984), *Lupo the Butcher* (1987), *Dog Brain* (1988) and *Pink Komkommer* (1991).

Sally Cruikshank

Sally Cruikshank has created some of the most original, entertaining shorts in animation. Her first film, *Quasi at the Quackadero* (1975), along with *Make Me Psychic* (1978) and *Quasi's Cabaret Trailer* (1980), forms an Art-Deco trilogy. In 1987 she directed *Face like a Frog*, with music by Danny Elfman. She has animated sequences for *Twilight Zone: The Movie* (1982) and *Ruthless People* (1986), and has contributed to Marv Newland's *Anijam*. From 1989–96 she animated and produced music videos for *Sesame Street*.

Paul Fierlinger

Paul Fierlinger was born in Japan, the son of Czechoslovakian diplomats, and was raised in America before returning to Czechoslovakia. In 1967 he escaped to Holland, eventually making his way back to the States. After forming AR&T Associates in 1971, Fierlinger animated sequences for *Sesame Street* ('Teeny Little Super Guy'). In 1979 his *It's So Nice*

Your Face

Done primarily in colored pencils, this film set Bill Plympton's signature style and launched his animation career. The loose, sketchy drawing style plays with the man's face, stretching it into every conceivable (and inconceivable) shape, mood and expression.

Hair High

Plympton's unique style, in which he sees the sense of the ridiculous in everyday life, is shown in this parody of high-school America. His animations are all done by hand, and he uses only four to six drawings per second, less than a Saturday-morning series. Disney-style animation requires 12 to 24 drawings per second.

Independents Grow » 250

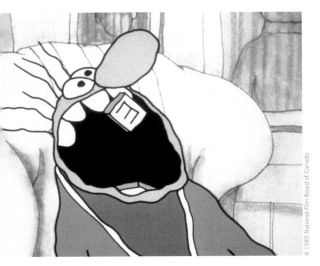

© 1985 National Film Board of Canada

The Big Snit

Richard Condie's short received an Oscar nomination and 16 other international awards. The squabbling husband and wife are typical of his insanely honest and humorous character portrayals, and the short, in which the characters are unaware a nuclear war has begun, is a perfect vehicle for his raw visual style and concern for environmental issues

The Cat Came Back

Animator Cordell Barker has worked behind the scenes making commercials; his short *The Cat Came Back* earned him an Oscar nomination and renown for his unique hand-drawn style and darkly comic cautionary tales.

© 1988 National Film Board of Canada

to Have a Wolf Around the House received an Oscar nomination. His alcohol and drug abuse film *And Then I'll Stop... Does Any of This Sound Familiar?* (1989) led to Fierlinger receiving a commission from PBS to create a one-hour autobiography called *Drawn from Memory* (1995).

George Griffin

Influenced by the films of Stan Brackhage, Robert Breer and Fred Mogubgub, with a nod to the golden-age cartoons, George Griffin is a pivotal figure among independent animators. Many of his films deal with the process of animation – *Trickfilm* (1973), *Head* (1975), *Viewmaster* (1975) and *Flying Fur* (1981), in which Griffin animates to a soundtrack from a Tom and Jerry cartoon. Other films include *Block Print* (1977), *Thicket* (1985), *Koko* (1988) and *New Fangled* (1992).

Joanna Priestly

Joanna Priestly studied painting and printmaking at the Rhode Island School of Design and the University of California, Berkeley, before receiving an MFA degree in film and video from the California Institute of the Arts. Using a wide variety of techniques, Priestley's films are imaginative and fun. Her films include *Voices* (1985), *She-Bop* (1988), *All My Relations* (1990), *Grown Up* (1993) and *Utopia Parkway* (1997).

Richard Condie

A former astrophysics student, teacher, social worker and musician, Richard Condie considered his drawing talent simply "fooling around" until he was awarded a grant from the Canada Council to animate his first film, *Oh Sure* (1972). The NFB commissioned Condie to make *John Law and the Mississippi Bubble* (1978), followed by the semi-autobiographical *Getting Started* (1982), also funded by the NFB. With *The Big Snit* (1985), Condie created one of the most uniquely funny cartoons since the golden age. *The Apprentice* (1991) and Condie's first foray into computer animation, *La Scalla* (1996), followed.

Other Film-Makers of Note

Others of influence during this period are John Dilworth (*The Dirty Birdy*, 1994), Jane Aaron (*Set In Motion*, 1988), Chris Hinton (*Blackfly*, 1991), David Fine and Alison Snowden (*Bob's Birthday*, 1994), Frank Mouris (*Frank Film*, 1973), Cordell Barker (*The Cat Came Back*, 1988), Wendy Tilby (*Strings*, 1991), Karen Aqua (*Nine Lives*, 1987), Flip Johnston (*Pulp*, 1990), Amy Kravitz (*The Trap*, 1988) and Stephen Hillenburg (*Wormholes*, 1992).

MUSIC TV & ANIMATION

Animation and music have a symbiotic relationship, a partnership that dates back to the beginnings of the art form. The Fleischer Studios were among the first to explore this partnership on film. Their series *Screen Songs* (1929–38) consisted of animated adaptations of popular songs. During the 1940s a "visual jukebox" called the Panoram made it possible not only to hear the hits of the day, but also to see the performers performing them. In the late 1950s a French company further developed a jukebox that played music film clips, and by the mid-1960s these "scopitones" could be seen throughout the US.

MTV Hits the Small Screen

As the pop-music industry grew, it became harder for music groups to make live television appearances. Bands like the Beatles began making films – *Strawberry Fields Forever* (1966) – to promote their records. In 1965 King Features created a Saturday-morning animated Beatles show, each week featuring two animated interpretations of a Beatles' song. During the 1970s pop groups filmed musical numbers that were used as video wallpaper in rock clubs and discotheques and on cable TV as fillers. Fast-forward to August 1981, the debut of MTV – music videos 24 hours a day, seven days a week

One of the first animation studios to have an impact on the music video medium was the London-based Cucumber Studio. Cucumber helped forge the marriage of animation and pop music in their video clips for the Tom Tom Club in 'Genius of Love' (1981), Elvis Costello's 'Accidents Will Happen' (1979) and Donald Fagen's 'New Frontier' (1983). Using a graphic but simple drawing style, their videos remain classics of the music-video form.

Video Classics

Winner of the MTV Award for Best Experimental Video, Art of Noise's 'Close to the Edit' (1984) launched the music-video directing career of Zbigniew Rybczynski (*Tango*, 1980). He would go on to direct videos for such artists as Grandmaster Flash, Simple Minds and Rush. A-ha's through-the-looking-glass-inspired 'Take On Me' (1985),

Radiohead – blipverts

The British band Radiohead, tired of the music video format, instead released "blipverts" to promote their 2000 album *Kid A*. These were a series of 10–40 second animated video "blips" that appeared on TV and MTV. The animation that formed these "blips" was inspired both from artwork by the band's graphic designer and by the music itself.

'Good Song'

The animated pop promo has survived into the twenty-first century: British video-makers Shynola produced this sequence for Blur's 'Good Song' which shows a love story between a squirrel and a fairy. Glasgow-based artist David Shirgley provided the surreal and charming drawings, and video won the 2004 British Animation Award for Best Music Video.

"Blipverts" – sequence

Shynola, directors of the "blipverts", were provided with photographs of paintings by the band's graphic designer and and unseen material from his sketchbooks. Having listened to the album, they set about creating the animation, sometimes bringing the pictures to life, other times making collages out of his work, or simply as a result of inspiration from the music.

directed by Steve Baron, made expressive use of the Rotoscope in combining the comic book world of a musician with that of a love-struck fan.

Two contrasting uses of computer animation can be seen in Mick Jagger's 'Hard Woman' (1985) and Dire Straits' 'Money For Nothing' (1985). Produced on a Cray X-MP Supercomputer (the most powerful computer at the time) at Digital Productions, 'Hard Woman' is a tour de force of animated imagery. Over 5,500 frames were computer generated to give the video its lush neon look. 'Money For Nothing', on the other hand, takes the opposite approach. Here, instead of fine line and fluid movement, the characters are big chunks of color.

Pioneers of the Medium

Ralph Bakshi has been making cartoons since the late 1950s. For the Rolling Stones' 'Harlem Shuffle', Bakshi, along with animator/designer and creator of *Ren & Stimpy*, John Kricfalusi, re-created the wild, fast-paced animation of the Warner Bros./MGM cartoons of the 1940s.

Director Jim Blashfield, whose film *Suspicious Circumstances* (1985) attracted the attention of head Talking Head David Byrne, has been using xerography in his animation for many years. Employing it in 'And She Was' (1985), Blashfield animates color photocopies of houses, furniture and, of course, the members of Talking Heads themselves. He would later use this technique to even greater effect on Michael Jackson's semi-autobiographical 'Leave Me Alone' (1988).

The pinnacle of animated music videos in the 1980s may be Peter Gabriel's 'Sledgehammer' (1986) and 'Big Time' (1987), both directed by Stephen Johnson. In 'Sledgehammer', Johnson utilizes the animation talents of the Quay brothers and Aardman Animation in mixing pixilation and three-dimensional animation to create a world of flapping chickens, flying fruit and frantic dances. It's a world in which Gabriel is used as much as a prop as the items surrounding him. For 'Big Time', Johnson employed many of the animators who worked with him on the first season of *Pee Wee's Playhouse*.

The 1990s and Beyond

At times it seemed that the tube had become a pop music *Fantasia* but by the end of the 1980s music video's fascination with animation was wearing thin (many of these videos were not cheap to produce, some costing upwards of $250,000). Throughout the 1990s and into the 2000s there has been an occasional return to animated music videos. Directors Magnus Carlssen ('Paranoid Android', Radiohead, 1997), Michel Gondry ('Fell In Love With A Girl' The White Stripes, 2002) and Shynola ('Good Song', Blur, 2003) among many others have directed entertaining and unique music videos employing animation.

CHANNEL 4 & ANIMATION

When Channel 4 was launched in the UK in November 1982, the company was young and enthusiastic, encouraging innovation and experimentation. They decided it would be more profitable to commission programs from outside rather than making their own. Film Four International got the idea of commissioning animation, and appointed Paul Madden as Channel 4's animation consultant. There were also schedulers who bought what was available to fill up the odd five-minute slot, and their financing of animated films did both Channel 4 and the film-makers a lot of good.

The Snowman

One of the initial involvements was with Raymond Briggs' (b. 1934) charming, bittersweet tale *The Snowman* (1982). This delightful, wordless fable was already popular in book form and, at the time, TVC was at a loss after the death of its driving force, George Dunning. They were therefore keen to make something that would provide them with an income. The simple story involves a lonely boy who builds a snowman that comes to life, taking the boy on a magical flight to the North Pole, where they meet Father Christmas and join in the snowmen's festivities until the boy has to return home.

The Snowman was directed by Dianne Jackson and, though initially bought for 10 British television runs, it has since been seen all over the world. With help from an evocative soundtrack, it is still a firm favorite for Christmas viewing. The guaranteed success of *The Snowman* meant that Channel 4's Paul Madden was able to get the best out of independent young animators. He began to finance the Quay brothers, who, with 4's backing, produced the highly successful *Street of Crocodiles* (1986).

Other Raymond Briggs favorites were to follow in *The Snowman*'s footsteps, since TVC had already bought the rights to several of Briggs' picture books. The next in line for the small screen was *When the Wind Blows* (1986), a poignant tale about two people isolated in their house after an atomic bomb has exploded. In the 1990s TVC went on to introduce a grumpy Santa in *Father Christmas* (1991) and tell the heart-warming tale of *The Bear* (1998).

Opportunities for Aardman

Alison De Vere's personal experience, as depicted in *The Black Dog* (1987), which came soon after *When the Wind Blows*, involves the tale of a woman who has a nightmare beginning with a black dog (representing depression) appearing at her window. But perhaps the most predominant

© Channel 4 Television Co Ltd. 1983

Conversation Pieces: Sales Pitch

Animating to soundtrack recordings, Aardman's *Conversation Pieces* feature a series of model animated films. Similar work was also produced by John and Faith Hubley, namely *Windy Day* in which they use a soundtrack of their children playing.

The Snowman – sketch and cel

The animators who worked on *The Snowman* retained the soft crayoned look of Raymond Briggs' original illustrations. It was nominated for an Oscar and won the BAFTA for best children's film in 1983. It has become one of the studio's best-loved films.

© Snowman Enterprises Ltd 1982, 2004

success story comes with Aardman Animations. Following screenings of their initial work on the BBC, Channel 4 offered to finance a series entitled *Conversation Pieces*. This series consisted of using a selection of 'vox pop' interviews, putting recorded words into the mouths of their animated characters. So successful were these *Conversation Pieces* that it led to another series entitled *Lip Synch*, featuring the *Creature Comforts* animals. This, in turn, led to the same characters being used for a series of hugely popular commercials, along with many other diversions that have been the backbone of Aardman.

Sadly, Channel 4's opportunity to create worthwhile television cartoons evaporated somewhere in the 1990s, and the system no longer exists to commission animated works of art. However, it was good while it lasted.

Raymond Briggs' The Snowman illustration

The film's success was helped by its original orchestral score by Howard Blake, Briggs's book avoided speech, and the film was reliant upon its images and music to move the story on, with occasional sound effects, such as the bells on a Christmas tree, or a motorbike.

© Snowman Enterprises Ltd 1982, 2004

THE QUAY BROTHERS

Heavily influenced by Eastern European cinema (particularly the surrealist Czech puppet animator Jan Svankmajer), twin brothers Stephen and Timothy Quay (b. 1947) have rekindled the kind of Gothic photoplay typical of the 1930s with their surrealistic stop-motion puppet films.

London-Bound

Natives of Norristown, Pennsylvania, the twins studied illustration at the Philadelphia College of Art, and in 1969 neatly avoided the draft by taking a course at London's Royal College of Art (RCA). They soon found London to be a cornucopia of decadence, overflowing with libraries, cinema, theater, opera, ballet and all the things that were not available in Norristown. When the course ended, and with money receding, the twins returned home and started preparing for a future visit.

During 1978, their friend and collaborator Keith Griffiths from the RCA informed the twins that he had managed to get them a grant from the British Film Institute so they would be able to make their first film. The Quays were soon back tramping the streets of London where, in 1980 with producer Keith Griffiths, they established their own studio. Their intention was to produce innovative puppet films that paid homage to the style of the early European puppeteers they so admired.

Nocturna Artificiala

Their first venture, *Nocturna Artificiala* ('Artificial Nocturne', 1979), involves the slight story of a man who, staring from a window, is mesmerized by a trolley car passing through an ill-lit city at night. He is seen back in his room and awakens with a start when he falls from his chair. This film was inspired by the boys' stay in an Amsterdam hotel, where passing trams cast menacing shadows throughout the room.

Nocturna Artificiala accentuates several causes and effects that were to become apparent in the Quay brothers' subsequent films: sets dominated by darkness; bizarre, unexplained nightmarish happenings; and odd camera angles – in short, all the things that put one in mind of the early French, German or Polish animators of the 1930s. Even the subtitles appear in four separate languages.

The Quays have always claimed that they "want to make a world that is seen through a dirty pane of glass". This perhaps explains their macabre, half-lit, miniaturized domain and the eerie feeling their work creates.

The Quay Brothers

The brothers Quay tend to avoid words in their films, relying instead on sound, music, objects, movement and light to convey meaning. Renowned for their craftsmanlike methods and unusual sources of inspiration, they make puppets that look like old dolls abused by many generations of children, construct the sets, arrange the lighting and do the photography.

Street of Crocodiles – character

This film has a dreamlike quality to it, partly due to its highly stylized direction. It has a shallow plane of focus that intentionally keeps certain objects blurred and a camera that moves with conspicuous mechanical precision.

© Brothers Quay/BFI Production Board, Channel 4, Konnick Studios

Street of Crocodiles

Their second film, *Ein Brudermord* ('A Fratricide', 1981), was founded on the writings of Franz Kafka. A series of animated documentaries built around people they held in high regard followed, capped by an affectionate homage to their particular hero in the documentary *The Cabinet of Jan Svankmajer – Prague's Alchemist of Film* (1984).

The claustrophobic *Street of Crocodiles* is perhaps their best-known work. Financed by the British Film Institute in conjunction with Channel 4 and based on a story by Polish writer Bruno Schulz, it depicts an aged museum watchman who, while on his rounds, falters at a kinescope machine. A drop of his saliva falls on the apparatus, putting it into motion, an action that also enlivens a puppet that severs his strings and begins to investigate the street

The Street of Crocodiles

The world invented by the Quay brothers for *Crocodiles* was the color of an old photograph: sepia, dirty, dark yellow, and brown. It seemed as if it was a locked room or glass cabinet that nobody had opened for years – dusty and cobwebby, almost a mystical land.

of crocodiles. There he encounters a collection of foreboding doors leading to equally foreboding rooms, one of which contains a robotic sweatshop where the puppet is taken apart, redesigned and reclothed.

Commercial Work

On the lighter side, the brothers have also been instrumental in providing pop promos for groups such as His Name Is Alive, Michael Penn, Sparklehorse, 16 Horsepower and Peter Gabriel's 'Sledgehammer' video. They also created a selection of innovative commercials for products such as Coca-Cola, MTV, Nikon, Slurpee and the Partnership for a Drug Free America.

The twins' more recent occupation has broadened to designing theater and opera sets, and in 1998 their staging for the Broadway production of Ionesco's *The Chairs* was nominated for a much-coveted Tony Award. In 1994 the Quays entered the world of live-action feature film-making with *Institute Benjamenta*, returning to animation in 2000 with the award-winning *In Absentia*, plus two dance films in 2002, *Duet* and *The Sandman*. Yet another departure from the animation tracks was the brothers' collaboration with composer Steve Martland in creating sets for a live event at the Tate Modern art museum in London.

A CAULDRON OF TALENT

The 1980s were a bubbling cauldron of gifted young animated film-makers, partially due to colleges now including animation in their curriculum and partially due to the arrival of Channel 4 and their policy of helping finance the cost of animated projects. These artists all had an extensive, spirited range, often paying tribute to artists and illustrators of yesteryear. Channel 4, itself, could well be considered as pioneers in the computer-graphics field through making early use of CGI for their logo (1982), which consisted of multicolored shapes flying around the screen, finally forming the number four.

Gifted Artists

Among the talents who sprang to light in this era was former teacher Sheila Graber (b.1940). She first decided to make animated films in 1970, but did not quite know how to go about it until she enlisted help from her local ciné club. With the success following from her films, Graber is now in a position to teach children every aspect of animation, "from Plasticine to pixels". Her trailblazing animated film *Heidi's Horse* (1987) pictures a child's artistic development.

Paul Vester had also been around since the 1970s, making unique use of cel animation in his musical cartoons such as *Football Freaks* (1971) and particularly *Sunbeam* (1980), in which he produced an animated version of a 1930s-style musical patterned after the early animated cartoons of that era.

The gifted Geoff Dunbar (b.1944), without any formal art training, began his career with Larkins studio in 1965 making advertising films. In 1968 he joined Halas & Bachelor, where he was made supervisor of a new commercials division. After a spell at Dragon Productions, he formed his own "Grand Slamm Animation" studio. He first caught the public's eye with his faithful representation of the paintings of Toulouse Lautrec with *Lautrec* (1974). The success of *Lautrec* was followed by Dunbar's interpretation of Alfred Jarry's anarchic nineteenth-century play *Ubu Roi* under the less complicated title of *Ubu* (1978). He has chalked up a number of awards along the way as well, having Paul McCartney's 'We All Sing Together' from *Rupert and the Frog Song* (1984) in the British top 10. Dunbar's latest project is the 58-minute film *The Cunning Little Vixen* (2003).

A Variety of Animation

Richard Ollive was influenced by turn-of-the-nineteenth-century artists such as Aubrey Beardsley and Arthur Rackham when he made *Night Visitors* (1974). The story involves a policeman, on night beat, who comes across Peter Pan and other nocturnal fantasy characters.

Face in Art

For over 20 years Sheila Graber has delighted audiences of all ages with her imaginative animated films about artists and art education. The films use a number of animation techniques in exploring the work of a certain artist as well as more general concepts in art.

Mondrian

This is from Sheila Graber's 1978 film *Mondrian*. She uses animation to stimulate an interest in art.

Twentieth Century Face

Having been an art teacher for 20 years, encouraging her pupils to find their creative outlet in paint, clay, wood, metal and finally animation, Graber still believes that animation is the "art of the future".

Satirical cartoonist Gerald Scarfe has also been known to dabble in animation. He first put his foot into the water by illustrating the early pop video, Pink Floyd's 'The Wall' (1981), which was animated straight onto film, providing a memorable image of hammers marching along to knock down the wall.

Barry Purves started his career by animating puppets at the Cosgrove-Hall studios, and then moved to computer animation with his five three-minute spots made for Channel 4, *The Very Models*, based on the songs of Gilbert and Sullivan.

Scotland-based Lesley Keen expanded on the Swiss artist Paul Klee's observation that "drawing is no more than taking a line for a walk" in his computer-animated tribute *Taking a Line For a Walk* (1983).

David Anderson included his *Dreamless Sleep* (1986) as part of the Channel 4 series *Sweet Disasters*. The film features the animation of wax figures that await a mysterious event in an atmosphere of pensive anticipation.

A protégé of Richard Williams, Tony White (b.1954) was thrown in at the deep end when he first joined the team as Williams' assistant on *A Christmas Carol* (1971). He was then left to direct the credit sequence for *The Pink Panther Strikes Again* (1976) while Williams was out of the country. However, it was his visual interpretation of the Japanese artist Hokusai's paintings in *Hokusai: An Animated Sketchbook* (1978) that brought him independent fame. He has since written a book on animating, *Animator's Workbook* (1988) and more recently has concentrated his talents on computer animation.

PANNONIA STUDIO

Hungarian animation reached new levels of international success in the 1980s. Pannonia was producing more films than ever before while winning international acclaim for their work. In 1981, Ferenc Rófusz's masterful short *The Fly* – about the killing of a fly from the fly's perspective – won the Oscar for Best Animated Short. A few months later, Pannonia won its third Golden Palm award for *Perpetual Motion* (about the incredible things that happen to a man each time he enters an elevator) by Béla Vajda.

TV and Features

Television production also reached a new peak. Pannonia was producing, on average, five series per year, including *Pom-Pom* by Attila Dargay, *The Curious Elephanny* by Zsolt Richly, *Csepke* by Ferenc Varsányi, *Trumpy and the Fire Troll* by Tamás Baksa, and, from two newcomers, *Never Mind Toby* by Ferenc Cakó and *Augusta* by Csaba Varga,

During this period, Pannonia produced an incredible 20 animated features, including *The Son of White Mare* (1980) by Marcell Jankovics, which in 1984 was acknowledged in Los Angeles as one of the best animation films ever made. The film combines various art styles (including Art Deco and Art Nouveau) with popular legends. Other notable features included the box office success *Vuk* (1981) by Attila Dargay, *Heroic Times* (1982) by József Gémes, *John the Boaster* (1983) by Zsolt Richly, *Saffi* (1984) by Attila Dargay, *The Captain of The Forest* (1987) by Attila Dargay and *Willy The Sparrow* (1988) by József Gémes.

Abundance of Talent

While veteran animators like Sándor Reisenbüchler of *Farewell Little Island* (1987) and István Orosz of *Ah, America!* (1984) continued to produce strong short films, the decade was dominated by a wealth of new talent who brought not only new ideas, but also a desire, perhaps encouraged by the Oscar success of *The Fly*, to try new animation techniques. Csaba Varga's *The Luncheon* (1980) used clay animation, Ferenc Cakó's *Ab*

© Pannonia Film

Vuk

Attila Dargay's *Vuk* was first in an impressive list of successful animated features made by Pannonia in the 1980s.

Vuk – character outlines

This was Hungary's second largest-ever box office hit. Also known as *The Little Fox*, it was concerned with a young fox whose family is killed by hunters and who is raised by his wise old uncle.

© Pannonia Film

© Pannonia Film

Ovo used a sand animation technique, *Ad Rem* (1989) used a combination of Plasticine and coal powder, Gyula Nagay animated real fingers in *Wave of Fingers* (1986) and Jánvári produced a computer-controlled sequence motion film called *Labyrinth* (1989). Other notable films by newcomers include *How to Scare a Lion* (1981), *Doors* (1983), *Sprinkling* (1989), *Ad Astra* (1982), *Augusta Dresses Up* (1984), *The Wind* (1984) and *Gravitation* (1984).

In 1985, the Kecskemét studio hosted Hungary's first animation festival. The festival was initially to be held every three years, but after the second edition in 1988, the festival was silent until 1993. Fortunately the festival has managed to survive.

Heroic Times

This was József Gémes' beautifully animated, award-winning feature from 1982. It won prizes at festivals during the early 1980s, such as Espinho, Annecy and Kecskemét.

Moving On

In 1986, the Hungarian animation landscape began to shift when the Pannonia Cartoon and Animated Film Studios became the independent company Pannonia Film Company. The artists now had full control over the company along with all distribution rights. But with independence came new problems. In 1988, Pannonia began to lose its monopoly over Hungarian animation when Varga Studios, the first private animation studio in Hungary, was formed by Csaba Varga and producer Andras Erkel. One of Varga's first jobs would be for an Hungarian émigré named Gabor Csupo, who was animating an American television series called *The Simpsons*.

POLAND, BULGARIA & RUSSIA

Poland

The 1980s saw the emergence of two prominent animators, Zbigniew Rybczynski (b. 1949) and Piotr Dumala (b. 1956), along with the continued maturity of another, Jerzy Kucia (b. 1942).

Kucia began making films in 1972 with *Return*, and his style was quite different from that of earlier Polish animators. His visually rich films are mysterious and elliptical, giving viewers impressions, glimpses and fragments rather than certainties. As such, the work is difficult and open to multiple interpretations. Kucia's notable films of this period include *Spring* (1980), *Splinters* (1984) and *The Parade* (1986).

One of animation's most outstanding talents, Piotr Dumala began making films during the 1980s. His early films, notably the fairy tale parody *The Black Hood* (1983), were crudely drawn black comedies. Later on, Dumala created a unique plaster technique that involved the use of slabs of plaster covered with normal glue (with hot water to make the surface stronger and smooth). Once it was dry, Dumala scratched on the plaster with sandpaper and painted it with oil paint. During this period the tone of Dumala's work changed, becoming more tranquil and elusive. He began using this technique in 1985, for the astonishing Dostoyevsky adaptation *Gentle*. Dumala also made *Flying Hair* (1984), *Walls* (1988) and the bizarre *Freedom of the Leg* (1989), about a man whose leg runs away while he is sleeping.

Another important animator from this period is Zbigniew Rybczynski, who made films that mixed live-action and animation. He started at the Semafor puppet studio in the 1970s and received some notice for his films *The Soup* and *Holiday*. In 1981 he made an extraordinary work, *Tango*, which won many awards including the Oscar for Best Animated Short. In this inventive and funny metaphor of human existence, people go in and out of a small room, repeating the same actions over and over again. Following *Tango*, Rybczynski left Poland for the US where he began experimenting with video.

Bulgaria

After a period of decline in the 1970s, Bulgarian animation was revitalized during the 1980s, thanks in part to two major artists, Anri Kulev (b. 1949) and Nikolai Todorov. Kulev debuted in 1976 with the cynical *Hypothesis*, and followed that with *Representation* (1979) and *Labyrinth* (1984). Kulev's films are full of impressive imagery, warmth and passion. Todorov's work includes the bleak hymn to nonconformity, *Odyssey* (1978), *A Day as a Flower* (1984) and *Successful Test* (1984).

© Pilot Moscow Animation Studio

The Dark Side of the Moon

Alexander Tatarsky, whose film *The Dark Side of the Moon* is pictured here, believes that to animate means above all to breathe life into something; he breathes rich and unusual life into various phenomena, objects and animals in his animation.

Polish & Bulgarian Animation in the 1950s » 194 » Polish & Bulgarian Animation in the 2000s » 362

© Piotr Dumala

Walls

Walls is a profound commentary on life in a totalitarian environment. In the film, a tiny man who is trapped and routinely observed within a small box responds to his situation at first with fear, madness and, finally, lethargy.

Other notable new talents during this decade include Boyko Kanev with *A Crushed World* (1986) – which won the Grand Prix at the 1987 Annecy Animation Festival – and Pencho Konchev with *Romance of the Wind* (1986).

Russia

In the 1980s Soyuzmultfilm's hierarchical structure had become so rigid that it was almost impossible for young animators to get into the studio. In fact, many, like Ivan Maximov and Mikhail Aldashin, did not even want to work at the studio. As government authority weakened during this period, Soyuzmultfilm's monopoly began to crumble. In 1989, the first private studio, Pilot, was formed by young animators Alexander Tatarsky (b. 1950) and Igor Kovalyov (b. 1963). Soon, over 25 studios appeared in Moscow. The new studios quickly began luring away Soyuzmultfilm talent. By the 1990s, Soyuzmultfilm was making a mere six films a year.

Pilot Studios in particular produced outstanding work. Tatarsky's preference for comedy and Kovalyov's more elliptical and deeply personal work proved to be a strong combination. The two worked well together on such films as *Wings, Tails, Legs* (1986) and *Investigation by the Kolobki Brothers* (1987). The Kolobki brothers became enormously popular in Russia, and later had their own video game and talk show. Alone, Tatarsky made *The Dark Side of the Moon* (1984) and Kovalyov created the very funny and strange *Hen, His Wife* (1989), which won the Grand Prix at the 1990 Ottawa International Animation Festival in Canada. The studio also produced newcomer Alexander Petrov's debut, *The Cow* (1989), Ivan Maximov's *5/4* (1990) and Mikhail Aldashin's *Poumse* (1989).

Other important animators to emerge during this period include Garry Bardin (*Break*, 1985), Nina Shorina (*The Door*, 1986), and Alexei Karaev (*Welcome*, 1986).

Soviet Animation in the 1960s » 234 Russian Animation in the 2000s » 362

ESTONIA

Estonian animation dates back to 1931 and a film titled *The Adventures of Juku the Dog*. However, the first Estonian animation studio, Nukufilm, a division of the state's live-action studio Tallinna Kinostuudio, was not created until 1957. Headed by Elbert Tuganov and Heino Pars, Nukufilm's early films, all puppet or cut-out animations, were aimed primarily at children, but as the films grew more satirical and at times poetic, the studio's output eventually became more tailored to an adult audience. In the 1960s, Kalju Kurepõld and Ants Looman made the first Estonian-drawn animation films for the Soviet Newsreel, *Fuse*, followed by commercials for Eesti Reklaamfilm (Estonian Advertisingfilm). Shortly thereafter Ants Kivirähk and Jaak Palmse made animation telefilms for Estonian television.

© Tallinnfilm Studios

Rein Raamat

In 1971, Rein Raamat (b. 1931), a classically trained artist who had worked as a designer with Tuganov, teamed up with Russian animator Fedor Chitruk to establish a cel-animation division (Joonisfilm) within Tallinnfilm (formerly Tallinna Kinostuudio). Under the direction of Raamat, Joonisfilm produced ambitious, philosophical films, many based on Estonian folklore, that won wide international acclaim and firmly planted Estonia on the international animation landscape.

Raamat's *Big Tyll* (1980) is based on an old Estonian legend about an Estonian folk hero who comes to the defense of his people and country when called upon. The film is beautifully designed and animated, and features a haunting score from famed Estonian composer Lepo Sumera.

Vision of Hell

Raamat's masterwork is *Hell* (1983). The film is based on the work of an Estonian artist named Eduard Viiralt; specifically, there are three prints in which he provides different interpretations of hell. The first image shows the punishment and destruction of human beings. The second reveals a hedonistic, anarchistic version of hell. And the third is a warning of what is to come. What Raamat did, echoing the work of Viiralt's

Triangle

Priit Pärn's style is both refreshing and startling. He rejects the rounded, pristinely drawn characters and landscapes that dominate traditional animation, and replaces them with a primitive style, bold colors and sketchy, childlike drawings.

© Tallinnfilm Studios

Estonian Animation in the 1950s » 194

contemporary, George Grosz, was to put the three images next to one another. He incorporated them all into one vision in order to create a multi-layered and contradictory vision of hell and, with it, society.

Priit Pärn Emerges

During Raamat's tenure at Joonisfilm – which ended after Estonian's re-independence in 1991 – a number of young artists emerged under his tutelage, most notably Priit Pärn (b. 1946), a former ecologist. In direct contrast to the traditional and heavily symbol-prone works of Raamat's animation, Pärn, influenced by black and absurd humor and the strong caricature tradition in Estonia, explored a more liberal and deceptively primitive manner of expression, producing complex and funny investigations into the human condition. Pärn's success and influence led to the development of a new generation of artists with backgrounds in political cartoons and surrealism rather than in classical arts: Mati Kütt, Janno Põldma, Heiki Ernits, Rao Heidmets, and, later, stop-motion animators Kalju Kivi, Hardi Volmer and Riho Unt.

Following his debut in 1977, *Is the Earth Round?*, along with the children's film, *And Plays Tricks* (1978), and the disappointing *Exercises for an Independent Life* (1980), Pärn made *Triangle*. Released in 1982, *Triangle* remains a landmark in Estonian animation for its examination of modern relations between a man and a woman; it fuses the personal and political into a witty observation of contemporary domestic politics.

A Golden Age

By the mid-1980s, as *glasnost* and *perestroika* emerged under Mikhail Gorbachev, censorship policies lightened. Not only was there little or no censorship, but there was also stable funding from Moscow. For many, this was the golden age of Estonian animation.

If there is one film that defines this new period it is Pärn's *Breakfast on The Grass* (1988), one of the masterpieces of animation. In examining a few moments in the daily lives of four Estonians, Pärn trenchantly critiques life in the Soviet Union by giving viewers a rare glimpse of the absurdities of communist society and what people endure on a daily basis just to survive. As with *Triangle*, *Breakfast on the Grass* astonished Russian audiences with its frank portrait of modern Soviet life.

During the 1980s, Nukufilm re-emerged under a new generation of animators. Riho Unt and Hardi Volmer had success with their decidedly adult puppet films like *The War* (1987), which depicts the Russian-German battle over Estonia, and the comical *Spring Fly* (1986) based on the work of Estonian writer Anton Hansen Tammsaare. Rao Heidmets has also made some significant puppet films including *Papa Carlo's Theater* (1988), while Kalju Kivi has made a number of highly original films including *Bride of the Star* (1984).

Breakfast on the Grass (head in hands)

In this film, Pärn examined a few moments in the daily lives of four Estonians. He gave viewers a glimpse of the absurdities of Communist society and what people endure on a daily basis just to survive.

Breakfast on the Grass

When describing this film, Pärn explained that it was the story of a society told in a realistic way using a dramatic structure that was close to a live-action feature. He used the usual tools of animation – visual gags, metamorphoses and different drawing styles to make his film funny, multileveled and ironic.

GROWTH IN ALL DIRECTIONS

During the 1980s Japanese animation continued to expand. The new direct-to-video market appeared, and it and the traditional areas of theatrical, TV and independent animation tended to blend together. Theatrical animation was still dominated by big screen spin-offs of popular TV series. But the decade saw many spectacular features, often sci-fi and based upon popular manga novels, such as *Harmagedon* (1983) by Rintaro, *The Wings of Honneamise: Royal Space Force* (1987) by Hiroyuki Yamaga (b. 1962) and *Akira* (1988) written, designed and directed by Katsuhiro Otomo (b. 1954).

Features

Features began appearing with 3D effects or experimental computer-graphics sequences, including director Osamu Dezaki's *Space Adventure Cobra* (1982), Dezaki's *Golgo 13: The Professional* (1983) and *Lensman* (1984) by Yoshiaki Kawajiri (b. 1950). Rumiko Takahashi's (b. 1957) manga-based *Urusei Yatsura* (1981) – a pun roughly translated as "those obnoxious aliens" – launched a new genre of high-school comedy-fantasy in which a shy, socially inept boy is suddenly surrounded by beautiful fantasy or outer-space girls.

Other Takahashi series – such as *Maison Ikkoku* (1986), a romantic comedy set in a boardinghouse, and *Ranma 1/2* (1989), a fantasy about a teen boy cursed with turning into a cute girl when he becomes wet – demonstrated that what was popular was the human-interest relationships between the likeable, believable characters rather than gags or fantasy elements.

DragonBall

The frenetically bizarre *Dr Slump* (1981) and *DragonBall* (1986), followed by *DragonBall Z*, won their audiences because of dynamic characterizations more than the dynamic action. This also held true for the giant-robot sci-fi genre. The most popular TV series were *Macross* (1982) and several *Gundam* sequels after 1985, all emphasizing complex character relationships in a realistic, futuristic war setting.

Other notable 1980s TV animation included the ultra-violent, post-apocalyptic *Fist of the North Star* (1984), by Tetsu Hara and "Buronson" (Sho Fumimura); *City Hunter* (1987), a private detective comedy-drama by Tsukasa Hojo; and *Creamy Mami, the Magical Angel* (1983), a magical little-girl series that made the reputations of new animation producer Studio Pierrot and character designer Akemi Takada (b. 1952).

Home Video

The first direct-to-video production, taking advantage of the home-video market created in 1975, was the four-episode *Dallos* (1983). The new market (called OAV or OVA for Original Animation Video) aimed to appeal to affluent young adult males. *Dirty Pair* (1985), a sci-fi comedy featuring two sexy interstellar "secret agents" in bikini uniforms,

DragonBall Z

One of the greatest manga franchises ever created, *DragonBall* has been adapted for many TV series and several movie features. It has also been translated into many languages and is extremely popular around the world. Goku (above) is the warrior leader, while Babidi (below) is one of the many ingenious villains of the series.

Japanese Animation in the 1970s » 260

Wicked City

Created by Yoshiaki Kawajiri, *Wicked City* is an example of anime noir: the darkly atmospheric telling of a high-tech urban crime story. Anime noir is characterized by black shadows, dark blue night-time exteriors and extreme camera angles.

Dirty Pair

The antics of the Dirty Pair were originally serialized in Japan's *SF Magazine* and later recounted in three novellas, by s-f author Haruka Takachiho. In 1984 the duo (Yuri, left, and Kei, right) made their animation debut with their own TV series, written by animation studio, Sunrise.

was a failed TV animation series that sold so well on OAV that new TV episodes plus OAV features and a theatrical feature were produced.

Successful OAVs, such as *Project A-Ko* (1986), *Gall Force* (1986), *Bubblegum Crisis* (1987), and *Mobile Police Patlabor* (1989) led not only to long OAV series, but also to TV series and/or theatrical features. The OAV market was also responsible for some theatrical features that were designed primarily for video sales following a short theatrical run, such as *Vampire Hunter D* (1985), directed by Toyoo Ashida (b. 1944), and *Wicked City* (1987), by Yoshiaki Kawajiri.

Art Animation

The OAV market also created opportunities for independent art animation. *Neo-Tokyo* (1987) and *Robot Carnival* (1987) were both funded as anthology features of three and nine short films respectively, showcasing the talents of individual animators such as Rintaro, Yoshiaki Kawajiri, Katsuhiro Otomo, Hiroyuki Kitakubo (b. 1963), Koji Morimoto (b. 1959), Takashi Nakamura (b. 1955) and others. The individual films could be shown at animation festivals, while their combined release as an OAV feature paid for their production.

World War Two drama emphasizing Japan's suffering civilians, seen through children's eyes, was an emerging genre. *Barefoot Gen* (1983), a semi-autobiographical account of the 1945 nuclear bombing of Hiroshima by cartoonist Keiji Nakazawa (b. 1939), who lived through it as a child, presents a harrowing contrast between the horrors of the event and the animation that is drawn in Nakazawa's personal "cute" art style. Director Isao Takahata's *Grave of the Fireflies* (1988) is a story told by the ghosts of two children who survive the 1945 firebombing of Kobe. Others in this genre included *Girls in Summer Dresses* (1988), *Raining Fire* (1988), *Kayoko's Diary* (1991) and *Rail of the Star* (1993).

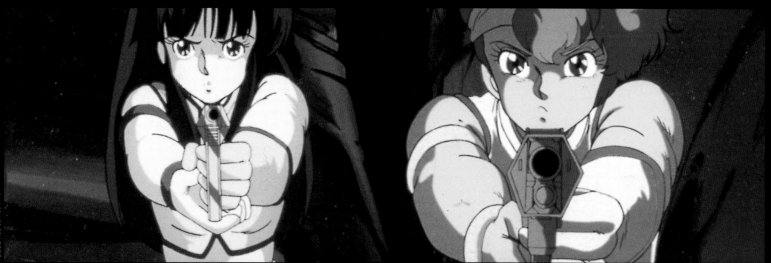

MIYAZAKI & OTOMO

Hayao Miyazaki (b. 1941), Osamu Tezuka's successor to the popular title of "the Disney of Japan", began at Toei Doga as an in-betweener in 1963, advancing by 1968 to set designer and key animator on *The Little Norse Prince*, directed by Isao Takahata (b. 1935) who had become a close friend. In 1971 both Miyazaki and Takahata left Toei.

Making His Name

After working on a variety of projects, Miyazaki's big break came in 1979 when TMS chose him to direct its second *Lupin III* theatrical feature, *The Castle of Cagliostro*. Miyazaki also wrote the story and designed the characters. In Japan's premiere animation magazine *Animage* (published by Tokuma Shoten) in 1978, editor Toshio Suzuki (b. 1948) interviewed Miyazaki extensively for coverage of *Cagliostro*. This led to a close relationship between them. In 1982 Suzuki asked Miyazaki to create a graphic novel for serialization in *Animage*. The result was *Nausicaä of the Valley of the Winds*, which Miyazaki animated in 1984. The result pleased Tokuma so much that it offered to finance a new animation studio under Miyazaki's leadership. Miyazaki agreed only if his friend Takahata could be a co-director.

Studio Ghibli, which Suzuki eventually became president of, became known for features by Miyazaki and Takahata such as *The Castle in the Sky* (1986), *My Neighbor Totoro*, *Grave of the Fireflies* (both 1988), *Kiki's Delivery Service* (1989) and *Only Yesterday* (1991), which were critical successes but barely successful. When Miyazaki reluctantly gave up his aversion to commercialism and allowed the beloved characters from his movies to be merchandised, they — and the movies — became tremendously popular throughout Japan. Miyazaki's *Porco Rosso* (1992) and Takahata's *Pom Poko* (1994) became Japan's top-grossing films of those years, animation or live-action. Miyazaki's *Princess Mononoke* (1997) broke new box office records in Japan, and *Spirited Away* (2001) set a new world box office record for a non-US theatrical feature — and ultimately won an Academy Award.

Cel Champion

Miyazaki is known for only taking on film projects in which he becomes personally interested. He has championed hand-drawn cel animation, although he is not adverse to using computer graphics to enhance the traditional art. Miyazaki groomed a successor, Yoshifumi Kondo (1950–98). Unfortunately Kondo, who directed only one feature, *Whisper of the Heart* (1995), died within a month after Miyazaki's retirement. He returned to Ghibli to keep the studio going until new directors could be groomed. *Spirited Away* did this with honours, and Miyazaki has expressed satisfaction with Ghibli's next feature, *The Cat Returns* (2002) by director Hiroyuki Morita (b. 1964). Miyazaki's adaptation of the novel *Howl's Moving Castle*, by British author Diana Wynne Jones, was released in 2004.

Akira

This was first published in the magazine *Young*, and is considered by many to be the finest work of graphic fiction ever created. When the animated version was made, it was one of the first Japanese anime films to have the character's voices recorded before they were animated. Although this is the norm in US animation, in Japan the animation is generally produced first.

My Neighbor Totoro – sequence

Miyazaki's films are visually enchanting, using a watercolor look for the backgrounds. His characters are drawn in the distinctive Japanese anime style, having large, round eyes and mouths that can be as small as a dot or as big as a cavern. They also have an unforced realism in the way they notice details; early in *Totoro*, for example, the children look at a little waterfall near their home, and there on the bottom, unremarked, is a bottle someone threw into the stream.

Akira's Creator

Katsuhiro Otomo, a fan of American movies and comic books, was first published as a teen comic book creator in 1973. By the end of the decade he was specializing in science-fiction manga with complex plots. In 1982 Otomo began serialization of his manga magnum opus *Akira*. His reputation as a serious sci-fi artist got him invited to become the character designer for the theatrical sci-fi feature *Harmagedon*. Although it was a popular success, for Otomo it was an unpleasant experience due to his lack of creative control. As a result, when major financial interests wanted to make *Akira* (which was still being serialized) into a major theatrical feature, Otomo refused unless he could have total control as its director.

Akira, released in 1988, was such a success, both commercially and creatively, that Otomo switched his career from writing and drawing cartoon fiction to directing and producing both animated and live-action films. During the early 1990s Otomo took fellow manga creator Satoshi Kon (b. 1963) under his wing and helped his entry into the animation industry.

Keeping Busy

Simultaneously with the production of *Akira*, Otomo worked on short art films for the *Neo-Tokyo* and *Robot Carnival* anthology features. In 1991 Otomo and Kon worked together on two features, the animated *Old Man Z* (written by Otomo and directed by Hiroyuki Kitakubo) and the live-action *World Apartment Horror* (directed by Otomo). During 1995 Otomo was the general director of *Memories*, an anthology feature adaptation of three of his most popular manga sci-fi short stories, individually written and directed by different animators; he personally directed the "Cannon Fodder" segment.

In 1998, Otomo got a supervisor credit on *Spriggan*, which he was popularly believed to have directed because of the artistic similarity between it and *Akira*. In 2001 he scripted and produced *Metropolis*, directed by Rintaro. Otomo's most recent project was *Steamboy* (2004).

© Nibariki-Takuma Shoten

My Neighbor Totoro

Totoro was released as a double-bill in 1988 with *Grave of the Fireflies*. Until recently, Miyazaki did not use computers to assist in the animation process; they are drawn a frame at a time, with Miyazaki himself contributing tens of thousands of frames.

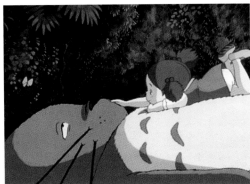

© Nibariki-Takuma Shoten

CHINA IN THE 1980s

The period following the fall of the infamous Gang of Four in 1976, which ended the Cultural Revolution, saw a new burst of creativity from the Shanghai Animation Studio after over 10 years of repression, especially apparent in the popular short *One Night in an Art Gallery* (1978) by A Da (1934–87) and Lin Wenxiao. Based on caricatures of the Gang of Four secretly drawn by A Da in a labor camp, it tells a tale of four functionaries who censored paintings they do not understand; the ending, when the four are chased off by children, signalled to Chinese audiences that the nightmare years were really over. During the following decade, A Da would become the dominant animation film-maker in China and a major international figure as well. And it was this film's critical and public reception that heralded what was called the Second Golden Age of Chinese animation.

Influential A Da

A Da's most famous film is *The Three Monks* (1980), a reworking of an old Chinese proverb that made a plea for co-operation to help heal the divisions caused by the Cultural Revolution. The film, which won awards at major film festivals and was widely shown on TV around the world, was praised for its blending of traditional Chinese and modern Western animation techniques. This was followed by *Butterfly Spring* (1983), a love story which was also the country's first animated film for adults. The year 1984 saw the release of *The Wanderings of San Mao* – based on a comic strip he read as a boy about an orphan boy's survival during the war with Japan – and *36 Characters*, an educational film inspired by films he made with children. His last work was two segments for David Ehrlich's *anijam* film *Academy Leader Variations* (1987), which premiered after he died.

During this period, the Shanghai Animation Studio was divided into three sections, reflecting the three basic techniques being used at the time: puppet, cut-out and cel animation. The most significant puppet films made during this period were the *Effendi* series based on an *Uigur* folk tale, first done by Jin Shi in 1980 and followed by Qu Jianfang (b. 1935) several years later.

Cut-Out Masterpieces

Given the long folk tradition of paper cut-outs, it is not surprising that this form of animation reached new heights in China. This was clearly evident in three films that won wide acclaim on the festival circuit: *Fox Hunts the Hunter* (1978) by Hu Xionghua, *Monkeys Fish for the Moon* (1981) by Zhou Keqin (b. 1941), and most famously *Snipe-Clam Grapple* (1983) by Hu Jinqing, based on the proverb: "In the fight between the snipe and the clam, the fisherman has the best of it." The film was especially lauded for the director's approach to nature. Hu Jinqing further developed his technique in such films as *The Straw Man* (1988), *Cockfighting* and *The Stronger Get Hooked* (1988).

© Shanghai Animation Film Studio

The Three Monks

With a simple and fresh directing style, A Da's film is an adaptation of a folk proverb: one monk will shoulder two buckets of water, two monks will share the load, but add a third and no-one will want to fetch water. *The Three Monks* (which had no dialog) made use of caricature – each monk had his own personality, defined as economically as possible through movement and actions.

Monkeys Fish for the Moon

Monkeys Fish for the Moon echoes a theme common in many post-Cultural Revolution films: the feeling of a great sense of loss. It tells the story of a group of apes who embark on a mission to obtain the unobtainable, a quest which is bound to end in disappointment.

Snipe-Clam Grapple

This delicate paper cut-out animation by Hu Jinqing lasts seven minutes and is based on an old Chinese proverb.

The Shanghai Studio » 175 *Tadahito Mochinaga and Puppet Animation* » 261

Other films of note using this technique include *Zhang Fei Judges the Theft of a Watermelon* (1979) by Qian Yunda and Ge Guiyun (b. 1933). Based on a character in the classic tale *Chronicles of the Three Kingdoms*, it exhibits the influence of Chinese opera and shadow theater. In addition, there is Qian Jiaxin's *Mr Nanguo* (1981), about a court musician who does not know anything about music; it was inspired by ancient Chinese bas-reliefs.

Powerful Themes

In terms of cel animation, 1979 saw the release of China's first widescreen feature, *Nezha Conquers the Dragon*, directed by A Da, Wang Shuchen and Yan Dingxian. The story has echoes of the fall of the Gang of Four in its tale of a boy rescuing a girl from four evil forces.

This period also saw director Te Wei return to his widely praised brush-animation technique after more than 20 years, with his final masterpiece in this unique style being *Feeling From Mountain and Water* (1988). Made after he retired as head of the Shanghai Animation Studio, and co-directed with Yan Sanchun (b. 1934) and Ma Kexuan (b. 1939), it has been characterized as a "painting-in-process". It tells the sad tale of a musician and his protégé, a story which seems symbolic of Te Wei passing on his art to his own younger disciples.

Shanghai Animation Studio in the 1960s » 240

KOREA IN THE 1980s

North Korea

Animation in Korea began with the opening of the state-owned Pyongyang Studios in North Korea soon after the establishment of the Democratic People's Republic of Korea in 1948 which, like the live-action film industry, had strong support from President Kim Il Sung. Their films emphasized ideological education for children, including many stories told by Kim Il Sung, and were strongly influenced by Soviet films of the period.

The most highly praised North Korean film was Kim Chu Ok's feature *The Flying Horse* (1986), again based on a Kim Il Sung story about the youngest of a man's three sons who defeats foreign invaders by riding a flying horse. Another film that gained some international attention was *An Ant who Rolled a Canteloupe* (1985) by Ryu Chung Ung, about an ant whose intellectual skills help him compensate for his lack of physical strength.

In 1985, the April 26th Children's Film Studio of the Democratic People's Republic of Korea, or SEK Studio, was established as an overseas facility. As such, it has done work for French, Italian and Spanish companies, including animation on versions of *The Arabian Nights* and *Les Miserables*, as well as *Corto Maltese*. It also produces children's films for its domestic market, which are often exported to other parts of Asia.

South Korea

Animation in South Korea, which dates back to TV commercials that began appearing in 1956, really got established with the work of Shin Dong Hun, who is considered the father of South Korean animation. After doing several commercials, he set up his own studio in 1960 and jump-started the local industry with the production of the popular feature-length *Hong Gil-Dong* (1967), based on Korea's first novel. Shin later deserted features to work on foreign TV productions, before abandoning animation.

Animated movies in South Korea flourished in fits and starts, with 62 features made between 1976 and 1985. This occurred despite primitive working conditions and competition for talent from the growing number of overseas studios servicing Japanese and Western studios that began appearing in 1966. Unlike *Hong Gil-Dong*, these movies tended to use Japanese animation as their model rather than indigenous graphic styles. Particularly influential was the Japanese TV series

Hong Gil-Dong – poster

One of the advertisements for Korea's first animated feature proclaimed: "125,300 pictures drawn for one year by 400 people. If one person did it, it would take 400 years." The film was a great success, and drew audiences of 100,000 in its first four days of release, sparking the start of an industry that continues to flourish to this day.

Majingâ Zetto (1972–74) which inspired a spurt of sci-fi movies, including *Taegwon Kids Maruchi and Arachi* (1976).

With South Korea set to host the Asian Games in 1986 and the summer Olympics in 1988, production of animated features dried up in favour of TV series, in order to serve the growth in tourism. This led to the first South Korean animated TV series, *Wandering Kkachi* (1987), produced for the Korean Broadcasting System.

Large Output

The period also saw a huge increase in the television production around the world, which in turn led to a huge growth in service studios. The major players in this area were AKOM, Sunwoo Entertainment, Saerom Production, Rough Draft Korea and Hanshin. This, plus the growth of local production, would eventually make South Korea the third largest producer of animation after the United States and Japan.

Hong Gil-Dong

The creation of *Hong Gil-Dong* was a frustrating process for all involved. Severe shortages of film and equipment in the 1960s meant that Shin Dong Hun and his team had to improvize at virtually every stage of the production process. They used secondhand film thrown away by the US Air Force, adapted their own camera and stand from one they had seen and taught themselves how to apply special effects.

Corto Maltese

The SEK studio were commissioned by the French company Les Films de la Perrine to work on *Corto Maltese*, the 2002 French feature directed by Pascal Morelli. Due to the success of the North Korean animation industry, increasing numbers of animation companies from Western Europe and South East Asia are now travelling to the country in the hope of doing business.

XI

1990–2000:
RENAISSANCE

Box office grosses and prime-time television proved, at last, that great animation could appeal to adults as well as children. This led to a renaissance that expanded the field and brought renewed respect.

     The Simpsons was the most successful TV cartoon of all time, and its success initiated a boom in creator-driven, prime-time animated series aimed at adults. The victors include *South Park*, *Beavis & Butt-head* and *King of the Hill*. New niche cable networks created animated superstars: *Ren & Stimpy*, *Rugrats* and *The Powerpuff Girls*, who became household names. And anime rules as *Pokémon* became an international powerhouse.

     Disney's *Beauty and the Beast* earned an Academy Award nomination for Best Picture and *The Lion King* roared to epic box office proportions. Old-school stop-motion techniques continued to wow the public: Aardman's clay-made *Wallace and Gromit* and *Chicken Run*, and Henry Selick's puppet-toon *The Nightmare Before Christmas*, have become audience favorites. DreamWorks established itself with *The Prince of Egypt* and *Antz*. But the big news was Pixar and its first feature-length film, *Toy Story*.

     Animated computer graphics dazzled and delighted mainstream moviegoers. The charm, the heart and the realistic visuals won new fans young and old – and in the hands of master storytellers, animated features entered a new dimension.

DISNEY STRIKES BACK

The Disney studio followed up *The Little Mermaid* with *The Rescuers Down Under* (1990), the first time Disney made an animated feature film sequel. But the sequel did not do as well critically or financially as *The Little Mermaid*.

Award-Winning Animation

However, *Beauty and the Beast* (1991), directed by Kirk Wise and Gary Trousdale, was a massive hit. Once again, Howard Ashman and Alan Mencken provided the music, with Ashman also producing and contributing to the story. It was the first animated feature in history to be nominated for the Academy Award for Best Picture. *Aladdin* (1992), John Musker and Ron Clements' follow-up to *The Little Mermaid*, did even better at the box office. The character of the Genie, voiced by Robin Williams and animated by Eric Goldberg, stole the show.

The Lion King (1994), directed by Roger Allers and Rob Minkoff, set the record for the highest-grossing traditionally animated film. Loosely based on *Hamlet*, the film told the mythical story of a son having to avenge the death of his father. Ironically, the studio did not have high expectations for the film. They were convinced that

Simba and Mufassa

While most of *The Lion King* was hand-drawn, there were certain effects the director wanted that would be extremely time-consuming to draw by hand. The wildebeest stampede, for example, was based on a wildebeest from a character designer's hand-drawn artwork. A 3D-computer model was created and replicated in order to produce the stampede seen on the film.

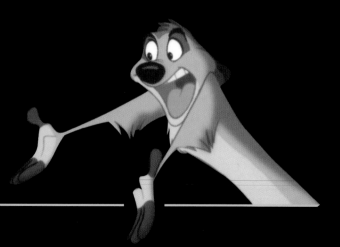

© The Walt Disney Company

Pumbaa and Timon

Producing a hand-drawn animated film is extremely labor-intensive: more than 600 artists, animators and technicians contributed to *The Lion King* and more than a million drawings were created for it. It is made up of 1,197 hand-painted backgrounds and 119,058 individually colored frames of film.

Simba and Scar

The Lion King's working title was "King of the Jungle", and when production began on it, the artistic team traveled to Africa to research how best to portray the different locations on-screen. Lions and other animals were brought to the studio so the animators could study them.

Pocahontas (1995) was the one that would be a blockbuster. *Pocahontas* did not do as well as *The Lion King* and was the start of a decline in the success of Disney animation.

All Change

Several factors contributed to changes at the studio. Howard Ashman died during the production of *Aladdin*. The success of *Beauty and the Beast* and *The Lion King* caused other companies to start producing animated features. This diluted the talent pool and forced up wages and budgets. Because Disney animation represented such a large investment and potential profit, management interfered more in the making of the films.

Pretentiousness also crept into the Disney features. *Pocahontas* and *The Hunchback of Notre Dame* (1996) were films that seemed more interested in critical accolades than in entertaining audiences. The warmth that marked films like *The Little Mermaid* was in short supply in later films such as *Hercules* (1997), *Tarzan* (1999), *The Emperor's New Groove* (2000), *Atlantis* (2001) and *Treasure Planet* (2002).

To increase production, Disney opened up a satellite studio in Orlando, Florida. Perhaps because they were separated from Disney management by distance, the studio produced more successful films. *Mulan* (1998) followed the formula of earlier Disney successes, but followed it in an entertaining fashion. *Lilo and Stitch* (2002) attempted to duplicate the spirit of *Dumbo* and met with great box office success. *Brother Bear* (2003) was their swan song. While it had story problems, it attempted to grapple with larger themes than the typical Disney film and did better with audiences than the studio expected.

By 2004, Disney had closed the studio in Florida and drastically reduced the size of the California studio. Management decided to abandon drawn animation in favor of computer animation. Sadly *Home on the Range* (2004) marked the end of traditional Disney animation as practiced by Walt Disney.

DIGITAL DOMAIN

When *Tron* was released in 1982, computer animation was still in its infancy. It cost over $20 million, and its lackluster box office gave Hollywood little incentive to invest in digital animation.

Technology Not Ready

In some respects, that may have been a good decision. Computers of the time were relatively slow and very expensive, and there were very few artists who had the patience to put up with the difficult software available at the time. In the early 1980s, computer animation was simply not ready for prime-time.

The rest of the decade served as the industry's adolescence. The people involved in the CGI community had to figure out ways to turn the technology into a real business. Digital studios had to find ways to hit production deadlines and meet budgets that matched those of more traditional studios. As the decade progressed, the animation itself improved as more artists became involved, the software matured and workstations got faster and cheaper.

Most of the major digital studios got their start in the 1980s. Industrial Light and Magic (ILM) experimented with digital techniques throughout the decade, mostly in the area of editing, but also with feature-film effects. Pacific Data Images (PDI) was one of the first successful independent studios. Founded in 1980, the company found its early niche in the field of broadcast graphics. Pixar was founded in 1986, while 1987 saw the opening of Rhythm & Hues and Blue Sky.

CGI Revolution

The large studios were also dabbling in digital. In 1986, Disney made its first use of computer graphics in the film *The Great Mouse Detective*. In this pioneering attempt, they used a computer to calculate and draw the inside of a clock for the final chase sequence. Subsequently, the studio began using other digital techniques on traditionally animated films.

By the end of the decade, the talent and tools were in place for digital animation to take a leading role in Hollywood. The first big splash came from ILM with an effect for an underwater movie called *The Abyss* (1989). ILM created a creature made of water that interacted with the live-action

Jurassic Park

The dinosaurs were created using a mixture of digital animation and animatronics. As a general rule, if the dinosaur was shown in full, then it had been rendered digitally, while shots of the dinosaurs' body parts were of animatronics.

Drawing from Jurassic Park

The digital technology used in *Jurassic Park* was able, for the first time, to create realistic, living, breathing characters with skin, muscles and texture. This breakthrough expanded the filmmaker's canvas and changed the cinematic art of storytelling.

Terminator 2

In this film, the T-1000 changes from one form to another via a computer process known as morphing. This involves taking two images or series of images and finding similarities between the pixels or shape of one and the pixels or shape of another. Recognizable structures are often shaped or changed from one image to another, while other parts are blurred or their color palettes reduced so one image or one pixel can become the same as the other.

© Universal Studios

© Universal Studios

actors. This sequence demonstrated a new level of realism and showed just how far CGI had come. The success of *The Abyss* gave ILM the courage to attempt bigger digital projects.

ILM scored another big success in 1991 with *Terminator 2: Judgment Day*. This film contained dozens of digital effects, including a digital representation of Robert Patrick as the liquid metal T-1000. The next huge leap forward was *Jurassic Park*. The dinosaurs in the film proved CGI could compete against traditional animation and effects, and in many ways with better results.

A revolution was under way in Hollywood. The maturing of CGI in the early 1990s changed the way traditional live-action movies were made. It was also about to revolutionize the process of creating animated films.

PIXAR & TOY STORY

By 1991, Pixar was one of the leading computer-animation studios and very confident in its production methods. That year, Disney announced an agreement with Pixar to create the first computer-animated full-length feature film: *Toy Story* (1995). For many of the people at the studio this was a dream come true, a dream that had started 20 years earlier in the quiet of the university research labs.

In the Making

Toy Story was the moment when computer animation became a true force in Hollywood. Just as *Snow White* was the point where traditional animation matured into a true art form, *Toy Story* was the point where computer animation truly came of age. Since its release, computer-animated films have taken Hollywood by storm.

Toy Story took almost four years to make. Until 1991, when Disney gave them the financing to create a full-length feature film, Pixar had only produced a few short films and a string of 30-second commercials. Creating almost an hour and a half of quality feature footage was a very high mark to hit, and they had to devise a new way of making movies on computers.

Pixar pitched a story to Disney about something they knew – toys. This subject was chosen partly on the success of *Tin Toy*, and partly because Pixar knew that toys could be animated much more realistically than other types of characters with the technology available. The story was a classic "buddy" picture exploring the tenuous relationship between cowboy Woody and space cadet Buzz Lightyear, whose arrival threatens Woody's position as Andy's favorite toy. The two heroes hit it off poorly, but finally find a way to work together when they land in the hands of Sid, a demented kid with a taste for explosives.

The story process for *Toy Story* was the same as for any animated feature, with a script, hand-drawn storyboards and plenty of conceptual art. It went through a number of revisions and, after almost 18 months, was ready for production.

Teamwork

While the story was taking shape, Pixar employed large numbers of new staff for the film. The animators' backgrounds were largely in traditional cel and stop-motion animation; other traditional artists were hired to paint textures and provide lighting. In addition, the studio engaged an equally large team of computer scientists and engineers to assist with the technical side of things.

Pixar developed an animation pipeline that bridged the unique talents of artists, scientists and engineers. Artists focused on making the movie look good, while the technical staff backed them up by managing the computers and writing custom software to help the artists realize their visions.

Buzz Lightyear

In order to make their characters' movements look realistic, the animators looked at what the toys were made of: Buzz was rigid, and his ball-and-socket joints gave him a purposeful stride; Woody was a floppy, loose, limp rag doll.

Toy Story

With *Toy Story*, Pixar formulated the technique of constructing characters as a series of digital models with limbs and facial expressions that could then be moved in any direction inside the computer environment. The result was that the animation camera could track and move through the CG action in almost exactly the same way that a tracking shot could do with live-action.

Woody

After completing the characters' body animations, the animators created the facial animation and lip sync. To create the facial animation, each main character was modeled with "pull points" for facial muscles. The animator-performer could pull down Woody's forehead into a frown – he had eight controls for his eyebrows alone.

© Pixar Animation Studios, Walt Disney Studios

Character Creation

Many of the tasks, such as art direction, were done by hand. Special care was taken to give the environments a stylized storybook look. Instead of the painted backgrounds used in most animated films, Pixar created 3D-digital sets, modeled by artists and technicians. The sets were then textured, using paintings as well as photographs to give the film a realistic yet "cartoony" feel.

Characters were first created on paper, then sculpted in clay and digitized into the computer. A team of computer-savvy technical directors then "wired" the digital characters with virtual controls for the animators to manipulate. An animator might have several dozen controls for creating facial expressions, for example.

Animating 3D characters on a computer is different from other types of animation. Animators pose their characters much like real-world puppets, but through the flat screen of a computer. Unlike stop-motion, however, the animators have the ability to finesse the animation as much as they want, giving supersmooth and controllable results.

The Final Result

The animation was then passed off to a lighting and rendering team, who brought the final product to the screen. Sets and characters were lit with digital lights much like in any live-action feature, and the resulting frames were rendered on a bank of several hundred computers into a final film.

Despite all the technical hurdles Pixar had to endure during its creation, they managed to create a film with great characters and an engaging story. *Toy Story* was the top animated hit of 1995. It was the first of a string of successes Pixar would rack up over the next few years, putting traditionally animated features on the defensive and making digitally animated features the new rage in Hollywood.

FEATURE PLAYERS

In August 1994, two months after the opening of Disney's hugely successful *The Lion King*, Jeffrey Katzenberg, Steven Spielberg and David Geffen formed DreamWorks SKG. From the very start, the new company had instant credibility in terms of animation; after all, Katzenberg had been a key figure in the revival of Disney's animation fortunes, and Spielberg had been involved in such groundbreaking films as *An American Tail* and *Who Framed Roger Rabbit?*.

Competing with Disney

DreamWorks' formation followed closely on moves by Warner Bros. and Twentieth Century Fox to set up their own feature animation divisions. All three aimed to compete head-on with Disney in producing big-budget animation blockbusters, a field the "mouse house" had had all to itself since Don Bluth's arrangement with Spielberg fell apart.

Warner Bros.

Warner's first animated feature in the new gold rush was the live-action/animated *Space Jam* (1996). Inspired by the Air Jordan TV commercials, it featured Michael Jordan and the classic *Looney Tunes* characters. Though often overwrought, it proved both popular and profitable. The unit's first all-animated effort, Frederik Du Chau's *Quest for Camelot* (1998), proved to be a rather inept Arthurian romance.

However, this was followed by Brad Bird's wonderful *The Iron Giant* (1999), based on Ted Hughes' book about a boy who befriends a robot from outer space. Although widely acclaimed by critics and animators alike, it failed at the box office. *Looney Tunes: Back in Action* (2003), by Joe Dante and Eric Goldberg, a surprisingly good follow-up to *Space Jam*, also failed to capture the public's attention.

Twentieth Century Fox

For the new Fox Animation Studios in Phoenix, Arizona, Don Bluth and Gary Goldman were brought in from Ireland as producers. Their first effort was *Anastasia* (1997), a smartly done musical remake of Anatole Litvak's 1956 movie, which seemed to herald a comeback for Bluth. However, *Bartok the Magnificent* (1999), the film's direct-to-video prequel, and *Titan A.E.* (2000), a poorly received sci-fi adventure blending cel and CG animation, spelled the end of the Phoenix operation. Fox instead shifted from traditional cel animation to CGI, and specifically to its newly acquired Blue Sky Studios, a company that traced its pedigree to MAGI SynthaVision, one of the two companies that did the computer animation for Disney's *Tron*. The result was Chris Wedge's *Ice Age* (2002), a hilarious takeoff of Peter B. Kyne's often-filmed book *The Three Godfathers*. Particularly striking were the stylized character designs by famed illustrator Peter DeSève, which dramatically broke away from the Pixar-style realism that had previously dominated computer-animated movies.

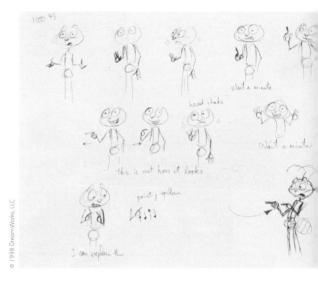

Antz – model sheet

PDI devised new facial-animation tools to create detailed expressions for Z and his fellow colony members based on an anatomical model of a face. Animators used combinations of controls that could raise an eyebrow, widen the eyes or dilate the pupils. There was also a less-detailed system that used shape interpolation and deformations rather than direct muscle control to animate faces.

Antz – crowd

Antz's animators needed to animate everything from a small group of background characters to thousands of ants in a battle scene. The technical directors created two types of crowd systems: the first was used for groups of fewer than 50 ants, which blended a mixture of body types and motions; and the second was used for larger crowds, which gave animators less control and more automation.

Z and Weaver

Antz's characters, with their organic body shapes and expressive faces, were a breakthrough in CG film. The facial animation system developed by PDI paid great attention to detail, and in particular offered a lot of eye control. For instance, when an eyeball turned, it actually grabbed the eyelid. Instances such as this added greater depth to the film.

Don Bluth » 274 DreamWorks » 344 Blue Sky & *Ice Age* » 346

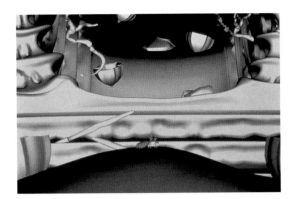

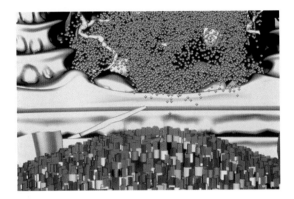

DreamWorks

Initially, DreamWorks poured most of its efforts into traditional Disney-style blockbusters, supplemented with lower-budgeted CGI films from PDI, a studio it later bought out. Its initial animated release was from PDI, Eric Darnell and Tim Johnson's *Antz* (1998), a Woody Allen-style comedy (featuring Allen's vocal talents) about a neurotic ant who rebels against the tyranny of his colony.

This was almost immediately followed by the more portentous *The Prince of Egypt* (1998), an operatic biography of Moses directed by Brenda Chapman, Steve Hickner and Simon Wells – done very much in the classic Disney manner, but lacking classic Disney warmth. Its reception was respectful, though its box office results were not much better than for *Antz*. Nevertheless, it proved to be the studio's most successful traditionally animated film.

Eric Bergeron and Don Paul's *The Road to El Dorado* (2000), about a pair of seventeenth-century Spanish con men in the New World, was in the vein of the traditional classic buddy movie, and was overshadowed by the company's subsequent release of Peter Lord and Nick Park's *Chicken Run*.

Big Success

However, DreamWorks' biggest success came from directors Andrew Adamson and Vicky Jenson's *Shrek* (2001), based on William Steig's popular children's book. *Shrek* spoofed both fairy tales and the Disney empire, and earned DreamWorks the first Oscar for Best Animated Feature. The wide popularity of *Shrek* and *Ice Age* not only helped bring an end to Disney's long-standing dominance, but it also proved to be a psychological deathblow to future production of large-scale cel-animated movies.

DreamWorks came out with two more hand-drawn movies: Kelly Asbury and Lorna Cook's *Spirit: Stallion of the Cimmaron* (2002), a modestly successful western about a wild mustang, and Tim Johnson and Patrick Gilmore's *Sinbad: Legend of the Seven Seas* (2003), a poorly received but sincere tribute to the films of Ray Harryhausen.

Ray Harryhausen » 158   Aardman Animation » 322   *Shrek* » 344

THE SIMPSONS

By the end of the 1980s, animated programs airing in prime-time were a distant memory. Cartoons had become strictly kids' stuff and were relegated to Saturday mornings. However, by the end of the decade, the fledgling Fox network would help change this perception, as well as television history.

Meet The Simpsons

It all began when Oscar-winning producer and director James L. Brooks contacted Matt Groening (b. 1954), who had garnered underground fame with his alienation-filled comic strip *Life Is Hell*, about bringing his characters to television. Worried about losing the rights to his work, Groening created the roughly drawn Simpson family, which made their television debuts in 1987 in short segments on Brooks's sketch comedy series *The Tracey Ullman Show*.

Named after Groening's own parents and sisters, the dysfunctional family was something that TV viewers had never seen before. The tone was not like other sitcoms where families fought civilly and triumphed over common crises in a half hour each week. These animated characters fitted in perfectly with Fox's other edgy programs, such as *Married with Children* and *In Living Color*.

Fox decided to take a chance and gave co-creators Groening, Brooks and Sam Simon an opportunity to create a Simpsons series, breaking the 20-year hiatus of animation in prime-time. The three played key roles in crafting the series' eventual success from the beginning. Groening brought the initial spark, and Simon hired many of the famed members of the writing staff, including George Meyer and Brooks, whose fame gave the entire creative team breathing room to experiment without having to answer constantly to network executives. With a slicker look that would be even more refined in time, *The Simpsons*' inaugural Christmas special aired on December 17, 1989.

Groening said he wanted the series to show that "your moral authorities don't always have your best interests in mind. I think that's a great message for kids."

Irreverent Style

Thus began a revolution on television, bringing irreverence out from its segregated life in late-night programming and into the "family hour". From the beginning, the writers loaded each episode with dozens of sly cultural references, including homages to distinct animation styles like those of the Dr Seuss animated specials

The Simpsons

When *The Simpsons* first began, it was all hand-drawn and colored. Although the traditional hand-painting of cels has now been superseded by computer digital ink and paint technology, the hand-drawn style still remains.

The Simpsons – singing

One episode of *The Simpsons* usually takes six to eight months to complete, from start to finish. This includes writing, re-writing, voice recording, storyboards, animatics, coloring (which is done in Korea), music scoring and post-production. Several episodes are in different stages of production at any given time, sometimes as many as ten.

© Gracie Films/20th Century Fox

and *School House Rock* series. The show received instant popularity, as well as a quick backlash. Then US President George H. W. Bush famously said, "We need a nation closer to the Waltons than to the Simpsons." Unafraid to take on critics and poke fun at just about anything, the show's creators had Bart counter, "Hey, we're just like the Waltons. We're praying for an end to the depression, too."

Voices Behind the Characters

Another cornerstone of the series is its voice cast, which began work on the characters in the original shorts. Dan Castellaneta and Julie Kavner were actors on *The Tracey Ullman Show* when they won the roles of Homer and Marge respectively, and they would later create other series regulars. Rounding out the family were actresses Nancy Cartwright as Bart and Yeardley Smith as Lisa. Adding to the show's depth was the enormous cast of supporting characters brought to life by such performers as *This Is Spinal Tap*'s Harry Shearer, *Saturday Night Live*'s Phil Hartman, *The Bob Newhart Show*'s Marcia Wallace and character actor Hank Azaria. In 2001, the cast fruitfully negotiated lucrative contracts, putting them among the highest-paid actors on television. The cultural-icon status of the show became so great that it has attracted legions of celebrity guests including Sir Paul McCartney, Elizabeth Taylor and even British Prime Minister Tony Blair.

The show's consistent ratings success and merchandising bonanza both helped solidify the future of the Fox network. Moreover, the series began to influence pop culture while continuing to comment on it. Homer's exclamation "d'oh" has been added to *Webster's New World Dictionary*, and "Don't have a cow, man" and "Ay, Carumba" are catchphrases synonymous with Bart Simpson. With the renewal of the series into at least a 16th season, *The Simpsons* will become the longest-running comedy in television history, besting the 1950s sitcom *Ozzie and Harriet*. So the question is, has America become more like the Simpsons or are the Simpsons more like America?

Homer with Mick and Keith

Rolling Stones legends Mick and Keith are just two in a long line of celebrities who have appeared (as themselves) on *The Simpsons*. Other musical guest stars have included Barry White, The Red Hot Chili Peppers, George Harrison, Johnny Cash and Britney Spears.

With the success of *The Simpsons*, network executives started reconsidering the notion that animation was only for children. Cable television quickly embraced adult-oriented animation; however, the networks were slower to respond.

New Characters

Both *The Tick* and *The Critic* debuted in 1994 on Fox and ABC respectively, but neither lasted longer than three seasons. Then, in 1997, Fox took another chance on animation when it gave *Beavis & Butt-head* creator Mike Judge and *Seinfeld* writer Greg Daniels the go-ahead on *King of the Hill*. The series centered on the working-class Hill family – conservative propane salesman Hank, his plucky wife Peggy, son Bobby and niece Luanne. Its witty, socially conscious writing and memorable supporting characters distinguished the series. However, the show's sitcom-like approach made some wonder why 'the series was animated in the first place. Nonetheless, the series has become a critical and ratings success, winning the 1999 Emmy for Outstanding Animated Program.

Futurama – sketch

This is a pre-production sketch of some of the characters from the show, which is an integration of traditional and computer animation. The backgrounds are animated by computer, and the figures are hand-drawn, but the two styles fit together so seamlessly that it is difficult to tell that one has been superimposed on the other.

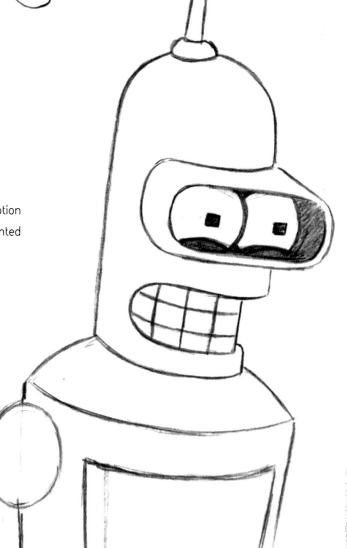

Mixed Successes

NBC ventured into prime-time cartoons in 1998 with the British import *Stressed Eric*, but it only lasted for two episodes. In 1999, six animated programs debuted with varying success. The WB aired *Mission Hill* (six episodes) and UPN showed *Home Movies* (10 episodes). Both series, as well as *Baby Blues*, which originally aired on the WB in 2000, would return to TV on Cartoon Network's *Adult Swim*. UPN put its hopes in bringing Scott Adams' satirical comic strip *Dilbert* to television. Featuring the voices of comic actors Daniel Stern and Chris Elliott, the show was terminated after 30 episodes.

Now with two animated hits, Fox launched three new series. Eddie Murphy, who voiced Thurgoode Stubbs, produced *The PJs* (1999), along with *Simpsons* producer Steve Tompkins and *In Living Color* writer Larry Wilmore. Animated by Claymation creators Will Vinton Studios, the rare African-American-themed cartoon moved to the WB in 2000 for one additional season. *Family Guy* (1999) followed the exploits of the Griffin family, featuring the maniacal baby Stewie, voiced by creator Seth MacFarlane. The show was canceled in 2002; however, its unexpected success on DVD spurred Fox to renew the series for 2005. To prove he could create a series on his own, in 1999 Matt Groening produced *Futurama*, a sci-fi satire featuring Fry, a pizza delivery man who has awoken from a cryogenic slumber 1,000 years in the future. The series was canceled in 2003 after winning three Emmy awards.

Family Guy

Peter, the father in *Family Guy*, pictured here, heads up a family that includes a smart-aleck dog and a neurotic baby. The show makes many references to the real world, especially the entertainment industry; William Shatner, *Star Wars* and President Clinton have all been included at some point or another.

Futurama

Due to the futuristic setting of *Futurama*, Matt Groening and his team are given great freedom, since the show is not restricted to one locale, like Springfield in *The Simpsons*, and the exploration of the galaxy opens many doors. The screenwriters use the conventions of sci-fi and run with them, often with hilarious consequences.

Cable TV

In 2000, ABC's *Clerks*, based on Kevin Smith's independent film; NBC's *God, the Devil and Bob* (2000), featuring a controversial Jerry Garcia-like *Almighty*; and NBC's *Sammy*, based on comedian David Spade's relationship with his deadbeat dad, only lasted two

episodes each. In 2001, UPN aired 13 episodes of the clay-animated *Gary & Mike*, and the WB's *The Oblongs*, featuring the voice of comedian Will Ferrell, only lasted eight episodes. Though there were many failures, some series found new life on cable, proving that the US was ready for adult animation.

Will Vinton and Claymation » 250   Cable Toons » 318

An animation boom exploded across the American cartoon industry in the 1990s. Feature films, cable TV, direct-to-video, syndication and broadcast television – all had needs for new cartoon fare. This great demand for programming led to a greater diversity of animation styles, and fresh products aimed at new audience segments (as "preschool" and "tweens" became hot new demographics). Renewed interest in television animation brought high-quality cartoon production from two powerful, though unlikely, sources: Disney and Steven Spielberg.

Tiny Toons

Spielberg, a long time cartoon fan, had produced the hit animated feature *An American Tail*, which gave Disney quite a run for its money. Spielberg collaborated with Warner Bros. Animation on a series of younger *Looney Tunes* characters in a new show, *Tiny Toon Adventures* (1990). Recruiting a young staff of renegade cartoonists (and a few old veterans), *Tiny Toons* brought "stretch and squash" to TV animation. The characters were derivative of the classic Bugs Bunny, Porky Pig and crew – junior versions with names like Plucky Duck and Babs Bunny – in a hodge podge "homage" to the classic Warner Bros. cartoons.

However, the most exciting thing to emerge from these shows was the teaming of *Tiny Toons* writers Paul Dini and artists Bruce Timm and Eric Radomski. Their reconception of the caped crusader, *Batman: The Animated Series* (1992), was a bold rethinking of how animated action cartoons could be done – its innovative influence still felt today. The writing was adult, the acting subdued, the artwork stylized and strong. Based partially on Tim Burton's live-action Batman movies, and influenced by Max Fleischer's Superman cartoons and Will Eisner's *Spirit* comic strip, *Batman: The Animated Series* was a rare animated triumph to transcend the children's audience it was intended for.

Baloo

Baloo, Shere Khan and King Louie were all in Disney's *Jungle Book*. Baloo, in *TaleSpin*, is listless, slobby and unreliable, with a failed business. Shere Khan stands upright and wears a business suit, and is a wealthy and astute businessman. King Louie runs the local bar.

© The Walt Disney Company

© MTV Productions

Beavis and Butt-head

The Spike and Mike Sick and Twisted Festival of Animation produced the first two *Beavis & Butt-head* shorts long before the characters debuted on MTV. Spike and Mike also premiered *The Spirit of Christmas*, the original, uncensored *South Park* short by Matt Stone and Trey Parker.

South Park

The pilot episode of *South Park* was made using paper cut-outs and stop-motion photography, but this process was too time-consuming and costly for a TV series. The creative team devised a way to retain the appearance of cut-outs being dragged across a screen while using computer-animation software, which sped the production up immensely. A feature-length theatrical film, *South Park: Bigger, Longer, and Uncut*, was released in 1999.

The Spirit Of Christmas (1995) was intended as a private Christmas joke, but it ended up becoming a serious hit: *South Park* (1997). The outrageous antics of a group of foul-mouthed kids were used by Parker and Stone to parody everything from President George W. Bush to Osama bin Laden. And it made a perfect fit with Comedy Central's programming agenda. Reruns of *The Tick* (1994) joined Nelvana's *Bob and Margaret* (1998), adapted from an NFB Academy Award-winning short, *Bob's Birthday* (1994) — which continued Comedy Central's commitment to animation.

Sex and Violence

HBO also tried to tap the adult market with a few series that pushed the envelope with sex and violence. Todd McFarlane's *Spawn* (1996), based on his comic book, was a very dark, violent animated show about a soul who'd been to hell and was not planning to return, and Ralph Bakshi's *Spicy City* was a film-noir sci-fi sex anthology. Neither grabbed ratings — though both have cult followings. Within a few years, HBO decided to leave grown-up animated cartoons to MTV, Comedy Central, Fox and Japanese animators, who had a head start.

Ralph Bakshi » 244 Anime in the 1990s » 330

THE AARDMAN STORY

Aardman Animation has made a name for itself over the past 30 years as not only being the home of Wallace and Gromit and *Creature Comforts*, but also as the company that introduced the highly inventive feature *Chicken Run* (2000).

Humble Beginnings

The founders of Aardman, Peter Lord (b. 1953) and David Sproxton (b. 1954), began their partnership as high school students working together on an amateur film. Influenced by television animation, they structured some cut-out and cel animation featuring a superhero character named "Aardman", his name being a combination of 'aardvark' and 'superman'. They photographed the result on a 16 mm Bolex camera borrowed from David's father, and their 15-second effort emerged as *Secret of the Bee*

Wallace and Gromit » 324 *Chicken Run* » 358

The Little Mole

Kratky Film's series *The Little Mole*, 70 percent funded by a German broadcaster, is an example of one of the international series currently being made in the formerly state-run studios of Eastern Europe.

gigantic dog, designed by another great Czech illustrator, Jiri Salamoun, and directed by Vaclav Bedrich. Probably the best-known animated films produced at the Prague studio are dozens of shorts starring the Little Mole, based on books by Zdenek Miler. The studio has also recently received commissions from the Czech Ministry of Education, including one on stress by Milan Klikar.

Reputation to Uphold

Founded in 1945, Bratri v Triku has an illustrious history to live up to. Jiri Trnka was one of its founders, along with other Czech masters like Bretislav Pojar, Jiri Brdecka and Zdenek Miler. The studio currently employs 35 full-time animators, with another 35 or so regular freelancers, who produce more than 200 minutes of animation each year.

By the 1990s, there were accusations that Japanese animation had become creatively bankrupt. There were no new concepts — just variations on worn-out themes and remakes of past hits. Despite this complaint, the popularity of animation grew to new global proportions.

New Creativity Emerges

Leading feature directors of the decade (besides Miyazaki and Takahata) include Mamoru Oshii, Yoshiaki Kawajiri, Rintaro, Satoshi Kon, Takashi Nakamura, Hiroyuki Okiura and Hiroyuki Kitakubo. Oshii stands out, not only for the features he directed, including *Patlabor: The Movie* (1990), *Patlabor 2* (1993) and *Ghost in the Shell* (1995), but for overseeing the creative teams that would produce cutting-edge animation features *Jin-Roh: The Wolf Brigade* (1999), directed by Okiura, and *Blood: The Last Vampire* (2000), directed by Kitakubo.

Ghost, *Jin-Roh* and *Blood* were productions of Production I.G, one of the more prominent new animation studios of this decade — co-founded in 1987 by character designer Takayuki Goto and Mitsuhisa Ishikawa (b. 1958).

The Madhouse studio, and its distinctive character designer/director Yoshiaki Kawajiri, established a trademark style of adult situations featuring characters who are sophisticated, sensual and dangerous. Kawajiri's *Ninja Scroll* (1993) made his often-delayed *Vampire Hunter D: Bloodlust* (2001) eagerly anticipated throughout the 1990s. Madhouse was also responsible for the critically acclaimed features of Satoshi Kon, starting with *Perfect Blue* (1997). Also of note is *Catnapped!* (1995) — a witty and visually imaginative children's film directed by Takashi Nakamura.

For Boys and Girls

Millions around the world who had never heard of Japanese animation learned of it in the 1990s because of international headlines in December 1997 that claimed a strobing-light effect in an episode of *Pocket Monsters* (a.k.a. *Pokémon*) had given "up to 12,000" children epileptic fits.

For boys, TV animation continued to be dominated by *Dragon Ball* and its *Dragon Ball Z* (1989–96) and *Dragon Ball GT* (1996–97) sequels. Also extremely popular were programs spun off from popular video games featuring young heroes who befriend cute fantasy animals with special powers. *Pokémon*, a 1997 TV series based upon a 1996 video game with 151 pocket-size "monsters", established itself as a worldwide fad. *Digimon* (1999) and *Monster Rancher* (1999) have been the most popular of its imitators. *Detective Conan* (a.k.a. *Case Closed*, 1996) presented a skilled

Princess Mononoke

This 1997 feature was a tour de force. Hayao Miyazaki and his team created a primeval forest where the gods still rule and the life force of the forest is intact, manifested in the presence of forest sprites. The rich, dark greens and the delicately drawn texture of the trees, moss, rocks, and water surfaces create a world as realistic as any live-action setting.

© Miramax Films

The Sandwiches

Yamamura's 1993 short won various prizes at festivals, including Chicago International Children's Festival and World Youth Film Festival.

The Sandwiches – work in progress

Koji Yamamura eschews the assembly-line approach to animation, and prefers working alone. His pieces contain few words, and he uses pencils, markers, clay or a combination of several materials. *The Sandwiches* was created with clay, puppets, photos and drawings on cel.

Pokémon

© Kids WB, Nintendo, Pikachu Project 1999

After the success of the TV series, *Pokémon: The First Movie* was released in 1998, and a second in 2000 (pictured). The success of the franchise has been perpetuated by further films, and parents continue to be pestered by their children for the spin-off cards and games as the merchandising continues unabated.

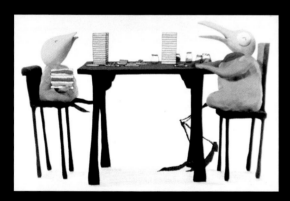

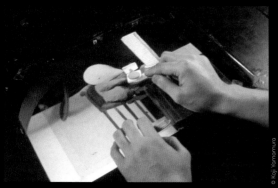

© Koji Yamamura

detective who is physically transformed into a seven-year-old boy and uses this handicap as an excellent disguise. For younger girls, the decade's most popular TV series were *Sailor Moon* (1992) and *Card Captor Sakura* (1998). *Sailor Moon*'s original director, Kunihiko Ikuhara (b. 1964), went on to guide the more surrealistic schoolgirl fantasy *Revolutionary Girl Utena* (1997), set in a vast ethereal high school.

Other notable TV animation included *Neon Genesis Evangelion* (1995), a giant robot drama that evolved in darkly psychological directions. *Evangelion* and the earlier *Nadia: The Secret of Blue Water* (1990) helped establish the Gainax studio's reputation for imaginative TV animation. Sophisticated adults swung to *Cowboy Bebop* (1998), a jazzy meld of futuristic space opera, noir private investigator drama, cynical comedy, hand-drawn and cel animation, and in-group references to the favorite cinematic influences of director Shinichiro Watanabe (b. 1965).

Serial Experiments Lain (1998), a sci-fi drama about the nature of reality, demonstrated how imaginative direction, by Ryutaro Nakamura; intelligent writing, by Chiaki Konaka (b.1961); and experimental art design, by Yoshitoshi Abe (b. 1971), could make what was clearly a low-budget TV series tense and gripping.

OAVs: From Medieval Fantasy to High-Tech

Highlights included *Record of Lodoss War* (1990), which introduced heroic sword and sorcery fantasy to animation, with humans, elves and dwarves fighting evil in a medieval Europe, and the comedy-adventure *Slayers* (1995) featuring tomboy sorceress Lina Inverse. Director/character designer Hiroyuki Ochi made the 1995 four-episode *Armitage III: Poly-Matrix* as an imaginative tribute to the sci-fi cyber-technology themes of Philip K. Dick, with enough flair and quality that the OAV series was released internationally as a theatrical feature.

Shoji Kawamori (b. 1958) proved equally adept at various genres, directing the sci-fi sequel *Macross Plus* (1995); directing the hauntingly surrealistic biography of author Kenji Miyazawa, *Spring and Chaos* (1996); and plotting the hit TV series *The Vision of Escaflowne* (1996), an adventure-romance of a Japanese high school girl who is transported to a fantasy world. Computer graphics appeared even more spectacularly in the OAV sci-fi series *Blue Submarine No. 6* (1998), the first that the public saw of new CGI-intensive Studio Gonzo (founded 1993) and its director Mahiro Maeda (b. 1963).

In the film festival world, Koji Yamamura (b. 1964) emerged as a major new talent of the 1990s, averaging one new film per year. His prizewinning films include *The Elevator* (1991); *A House* (1993), *The Sandwiches* (1993) and *Imagination* (1993), all featuring his characters Karo and Piyobupt; *Bavel's Book* (1996); and *Your Choice!* (1999). His Yamamura Animation, Inc. (founded 1993) also produces TV commercials.

THE
NEW CENTURY

As we begin a new millennium, animation art enters an era of change – a new phase of popular acceptance – and has artists redefining themselves.

Computer animation has taken over Hollywood. Due to the success of numerous CG cartoon features (*Finding Nemo*, *Ice Age*, *Shrek*), Hollywood studios have abandoned traditional hand-drawn techniques, Disney has down-sized, and Pixar has triumphed.

Hollywood has utilized the CG techniques to aid its live-action agenda – now many impossible situations (think *Titanic*, *The Matrix* and *Lord of the Rings*) are easier to accomplish. New hybrid movies integrating "cartoon" stars into live-action (*Garfield*, *Scooby-Doo* and *Rocky & Bullwinkle*) have found supersized success at the box office.

New techniques, derived from computer graphics, have provided pioneer opportunities: low-cost Flash animation has made TV-animation production more economical, while upscale motion capture technology (*The Polar Express*) has allowed animated actors to emote realistically.

And yet hand-drawn cartoons have not completely disappeared. Anime has sustained its worldwide grasp, as Japan's TV programs get more stylized and its theatrical features become more elaborate. Hayao Miyazaki's *Spirited Away* and Sylvain Chomet's *The Triplets of Belleville* have garnered global acclaim – and *The Simpsons* just keeps on going.

Animation Art is alive and well – and here to stay!

CGI VICTORIOUS

Courtesy of DreamWorks Pictures, Shrek™ and © 2001 DreamWorks L.L.C.

A little over five years after the release of *Toy Story*, CGI animated features were dominating the box office. Films like *Shrek*, *Monsters, Inc.* (2001) and *Ice Age* proved to be wildly successful with audiences, setting box office records and leaving traditionally animated films in the dust. While some cel-animated films, such as *Lilo & Stitch* did quite well, they were the exception rather than the rule. In a very short amount of time, CGI went from being the exception to being the rule.

Going Digital

This sudden change of fortune caused traditional animation studios to rethink their production methods. In 2003, after a string of mediocre box-office returns, Disney announced they were going digital for all future animated productions, ending almost 65 years of traditional cel animation at the studio. DreamWorks, though a much younger studio, made a similar decision at about the same time. While this was by no means the end of cel animation, the light table had certainly lost the position of dominance it once had.

Fiona and Shrek

Shrek signaled a major advance in CG technology. For example, the animators managed to create realistic-looking clothing with fabric that wrinkled and moved as it would in real life, such as Fiona's velvet dress and Shrek's rough tunic. They were also able to "grow" forests with millions of leaves that would rustle in the breeze.

Ice Age

Sid the Sloth started life on an artist's drawing board. From the initial pencil sketches, a 3D-clay model was created and then transferred to a computer. To do this, a grid was created on the model to allow the computer to recognize Sid's shape by recording the intersections of the lines. From those points of intersection the computer generated hundreds of curves, forming Sid's basic outline.

© 2002 20th Century Fox

While the visual novelty of CGI features was certainly a factor in this sudden change, these films also told a different type of story. Pixar avoided the cliché of the musical fairy tale, while *Shrek* simply slapped it in the face. These films had a very broad appeal, with complex characters, fewer formulas and plenty of jokes aimed directly at adults. They could be enjoyed by everyone, not just children, and were really good films. Hollywood put its money on these emerging studios and thereby attracted the best veteran artists and top young talent.

Stuart Little 2

The wireframe model used to create Stuart's face was extremely mobile, having been divided and subdivided into independently moveable parts. This allowed the animators maximum flexibility in choosing facial gestures and expressions. By animating more aspects of Stuart's facial gestures, more believable expressions were achieved.

Digital Domination

Digital characters were not only dominating animated features, they also were taking big roles in live-action films as well. During the 1990s, digital characters went from being one-dimensional monsters to fully integrated cast members. Films such as *Stuart Little* (1999) and *Star Wars: Episode I – The Phantom Menace* (1999) featured digital characters in starring roles.

This overlap started to blur the line between live-action and animation. How should films such as *Stuart Little*, which stars a computer-animated mouse in the title role, be defined? Is it a live-action film or an animated one? This question became even more relevant as an Academy Award was created for Best Animated Feature. The first of these Oscars was given to *Shrek* in 2002, showing just how far the art form had come in a few years.

Digital techniques have completely changed the landscape of Hollywood film-making within the span of a decade. Animation, once relegated to Termite Terraces on the studio back lot, was now part of the mainstream. The landscape has been permanently changed, and, thanks to the innovations of CGI, animation is hotter than ever.

© Columbia Pictures

BRITISH ANIMATION

The boom in British animation that began in the 1990s continued into the new millennium, the highlight of 2000 being the release of Aardman Animation's first feature *Chicken Run*. It was the first of four features in a partnership between Aardman and DreamWorks.

Revitalization

Animation festivals were on the increase everywhere, and Britain was no exception. Small animation festivals began and continue to thrive in Bradford, Norwich and Exeter, and there was a revival of the Bristol festival in the shape of Animated Encounters. Thanks to the presence of Aardman, the BBC Animation Unit and a number of leading studios, the city of Bristol became a major center of animation, as did Cardiff in Wales, with several notable production companies. The Surrey Institute of Art created an Animation Research Center with an archive that includes the work of Halas & Batchelor. The British Animation Awards, begun in 1998, continued to show appreciation of the industry's finest.

The year 2000 brought to the screen Michael Dudok de Wit's (b. 1953) serenely beautiful film *Father and Daughter*, winner of many prizes, including a British Film Academy Award and an Oscar. De Wit is a master of the use of light and shadow for dramatic effect. Also from the Aardman studio in 2000, Peter Peake's *Humdrum*, a witty short using shadow characters, gained an Oscar nomination.

It's a Dog's Life

In 2001, Suzie Templeton's short film *Dog* won awards all round the world. In lifelike model animation, the film tells a harrowing tale of a grieving family and their dog. Due to policy changes by Channel 4 television that had always championed short animated film, British animation began to suffer from a lack of commissioned work, and commercials became one of the main sources of studio income. This caused some long-established London production companies to close. New technologies were changing the face of animation, and many UK studios found easier ways to fulfil the tedious tasks of trace and paint.

Nick Park with camera

The cameras used to film *Chicken Run* were 35 mm film cameras that were considerably adapted for Aardman's purposes. They had video-assist cameras that looked through the lenses on the film cameras so the animators could see the picture that would be recorded on each frame of film.

Chicken Run

Some 300 full-size chicken models were made for the shoot, along with 140 smaller ones for the crowd scenes. The chickens contained a wire skeleton beneath a body of foam latex and silicone-based plasticine. A series of different beaks and mouths were produced, each molded to match the phonetic pronunciations of the alphabet – a technique pioneered by Aardman during production of *A Close Shave*.

© Aardman Animations, Allied Filmmakers, DreamWorks SKG

© Aardman Animations, Allied Filmmakers, DreamWorks SKG

The Sound of Music

In the next two years UK music videos broke new ground. The first to stun audiences were award-winning pop promos by Jamie Hewlett and Pete Candeland who created an animated rock band for the Gorillaz ('Rock da House', 2001, and 'Clint Eastwood', 2001). Tim Hope's award-winning shorts blend live-action and computer graphics in a distinctive collage style. These include 'Trouble' (2001) and 'Don't Panic' (2001) for Coldplay, and his stunning latest creation for One Giant Leap in 'My Culture' (2002), featuring Robbie Williams. A new British feature, *A Christmas Carol* (2002), directed by Jimmy Murakami using traditional drawn animation, was successful in UK cinemas. Animation on the Internet took off with a bang but soon faded, leaving the field to the amateurs.

Studios continue to be prolific in the commercials market, providing a wide range of high-quality ads and music promos. Because of the relatively large budgets, the work is amazingly fresh, and makes use of innovative techniques and novel solutions. The latest feature now in production is *Valiant*, the tale of a brave carrier pigeon, by Vanguard at Ealing Studios. Aardman's *Wallace and Gromit* feature is due for release in 2005. In spite of ups and downs, British animation, which began more than a century ago, is still going strong.

A Christmas Carol

A Christmas Carol begins and ends with live-action sequences starring Simon Callow as Charles Dickens. In order to capture the atmosphere of the classic Dickens story, the animation was hand-drawn, the colors muted, and the film did not make use of modern animation techniques.

© Illuminated Films / MBP

EUROPEAN INNOVATIONS

Over the last few years, features have played a major role in European animation, with France and Italy dominating the field, often in co-productions. The European funding body Cartoon Movie, based in France, reported that more than 30 feature projects had applied for money in 2000. Production of short films and series for children also increased significantly. Spain became the third-largest producer of animated film in Europe after France and the UK, production costs being considerably less than in other European countries. Animation festivals play an important role, one of the most prestigious being Annecy Festival and Film Market in France, attracting delegates from all over the world. Cinanima in Espinho, Portugal; Anima Festival in Brussels; Stuttgart Festival in Germany; and Holland Animation Festival are also important events for the industry.

Setting Standards

There was a significant breakthrough for European animation in territories other than the domestic market, one of the most successful being the French feature *Kirikou and the Sorceress*, released in 2000. This mythical tale of witchcraft and innocence, directed by Michel Ocelot, is a kaleidoscope of color, with its exotic imagery inspired by African art. Using pencil drawing on paper and 2D-computer, it set a new standard by which all future serious animated film should be measured.

Also in 2000, Italy and Germany joined forces to make *Momo: The Conquest of Time*, a feature directed by Enzo d'Alo (b. 1953), one of the most prolific feature directors in Europe. Using traditional hand-drawn animation on cel, this is the story of Momo, an orphan girl who discovers that the sinister Gray Men are stealing time. Enzo d'Alo's earlier films *The Blue Arrow* (1996) and *Lucky and Zorba* (1998) had already achieved major success, and he brought yet another feature to the screen at the end of 2003 with *Opopomoz*, the story of a Neapolitan family who are about to celebrate Christmas and the birth of their own child.

The 2003 animated feature from Spain, *El Cid: The Legend*, directed by José Pozo, is the tale of Spain's greatest hero. Technically well made, blending traditional cel with computer-generated images, the film uses odd perspectives both for its majestic landscapes and for its stylized characters.

French Resistance

The award-winning Folimage Studio in France, usually devoted to short- and medium-length films, believes in quality combined with artistic freedom. Their annual Artist in Residence program has produced dozens of first-class films by animators from all around the world. Their first feature, *Raining Cats and Frogs*, six years in the making, was released in 2004. Directed by Jacques-Rémy Girerd, this is the first animated feature in 20 years to be made entirely in France. A rather unconventional family and

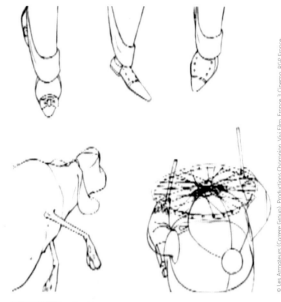

© Les Armateurs (Carrere Group), Productions Champion, Vivi Film, France 3 Cinema, RGP France

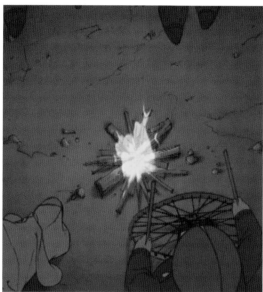

The Triplets of Belleville

Sylvain Chomet believes that animation without the constraints of spoken words is stronger, and that if you have to fit everything to the words, all the gestural movement revolves around the mouth. Without speech, he says, the animator is much freer to create true animation, whereas animation modeled around the dialogue has already been set in stone. Each animator who worked on the film was able to bring something different to it.

© Les Armateurs (Carrere Group), Productions Champion, Vivi Film, France 3 Cinema, RGP France

the animals from a small zoo are adrift in an ark at the beginning of a flood of biblical proportions. The storyline deals with important issues and how we, as human beings, cope with them.

International Success

Short films continued to emerge from studios all over Europe, but they rarely found an outlet beyond the animation festivals. Dutch director Paul Driessen, who also works in Canada, displayed a strongly personal style, often using a split-screen technique and inventing crazy enclosed worlds with their own inverted logic. Also from Holland, Gerrit van Dijk created works of art within animated film. Georges Schwizgebel from Switzerland painted in acrylic gouache on cel to make vibrant moving images.

Short films that have succeeded internationally include *The Periwig Maker* (2001), directed by Steffen Schaeffler from Germany. Using puppet animation, the film is set in London during the plague years, and perfectly captures the horror and tragedy of the time. Andreas Hykade, also from Germany, won a string of awards for *Ring of Fire* (2002), which used stark black-and-white imagery in its portrayal of two lonely cowboys.

C'est la Vie

One of the most successful features of 2004 was *The Triplets of Belleville* (a.k.a. *Belleville Rendezvous*), a co-production between France, Belgium and Canada, directed by Sylvain Chomet. Acclaimed by audiences and nominated for both British and Hollywood Academy Awards, it did not rely on famous voice artists; it is almost a silent film apart from music, minimal sound effects and background murmurs. This enhanced rather than detracted from the enjoyment. It was a visual delight. Every frame was meticulously drawn and colored using hand-drawn animation and computer-generated images, and the film emerges triumphant on the big screen.

The European animation industry is spreading its wings with the enormous potential for children's television series within Europe and animated features finding outlets throughout the world.

The Triplets of Belleville

In *Triplets*, director Sylvain Chomet combines his two loves, comics and film. The film borrows influences from contemporary French comic strips and filmmakers like Jean Pierre Jeunet (*Amélie*) and Marc Caro (*Delicatessen*). Chomet was very involved with the team working on the physical production of the film, animating scenes himself and relishing the moments at the end of the day when he could see the drawings move.

The collapse of Communism and the outbreak of war in the former Yugoslavia dealt animation throughout Eastern Europe and Russia a major blow during the last decade of the twentieth century and into the twenty-first century. When Communism collapsed, state funding of culture went with it, leaving many animators (and artists in general) to fend for themselves in a brave new world where art is seemingly no longer a priority.

Poland

As Polish animation struggles for funding and identity in the twenty-first century, Jerzy Kucia and Piotr Dumala continue to lead the way. In 2000, Kucia released *Tuning the Instruments*, a delicious feast of image and sound, while Dumala gave us the masterful, *Crime and Punishment*. Dumala's take on Dostoyevsky's novel is more of an essay than an adaptation. What interests Dumala is less the crime and more the emotional and mental state of the troubled soul before and after a murder.

Hungary

Hungarian animation has undergone dramatic changes over the last decade. In the early 1990s, Pannonia lost its monopoly on animation when new studios like Varga appeared, and when branch studios in Kecskemét and Pécs split from Pannonia. At the same time, state funding decreased and Hungarian Television stopped supporting TV series.

Despite these setbacks, Pannonia has managed to survive by doing what it has always done: producing a careful combination of artistic and commercial work while developing international co-production partnerships.

Varga Studio has now superseded Pannonia as Hungary's most important animation studio. Their work on *The Simpsons* in the early 1990s led to many contracts, including financial backing from a group of investors in London. Varga Holding has become a major international player on the world animation scene. Aside from their head office in Budapest, they now have satellite studios in Moscow, Sofia and London.

Zagreb

When Croatia declared its independence in 1991, Zagreb film production came to a complete stop. Despite the studio's achievements, the government was not prepared to continue its support – especially with war raging around them.

In 1995, Zagreb film was taken over by the city and restructured. The animators now work as freelancers and are paid out of the budgets for their films. The year 2006, however, was set as the date for privatization. The studio will have to exploit its vast library, and find co-production and service work if it is to manage.

Unfortunately, short personal animation films have now taken a backseat as Zagreb struggles to find a place within the international marketplace.

© Pilot Moscow Animation Studio

Nativity

Mikhail Aldashin, who made the 1997 short *Nativity*, pictured, works at Pilot as a director and producer and has also done freelance work for other companies including America's Cartoon Network, where he created the TV series *Mike, Lu and Og* (1999).

Pannonia Studio in the 1990s » 288 Eastern European Animation in the 1980s » 290

© Pilot Moscow Animation Studio

Switchcraft

This short won the Grand Prix at the Annecy Festival in 1995. Animator Konstantin Bronzit's animation style has been described as non-linear storytelling combined with a great deal of humor.

Crime and Punishment

The striking opening sequence of *Crime and Punishment* is dominated by a thumping and repetitive piano piece and reddish-brown images emerging and returning to the shadows. The series of images includes the murder scene, thus letting the viewer know what will follow in the film. Dumala's focus in the film is not the crime itself but the disturbed emotional state of the murderer before and after his crime is committed.

© Piotr Dumala

Bulgaria

Because of decreased government funding, Bulgarian animation, like that of almost every other country, must now face the pressures and demands of the global marketplace. Hence they have moved away from independent short films toward mass-market animation features and TV series. There are now many studios in Bulgaria, but while they are trying to develop their own indigenous projects, most of the studios simply provide services for international projects. Boyana Film is now Bulgaria's largest animation studio.

The future is not so dim however. The National Academy of Theater and Film Art and the New Bulgarian University have produced a number of new talents, and a number of relative newcomers have produced some interesting work. These include Theodore Ushev (*The Attempt Counts*), Vitko Boyanov (who has made a few fantastic, frenzied pieces including *Sister*, 2000), Boris Despodov (*Mythology*, 2002) and Ivan Rusev (*Yellow*, 2001).

Russia

Post-Soviet Russia has not been without its problems, especially in terms of financing. Soyuzmultfilm's influence has waned dramatically, and in 1993, Soyuzmultfilm's most prominent animators – Yuri Norstein, Fjodor Chitruk, Andrey Khrjanovsky and Edward Nazarov – left the studio to establish the animation school "Shar".

Despite the emigration of co-founder Igor Kovalyov to Hollywood in the early 1990s, Pilot continues to be the leading animation studio in Russia. Like Soyuzmultfilm before them, Pilot has taught a new generation of animators, such as Alexander Petrov, Mikhail Aldashin and Ivan Maximov.

Petrov, whose first two films were produced at Pilot, has since achieved international fame with *The Mermaid* (1996, an Oscar nominee) and the technically astonishing Imax film *The Old Man and the Sea* (which won the Oscar for Best Animated Short in 2000).

Konstantin Bronzit is perhaps the funniest of the new Russian masters. He likes to place his characters in the most uncomfortable and seemingly impossible situations so that we can laugh at how they confront them. His award-winning films include *Switchcraft* (1995) and *At the Ends of the Earth* (1999).

Alexander Tatarsky has also continued to make his own films, including *Gone With the Wind* (1999) and the nostalgic *The Red Gates of Rashomon* (2002, co-directed with Valentin Telegin).

Czech Animation in the 1990s » 328

As the first decade of the twenty-first century has begun, anime has joined the evolution from traditional hand-drawn animation to hand-drawn animation enhanced by computer graphics. The Japanese animation industry has also come to interrelate more closely with the American animation market.

Theatrical Animation

Theatrical animation from 2001 to 2004 has still been dominated by annual feature-length adventures of the most popular children's TV series: *Doraemon*, *Pokémon*, *Detective Conan*, *Crayon Shin-chan*, and new TV programs which have established their popularity since 2000 such as *Inu Yasha* and *Hamtaro Tales*.

Theatrical releases for older audiences included some impressive adaptations of older anime and manga works during 2001: *Cowboy Bebop: The Movie*, by Shinichiro Watanabe and the other creators of the TV series, and *Vampire Hunter D: Bloodlust* by Yoshiaki Kawajiri. Both took advantage of longer theatrical running times and larger production budgets to improve on their already-popular original versions. Osamu Tezuka's *Metropolis* was a 2001 prestige production by the Madhouse studio of one of Tezuka's early manga classics, a variation of the famous Fritz Lang sci-fi movie. Adapted by Katsuhiro Otomo and directed by Rintaro, *Metropolis* was an imaginative "retro" presentation of Tezuka's well-known 1949 visualization of a futuristic world as seen through 1920s art design, but with a cutting-edge hand-drawn/computer-animation sparkle.

In the Shadow?

The success of Hayao Miyazaki's *Spirited Away* (2001) overshadowed other original theatrical features of the new century, but several were notable. Studio Ghibli's 2002 *The Cat Returns* was a charming fantasy for family audiences. The first *Patlabor* theatrical feature in a decade, *WXIII: Patlabor the Movie 3* (2002), directed by Takayama Fumihiko and Takushi Endo at Madhouse, was a taut intellectual sci-fi/detective thriller. Similarly, Production I.G's popular 1990s *Ghost in the Shell* finally got a theatrical sequel in 2004: *Ghost in the Shell: Innocence*, directed again by Mamoru Oshii.

Animated features intended for the art-festival circuit included Satoshi Kon's *Millennium Actress* (2001) and *Tokyo Godfathers* (2003), both premiering at North American film festivals and winning awards internationally before their Japanese theatrical releases. *A Tree of Palme* (2002), by Takashi Nakamura, was a blend of sci-fi and *Pinocchio*-like fantasy set on a visually bizarre distant world. *Tamala 2010: A Punk*

™ & © 2004 Go Fish Pictures

Millennium Actress – fighting

Recalling one of her greatest roles, Chiyoko Fujiwara is a ninja fighter battling the samurai. Being animated rather than live-action allows the film a more seamless transition through the scenes from the "real present" to the "real past".

Millennium Actress – cityscape

The animation is dark and realistic, with recurring themes and metaphors. Because the film takes place in recollection rather than reality – time periods and settings shift as Chiyoko relates the account of her life through the characters she played (geisha, noblewoman, astronaut, and more) – the anime emphasizes the timeless nature of the story.

Millennium Actress – head-shot

This is a hand-drawn film about legendary Japanese actress Chiyoko Fujiwara, who is persuaded to tell her story to a documentary maker and his cameraman. They become literal witnesses to her extraordinary story as she recounts her career, moving from space to feudal Japan in the process.

Cat in Space (2002), written/directed/scored by the rock-music duo "Tree of Life" a.k.a. "Kuno and Kazuka", was an imaginative space adventure featuring a funny animal cat that looked like a sluttish, foul-mouthed Goth parody of *Hello Kitty*, in the tradition of such American animation as *The Ren & Stimpy Show* and *Beavis & Butt-head*. It was popular enough to spin off a late-night TV series, *Tamala's Wild Party* (2004).

Japanese TV

New hit-TV animated series included the juvenile *Hamtaro Tales* (2000) about a young girl's happy pet hamster and his happy friends; *Inu Yasha* (2000), a fantasy-drama featuring supernatural monsters typical of medieval Japanese folklore (another adaptation of a popular manga by Rumiko Takahashi); and *Love Hina* (2000), a teen romantic comedy revolving around a shy, easily embarrassed boy forced to become the manager/caretaker of an all-girl student dorm. The allure of *DragonBall*-style art and light fantasy-adventure continued in *One Piece* (1999), a pirate-world burlesque epic by Eiichiro Oda (b. 1975), an acknowledged fan of DB's Akira Toriyama. *Beyblade* (2001) was the next *Pokémon*-like hit series based upon a heavily merchandised game or toy. An elaborate fantasy world in which boys everywhere compete for prestige in national and global Beyblade tournaments, it had its popularity reinforced by actual tournaments organized by the manufacturers of Beyblade spinning tops (including electronic and remote-controlled tops, and accessories). At the opposite extreme, *Hikaru no Go* (2001), based upon the manga by Yumi Hotta and Takeshi Obata, made news by unexpectedly revitalizing interest among the youth in the ancient Japanese chess-like game of Go. Hikaru, an undisciplined schoolboy, solves his modern social problems after learning to think and develop strategy after he is possessed by the friendly spirit of a ninth-century Go master.

SMALL-SCREEN SUCCESS

In the early part of the new century, there was a vogue for short (usually 12 or 13 episodes) futuristic sci-fi TV series in interstellar settings with visually spectacular CGI astronomical panoramas and complex shiny machines, often ending on a cliff-hanger; those that were popular were followed up with a "part 2" conclusion a year later. *Crest of the Stars* (1999), *Pilot Candidate* (2000), *Vandread* (2001) and *GeneShaft* (2001) were among the most outstanding of these. Broccoli, a new design company, took the "cute fantasy little girl" stereotype and emphasized it to the point of self-parody in such popular comedy-fantasy series as *Di Gi Charat* (1999) and *Galaxy Angel* (2001), both produced by the Madhouse studio, and *Sugar: A Little Snow Fairy* (2001), produced by J.C. Staff.

The Hit-Makers

Two TV series based upon their studios' hit theatrical features of the previous decade were Production I.G's *Ghost in the Shell: Stand Alone Complex* (2002) and Madhouse's *Ninja Scroll: The Series* (2003), while a new TV adaptation of *Astro Boy* was created by Tezuka Production Co. for his "birthday". He was said, in his 1953 manga origin story, to have been created in 2003 and his character was updated with state-of-the-art animation.

Two TV series achieved critical and popular success for quality and originality even though they were clearly inspired by foreign hit movies or TV series: *Noir* (2001), about young women professional killers, similar to *La Femme Nikita*; and *Witch Hunter Robin* (2002), about an agency assigned to hunt "witches" (people with psychic abilities such as teleportation and telepathy) who use their powers in criminal ways – a cross between a police-procedural series and *The X-Files*.

Something Different

TV series that stood out as imaginatively different included *Boogiepop Phantom* (2000), a psychological horror fantasy. *NieA_7* (2001) and *Haibane-Renmei* (2002) are both dreamlike fantasies, written and designed by Yoshitoshi Abe, that question the nature of reality. *Arjuna* (2001), directed by Shoji Kawamori, is a didactically pro-ecological fantasy. *Hellsing* (2001) pushed graphic horror on TV in new directions and to new limits. *.hack//SIGN* (2002) created a visually striking virtual fantasy gaming world in which role-playing fans could become trapped. *Last Exile* (2003) is a stunning creation of a socially grim nineteenth-

Noir

Tsukimura Ryoei's stylish TV series had opening credits featuring *James Bond*-inspired animation and a great soundtrack. Featuring two female assassins, *Noir* has plentiful shoot-outs that resemble the sword fights of samurai dramas, but no blood is spilled.

Noir – Mireille

Mireille is one of the two assassins that make up the "Noir" partnership. This model sheet shows some of the early sketches of this most stylish of assassins.

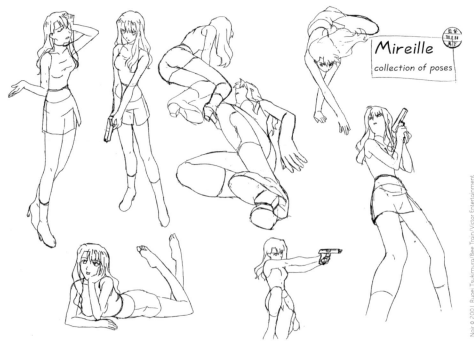

Mireille
collection of poses

© Nekojiru – Yamato Do Co. Ltd./ Nekojiru Family

century-style world with Vernean flying machines. *Wolf's Rain* (2003) is an impressive, though gloomy, tale of a hidden clan of werewolves trying to survive in a decaying over-urbanized future world. *Planetes* (2003) is a technologically accurate, hard-science sci-fi comedy about astronaut "garbage collectors" assigned to clean up debris in near-Earth orbits, and *Paranoia Agents* (2004), Satoshi Kon's first TV series, is a psychological thriller.

Art-House Influence

Two art films that got high-profile OAV releases were *Cat Soup* (2001), by director Tatsuo Sato (b. 1964), a tribute to an early 1990s surrealistic underground comic by "Nekojiru" (which was popular with animators and was produced shortly after the disturbed artist's suicide), and *Voices of a Distant Star*, by Makoto Shinkai (b. 1973), a 25-minute sci-fi romance that looked like a professional production, but was written and produced entirely by the prize-winning creator on home equipment.

© Nekojiru – Yamato Do Co. Ltd./ Nekojiru Family

Cat Soup

Director Tatsuo Sato explained that he and his staff constructed *Cat Soup* – an unconventional work – by creating a series of distinct images and then simply stitching them together. This visually stunning, free-form short used only the loose guidelines of the original manga to govern the narrative flow.

Final Fantasy » 372

JAPAN & AMERICA: CO-PRODUCTION

A significant development was a growing bond between Japanese and American animation production, both artistically and commercially. Whereas Japanese animation was originally produced entirely for the domestic market, with any later foreign sales considered as a pleasant bonus, new films began to be planned counting on the international market.

Early Enterprise

The Sunrise studio, which had done subcontract production for Warner Bros. TV Animation's *Batman: The Animated Series* (1992–95), produced its own extremely *Batman*-like (with giant robots) *The Big O* (1999), a 13-episode TV serial which ended with a cliff-hanger. *The Big O* was only moderately successful in Japan, but was popular enough in America on TV and in home-video sales to justify production of *The Big O II* in 2003, completing the adventure. During the 1990s anime fan conventions in America began inviting noted Japanese directors, character designers and voice actors as guests. During the 2000s Japanese animation studios began sending representatives and exhibiting at American fan conventions to promote sales.

The highest-profile examples of co-production started when Square Co., Ltd., the Japanese producer of the *Final Fantasy* video games, noted for high-quality computer animation, had its Square USA subsidiary create a new animation studio in 1997 in Honolulu named Square Pictures. They produced a theatrical sci-fi feature, *Final Fantasy: The Spirits Within* (2001) using newly developed computer-graphic technology to create "hyper-real" characters indistinguishable from real humans.

Final Fantasy

The studio was designed to be halfway between Japan and the US, taking advantage of the animation-industry talents of both nations. *Final Fantasy*, directed by Hironobu Sakaguchi with animation direction by Andy Jones, was admired as a daring artistic experiment and was generally technologically successful. The story, however, was neither exciting nor emotionally appealing, and was such a financial failure that Square Pictures was closed.

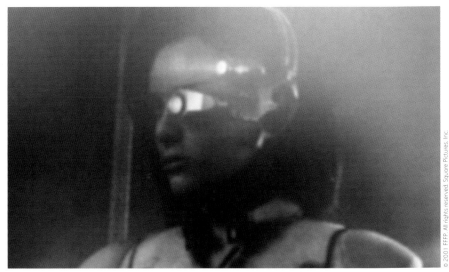

Final Fantasy: The Spirits Within

The work on *Final Fantasy* was undertaken by many departments including Storyboards, Layout, Sets/Props, Animation, Motion-capture, Lighting, FX, Rendering and Compositing. One shot could be made up of anywhere from nine to 498 composite layers.

The project, however, generated enough attention that Square Co., Ltd. and Disney Interactive, the Disney subsidiary producing Disney-character electronic games, co-produced *Kingdom Hearts* (2002), a video game featuring the well-known Disney animated characters in *Final Fantasy*-style CGI imagery. Additionally, Square Pictures was commissioned in 2000 to produce a short film for the composite feature *The Animatrix*. This film, *The Final Flight of the Osiris*, directed by Andy Jones, was the final production of Square Pictures.

The Animatrix

The Animatrix was the creation of American film-makers Larry and Andy Wachowski, writer/directors of the extremely popular sci-fi feature *The Matrix* trilogy. The Wachowski brothers were admitted fans of American and Japanese comic books and anime, and *The Matrix* was well-known for its look of "a live-action anime movie". It was the first of a live-action trilogy, but the Wachowskis also wanted to use its popularity to give themselves the opportunity to work with some of the most talented anime directors.

They conceived *The Animatrix* to be a collection of nine separate short films set in the *Matrix* world, showcasing the styles of such directors as Yoshiaki Kawajiri, Mahiro Maeda, Koji Morimoto, Shinichiro Watanabe and Takeshi Koike, as well as Americans Andy Jones and Korean-born Peter Chung. Some of the stories were written by the Wachowskis and others by their directors. Most of the animation was produced in Japan at the Madhouse and Studio 4°C studios. A theatrical release in Japan and a home-video release in America, *The Animatrix* was popular in both countries.

Popular Anime

A similar production was an untitled animation sequence with "the anime look" in director Quentin Tarantino's live-action 2003 *Kill Bill Volume I*. This tribute by Tarantino to his favorite Japanese and Chinese live-action martial arts and *yakuza* crime movies was filmed in China and Japan. The anime sequence was produced at Production I.G., and was so closely supervised by Tarantino that he is considered its director. Co-productions like *Final Fantasy: The Spirits Within*, *The Animatrix* and *Kill Bill* are encouraging indications of future American movie-industry utilization of Japanese animation styles and resources.

Final Fantasy: The Spirits Within

Considerable praise has been given for the incredibly realistic animation of skin and hair in *Final Fantasy*. For the facial animation, a set of sliders, such as "Left Lower Eyelid Twitch" were created to control each element of the face. Tools were created allowing the animators to control the movement of Aki's 60,000 strands of hair.

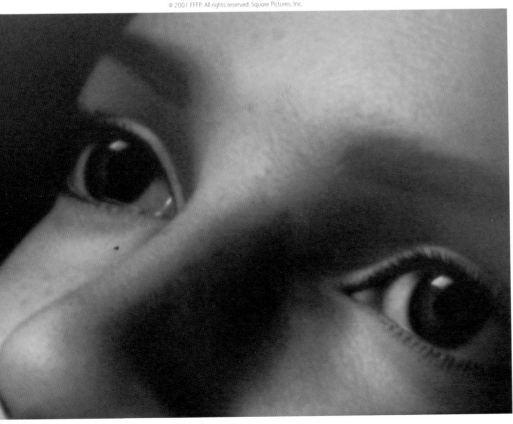

INDIA: ANIMATION IS BURGEONING

The modern Indian animation industry essentially dates back to 1956, when the Cartoon Film Unit of the Films Division of the Ministry of Information was formed. The unit, which is still active, was nurtured by Indian animation pioneer G.K. Gokhale and former Disney animator Clair Weeks, who grew up in India as the son of Christian missionaries; the two collaborated on the unit's first film, *Banyon Tree*, based on a Buddhist *Janaka* story.

Important Pioneer

The most significant figure to come out of the unit was Ram Mohan (b. 1931), who worked there from 1956 until 1967; he later established Ram Mohan Biographics in 1972, which not only produced such films as *Baap Re Baap* (1972), but also proved to be an important training ground for many animation artists. The company later merged with United Studios Ltd. to form what became UTV Toons, where Mohan produced several episodes of the widely praised *Meena and Sara* educational film series for UNICEF.

Despite the efforts of film-makers like Mohan, animation in India remained marginal until the mid-1990s, when studios servicing Western television producers began to form. A small independent sector also emerged in Mumbai, fed by graduates of the National Institute of Design's world-class animation program and nurtured by such broadcasters as MTV-India and Channel (V). Along with Cartoon Network India, they helped build a growing internal market for animation.

Attracted by India's low-cost labor force and computer expertise, several facilities were established to provide digital ink-and-paint services requiring a low level of artistic skill. These were followed by an increasing number of full-service animation studios, often funded by large industrial companies with no previous relationship to film or television, including India's huge live-action film industry.

The International Arena

A small number of studios have moved into original productions aimed at the international market; the most prolific has been Pentamedia, which, starting with *Sinbad: Beyond the Valley of the Mists* (1999), made a number of poorly received movies using CGI motion-capture animation. TV series production began in earnest with Toonz Animation India's *The Adventures of Tenali Raman* (2002), a traditional cel-animated show that exhibits a more professional approach. The number of shows increased rapidly after Cartoon Network India decided to commission original programming in 2003, including CB Media Ventures' *The Adventures of Chhota Birbal*.

In terms of quality, the most interesting work is found in projects commissioned by MTV-India and Channel (V) and their respective creative directors, Cyrus Oshidar and Arnab Chaudhuri, who rank among the most important figures in contemporary Indian animation. A number of these networks' most important

Poga

Poga was directed by Cyrus Oshidar, and made at Famous House of Animation, part of the Famous Cine Labs & Studios. Clay animation is a popular format of animation in India, and Famous House of Animation has been instrumental in popularizing this form with its highly successful commercials.

© Famous Animation

The Freedom Song

Based on a folk story that stressed the need to protect nature, the film made use of folk art and Madhubani and Kalighat styles of painting. It won some prestigious awards, including the Golden Conch and the Critics Award at the Mumbai International Film Festival and the Best Animation Film at the Japan Wildlife Film Festival.

Still I Rise

Inspired by the coincidental suicides in 1890 of Elephant Man Joseph Merrick and the painter Vincent van Gogh, this film fuses two events by presenting a fantasy visualization of Merrick's last dream. It was animated and rendered on Windows 2000 workstations, and the final renders were recorded on 35 mm film.

© Umesh Shukla

commissions, including many by Oshidar, have been fulfilled by Famous's House of Animation, which is located in Mumbai and is a division of Famous Cine Labs & Studios Ltd., the leading commercial house in India.

The Leading Animators

Chaudhuri's sometimes rough style hides his considerable skill in a variety of techniques, including mixing live-action and animation. He shows a particular affinity for clay animation, as seen in *Macho and Banjo: The Space Khalasis*, a wacky series about two Bengalese garbage men in space, which made his reputation.

In contrast, Oshidar's works are generally slicker in execution, but have an equally irreverent comic approach. Of note is his wacky clay-animated *Poga* (2000), an MTV station ID promoting a fusion of yoga and pogo sticks, and *Gaseous Clay* (2003), an outrageous CGI short about a boxer who uses an unusual tactic to beat his opponents.

Looking to the Future

In 1998, Famous Cine Labs & Studios, a live-action service facility hired NID (National Institute of Design) graduate E. Suresh as creative director to supervise the production of a TV series. The series did not go beyond the pilot stage, but a highly successful TV commercial for Novartis Pharmaceuticals led to other commissions, including work for MTV and Channel (V). On their own, they produced Narayan Shi's *The Freedom Song* (2000), a charming Indian version of *The Emperor's Nightingale*, which exhibits a high degree of craftsmanship and artistry, placing it more than a cut above most Indian studios.

Among Indian animators working abroad, the most promising is Umesh Shukla, whose independently made *Still I Rise* (2001) is a striking meditation on the last dream of Joseph Merrick, the Elephant Man, who died in 1890. He has worked for such major Hollywood studios as Disney and DreamWorks, and has ambitions to return to India to make animated movies.

WEB & FLASH ANIMATION

The explosive growth of Web animation paralleled the dot-com boom of the late 1990s and briefly brought about a major revival of the production of short animated films. It also saw the introduction of new, lower-cost technologies — most prominently Macromedia Flash software. Even after the boom collapsed, Internet animation continued to provide new opportunities for independent film-makers and a testing ground for more established producers.

Pioneering Events

The first major artistic event for Web animation was the launch of the Absolut Panushka Website, an experimental film showcase sponsored by Absolut Vodka and curated by independent film-maker Christine Panushka. A sensation when it premiered in February 1997, it included 33 brief films featuring the Absolut bottle by the likes of Jules Engel, Kihachiro Kawamota, Priit Pärn, Michaela Pawlatowa and Panushka herself. However, web animation itself did not come into its own until the introduction of Flash animation in 1996, which was soon adopted by MSN and Disney Online.

After producing *Weekend Pussy Hunt*, a short Flash animation, for MSN, *Ren & Stimpy* creator John Kricfalusi realized the possibilities offered by the technology; it not only allowed for rapid and inexpensive production, but also held out the promise of a way independents could bypass traditional means of financing and distribution. In October 1997, Kricfalusi came out with the Internet's first animated series, *@ The Goddamn George Liquor Program!* While the self-financed series was unable to maintain a regular schedule, its popularity spurred a mania for web animation that culminated in 2000, a year that might be called its golden hour.

Leading the Way

Small studios started to produce their own series in the hopes of eventually finding a home on television. One of the best was Will Ryan's delightful *Elmo Aardvark: Outer Space Detective!* (2000) from Snappytoons Amusement Company and Darryl Van Citter's Renegade Animation. Motion-capture pioneer Protozoa morphed into the DotComix Website, which featured Gary Trudeau's *Duke2000*, based on the Doonesbury comic strip.

On a much larger scale, Film Roman, best known for *The Simpsons*, launched the adult-oriented Level13.net site as a test bed for new TV shows. In France, Millimages (*64 Zoo Lane*) took a similar approach, but used the international co-production model, more familiar in Europe. New companies were formed specifically to showcase pilots for TV shows and feature films. Most prominent were Icebox, whose founders include former *King of the Hill* and *Simpsons* producers, and Urban Entertainment, which saw John Ridley's *Undercover Brother* become a live-action movie in 2002. Subsequently, the CBC broadcast March Entertainment's *Chilly Beach* (2003), a sort of Canadian *South Park*, based on a Web original.

TV Commercials » 184   Ren & Stimpy » 318

Elmo Aardvark — Earth

The *Elmo Aardvark* series received a special Annie Award from the International Animated Film Society (ASIFA-Hollywood) and the Monsieur Pluc Award at Annecy due its inventiveness. LokoMotion and Bisonic Aural Gratification Systems were developed especially for the series.

Elmo Aardvark & VaVa LaVoom

Pictured here are Elmo Aardvark and VaVa LaVoom. A feature film based on the outer-space adventures of Elmo has been on several development slates in the intervening years.

Atom Films & Bill Plympton

25 Ways to Quit Smoking, *How To Kiss*, *Parking* and *The Wiseman* are just four of Bill Plympton's films featured on AtomFilms.com. These and seven other Plympton films can be viewed online.

A Flash of Inspiration

AtomFilms.com, IFILM.com and Macromedia's Shockwave.com created the most excitement among independent film-makers by establishing a new marketplace for animated short films. For instance, IFILM had great success putting Spike and Mike's Festival of Animation online, while Shockwave linked up with comic-book and animation-legend Stan Lee to screen his popular *7th Portal* series. Aardman made the live-action/animated *Angry Kid* for AtomFilms, which also provided a venue for the films of Bill Plympton. It also signed Tim Burton, who produced the *Stainboy* series, as well as *South Park* creators Trey Parker and Matt Stone; however, the latter's first film was shelved after it proved too gross for AtomFilms' viewers.

Among broadcasters who got involved, the most interesting was the nascent Oxygen network, which simulcast its offbeat *X-Chromosome* anthology series online, including *Fat Girl* by Prudence Fenton, Allee Willis and April Winchell.

End of a Good Thing?

The lack of viable business models that caused the dot-bust eventually hit Web animation by the end of 2000. Many companies closed, and those that survived endured massive layoffs, with Shockwave taking over AtomFilms. A few major players survived, including Mondo Media, which was able to develop a viable syndication model for such series as *The God and Devil Show* (2000), and using DVD sales and merchandising to increase revenues from series like *Happy Tree Friends* (2002). For its part, AtomFilms has used a subscription model for such in-demand series as Aardman's *Wallace and Gromit's Cracking Contraptions*.

The use of Web technologies, especially Flash, has also found markets beyond the Internet itself. Thus, in 2001, Nelvana's prime-time show *Quads* became the first TV series produced using Flash, which also made it easier to show it on the Web.

In the late 1980s independent producers were looking for ways of financing their productions and started looking to the world market. And production companies like Hanna-Barbera were looking for new animation for their broadcasters. Mike Young, at Siriol Animation in Wales, could not sell a show directly to US broadcasters, so he partnered with Hanna-Barbera and Booker Entertainment to produce television series *Super Ted* (1985) and *Fantastic Max* (1988). Young also co-produced *Once Upon A Forest* (1993), a movie for FOX with Hanna-Barbera and HTV.

Plenty of Opportunities

There were advantages for animation producers to work in Europe or Canada. France had established in 1946 the government agency Centre National de la Cinematographie (CNC), which has helped to subsidize French productions. Canada established a tax incentive for production companies that shot films in the country. By partnering with French or Canadian production companies, US and other producers were able to reap the financial benefits.

In the United States, in the late 1980s, producers like Ted Kopplar, of World Events Productions, saw the financial benefits of co-production with a French company. World Events was already partnered with Calico Entertainment in 1988 on *Denver the Last Dinosaur*. During the second season World Events took on the French partner IDDH. Koplar exchanged production services and funding from the French company for international rights and toy deals.

Calico Entertainment later partnered with Zodiac Entertainment on *Widget* (1990–91). Calico also partnered with Zodiac and Alligator Films, a Belgium production company, for *Mr Bogus* (1991–93). In 1992 Zodiac and Calico partnered again on *Twinkle*, a series based on the popular Olympic mascot from the 1992 Korean Games. This co-production was led by the Korean broadcaster MBC, along with Sei Young Studios, a Korean production service that had worked on all of Calico's previous productions.

© 1999 BKN International AG / Ellipseanime / M6

Kong, The Animated Series

The story leading up to the series explains that a new Kong is born from DNA taken by Lorna Jenkins, from the original Kong and a small amount of human DNA taken from her grandson, Jason Jenkins. Kong and his prehistoric island are once again under threat, this time from gigantic prehistoric creatures and monstrous DNA mutants.

© 1999 BKN International AG/Ellipseanime/M6

Kong, The Animated Series

Jason Jenkins and his friend Tan bring their teacher Ramon De La Porta to the island to show him the beauty of it, and of course Kong. Unfortunately De La Porta has other plans and steals the island's Primal Stones which control its balance. In each episode Jason, Tan, a shaman girl named Lua and Kong travel around the world to find the stones, restore balance to the island and thwart De La Porta once and for all.

Multitude of Takeovers

In 1990, the broadcast networks' audiences dropped dramatically due to the advent of cable and the introduction of FOX-TV. The FCC relaxed Fin-Syn in 1991 and finally abolished it in 1995. This change opened up the opportunity for the major production companies like the Walt Disney Company to purchase the ABC network and for Warner Bros. to start WB TV network. These companies could now own what they aired.

The year 1995 was the turning point for many companies. Hanna-Barbera was purchased for its library of shows by the Turner Company (later to be a part of Warner Bros.), and the smaller studios like Fred Wolf Production, Ruby-Spears, Zodiac Entertainment, Calico Entertainment and many others started closing their doors for a lack of venues to sell their programs.

In 1990 Mike Young crossed over to the US to start Mike Young Productions. Using his connections in Europe he immediately produced the television series *Secret Garden* (1993–94) with S4C for ABC TV. He then produced Prince Charles' *Legend of Lochnagar* (1993) with ABC, Virgin and S4C.

International Co-Production

In the early part of the twenty-first century, international co-production has become a necessity. The television series *Kong: The Animated Series* (2000) was conceived in the US by Stephanie Graizano of BKN, and produced with Ellipse Anime (France) and pasi (Philippine Animation Studio, Inc.). Both Ellipse Anime and pasi worked with their own outside services, including services in Korea, the Philippines and India. Co-productions like this can offer many benefits to the contributing partners, including production services at cost in exchange for regional distribution revenues, revenues for all from the adjusted gross and tax points and credits where applicable. Working with so many partners can have its drawbacks in communications, cultural differences and time zones.

An example of a truly international co-production model is the animated series *Max and the Mechanicals* (2004) for PBS (US). This is a co-production between Mike Young Productions (US), Sony Television Animation (US), PBS (US), Telegael (Ireland) and jadooWorks Animation Studio (India). Deals like this allow for partners to put in either cash, cash and services, or services as their participation.

As we get further into the twenty-first century co-production will be borderless. IDT Entertainment, Inc. has established a proprietary system, the Global Animation Protocol, for working together with other production companies worldwide. IDT Entertainment is bringing the financial resources of its parent company, IDT Corp., an international telecommunications company, to assist in deficit financing of co-productions, along with providing their own production resources to creative partner companies for television and features.

REFERENCES

BIBLIOGRAPHY

Adamson, J., *Tex Avery, King of Cartoons*, DeCapo Press, 1985
Barrier, M., *Hollywood Cartoons*, Oxford University Press, 1999
Beck, J., *The 50 Greatest Cartoons*, Turner Publishing, 1994
Beck, J., and Friedwald, W., *Looney Tunes and Merrie Melodies: A Complete Illustrated Guide to the Warner Bros. Cartoons*, Henry Holt, 1989
Beckerman, H., *Animation: The Whole Story*, Allworth & School of Visual Arts, 2003
Bendazzi, G., *Cartoons: One Hundred Years of Cinema Animation*, Indiana University Press, 1994
Cabarga, L., *The Fleischer Story*, DeCapo Press, 1995
Canemaker, J., *Walt Disney's Nine Old Men*, Disney Editions, 2001
Canemaker, J., *Winsor McCay: His Life and Art*, Abbeville Press, 1987
Clements, J., and McCarthy, H., *The Anime Encyclopedia: A Guide to Japanese Animation Since 1917*, Stone Bridge Press, 2001
Crafton, D., *Before Mickey*, MIT Press, 1982
Culhane, S., *Talking Animals and Other People: The Autobiography of One of Animation's Legendary Figures*, St Martin's Press, 1994
Erickson, H., *Television Cartoon Shows: An Illustrated Encyclopedia, 1949–1993*, McFarland, 1995
Ledoux, T. (ed.), *Anime Interviews: The First Five Years of Animerica, Anime & Manga Monthly*, Cadence Books, 1997
Ledoux, T., and Ranney, D., *The Complete Anime Guide: Japanese Animation Film Directory & Resource Guide*, Tiger Mountain Press, 1997
Lent, J. (ed.), *Animation in Asia and the Pacific*, Indiana University Press, 2001
Levi, A., *Samurai From Outer Space: Understanding Japanese Animation*, Open Court Publishing Co., 1996
Maltin, L., *The Disney Films*, Disney Editions, 2000
Maltin, L., *Of Mice and Magic: A History of American Animated Cartoons*, Plume Books, New American Library, 1980
Mangels, A., *Animation on DVD: The Ultimate Guide*, Stone Bridge Press, 2003
McCarthy, H., *Hayao Miyazaki: Master of Japanese Animation*, Stone Bridge Press, 1999
Merritt, R., and Kaufman, J. B., *Walt in Wonderland*, Indiana University Press, 1992
Patten, F., *Watching Anime, Reading Manga: 25 Years of Essays and Reviews*, Stone Bridge Press, 2004
Pilling, J. (ed.), *A Reader in Animation Studies*, John Libbey, 1997
Robinson, C., *Between Genius and Utter Illiteracy: A Story of Estonian Animation*, Varrak Publishing, 2003
Schneider, S., *That's All Folks! The Art of Warner Bros. Animation*, Henry Holt, 1990
Scott, K., *The Moose That Roared*, St Martin's Press, 2000
Smith, D., *Disney A to Z*, Hyperion, 1998
Stephenson, R., *The Animated Film*, The Tantivy Press, 1981
Webb, G., *The Animated Film Encyclopedia, 1900–1979*, McFarland, 2000

MAGAZINES

Animation Magazine
Animation Blast
"Beyond Good and Evil: Piotr Dumala's Crime and Punishment", Issue 5.10, *Animation World Magazine*, January 2001
Janeva, M., "Bulgarian Animation: A Short Review", *Animation World Magazine*, June 2003
Knott, T. and Taylor F., "Bold and Beautiful: The Genius of Bulgarian Animation", pp. 72–73, *Ottawa 88 International Animation Festival Official Programme Book*, Canadian Film Institute, 1988
Matuszewski, W., "Animated Film in Poland", pp. 8–18, *Holland Animation Film Festival Catalogue*, Holland Animation Film Festival, 1996
Pavlov, B., "Sixty Years Soyuzmultfilm", pp. 48–52, *Holland Animation Film Festival Catalogue*, Holland Animation Film Festival, 1996

ORIGINAL JAPANESE & CHINESE FILM TITLES

I: The Origin of the Art: pages 30–31

Imokawa Mukuzo Genkanban no Maki = *Mukuzo Imokawa, the Concierge*
Sarukani Gassen = *The Battle of the Monkey and the Crab*
Hanahekonai Meitou no Maki = *Hanahekonai's New Sword*, a.k.a. *The Fine Sword*
Taro no Banpei: Senkotei = *Taro the Sentry: Submarine*
Kiatu to Mizuageponpu = *Atmospheric Pressure and the Suction Pump*
Ninki no Shouten ni Tateru Goto Shinpei = *The Spotlight is on Shinpei Goto*
Usagi to Kame = *The Tortoise and the Hare*
Ubasute-yama = *The Mountain Where Old Women Are Left to Die*
Shiohara Tasuke = *Tasuke Shiohara*
Nonkino Tosan Ryugu Mairi = *A Carefree Old Guy Visits the Ryugu*
Suzumi Bune = *Cooling Off on the Boat*
Nihonichi no Momotaro = *Momotaro is Japan's No. 1*
Tako no Hone = *Octopus Bones*
Bunbuku Chagama = *The Tale of the Lucky Teakettle*
Kaeru wa Kaeru = *A Frog is a Frog*
Dobutsu Olympiku Taikai = *The Animals' Olympics*
Oira no Yakyuu = *My Baseball*
Komori = *The Bat*
Son Goku Monogatari = *The Legend of Son Goku*
Kujira = *The Whale*
Kuro Nyago = *Black Kitty*

II: Finding Its Voice: pages 52–53

Nansensu Monogatari: dai 1 hen, Sarugashima = *A Shipwreck Tale: Part 1, Monkey Island*
Nansensu Monogatari: dai 2 hen, Kaizoku-bune = *A Shipwreck Tale: Part 2, The Pirate Ship* (Note: *Nansensu Monogatari* is a pun that means both "A Shipwreck Tale" and "A Nonsense Tale")
Chikara to Onna no Yokonaka = *The World of Power and Women*
Tahchan no Kaitei Ryokou = *Tahchan's Trip to the Bottom of the Sea*
Osaru no Taiyyo = *The Monkey's Big Catch*
Sora no Momotaro = *Aerial Momotaro*
Norakuro = *Black Dog*
Norakuro Nitohei – Kyoren no Maki = *Buck Private Norakuro – Training*
Norakuro Nitohei – Enshu no Maki = *Buck Private Norakuro – Drills*
Norakuro Gocho = *Sergeant Norakuro*
Norakuro Shoi – Nichiyobi no Kaijiken = *2nd Lieutenant Norakuro – The Sunday Mystery*
Koari no Itazura = *The Mischievous Little Ant*
Osaru Sankichi – Bokusen no Maki = *Sankichi the Monkey – Air Defense Military Exercise*
Kuroneko Banzai = *Black Cat Hooray!*

III: Technicolor Fantasies: pages 76–77

Genroku Koi Moyou: Sankichi to Osayo = *Love in the Genroku Era: Sankichi and Osayo*
Izakaya no Ichiya = *A Night at a Tavern*
Issun Boshi Chibisuke Monogatari = *The Tale of Tiny Issun Boshi's Rescue*
Benkei tai Ushiwaka = *Benkei versus Ushiwaka*
Kachikachiyama = *The Hare's Revenge on the Tanuki*
Musume Dojoji = *The Girl at Dojo's Temple*
Oira no Hijoji = *My Emergency*
Maabo no Shonen Kokuhei = *Maabo, the Boy Pilot*
Sora no Shanhai Sensen = *Skies Over the Shanghai Battlegrounds*
Sora no Arawashi = *Aerial Ace*

IV: The World War Two Era: pages 112–115

Ma-bo no Rakkasan Butai = *Ma-bo's Paratroop Unit*
Fuku-chan no Sensuikan = *Fuku-chan and the Submarine*
Spy Gekimetsu = *Spies Defeated*
Nippon Banzai = *Hooray for Japan!*
Osaru Sankichi – Bokunado no Kaiheidan = *Sankichi the Monkey's Marine Corps Air Defense*
Osaru Sankichi – Tatakau Sensuikan = *Sankichi the Monkey's Fighting Submarine*
Ocho-fujin no Genso = *Fantasy of the Butterfly Wife*
Kaguya Hime = *Princess Kaguya*
Momotaro no Umiwashi = *Momotaro's Sea Eagles*
Kumo to Tulip = *The Spider and the Tulip*
Ari-chan = *Ant Boy*
Momotaro – Umi no Washi = *Momotaro's Divinely-Blessed Sea Warriors*
Tieshan Gongzhu = *Princess Iron Fan or Princess with the Iron Fan*

V: The Post-War Era: pages 142–143

Maho no Pen = *The Magic Crayon*
Suteneko Tora-chan = *Tora-chan, the Abandoned Kitten*
Tora-chan to Hanayome = *Tora-chan and the Bride*
Ousama no Shippo = *The King's Tail*
Dobutsu Daiyakyu Sen = *The Animals' Great Baseball War*
Yuki no Yoru no Yume = *A Snowy Night's Dream*

VI: Cartoons Mature: pages 174–175

Mori no Ongakukai = *The Forest Concert*
Kobito to Aomushi = *The Gnome and the Green Caterpillar*
Ari to Hato = *The Ant and the Pigeon*
Ko Usagi Monogatari = *Story of the Little Rabbit*
Kawataro Kappa = *Kawataro the Kappa*
Ukari Violin = *The Happy Violin*
Onbu Obake = *Onbu, the Little Goblin*
Taisei Shakusan = *The Great Buddha*
Kujira = *The Whale*
Yuri-sen = *The Ghost Ship*
Aru Machikado no Monogatari = *Stories on a Street Corner*
Ma Liang = *The Magic Paintbrush*

VII: To The Tube: pages 196–197

Koneko no Rakugaki = *Doodling Kitty*
Koneko no Studio = *Kitty's Studio*
Hakuja Den (Legend of the White Snake Enchantress) = *Panda and the Magic Serpent*
Shonen Sarutobi Sasuke (Sasuke, the Ninja Boy) = *Magic Boy*
Saiyuki (History of the Journey to the West) = *Alakazam the Great*
Hyotan Suzume = *The Sparrow in the Empty Gourd*
Otogi no Sekai-Ryoko = *Otogi's World Tour*
Plus 50,000 Nen = *More Than 50,000*
Urikohime to Amanjaku = *The Little Devil and Princess Uriko*
Osama ni Natta Kitsune = *The Fox Who Became King*
Beer Mukashi Mukashi = *Once Upon a Time There Was Beer*
Chibi Kuro Sambo no Tora Taiji = *Little Black Sambo Conquers the Tigers*

VIII: International Explosion: pages 236–241

Anju to Zushiomaru/Anju and Zushiomaru = *The Littlest Warrior*
Wanpaku Oji no Orochi Taiji = *The Little Prince and the Eight-Headed Dragon*
Arabian Night: Sindbad no Boken = *Sinbad the Sailor*
Gulliver no Uchu Ryoko = *Gulliver's Adventures Beyond the Moon*
Andersen Monogatari = *The World of Hans Christian Andersen*
Nagagutsu o Haita Neko = *Puss in Boots*
Taiyo no Oji: Hols no Boken = *The Little Norse Prince*, a.k.a. *The Sun Prince: Hols' Great Adventure and The Little Norse Prince Valiant*
Cyborg 009: Kaiju Senso = *Cyborg 009: Fighting Monsters*
Soratobu Yureisen = *The Flying Phantom Ship*
Kaitei 30,000 Mile = *30,000 Miles Under the Sea*
Otogi Manga Calendar = *Otogi Cartoon Calendar*
Tetsuwan Atom = *Astro Boy*, a.k.a. *Mighty Atom*
Tetsujin 28-go = *Gigantor*, a.k.a. *Iron Man No. 28*
Eight Man = *8th Man*
Takarajima = *Treasure Island Revisited*
Jungle Taitei = *Kimba the White Lion*, a.k.a. *Jungle Emperor*
Mahotsukai Sally = *Sally the Little Witch*
Ribon no Kishi = *Princess Knight*, a.k.a. *Choppy and the Princess*
Ge Ge Ge no Kitaro = *Kitaro's (Scary Ghost Moon)*, a.k.a. *Kitaro's Booooo!*
Sabu to Ichi Torimono Hikae = *The Detective Stories of Sabu and Ichi*
Sazae-san = *Mrs Sazae*
Ashita no Joe = *Tomorrow's Joe*
Tenma no Torayan = *Torayan on the Boat*
Ningen Dobutsuen = *The Human Zoo*
Isu = *The Chair*
Satsujinkyo Jidai = *The Maniac Age*
Hana = *Flower*
Ookami Shonen Ken = *Ken the Wolf Boy*
Tsukiyo to Megane = *A Moonlit Night and Eyeglasses*
Gen-ei Toshi = *Fantasy City*
Ai = *Love*
Honoo no Fantasy = *A Fantasy of Flames*
Shin Takarajima = *New Treasure Island*
Ginga Shonentai = *Boys' Space Patrol*
Tenrankai no E = *Pictures at an Exhibition*
Sen-ya Ichi-ya Monogatari = *The Thousand and One Nights*
Cleopatra = *Cleopatra*, a.k.a. *Cleopatra, Queen of Sex*
Kanashimi no Belladonna = *The Tragedy of Belladonna*
Hinotori 2772: Ai no Cosmozone = *Phoenix 2772*, a.k.a. *Space Firebird*
Onboro Filumu = *Broken-Down Film*
Mori no densetsu = *Legend of the Forest*
Sun Wu Kong – Da Nao Tian Gong (Mandarin)/*Da No Tien Gu* (Cantonese) = *Havoc in Heaven*, a.k.a. *Uproar in Heaven*
Cao Yuan Ying Xiong Jie Mie = *Two Heroic Sisters of the Grasslands*
Mu Di = *Buffalo Boy and the Flute*

IX: Animation For Grown-Ups: pages 260–261

Lupin III = *Lupin III: The Mystery of Mamo*, a.k.a. *Lupin the 3rd: The Secret of Mamo and Lupin vs. the Clones*
Lupin III: Cagliostro no Shiro = *The Castle of Cagliostro*
Mazinger Z = *Mazinger Z*, a.k.a. *TranZor Z*
Kido Senshi Gundam = *Mobile Suit Gundam*
Uchu Senkan Yamato = *Space Cruiser Yamato*, a.k.a. *Space Battleship Yamato and Star Blazers*
Ginga Tetsudo 999 = *Galaxy Express 999*
Kagaku Ninja-Tai Gatchaman = *Battle of the Planets*, a.k.a. *G-Force*
Versailles no Bara = *The Rose of Versailles*
Pika-Don, a.k.a. *Pica-Don*
Ittai Yatsu wa Nanimonoda? = *What on Earth Is He?*
Nihonjin = *The Japanese*
Hana Ori = *Breaking Branches is Forbidden*
Oni = *The Devil*
Tabi = *The Journey*
Shijin no Shogai = *The Life of a Poet*
Dojoji = *Dojoji Temple*
Kataku = *House of Flames*
Fushigi na Kusuri = *Strange Medicine*
Hana to Mogura = *The Flowers and the Mole*
Mochi Mochi no Ki = *The Mochi-Mochi Tree*
Saru Kani = *The Crab's Vengeance on the Monkey*
Namu Ichibyo Sokusai = *Praise Be to Small Ills*
Mizu no Tane = *Water Seed*
Chikarabashi = *The Bridge of Strength*
Okon Joururi = *The Magic Fox*
Chumon No Oi Ryoriten = *A Well-Ordered Restaurant*

X: New Directions: pages 294–299

Genma Taisen = *Harmagedon*
Oneamisu no Tsubasa: Oritsu Uchugun = *The Wings of Honneamise: Royal Space Force*
Golgo 13 = *Golgo 13: The Professional*
Urusei Yatsura = often translated as *Those Obnoxious Aliens*, but released in the US under the Japanese title
Maison Ikkoku = the name of a boarding house, released in the US under the Japanese title
Ranma 1/2 = sometimes translated as *Ranma Half-and-Half* or *Halfway Ranma*, but released in the US under the Japanese title
Dr Slump Arale-chan = *Dr Slump (and) Little Arale*, unreleased in the US but well-known to anime fans as *Dr Slump*
Chojiku Yosai Macross = *Macross, the Super-Dimensional Fortress*, usually known as just *Macross*
Hokuto no Ken = *Fist of the North Star*
Maho no Tenshi Creamy Mami = *Creamy Mami, the Magical Angel*
Kido Keisatsu Patlabor = *Mobile Police Patlabor*
Yoju Toshi = *Wicked City*
Manie Manie Meikyu Monogatari = *Neo Tokyo*
Hadashi no Gen = *Barefoot Gen*
Hotaru no Haka = *Grave of the Fireflies*
Natsufuku no Shojotachi = *Girls in Summer Dresses*
Hi no Ame ga Furu = *Raining Fire*
Ushiro no Shomen Daaare = *Kayoko's Diary*
Ohoshi-sama no Rail = *Rail of the Star*
Kaze no Tani no Nausicaa = *Nausicaa of the Valley of the Winds*
Tenku no Shiro: Laputa = *Laputa: The Castle in the Sky*, a.k.a. *The Castle in the Sky*
Tonari no Totoro = *My Neighbor Totoro*
Majo no Takkyubin = *Kiki's Delivery Service*
Omohide Poroporo = *Only Yesterday*
Kurenai no Buta = *Porco Rosso*
Heisei Tanuki Gassen Pompoko = *Pom Poko*
Mononoke Hime = *Princess Mononoke*
Sen to Chihiro no Kamikakushi = *Spirited Away*
Mimi no Sumaseba = *Whisper of the Heart*
Neko no Ongaeshi = *The Cat Returns*
Roujin Z = *Old Man Z*
Metropolis = *Metropolis*, a.k.a. *Osamu Tezuka's Metropolis*
San Ge Heshang = *The Three Monks*
San Mao Liu Lang Ji = *The Wanderings of San Mao*
Yu Bang Xiang Zheng = *The Snipe-Clam Grapple*

XI: Renaissance: pages 330–331

Kido Keisatsu Patlabor = *Patlabor: The Movie*
Kido Keisatsu Patlabor 2 = *Patlabor 2*
Kokaku Kidotai = *Ghost in the Shell*
Blood = *Blood: The Last Vampire*
Jubei Ninpocho = *Ninja Scroll*
Totsuzen! Neko no Kuni Banipal Witt = *Catnapped!*
Pocket Monster = *Pokémon*
Digimon Adventure = *Digimon: Digital Monsters*
Monster Farm = *Monster Rancher*
Meitantei Conan = *Detective Conan* a.k.a. *Case Closed*
Bishojo Senshi Sailor Moon = *Sailor Moon*
Card Captor Sakura = *CardCaptors*
Shojo Kakumei Utena = *Revolutionary Girl Utena*
Shinseiki Evangelion = *Neon Genesis Evangelion*
Fushigi no Umi no Nadia = *Nadia: The Secret of Blue Water*
Lodoss to Senki = *Record of Lodoss War*
Ihatov no Kenso: Kenji no Haru = *Spring and Chaos*
Tenku no Escaflowne = *The Vision of Escaflowne*
Ao no Roku-go = *Blue Submarine No. 6*
Fushigina Elevator = *The Elevator*
Ouchi = *A House*
Sandoitti = *The Sandwiches*
Ame no Hi = *Imagination*
Bavel no Hon = *Bavel's Book*
Dottini Suru! = *Your Choice!*

XII: The New Century: pages 366–373

Cowboy Bebop: Tengoku no Tobira = *Cowboy Bebop: Knockin' on Heaven's Door* a.k.a. *Cowboy Bebop: The Movie*
WXIII: Patlabor the Movie 3 a.k.a. *Patlabor WXIII The Movie* and *Wasted 13 Patlabor the Movie*
Sennen Joyu = *Millennium Actress*
Palme no Ki = *A Tree of Palme*
Seikai no Monshou = *Crest of the Stars*
Megami Kouhosei = *Pilot Candidate*, a.k.a. *Candidate for Goddess*
Chitcha na Yukitsukai Sugar = *Sugar: A Little Snow Fairy*
Kokaku Kidotai: Stand Alone Complex = *Ghost in the Shell: Stand Alone Complex*
Jubei Ninpocho: Ryuhogyoku-hen = *Ninja Scroll: The Series*
Chikyu Shoujo Arjuna = *Arjuna*
Mousou Dairinin = *Paranoia Agents*
Nekojiru-so = *Cat Soup*
Hoshi no Koe = *Voices of a Distant Star*
Sentou Yousei Yukikaze = *Yukikaze*
Atama-yama = *Mt Head*
Wo Wei Ge Kuang = *Music Up*
Mai Dou Gu Shi (Mandarin)/*Mak Dau Goo Si* (Cantonese) = *My Life As McDull*
Final Fantasy: The Spirits Within, a.k.a. *Final Fantasy*

PICTURE CREDITS

Picture Courtesy of:

A1 Video: 22 (all), 23 (all)
Aardman Animations Ltd: 282 (t), 322, 323, 324, 325 (all)
ADV Films: 368 (all)
ARC Archive: 104 (all), 105, 166 (all), 167 (t), 168 (all), 169 (all), 250 (b), 251 (all)
Mark Baker: 326 (tr)
Nancy Beiman: 18 (t)
bfi Stills: 28, 48 (all), 49 (all), 71 (t), 72 (all), 73 (all), 74 (b), 75 (all), 134, 135 (all), 136 (all), 137 (all), 141 (all), 158, 159 (all), 170 (all), 171 (all), 188 (all), 189, 220 (all), 224, 225 (all), 231 (t), 252, 253 (all), 254 (all), 257, 258, 259 (all), 284 (all), 285, 326 (br)
BKN New Media Limited: 378 (all), 379 (all)
Bruno Bozzetto/www.bozzetto.com: 222 (all), 223 (all)
Cartoon Research Co.: 14, 15 (t), 16, 17 (all), 18 (b), 19 (all), 20 (all), 21, 26 (tl), 27, 34 (all), 35, 36 (all), 37 (all), 38, 39 (all), 41 (t), 42, 43 (all), 44, 45, 46, 47 (all), 56 (all), 57 (t), 58 (b), 60 (all), 61 (all), 63 (b), 64, 65 (all), 66, 70, 71 (b), 80 (all), 81, 84, 85 (all), 86 (b), 87, 88, 89 (b), 90, 91 (b), 92 (all), 93, 94, 95 (all), 97 (all), 98, 124 (all), 125 (tl & r), 128 (b), 129 (all), 131 (b), 146 (t), 147 (bl & r), 148 (all), 154 (b), 155 (t), 156, 157 (c & br), 162 (all), 163 (all), 178, 179 (all), 181 (t), 183 (t), 184 (all), 185 (t), 187 (all), 202 (b), 204 (all), 205 (t), 206, 207 (bl), 209 (all), 218 (b), 236 (all), 241 (all), 244 (b), 245 (all), 250 (t), 270, 271 (all), 272 (all), 273, 274, 275 (t & bl), 295 (all), 296, 297 (all), 309, 318 (t), 330, 350, 351 (b)
Cartoon Research Co./David Gerstein: 40 (t)
Center for Visual Music: 216 (all), 217; The Fischinger Archive/www.oskarfischinger.org: 68, 69 (all)
Central Park Media: 369 (all)
Christie's Images: 57 (b), 58 (t), 59, 82 (all), 83, 120, 150, 151 (all), 152, 153 (all), 154 (t), 210 (all), 211 (all), 213 (all), 277 (b)
Cyberroach/www.cyberroach.com: 268 (all)
Harvey Deneroff: 374 (all), 375 (all)
DreamWorks SKG: 310, 311 (all), 338, 344 (all), 345, 358, 359 (t), 366, 367 (all)
Eesti Joonisfilm/www.joonisfilm.ee: 292 (all), 293 (all)
Sheila Graber/www.graber-miller.com: 286, 287 (all)
Benjamin Gross: 67 (all)
The Halas & Batchelor Collection Ltd: 167 (b)
Heritage Comics Auctions: 99, 207 (tl)
The Hubley Studio, Inc.: 214, 215 (all)
The Illuminated Film Company: 359 (bl & r)
The Internet Archive: 164 (all), 165 (all)
Jove Film/www.russiananimation.com: 110 (all), 111 (all), 140 (all), 234 (all), 235 (all)
Renzo Kinoshita/Studio Lotus: 261 (t)
The Kobal Collection: 15 (b), 62, 63 (t); Carolco: 306; Touchstone: 320 (t), 321
Kratky Film Praha a.s.: 328 (all), 329 (all)
John A. Lent: 76 (bl & r), 114 (all), 174 (t), 175, 240, 298, 299 (all), 300, 301 (t), 332 (all), 333, 334 (all), 335; Walter and Wendy Hucker & Jan Begg/Silicon Pulp Animation Gallery: 262 (all)
Library of Congress: 12 (all), 13 (all)
Pam and Bob Martin: 121 (all), 180 (t), 182 (t), 183 (b), 205 (b), 316, 317
William Moritz/AWN.com: 108 (all), 109 (b)
National Film Board of Canada: 100, 101 (all), 102 (all), 103 (all), 160 (all), 161 (all), 248 (all), 249 (all), 256 (all), 279 (all)
Nukufilm/www.nukufilm.ee: 194 (t), 195 (all)
Parlophone Records & Shynola: 280, 281 (all)
Fred Patten: 30, 31 (all), 52 (all), 53, 112 (all), 113 (all), 115, 142 (all), 143 (all), 196 (all), 197 (all), 230 (all), 231 (b), 237, 238, 239 (all), 260, 261 (b), 288 (all), 289 (all)
Pilot Moscow Animation Studio: 290 (all), 362 (all), 363 (t)
Bill Plympton: 278 (all), 376 (all)
Chris Robinson & André Coutu/Ottowa International Animation Festival: 172, 173 (all), 291, 363 (b), 364 (all), 365 (all)
Will Ryan/SnappyToons Amusement Company: 377 (all)
Screensound Australia - The National Screen and Sound Archive: 263
Pietro Shakarian & David Gerstein: 40 (bl & r)
Snowman Enterprises Ltd: 282 (bl & r), 283; TVC Ltd: 327 (all)
Adam Snyder/Rembrandt Films: 192 (all), 193, 194 (c), 232 (all), 233
Toon Tracker/www.toontracker.com: 122 (all)
Topham Picturepoint: 26 (r), 29, 218 (t), 219, 221, 276, 277 (t), 294 (all), 304, 305 (all), 307 (all), 308 (all), 319 (all), 320 (b), 331 (t), 339 (all), 340, 342, 343 (all), 346, 347 (all), 348, 349 (all), 352, 353 (all), 354, 355 (all), 356, 357; UPPA.co.uk: 212; Universal Pictorial Press Photo: 312 (all), 313
Van Eaton Galleries: 86 (t), 89 (t), 132, 133 (all), 155 (b), 200, 202 (t), 203 (t), 246 (all), 247 (all), 255 (all), 269 (all), 314 (all), 315 (all), 318 (b), 351 (t)
Graham Webb: 24 (all), 25, 91 (t), 96 (all), 106, 107 (all), 118 (all), 119 (all), 123 (all), 125 (br), 126 (all), 127 (all), 128 (t), 130 (all), 131 (t), 146 (b), 147 (tl & r), 149 (all), 157 (tl), 180 (b), 181 (b), 185 (b), 201 (all), 203 (b), 208 (all), 244 (tl & tr), 275 (br)
Yamamura Animation, Inc.: 186 (all), 331 (c & b), 370, 371 (all)
Yoram Gross Film Studios: 264, 265 (all)
Zagreb Film: 138 (all), 139 (all), 190, 191 (all), 226 (all), 227 (all), 228, 229 (all)

AUTHOR BIOGRAPHIES

Jerry Beck (General Editor; Author: chapter openers, pages 118–121, 130–131, 162–163, 182–185, 204–205, 246–247, 316–321)

Jerry Beck is a noted animation historian who has written numerous articles and books on the subject including Looney Tunes: The Ultimate Visual Guide, Outlaw Animation, and The 50 Greatest Cartoons. He is also an animation industry executive and cartoon producer. Beck has taught History of Animation at UCLA, NYU, The American Film Institute and The School of Visual Arts. He has produced many best-selling DVD compilations of classic cartoons, including The Looney Tunes Golden Collection and The Definitive Betty Boop. Beck lives in Los Angeles and is on the board of directors of ASIFA-Hollywood.

Will Ryan (Consultant Editor; Author: pages 12–15, 154–155)

Will Ryan is past-president of the International Animated Film Society and a charter member of the Society for Animation Studies. He has contributed hundreds of articles, interviews, editor-ials and reviews to many publications, including Animation Magazine, for which he is currently Contributing Editor. He is perhaps best known as a cineloquist with voice credits in many Academy Award nominated films. He is the creator of the Annie Award-winning series Elmo Aardvark: Outer Space Detective!, based upon the classic character. Musical recordings written and produced by Will Ryan can be found at CDBaby.com. He serves on the Executive Committee of the Animation Branch of the Academy of Motion Picture Arts and Sciences in Los Angeles.

Jeffrey Katzenberg (Foreword)

A native New Yorker, Jeffrey Katzenberg began his career in entertainment as the assistant to David Picker, then President of United Artists. In 1974, he joined Paramount Studios as an assistant to Barry Diller. Three years later, he became a production executive in the motion picture division, and in May 1982, he was promoted to President of the studio. From 1984 to 1994 Katzenberg served as Chairman of The Walt Disney Studios. In 1994 Katzenberg co-founded DreamWorks SKG with Steven Spielberg and David Geffen. Under Katzenberg's leadership, DreamWorks' animation division has enjoyed several successes, including Shrek (2001) which won the first-ever Academy Award for Best Animated Feature (and on which he served as a producer) and Shrek 2 (2004), which has become the top-grossing animated film in history. In 2002, Katzenberg received an Academy Award nomination for Best Animated Feature as a producer of Spirit: Stallion of the Cimarron and he received the Hollywood Tex Avery Award for Achievement in Animation. Katzenberg is currently the Chairman of the Motion Picture & Television Fund.

Bill Plympton (Foreword)

Bill Plympton was born and raised in Portland, Oregon. On graduation from Portland State University in Graphic Design he moved to New York City and began his career creating cartoons for publications such as the New York Times, National Lampoon, Playboy and Screw. In 1987 he was nominated for an Oscar for his first short film, Your Face. After producing many shorts which appeared on MTV and in Spike and Mike's festivals, he turned his talent to features. Since 1991 he has made seven feature films, four of them (The Tune, Mondo Plympton, I Married a Strange Person and Mutant Aliens) animated features. He completed his fifth animated feature, Hair High, in 2004.

Ryan Ball (Author: pages 92–93, 158–159)

Ryan Ball is the web editor for Animation magazine. He is a specialist in stop-motion animation, and is particularly interested in the work of legendary animator Ray Harryhausen.

Rick DeMott (Author: pages 56–59, 206–207, 312–315, 348–351)

Rick DeMott, serving as marshal of his class, graduated with honors from Penn State University, majoring in Film and Video and minoring in World Literature. In 1999, he became the associate editor of Animation World Network (www.awn.com). After a stint as a freelance writer, he served as Production Co-ordinator for sound production company BadaBing BadaBoom Productions and animation house Perky Pickle Studios. In 2002, he returned to AWN as its managing editor.

Harvey Deneroff (Author: pages 26–29, 122–123, 214–217, 244–245, 250–251, 272–275, 298–301, 310–311, 332–335, 374–377)

Harvey Deneroff is the founder and past president of the Society for Animation Studies, was editor of Graffiti, Animation Magazine and Animation World Magazine, and published The Animation Report, an industry newsletter. The author of The Art of Anastasia (HarperCollins, 1997), he has also written for The Hollywood Reporter, Animatoon, Sight and Sound, Film History and Asian Cinema; he was also Festival Director of the Week With the Masters Animation Celebration, in Trivandrum, India.

David Gerstein (Author: pages 18–19, 20–21, 34–37, 40–43, 46–47, 94–99)

David Gerstein is an animation and comics researcher, writer and editor working with Gemstone Publishing and Egmont Creative A/S. His published work includes Nine Lives To Live: A Classic Felix Celebration (Fantagraphics, 1996), The Walt Disney Centennial Book (Egmont Serieforlaget, 2001), and various issues of Uncle Scrooge. In real life he dislikes cats, fears mice and considers ducks a fine dinner.

Frank Gladstone (Author: pages 90–91, 124–127, 146–149, 156–157)

Frank Gladstone has been working as a professional animator, producer, director, writer and teacher for more than 30 years. He managed his own Emmy award-winning studio, Persistence of Vision, Inc., producing commercials and educational films, and has since worked for the feature animation divisions at Disney, Warner Bros. and DreamWorks. Frank has spoken on animation at schools and institutions around the US, in the Caribbean, Europe and Asia and has given animation and cinematography workshops for the University of Miami, VIFX, Cinesite, UNICEF, Gnomon Digital, Vancouver Film School, Nickelodeon, UCLA, San Jose State, Stanford and USC. Currently, Frank is the head of artistic development at DreamWorks SKG Animation. He also programs independent films for DreamWorks' "Go Fish Pictures" division.

Tom Knott (Author: pages 100–103, 160–161, 186–187, 248–249, 278–281)

Prior to joining Warner Bros. Animation as director of recruiting, Tom Knott was the director of the Ottawa International Animation Festival. He has also worked with Colossal Pictures, MTV, the National Film Board of Canada, the Tournee of Animation, Animation World Magazine, the Los Angeles International Animation Celebration, Algonquin College and the Canadian Film Institute. He is currently an animation consultant.

Andrew Leal (Author: pages 80–83, 208–209)

Andrew Leal serves as lead contributor for the animation voice actor info site Voicechasers.com, and has compiled a database of US feature animation credits, Toonjunkies.com, a work in progress. He writes regularly for APAToons, been published in the genre film magazine Scarlet Street and was a presenter at last year's Comic Arts Conference at the San Diego Comic-Con. He is currently working on expanding a thesis on narrative and imagery in US World War Two propaganda cartoons for eventual publication.

George Maestri (Author: pages 268–271, 306–309, 338–347, 352–357)

George Maestri has worked as a writer, director and producer for studios such as Warner Bros., Disney, Nickelodeon and Comedy Central. He has written a number of books on computer animation, including (digital) Character Animation, a standard textbook on character animation techniques.

Michael Mallory (Author: pages 178–181, 200–203)

Michael Mallory is the author of the books Hanna-Barbera Cartoons and Marvel: The Characters and their Universe, as well as more than 250 articles on animation that have regularly appeared in the Los Angeles Times, Daily Variety, Animation Magazine and Millimeter. He lives in Southern California.

Mark Mayerson (Author: pages 64–65, 128–129, 210–213, 276–277, 304–305)

Mark Mayerson has worked professionally in both drawn and computer animation. His jobs have included producer, director, writer and animator. He is the creator of Monster By Mistake, a computer animated television series that runs in over 30 countries. Mark has written about animation history and techniques for Animation Magazine, awn.com, fps, Animato, The Velvet Light Trap and The Comics Journal. He lives in Toronto with his wife and two children.

Harry McCracken (Author: pages 44–45, 150–153)

Harry McCracken is the editor of PC World, the world's largest monthly technology magazine. A longtime cartoon buff, McCracken was the editor of Animato, a popular animation magazine, from 1987 to 1991. He has also written about cartoons and comics for numerous other publications, and operates www.harrymccracken.com, a website on cartoons and related topics.

Dewey McGuire (Author: pages 66–67, 84–89)

Dewey McGuire is a graphic artist and cartoonist whose artwork has been published in both the US and Japan. He has contributed to Video Ratings Guide, Animato and Apatoons, as well as his own self-published newsletter, McBoing Boing's (1994–98). He lives with his wife and six cats in Iowa City.

Jan Nagel (Author: pages 378–379)

Jan Nagel has worked with award-winning feature and television production studios, and acts as a consultant to animation and visual effects production companies. She is a founding member and current president of the board of directors of Women In Animation, as well as an active member of other entertainment organizations including Academy of Television Arts and Sciences and ASIFA-Hollywood. Jan is a frequent guest lecturer on animation and entertainment careers at colleges and universities.

Fred Patten (Author: pages 30–31, 52–53, 76–77, 112–115, 142–143, 174–175, 196–197, 236–241, 260–261, 294–297, 330–331, 366–373)

Fred Patten discovered manga and anime in the 1970s, and was a co-founder of the first American anime fan club in 1977. He has been writing about anime since the early 1980s for popular culture magazines like Starlog, and for specialty magazines like Manga Max. He has also served as a consultant on anime for international film festivals. He currently writes regular anime columns for Animation World Magazine and Newtype USA.

Ray Pointer (Author: pages 16–17, 18–19, 38–39, 60–63, 164–165)

Ray received the first Student Oscar in 1973 for his cartoon short, Goldnavel. In the 1980s, he was a producer of animated and live action television spots for Navy Broadcasting, and in the 1990s he was an assistant animator on the features Tom and Jerry: The Movie and Bebe's Kids. He was an animator on commercials and directed industrial-animation videos and directed numerous cartoons for Nickelodeon. For the past 30 years Ray has been researching various aspects of animation history, and is one of the foremost experts on Max Fleischer and the Fleischer Studios. Through his company, Inkwell Images, Ray has produced several award-winning programs on animation for the home video market.

Pat Raine Webb (Author: pages 358–361)

Pat Raine Webb worked at the Halas & Batchelor Studios from 1977 to 1992 as assistant to John Halas and was appointed director in 1989. In 1993/94 she was administrator of the Cardiff Animation Festival. She has organized exhibitions and retrospectives of animated film in London, Belgium and Croatia including the UK's first Computer Animation Conference. She was on the board of the International Animated Film Association from 1988, and was vice president from 1991 to 2001. She is currently president of the UK office, responsible for writing and editing the group's magazine. Since 1993 Pat has also been the European reporter for Animatoon, a Korean magazine.

Chris Robinson (Author: pages 50–51, 74–75, 110–111, 140–141, 172–173, 194–195, 230–231, 234–235, 258–259, 288–293, 362–365)

Chris Robinson writes for Magma magazine in Canada. He has directed many animation festivals, including the 2002 Ottawa Animation Festival. He is particularly interested in Eastern European animation.

Keith Scott (Author: pages 132–133, 262–265)

Keith Scott is a veteran animation voice artist based in Sydney. Since 1973, he has created hundreds of character voices for TV commercials and cartoons in Australia and in the US. He is a respected animation historian, with several articles published in American cartoon journals. His first book, The Moose That Roared, was published in 2000 by St Martin's Press. His special interest lies in the theatrical cartoons made from 1930–60 by America's five West Coast based studios: Disney, Warner Bros., MGM, Walter Lantz and Columbia. He is presently working on a book about the great cartoon voice artists of the Golden Age.

Adam Snyder (Author: pages 138–139, 190–193, 226–229, 232–233, 328–329)

Adam Snyder is president of the animation company Rembrandt Films, which in the 1960s received four Academy Award nominations and an Oscar for Munro. In 1993, Adam revived Rembrandt Films with the production of the 13-part half-hour animation series, The Nudnik Show, which has now aired in more than 20 countries. He is also the exclusive distributor of a number of classic properties, including the animation library of Zagreb Film and the US television series Winky Dink and You. Most recently, Adam co-wrote, directed and produced The Animation Century, a two-hour television special on the history of animation that aired on Bravo in the United States in late 2003.

Graham Webb (Author: pages 22–25, 48–49, 68–73, 104–109, 134–137, 166–171, 188–189, 218–225, 252–257, 282–287, 322–327)

Graham Webb's formative years were spent endeavoring to become an animator. This ambition was finally realised by his animating on the Beatles' feature cartoon, Yellow Submarine. Since then he has worked for children's comics, researched stage musicals and written for FunnyWorld, Animation Magazine, Animator and Animato! as well as contributing to various books, including The Great Movie Cartoon Parade (Tribune) and The Great Cartoon Stars (Jupiter). Graham has also researched and written The Animated Film Encyclopedia (McFarland, 2000).

Acknowledgements

Jerry Beck would like to thank the following: Marea Boylan, Karl Cohen, Nancy Beiman, Antran Manoogian (ASIFA-Hollywood), Benny Gross, Leonard Maltin, Mike Barrier and John Canemaker.

Chris Robinson would like to thank the following people:

I would like to acknowledge an email (13 February 2004) from Bordo Dovnikovic which is the basis for the section on Zagreb Animation during the 1980s.

Many thanks to Joan Borsten of Films By Jove for providing details about Soviet World War Two propaganda films.